EVERYMAN,
I WILL GO WITH THEE,
AND BE THY GUIDE,
IN THY MOST NEED
TO GO BY THY SIDE

WILLIAM LANGLAND

Piers Plowman
with Sir Gawain and the
Green Knight, Pearl
and Sir Orfeo (anon.)

Piers Plowman translated by Terence Tiller
Sir Gawain, *Pearl* and *Sir Orfeo* translated by
J. R. R. Tolkien and edited by
Christopher Tolkien

with an Introduction by John Burrow

EVERYMAN'S LIBRARY

224

This book is one of 250 volumes in Everyman's Library
which have been distributed to 4500 state schools
throughout the United Kingdom.
The project has been supported by a grant of £4 million
from the Millennium Commission.

Typography by Peter B. Willberg

ISBN 1-85715-224-7

Published by Everyman Publishers plc,
Gloucester Mansions, 140A Shaftesbury Avenue,
London WC2H 8HD

Distributed by Random House (UK) Ltd.,
20 Vauxhall Bridge Road, London SW1V 2SA

C O N T E N T S

INTRODUCTION

In a book entitled *The Art of English Poetry* published in 1589, the author declares that he 'will not reach above the time of King Edward the Third and Richard the Second for any that wrote in English metre', because, he says, 'beyond that time there is little or nothing worth commendation to be found written in this art'. Although scholars and enthusiasts will protest at this judgement, it remains true that the earliest poems which might confidently be expected to figure in an Oxford Book of English Verse were produced in the 'Age of Chaucer', during the reigns of Edward III (1327–77) and Richard II (1377–99). The Elizabethan writer's historical sketch puts Chaucer and Gower first, followed by Lydgate and 'that nameless who wrote the satire called "Piers Plowman"'. These four poets were all available in printed editions to sixteenth-century readers and their successors; so *Piers Plowman*, like the work of the others, has been a continuous presence in the English poetic tradition, available to be admired by Edmund Spenser and disliked by Gerard Manley Hopkins. By contrast, the other two major poems represented in this book, *Pearl* and *Sir Gawain and the Green Knight*, survived for centuries in just one manuscript copy and remained generally unknown until nineteenth-century scholars printed them. So they are still, one might say, in the process of being digested by readers of English poetry. This process has not been helped by the difficulties their language presents. All the poets known to the author of *The Art of English Poetry* were southerners; and even *Piers Plowman*, though its author evidently grew up in the West Country, shows a form of English not very unlike Chaucer's (the London English from which the modern standard language descends) and so can be read in the original without too much difficulty. The nameless author of *Sir Gawain* and *Pearl*, however, learnt his English in the north-west of England, somewhere near the borders of Staffordshire and Cheshire; and, in the absence then of a standard literary form of the language, he wrote in his native dialect. So his poems are distinctly harder for a modern reader than those of Chaucer, Gower or Langland. Compare the opening of *Sir Gawain* with that of *Piers Plowman*. First *Gawain*:

> Sithen the sege and the assaut watz sesed at Troye,
> The borgh brittened and brent to brondez and askez,
> The tulk that the trammes of tresoun there wroght...

And *Piers*:

> In a somer seson, whan softe was the sonne,
> I shoop me into shroudes as I a sheep were,
> In habite as an heremite unholy of werkes...

The author of the latter lines, to take him first, is no longer 'nameless'. His name was William Langland. Yet little is known about his life. Born about the year 1330, he was the son of an Oxfordshire gentleman, according to a note in one of the many early manuscripts of the poem; but his dialect shows that he was brought up further west, in the vicinity of those Malvern Hills on which he places his narrator as the poem opens. That narrator, known as Long Will, cannot simply be identified with the author, yet the adult Langland is generally supposed to have lived a life much like his. Long Will describes himself as living in London, in a little house on Cornhill, with his wife and daughter; he wears the long clothes of a cleric, though, as a married man, he could only be in minor orders; and he makes an irregular living by saying prayers for his benefactors and their dead relatives. In his last years, Langland perhaps returned to the West Country. The date of his death, probably after 1388, is unknown. *Piers Plowman* is the only poem of his that has survived, and he evidently devoted many years to its composition and revision. The great Victorian editor W. W. Skeat distinguished three versions in the manuscripts, still known as the A, B and C Texts. These can be roughly dated from their allusions to public events, which suggest that the poet was working on the A Text in the 1360s, on B in the 1370s, and on C in the 1380s.

None of these versions is final. The A Text breaks off abruptly without an ending, at a moment of acute theological difficulty; the B Text rewrites some of the A section and takes up the narrative at length, arriving at a rather inconclusive conclusion; but Langland was still not satisfied, and he embarked on, though evidently never completed, yet another revision of the whole work, the C Text. It is not only comparison of these three versions that gives the sense of a work constantly in transit. As a reader of the present translation of the B Text will see, *Piers* is a poem of restless search. It belongs to a common medieval type, the dream poem; but, unlike almost all other examples, it describes a series of no less than ten dreams (two of them dreams-within-dreams), and from all but one of these the dreamer Will wakes up sadly puzzled and dissatisfied in his quest for visionary understanding. Since readers are often puzzled too, it may be helpful to offer a very broad summary of the poem's progress. The first two dreams, which occupy Passus I to VII, are primarily concerned with the possibilities of reform in contemporary society, imagined as the overcoming of corruption in the person of Lady Meed, and then the undertaking of a communal pilgrimage to Truth, that is, to God. It is God's promise of salvation for those who do well on this pilgrimage, communicated by his pardon, that sets the poem off on its long second phase (Passus VIII to XV). This is primarily concerned with the moral life of the individual. Long Will seeks to understand that good life, 'Do Well', upon which his salvation may depend; and he progresses through a series of encounters with intellectual powers, whose instruction fails to satisfy him, to more rewarding visions of patience and of charity. The third and final phase of the poem (Passus XVI to XX) begins when charity is identified in the person of Christ, with his forerunners Abraham (faith) and Moses (hope). After the climactic vision of Christ's passion (Passus XVIII), the poem goes on to contrast the spiritual power of the early Church with its present decline into near collapse, ending on a note of uncertainty.

Such a summary, however, disguises the fact that Langland by no means distinguishes, as we commonly do, between social, moral and religious issues. On the contrary, though his emphases change, he is concerned with all three nearly all the time. Thus, in the second dream, of the Pilgrimage to Truth (V–VII), he does indeed imagine the reform of his society, but as a matter of individual contrition, confession (of the Seven Deadly Sins) and penance, following the order of the Sacrament of Penance. Conversely, in the last part of the poem, the vision of the degenerate latterday Church embraces unscrupulous physicians as well as corrupt friars. Ideally, for Langland, the Church and society were one and the same. Hence the poem's titular hero, Piers the Plowman, can carry the weight of all Langland's hopes. When he is first encountered, ploughing his half-acre in Passus VI, by the people on their pilgrimage to Truth, he embodies an ideal of God-fearing fidelity to one's vocation in the social order. He is a true agricultural worker, such that he could be invoked in 1381 by the leaders of the Peasants' Revolt in letters to their followers; but he also has a special relationship with Truth, such that he can be the chosen recipient, on behalf of the people, of Truth's pardon. His tearing up of that pardon, so perplexing to all readers, may be taken to anticipate the later apotheosis of Piers as the champion of inner, spiritual realities, as against external forms (here, paper pardons). Very much later in the poem, after just two strange references to him as one who teaches and knows the supreme virtue of charity, he at last reappears. He tends the Tree of Charity which grows in man's heart (Passus XVI); and he comes to be associated, through that same virtue, with Christ in his human nature. Finally, in the last phase of the poem, he represents for Langland the true spirit of Christ's Church on earth, embodied in its first great leader, St Peter ('Piers' is a familiar form of that name), but sadly lacking in the world the poet saw around him. So when, in the last lines of the poem, Conscience sets out to seek Piers the Plowman, that visionary figure stands for all the highest potentialities of human nature, social, moral and spiritual.

Langland was a near contemporary of Geoffrey Chaucer and may, for a time, have been his near neighbour in London; but there is no definite evidence that either knew the other's work. The two men are indeed very different kinds of writer. Langland addresses contemporary conditions much more directly than the elusive, 'elvish' Chaucer; and his poem displays a wider range of English, and London, life than even the *Canterbury Tales* – especially the dispossessed, whom Langland must have had more opportunities to encounter, as a member of what modern historians call the 'clerical proletariat'. *Piers* also belongs to a different tradition of English poetic technique, that of alliterative verse. In the *Canterbury Tales* Chaucer's Parson declares that, being a 'Southren man', he cannot tell his tale ' "rum, ram, ruf" by lettre' – evidence, not that Chaucer himself despised the form (for the Parson is a puritanical cleric who does not like rhyme either), but that he associated alliterative writing with parts of England other than the south-east, regions such as Worcestershire, where Langland grew up. Alliterative verse, unlike Chaucer's, does not rhyme or count syllables. Its line consists of two half-lines, each normally with two stressed syllables, linked by alliteration: 'I shoop me into shroudes/as I a sheep were'.

Langland handles this ancient metre (going back to Anglo-Saxon times and beyond) with great freedom and flexibility, as the varying demands of his long poem dictate. Although much of the expository writing is, inevitably, rather plain, the arguments often turn on inventive wordplay, as when Holy Church explains human knowledge of the virtue of love: 'In the herte there is the heed and the heighe welle'. The word 'head' here contrasts with 'heart', for true knowledge is feeling, but it also combines with 'well' (a spring or water-source in Middle English) to suggest the head of a stream from which that knowledge naturally flows. Elsewhere, Langland displays an ability, unmatched among alliterative poets, to create lines of easy, informal speech. Thus, in the confessions of the Seven Deadly Sins, Covetousness is asked by his confessor whether he has shown pity on the poor and replies: 'I have as muche pité of povere men as pedlere hath of cattes'. These confessions are rich in such commonplace realities, like Envy's preoccupation with his loss of a bowl and a torn sheet:

> And whan I come to the kirke and sholde knele to the roode
> And preye for the peple as the preest techeth,
> For pilgrymes and for palmeres, for al the peple after,
> Thanne I crye on my knees that Crist gyve hem sorwe
> That baren awey my bolle and my broke shete.

[*kirke* church, *roode* cross, *palmeres* pilgrims, *baren* carried, *bolle* bowl, *broke* torn].

Yet the same episode has the extraordinary grandeur of the confessor's prayer on behalf of the penitent Sins, in which he recalls the events of their redemption. Thus he speaks of the darkness at noon during the crucifixion as a moment when those waiting in the darkness of hell were fed by the blood of Christ:

> The sonne for sorwe therof lees sight for a tyme
> Aboute mydday whan moost light is and meeltyme of seintes;
> Feddest tho with thi fresshe blood oure forefadres in derknesse.

[*sonne* sun, *lees* lost, *tho* then].

The sublime strangeness of that last line is matched elsewhere in the poem, notably at its climax in the account (Passus XVIII) of the crucified Christ's appearance before 'our forefathers in darkness' at the harrowing of hell, and his triumphant speech there, with its riddling reference to the general resurrection at the end of time:

> For I that am lord of lif, love is my drynke,
> And for that drynke today I deide upon erthe.
> I faught so, me thursteth yet, for mannes soule sake;
> May no drynke me moiste, ne my thurst slake,
> Til the vendage falle in the vale of Josaphat,
> That I drynke right ripe must, *resureccio mortuorum*.

[*me thursteth* I thirst (John 19.28), *vendage* wine-harvest, *Josaphat* (Joel Chapter 3), *must* new wine].

*

A small manuscript book in the British Library in London (commonly on display there) contains the only surviving record of four poems: *Sir Gawain and the Green Knight*, *Pearl*, and two other pieces, *Patience* and *Cleanness*. These poems are widely believed, on internal evidence, to be the work of a single author; but his identity is quite unknown. The manuscript copy can be dated around the year 1400, and its contents were probably composed not very long before that. Their form of English, from Cheshire or Staffordshire, proves that the author was not a 'Southren man'; and *Sir Gawain* shows familiarity with what was evidently his home territory. The hero of that poem, on his quest, fords the river Dee, passes through the

Wirral, and enters a hilly country where he eventually arrives at a 'Green Chapel' described with such particularity that it is hard to believe that the author did not have some specific local spot in mind (and scholars have looked for it). Whoever he was, though, the *Gawain*-poet was no narrow provincial. His four poems display a real familiarity and inwardness with the speech and manners of aristocratic society; he knew courtly French writings such as the *Romance of the Rose* and Arthurian romances; and he shared with Langland an informed interest in theological thought and the interpretation of the Bible. These attributes have led some to speculate that he may have been a cleric in service, as a chaplain or suchlike, in the household of a great man – outside his native territory, probably, and perhaps even in London. But this is no more than speculation.

Sir Gawain and the Green Knight belongs to that type of Arthurian writing which takes as its subject a single adventure (where Malory's *Morte Darthur*, for instance, embraces the whole history of Arthur and his knights). It confines itself to the Adventure of the Green Chapel, which Sir Gawain undertakes in response to the challenging offer by the Green Knight of a 'Beheading Game'. This bizarre test requires the hero to agree to decapitate the challenger on condition that he submit to a return blow from him on a later occasion. The English poet derived this story from French romance; but he complicates and enriches the action by nesting within it another set of events, the so-called 'Exchange of Winnings'. For his hero, on his way to the Green Chapel where the return blow is to be delivered on New Year's Day, is entertained over Christmas by a host who proposes, to pass the last three days of the old year, that they should exchange each day whatever they have acquired – Gawain at ease in the castle, the host out hunting. This subplot has the effect of making the outcome of the whole adventure much more interesting. Gawain approaches the Green Chapel on New Year's Day expecting certain death at the hands of an apparently supernatural adversary; but readers know the logic of such traditional tales and will expect him to be spared if he loyally keeps his tryst. And spared he is; but even readers may be surprised, as

Gawain certainly is, when the Green Knight identifies himself as the host of the castle, and explains that he has spared the hero because of his performance in the Exchange of Winnings. What had appeared to be just a Christmas house-party game turns out to have been a critical test.

Similar play with the expectations of hero and reader alike occurs elsewhere in the poem, notably in the treatment of Gawain's failure – for he does not simply succeed. On the three days of the Exchange, he has been visited in his bedchamber by the host's beautiful wife, offering him favours which he could not possibly pay over to her husband when evening comes. As courteously as he can, Gawain resists her advances, and so, on the third visit, she finally declares that she gives him up; but, as no more than a parting keepsake, she offers him a belt (ominously green) which has, she says, the power of saving its wearer's life. Gawain accepts the gift on her condition, that he will conceal it from her husband; and so, to save his life (as he thinks), he breaks his promise on the third evening when winnings are exchanged. This failing, incurred at a moment of relaxation and relief, comes home to the hero only on the following day, when the Green Knight, after sparing his life, explains that he knows what Gawain did and has just nicked his neck with the axe because of it. He indeed praises Gawain more than he blames him; but the hero, caught out again when he least expects it, reacts to the revelation with intense shame and self-reproach. When he finally returns to Camelot, to be welcomed as a hero by Arthur and the knights of the Round Table, he remains inconsolable, vowing that he will wear the green belt for the rest of his life as a mortifying sign of his weakness.

What Gawain chiefly accuses himself of, before both the Green Knight and his comrades at Camelot, is 'treachery and untruth'; and these words identify the main moral issue in a poem deeply concerned with the values of Christian chivalry. When Gawain sets out, at the beginning of the second of the poem's four books or 'fitts', to seek the Green Chapel, he is ceremoniously invested with his armour; and the poet lays particular emphasis on the heraldic sign which he bears on his shield, a pentangle. This sign symbolizes, we are told, the multiple moral and spiritual values by which the hero lives, including the courtesy and sexual purity which are to be tested together in the scenes with the host's wife. What it primarily signifies, however, is 'trawthe' or troth, and this is what the Adventure of the Green Chapel chiefly tests. The key moments in the story are when the hero gives his word or, better, plights his troth – first to the Green Knight at Arthur's court, and then three times to his host at the Christmas castle. Gawain fulfils to the letter the terms of his promises given at Camelot – turning up on time at the mysterious Green Chapel, submitting to the return blow without resistance – and so vindicates the honour of the Round Table, as his fellow knights recognize at the end of the poem. Yet he cannot forgive himself for failing to honour his promise to the host on the third day of the Exchange. For he failed on that occasion to redeem his pledged word and so, as it were, lost it. Hence his shame and mortification. As one later knight put it, in Tudor times: 'He that promiseth to be true to one, and deceiveth him, may be called a traitor; for what is a man but his promise?'

As a narrative poem, *Sir Gawain* is matched only in its period by Chaucer's *Troilus and Criseyde*. Since both poets choose to tell a single story at length, they can accommodate details of setting and behaviour for which more cursory narratives have no time. They both, indeed, take a long step towards that rich 'scenic art' which Henry James saw as the novelist's ideal. Although *Gawain* is not a novel, it does convey a powerful sense of the reality of the events it describes. On the morning of Gawain's final encounter, for instance, he wakes and lies in bed listening to the wild northern weather outdoors and counting the crowings of the cock; and this chill sense of apprehension persists as he rides out from the castle through mist and snow, down to the wild valley of the Green Chapel, and hears, somewhere in the surrounding crags, a mysterious sound of grinding. These experiences call for more than the weightless heroism of many romance knights: Gawain is heroic, but he is also afraid. Fear of death is one of the many common realities for which, despite its romantic and aristocratic setting in the days of King Arthur, this poem finds ample room.

*

Although probably written by the same man, *Pearl* is a different kind of work from *Sir Gawain*. It is a dream poem, like *Piers Plowman*; but, unlike Langland's poem, it focuses on a single vision: a father's vision of his dead infant daughter, appearing to him from the world beyond the grave. It may well be that the poet himself, or a patron, had in reality suffered the loss of a one-year-old girl ('you lived in our country not two years', the dreamer says to her). She may even have been christened Margery, for that name has the same meaning as 'pearl', which is how the father addresses her. Such play on names was not uncommon at the time. William Langland, like William Shakespeare in his sonnets, made the most of his first name in its familiar form, as both 'Will' and 'will'. If the poem is indeed, among other things, a monument to the dead, this may help to explain its extreme formal elaboration, comparable to what stonemasons created in the intricate Gothic tombs and chantries of the time. In *Gawain*, unrhymed alliterative lines are divided by short rhyming units into one hundred and one paragraphs of varying length, giving the poet considerable elbow-room; but he allowed himself no such liberties in *Pearl*, which consists of stanzas (one hundred and one, again) of twelve short lines each. The demanding rhyme-scheme of these stanzas is well preserved in the present translation, as is that system of repeated words which links them into groups of five stanzas, links those groups together, and links the last stanza to the first as if to complete a circle.

One does not nowadays expect poems – and particularly not poems of such rich formal complexity – to pursue arguments; but *Pearl*, like *Piers* and indeed Dante's *Comedy*, admits theological argument as part of its proper business. The issue in *Pearl* arises directly from its real or imagined occasion, the death of an infant, and concerns the heavenly rewards that God may be supposed to grant in such a case. In his vision, after a prologue enigmatically representing his loss, the dreamer finds himself in an otherworldly landscape; and there he encounters his daughter in her spiritual form as a grown lady, beautiful and crowned with a crown of pearls. She is, she tells him, a queen of heaven. The dreamer responds with natural delight and pride, but he is also puzzled and even indignant. How can it be right for one who lived only as a baby to be so honoured? What about those others who have faced and conquered the challenges of adult life? What, he almost says, about me? The poem offers what would have been taken as convincing answers to these questions. Thus, if a child has been cleansed of original sin by baptism and has had no opportunity to sin on her own account, then she is a complete innocent, and there is nothing for God to hold against her. Another of the pearl maiden's arguments rests not on reason but on authority: Christ's parable of the vineyard teaches that there can be no question of 'more and less' in the kingdom of God. Like Langland and Dante (both of whom address the somewhat similar problem known as the Salvation of the Righteous Heathen), the *Pearl* poet clearly regarded such thorny difficulties as proper matter for serious poetry.

Yet most readers will find more human than theological interest in the poem. The relationship between the dreamer and the pearl maiden drastically reverses the normal balance of power and knowledge between a male parent and a small female child. When they first meet, the maiden deferentially acknowledges her daughterhood by bowing and doffing her crown; but she then shortly resumes her crown and for the rest of their encounter treats her father with the absolute authority of a blessed spirit. For she is no longer subject to the limitations and distortions imposed upon the human mind by the body. She is pure spirit and, as she says, enjoys utter clarity and fulness of knowledge. So her behaviour cannot be taken as that of an ordinary living person, let alone an ordinary girl. Like another blessed spirit, Beatrice in Dante's *Comedy*, she has little time for earthly affections; and consequently readers find her, like Beatrice, rather difficult to love. But the dreamer still does love her, and there is pathos in his repeated appeals to their former relationship. Throughout the poem, indeed, the dreamer proves slow to comprehend the spiritual realities with which his vision confronts him, and slow to be consoled by them for the loss which he has suffered. Even at the very end of the dream, when he is granted a sight of what St John described in the Book of Revelation, the procession of maidens in the Heavenly Jerusalem, he at once singles out what he calls 'my little queen' and jumps to cross the river that divides him from her. His incomprehension may sometimes appear comic; but it is best understood as testifying to real human difficulties, and especially to the difficulty of what Freud called 'the work of mourning'. It is only after he has been woken by his sudden jump towards the stream that the narrator finds himself able to give his dead daughter up into God's keeping, and even there he reserves a muted parental claim when he gives her 'Christ's dear blessing and mine' – a parting formula used at the time in letters from parents to children.

The narrator of *Pearl* several times refers to himself as a 'jeweller', and the poem itself has been justly characterized as a luxury product from an age of aristocratic opulence. Its world is one in which cheap and common things play little part, except in the maiden's vivid retelling of the parable of the vineyard. It is a world of precious metals and stones. When the dreamer first finds himself in the other world, he sees gravelstones of pearl and a river running between banks of beryl over beds of sapphire and emerald, and the Heavenly Jerusalem is all of gold on foundations of twelve precious stones. These extravagances are not much to modern taste; but the symbolism of pearls lies at the heart of the poem, as the title given by modern editors correctly indicates. The maiden is identified as herself a pearl, and she wears a crown set with pearls, garments edged with pearls, and a single great pearl at her breast. Because it is white and spherical, the pearl symbolizes completeness and perfection. Towards the end of *Sir Gawain*, the hero is praised by his adversary as one who surpasses other knights just as much as pearls surpass dried peas; but the pearl maiden embodies an absolute, not relative, perfection of white innocence. At the same time, as she herself explains, the single pearl on her breast betokens the kingdom of heaven itself, in accordance with the parable of the merchant 'who, when he had found one pearl of great price, went his way and sold all that he had and bought it' (Matthew 13.45–6). To win that pearl, human beings must themselves either be or become pearls. Hence, whereas the poem began by referring to the pearl as a luxury item treasured by earthly princes, it echoes that opening line with altered reference at the end, substituting Christ for the prince:

> He gef us to be his homly hyne
> And precious perlez unto his pay.

[*gef* grant, *homly hyne* household servants, *pay* pleasure]

John Burrow

SELECT BIBLIOGRAPHY

EDITIONS

ANDREW, M., and WALDRON, R., eds, *The Poems of the Pearl Manuscript*, 3rd edn, University of Exeter Press, Exeter, 1996.

GORDON, E. V., ed., *Pearl*, Clarendon Press, Oxford, 1953.

SCHMIDT, A. V. C., ed., *William Langland: The Vision of Piers Plowman*, 2nd edn, Dent, London, 1995.

TOLKIEN, J. R. R., and GORDON, E. V., eds, *Sir Gawain and the Green Knight*, 2nd edn, revised N. Davis, Clarendon Press, Oxford, 1967.

'PIERS PLOWMAN': STUDIES

ALFORD, J. A., ed., *A Companion to 'Piers Plowman'*, University of California Press, Berkeley, California, 1988.

FRANK, R. W., *'Piers Plowman' and the Scheme of Salvation*, Yale University Press, New Haven, Connecticut, 1957.

GODDEN, M., *The Making of 'Piers Plowman'*, Longman, London, 1990.

KANE, G., *'Piers Plowman': The Evidence for Authorship*, Athlone Press, London, 1965.

SIMPSON, J., *'Piers Plowman': An Introduction to the B-Text*, Longman, London, 1990.

THE 'GAWAIN'-POET: STUDIES

BREWER, D., and GIBSON, J., eds, *A Companion to the 'Gawain'-Poet*, Brewer, Cambridge, 1997.

PUTTER, A., *An Introduction to the 'Gawain'-Poet*, Longman, London, 1996.

SPEARING, A. C., *The 'Gawain'-Poet: A Critical Study*, Cambridge University Press, Cambridge, 1970.

'SIR GAWAIN AND THE GREEN KNIGHT': STUDIES

BENSON, L. D., *Art and Tradition in 'Sir Gawain and the Green Knight'*, Rutgers University Press, New Brunswick, New Jersey, 1965.

BORROFF, M., *'Sir Gawain and the Green Knight': A Stylistic and Metrical Study*, Yale University Press, New Haven, Connecticut, 1962.

BURROW, J. A., *A Reading of 'Sir Gawain and the Green Knight'*, Routledge, London, 1965.

PUTTER, A., *'Sir Gawain and the Green Knight' and French Arthurian Romance*, Clarendon Press, Oxford, 1995.

'PEARL': STUDIES

BISHOP, I., *'Pearl' in its Setting*, Blackwell, Oxford, 1968.

KEAN, P. M., *The 'Pearl': An Interpretation*, Routledge, London, 1967.

THE LITERATURE OF THE PERIOD: STUDIES

AERS, D., *Community, Gender, and Individual Identity: English Writing 1360–1430*, Routledge, London, 1988.

BURROW, J. A., *Ricardian Poetry: Chaucer, Gower, Langland and the 'Gawain'-Poet*, Routledge, London, 1971.

MUSCATINE, C., *Poetry and Crisis in the Age of Chaucer*, Notre Dame University Press, Notre Dame, Indiana, 1972.

SALTER, E., *Fourteenth-Century English Poetry: Contexts and Readings*, Clarendon Press, Oxford, 1983.

SPEARING, A. C., *Medieval Dream-Poetry*, Cambridge University Press, Cambridge, 1976.

TURVILLE-PETRE, T., *The Alliterative Revival*, Brewer, Cambridge, 1977.

CHRONOLOGY

DATE	AUTHOR'S LIFE/ TEXTUAL HISTORY	LITERARY CONTEXT
1327–77		
1330	Probable birth of William Langland, son of an Oxfordshire gentleman, and author of *Piers Plowman*.	*c.* 1330 MS Advocates' MS 19.2.1 (the Auchinleck MS), a large compilation of English romances and other poems, including *Sir Orfeo*.
1335		
1337		Boccaccio completes *Il Filostrato*.
Early 1340s	Langland may have gone to school at the Great Malvern Priory.	Birth of Chaucer. Completion of copying of National Library of Scotland, Edinburgh.
1341		Boccaccio completes his *Teseida delle Nozze d'Emilia*.
1346		
1347		
1348–9		Boccaccio begins writing *The Decameron*.
1349		Death of Richard Rolle, English mystic, and of the scholars and theologians Robert Holcot, William of Ockham and Thomas Bradwardine.
1350s	It is probable that Langland took minor orders but never became a priest.	Beginnings of reflourishing of alliterative poetry in the west and north-west. *Ywain and Gawain* (poetry), translation of Chrétien's *Ywain*.
1351		
1356		
1360s	Langland begins *Piers Plowman*, A Text.	
1360	*c.* 1360 In London, Langland possibly eked out his living by saying prayers for benefactors.	*c.* 1360 Alliterative *Morte Arthur* based loosely on Wace.

xxii

Reign of King Edward III.

Hundred Years' War between England and France begins.
Edward formally assumes title of King of France. French influence within the Church increases (popes based in Avignon 1309–77).

English victory at the battle of Crécy. Battle of Neville's Cross: David II of Scotland defeated and captured.
Fall of Calais.
The Black Death reaches England and kills between one third and one half of the country's population. Order of the Garter thought to have been formally inaugurated.
Ordinance of Labourers in which the king attempts to freeze wages to pre-plague levels and control the movement of labour.

Statute of Labourers: vain attempt to enforce the Ordinance. Statute of Provisors: first of a series of anti-papal statutes (1353, 1365, 1390, 1393).
English victory at the battle of Poitiers; King John of France captured; lives at the English court 1357–60 in luxurious captivity, with much of the French royal household.

Treaty of Brétigny begins period of uneasy peace with France. Introduction of oil painting to western Europe.

DATE	AUTHOR'S LIFE/ TEXTUAL HISTORY	LITERARY CONTEXT
1361		Jean Froissart, French poet and chronicler, in the household of Queen Philippa as 'clerc de la chambre' (to 1367).
1362		
1364		
1367		
1368		Chaucer: *The Book of the Duchess*. Oton de Granson (the poet of Savoy) settles at the English court.
1369		
Late 1360s		Chaucer translates (part of) *The Romance of the Rose*.
1370s	Langland revising *Piers Plowman*, B Text.	Chaucer: *Anelida and Arcite*.
1370		*c.* 1370 John Lydgate born (later one of the most prolific writers of the 15th century, whose works include *Fall of Princes*).
1371		
1373		
1374		Death of Petrarch.
1375		Death of Boccaccio. John Barbour's Scots poem *The Bruce* completed.
c. 1375		Gower begins his Anglo-Norman *Mirour de l'Omme*. *Antwyrs of Arthure* (poetry).
1376		
1377		Death of Guillaume de Machaut, French poet.
1377–99		
1378		First record of York cycle of Mystery Plays. Chaucer completes *House of Fame* around this time.
1380s	Langland at work on *Piers Plowman*, C Text.	Gower completes his Latin poem, *Vox Clamantis*.

CHRONOLOGY

DATE	AUTHOR'S LIFE/ TEXTUAL HISTORY	LITERARY CONTEXT
c. 1380		Chaucer: *The Parliament of Fowls*, probably written with some allusion to the negotiations that ended with Richard II's marriage to Anne of Bohemia on 3 May, 1381.
1381		
c. 1381–6		Chaucer: *Troilus and Criseyde*; probably simultaneously with *Boece*, the prose translation of *De Consolatione Philosophiae* by Boethius.
1382		*c.* 1382 First English translation of the whole Bible issued by Lollard followers of John Wyclif.
Mid-1380s		Sir John Clanvowe writes *The Book of Cupid*, with quotation from *Palamon and Arcite*.
1385		The French poet Eustache Deschamps sends a poem of praise to Chaucer.
c. 1385–7		Thomas Usk: *Testament of Love*.
1386		
c. 1386–7		Chaucer: *The Legend of Good Women*.
1387		John Gower begins his *Confessio Amantis*. John Trevisa writing his English prose translation of Higden's universal history, the *Polychronicon*.
c. 1387		Chaucer begins the *Canterbury Tales*.
1388	*c.* 1388 Death of Langland.	*c.* 1388 Birth of Jean Froissart, French poet and chronicler.
1389		Christine de Pisan begins her writing career at the French court.

CHRONOLOGY

The Peasants' Revolt (June) led by Wat Tyler. They use *Piers Plowman* as a reference.

Official condemnation of the heretical opinions of John Wyclif.

Robert de Vere, Earl of Oxford, the king's favourite, made Duke of Ireland. Death of Princess Joan of Kent, the king's mother.

Gaunt sails for Spain (9 July); away until November 1389. The Duke of Gloucester and his adherents seek to curb the king's power at the 'Wonderful Parliament' (October–November).

Battle of Radcot Bridge; De Vere routed (20 December).

The 'Merciless Parliament': the Lords Appellant secure the removal of some of the king's closest advisers, and the execution of other adherents, including Thomas Usk.
Richard resumes his regality (3 May).

DATE	AUTHOR'S LIFE / TEXTUAL HISTORY	LITERARY CONTEXT
1391		Chaucer: *Treatise on the Astrolabe*; continuing work on the *Canterbury Tales*.
1392		*The Equatorie of the Planetis*, attributed by some to Chaucer.
1394		
1394–5		Chaucer revises *Prologue to Legend of Good Women*.
1395		*c.* 1395 Second version of the Wycliffite Bible in English.
1396		Death of Walter Hilton, canon of Thurgarton, author of *The Scale of Perfection*.
1396 (?)		Chaucer: *Envoy to Bukton* which mentions Wife of Bath.
1397		
1398		
Late 14th century		Copying of Bodleian Library MS Eng.poet.a.I (the Vernon MS), a massive compilation of English religious and didactic writing in prose and verse.
1399		
1399–1413		
1400	*c.* 1400 Copying of British Library MS Cotton Nero A.x, containing *Sir Gawain and the Green Knight*, *Pearl*, *Patience* and *Cleanness* (the only extant MS of these poems). Probably the work of one author, originating from Cheshire or Staffordshire.	Chaucer: *Complaint to his Purse*. *c.* 1400 Stanzaic version of *Le Morte Arthur*. *Sir Gawain and the Carl of Carlisle*.
1401		

HISTORICAL EVENTS

Death of Queen Anne.

Lollard 'manifesto' affixed to the doors of Westminster Hall.

Truce between England and France. Richard married by proxy to Isabella, seven-year-old daughter of Charles VI.

Richard takes his revenge upon the Appellants; Duke of Gloucester murdered at Calais.
Shrewsbury Parliament; beginning of Richard's 'tyranny'. Concordat between Richard and the pope.

Death of John of Gaunt (3 February). Deposition of Richard II; accession of Henry IV (30 September).
REIGN OF KING HENRY IV.
Owen Glendower's revolt suppressed.

The death penalty becomes the punishment for heresy.

NOTE ON THE TEXTS

SIR GAWAIN AND THE GREEN KNIGHT, PEARL, SIR ORFEO

EDITIONS

Sir Gawain and the Green Knight, edited by J. R. R. Tolkien and E. V. Gordon, Oxford University Press, 1925. This has been extensively revised in a second edition by Norman Davis, Clarendon Press, 1967.

Pearl, edited by E. V. Gordon, Clarendon University Press, 1953.

Sir Orfeo, edited by A. J. Bliss, second edition Oxford University Press, 1966. This edition contains all three texts of the poem, and a discussion of the origins of this treatment of the legend of Orpheus and Eurydice.

The Auchinleck text, with the same insertions as are made in the translation, is given in *Fourteenth Century Verse and Prose*, edited by Kenneth Sisam, with a glossary by J. R. R. Tolkien (Oxford University Press).

THE TRANSLATIONS BY J. R. R. TOLKIEN

The details of presentation (most notably the absence of line numbers in *Sir Gawain* and *Pearl*, and the use of inverted commas in interior quotations from *Pearl*) are in accordance with my father's wishes.

Line 4 in stanza 42, and line 18 in stanza 98, of the translation of *Sir Gawain* are not in the original. These were introduced into the tranlasion on the assumption that at these points lines had been lost from the original poem, and they are based on suggestions by Sir Israel Gollancz (edition of *Sir Gawain and the Green Knight*, Early English Text Society, 1940).

Since a primary object of these translations was the close preservation of the metres of the originals, I thought that the book should contain, for those who want it, an account of the verse-forms of *Sir Gawain* and *Pearl*. The section on *Sir Gawain* is composed from drafts made for, but not used in, the introductory talk to the broadcasts of the translation [1953]; and that on the verse-form of *Pearl* from other unpublished notes. There is very little in these accounts (and nothing that is a matter of opinion) that is not in my father's own words.

At the end of the book I have provided a short glossary. On the last page will be found some verses translated by my father from a medieval English poem. He called them 'Gawain's Leave-taking', clearly with reference to the passage in *Sir Gawain* where Gawain leaves the castle of Sir Bertilak to go to the tryst at the Green Chapel. The original poem has no connection with Sir Gawain; the verses translated are in fact the first three stanzas, and the last, of a somewhat longer poem found among a group of fourteenth-century lyrics with refrains in the Vernon manuscript in the Bodleian Library at Oxford.

Christopher Tolkien

PIERS PLOWMAN

Terence Tiller's translation of the B Text is based on: W. W. Skeat, *The Vision of William concerning Piers the Plowman: Text-B* (with notes, general preface and indexes), Oxford University Press, 1972; and J. A. W. Bennett, *Piers Plowman: The Prologue and Passus I-VII*, Oxford University Press, 1972. Tiller also refers to the lively and learned prose translation by J. F. Goodridge, Penguin, revised edition 1966.

Priscilla Martin's translation of the 'Autobiographical Episode' (C, 5, 1–104) is based on: Derek Pearsall, *Piers Plowman by William Langland: An Edition of the C-text*, University of California Press, 1979.

PIERS PLOWMAN

PROLOGUE

One summer season, when the sun was soothing,
I shrouded myself in a shaggy sheepskin coat;
Thus habited like a hermit of unholy life,
I walked into the wide world to hear of wonders.
But one May morning in the Malvern Hills,
I met with a marvel that seemed made by magic:
I was weary with wandering, and went to rest
Under a broad bank by the side of a brook;
And as I lay, and leaned to look into the waters,
They sounded so sweetly that I sank into sleep ...   10
    There I dreamed a dream that was indeed wonderful:
I was in a wilderness, but *where* I knew not.
I set my face eastward, where, high against the sun,
I saw a tower, trim-built on the top of a hill;
And a deep dale beneath it, and a dungeon in it,
With deep dark dykes that were dreadful to see.
A pleasant plain full of people lay between these places,
With every manner of man, poor, middling, and rich,
Toiling or travelling as the world's way took them.
Some spent their lives at the plough, and were seldom idle,   20
Seeding and sowing and strongly labouring
To gather what the gluttony of wastrels would again scatter.
Some spent their lives in pride, and were dressed in apt style,
Coming all tricked-out in conspicuous clothing.
In prayers and in penance many passed their days,
And for love of Our Lord lived rigorous lives
In hope of having happiness in Heaven;
Such are hermits and anchoresses who hold to their cells
And do not care to career about the country
Or flatter their flesh with dainty food and living.   30
    And some were sellers and buyers; they were served better,
For in *our* sight it seems always that such men thrive.
Some came to make men merry, as minstrels know how,
Getting money for glad music – and are guiltless, I think.

But jokesters and jabberers, Judas's children,
With feigning and with fantasy pretend to be fools,
Yet have wits enough to work, at will or at need:
That St Paul[1] has preached of them I shall not prove in full,
Save that 'he who speaks foulness' is in the service of Lucifer.

    Cadgers and beggars were bustling all about,   40
Their bellies and their back-packs crammed with bread;
They were fed by their feigning, and fought over their ale;
And in gluttony, God knows, do they go to bed,
And arise with ribaldry, the robberly rogues:
Sleep and shabby sloth pursue them for ever.

    Pilgrims and palmers were compacting together
To seek Spanish St James's,[2] or saints' relics in Rome.
They went upon their way with much wise talk,
And had licence to lie for the rest of their lives.
I saw some that said they had sought-out saints: 50
Whatever tale they told, their tongues were attuned to lying
More than to speaking the truth, as their style of speech
    proved.

    Hermits in hordes, with their hooked staves,
Were away to Walsingham[3] – and their wenches followed
    them.
Great long-bodied lubbers that were loth to work, they were,
And clad themselves as clergy for their kind to be known,
And were habited as hermits to have easy times.

    I found there friars, all the four orders,
Who preached to the people for their own profit,
And glossed the Gospel for the good will of their patrons,   60
Construing it comfortably, they so coveted new cloaks.
Many of these master-friars may dress as they please,
For their merchandise and their money move on
    hand-in-hand.
For since Charity turned chafferer, and the chief-confessor
    to nobles,
Many strange things have we seen in the space of few years.
If the friars and Holy Church form no better friendship,
The greatest evil on Earth will come early upon us.

    There was a pardoner[4] preaching as if he were a priest;

He brought forth a pope's Bull, with bishops' seals on it,
And said that he himself could absolve all men   70
From falsehoods, fast-breaking, and forsworn vows.
The unlettered quite believed him, and liked his words;
They came and knelt and kissed his credentials.
He brow-beat them with his brevet, and blinded their eyes,
And raked-in with his great roll their rings and brooches.
Thus people give their gold, to maintain gluttons,
And believe in such wastrels who live in lechery.
Were the bishop truly blessèd, and his whole brain working,
His seal would not thus be sent to deceive the people.
But it is not by the bishop's word that this biter preaches,   80
For the parish priest and the pardoner share the plunder –
Which the poor folk of the parish would have, apart from
      those two.
   Parsons and parish priests pleaded with the bishop,
Their parishes being poor since the time of the Plague,[5]
To have licence to leave, and live in London,
And sing simoniac Mass there (for silver is sweet).
Brethren and bishops, both masters and doctors,
Curates under Christ, their crown shaven in token
That they should all of them shrive their parishioners,
And preach to them, and pray for them, and feed the poor – 90
There they were, living in London, even during Lent:
Some as the King's servants, counting his silver,
In Chancery or the Exchequer keeping charge of his dues
From wards and wardships and waifs and strays.
And some enlisted as lords' or ladies' servants,
Sitting and making decisions in the office of steward,
Their Masses and their Matins, and most of their
      set prayers,
Being done undevoutly: and they are in danger
Lest at Christ's final Consistory[6] many are accursed.
I perceived then some of the power in St Peter's charge,   100
'To bind and unbind', as the Bible tells us.[7]
He left that power to Love, as Our Lord commanded –
The greatest Virtue of all, among those four Virtues
Called by men 'Cardinal':[8] hinges that close

The gates of the Kingdom of Christ, or *dis*close to others
All Heaven open, and its happiness at hand.
But the *Cardinals* of Rome's Curia, who claimed that title,
And pre-empted for themselves the power of pope-making,
With all the potency of Peter: impugn them I will not;
For such elections belong to both love and learning;   110
Therefore I may not – though I might – say more of
    that Court.

  Then there came a King; with a convoy of Knights; [9]
By consent of the common-folk was his kingship gained,
But Mother Wit came amain and found men of learning
To counsel the King and protect the common-weal.
The King and his knightly cohort, and the clergy too,
Planned that the People should provide for all.
With Mother Wit, the commoners contrived crafts for
    themselves;
And, that all the People might profit, appointed ploughmen
To till the earth, and to toil as trusty men should.   120
Thus the King and the Commons, accompanied by
    Mother Wit,
Laid down law and fair-dealing, their duties and rights
    known by all.

  Then a lunatic looked in on them – and a long lean
    creature he was –
And said, on his knees to the King, in formal style:
'Christ keep you, my lord King, and all your kingdom,
And let you so rule your realm that the loyal shall love you,
And you for your righteous reign be rewarded in Heaven.'
And then, from the air on high, a heavenly angel
Stooped low, and spoke in Latin – for the unlettered had not
The judgment or the jargon for what should gain them
    justice,   130
But must suffer and serve. Therefore, thus spoke the angel:
    '*Sum rex, sum princeps: neutrum forasse deinceps;*
    O qui jura regis Christi specialia regis,
    Hoc quod agas melius justus es, esto pius!
    Nudum jus a te vestiri vult pietate;
    Qualia vis metere talia grana sere.

Si jus nudatur nudo de jure metatur;
Si seritur pietas de pietate metas!'
('I am King, I am Prince, you say: perhaps neither,
    after today;
You wield the laws most high of Christ's own Majesty;
The better so to do, be just and ruthful too!
Justice in nakedness needs from you Mercy's dress;
That harvest you would see, such let your sowing be.
If you strip Justice bare, such too may be your share;
Mercy by you once sown, *you* shall be mercy shown.')
Then a goliard,[10] a glutton for words, made this a grievance:
And to the angel on high he gave this answer: 140
    'Dum rex a regere dicatur nomen habere,
    Nomen habet sine re nisi studet jura tenere.'
('Since by his reign alone the king *as* king is known,
He holds the name alone if laws be overthrown.')
Then all the Commoners called out a catchword in Latin,
To counsel the King, construe it who wished.
    'Praecepta regis sunt nobis vincula legis!'
('All that the King ordains binds us with legal chains.')
  Then all at once there ran out a riot of rats,
And little mice among them, more than a thousand,
Who came to confer for their common profit.
For a Cat from a certain Court came whenever he chose
And lighted on them laughingly, and did what he liked   150
To play with them perilously, and paw them, and toss
    them about.
'For dangers and dreads of all kinds we dare scarcely stir;
And if we grumble at his games, he will grieve us the more –
Scratch us and scrape us, or seize us in his claws
Till life is not worth living until he leaves us alone.
Were we but wise enough to withstand his will,
We too might be lofty lords and live at our ease.'
  One rat of renown, with a free-running tongue,
Offered an ideal scheme of his own invention.
Said he: 'I have seen certain fellows, in the City of London, 160
Bearing bright golden chains about their necks,
And cleverly fashioned collars; they are unconfined,

They walk in warrens or wastelands wherever they please
(And at other times, I am told, they take themselves elsewhere).
It seems to me, by Jesus, if their bright chains carried a bell,
People would hear where they went, and could run away.
I have reasoned this out,' said the rat, 'and our right course
Is to buy a bell, of brass or of bright silver,
And, for our common cause, to fix it on a collar
And hang it round the Cat's neck. We shall hear him then   170
When he takes the road, or rests, or runs out to play.
If he is disposed for sport, we may spy on him,
Present only in part while his mood is playful;
And should he wax wroth, beware, and avoid his ways.'
   All that rout of rats agreed with his reasoning.
But when the bell had been bought, and hung on the chain,
There was never a rat in the rout – not for the realm of France
– That dared to bind the bell about the Cat's neck,
Nor to hang it over his head, for the whole of England.
They confessed themselves fearful, and their plan feeble,   180
And allowed that their labour was lost, and all their long
      scheming.
   Then a mouse that seemed to me to have much wisdom
Strode forward strongly, and stood before them all,
And, as follows, addressed the assembly of rats.
'Even if we killed the Cat, another would come
To claw us and all our kinsmen, though we crept under
      benches.
Therefore I counsel the commoners to leave the Cat alone,
And let us never be so bold as even to *show* him the bell.
For I heard my father say, these seven years since,
That when the Cat is a kitten, the Court is wretched.   190
Thus too runs Holy Writ, for anyone to read:
      Vae terrae ubi puer rex est.
      (Woe to thee, O land, when thy King is a child.)[11]
For there no resident can rest, for the rats at night.
More: while the Cat chases conies, he does not covet
      our corpses,
But (not to defame him) feeds on game from the fields.
Better a little loss than a long sorrow,

And the trouble among us today than the *loss* of our troubles.
For then we mice would destroy the malt of many a man,
And all you riot of rats would rend men's clothing,
Could not the Cat in this Court pounce and catch us.
Were you given your own way, you rats could not rule
      yourselves.   200
For *my* part,' said this mouse, 'I foresee such an aftermath,
My counsel is to vex neither Cat nor Kitten,
Nor collogue about this collar (that cost *me* nothing,
Though even if it *had* cost me cash I should never confess it),
But to let each one of them do as either pleases –
Whether paired or in private – to take what prey he can.
So, a warning to the wise: watch *your own* affairs.'
   Now, the meaning of my dream, you merry men all,
Decide for yourselves, for *I* dare not, by dear God in Heaven!
   Now a hundred men hovered there, in silken headgear,   210
Serjeants-at-Law, it seemed, that served at the Bar
And presented their pleas for pennies or for pounds;
Not for love of Our Lord did their lips ever open;
You might sooner measure the mist on the Malvern Hills
Than get one murmur from their mouths without
      showing money.
   Barons and burgesses and bondsmen too
I saw in the assembly, as you shall soon hear;
Batches of bakers and brewers and butchers,
Weavers of wool and weavers of linen,
Tailors and tinkers and market-toll-takers,   220
Masons and miners, and many other craftsmen.
No kind of labourer living, but some leapt forward,
Such as ditchers and delvers that do their work badly
And spend the long day singing *Dieu vous sauve,*
    Dame Emme.[12]
There cooks and their kitchen-boys cried, 'Hot pies! Hot!
Good pigs and geese! Come and get your dinner!'
And taverners told the same tale to the world –
'White wine of Alsace! Red wine of Gascony!
Rhine wine or La Rochelle to digest the roast!'
All this I saw in my dream, and seven times more.   230

PASSUS 1

Now, what that mountain meant, and that murky valley,
And the plain full of people, I shall presently show you.
A Lady, lovely to look upon, clothed in linen,
Came down from a castle and called to me kindly,
Saying, 'Are you asleep, my son? Do you see these people,
How busily they bustle about their maze?
The greater part of the people that pass through this world,
If honoured upon Earth, ask nothing better;
Of a Heaven, other than here, they have no thought.'

    Her face made me fear her, fair though she was. 10
'Madame,' I said, 'if you please, what may all this mean?'
She said, 'The tower on the hill-top is where Truth dwells,
He who would have your works accord with His word;
For He is Father of Faith, and fashioned you all
With a figure and a face, and gave you five senses
With which to worship Him while you dwell here.
Therefore he ordered the earth to afford all men
Linen enough, and wool, and their livelihood,
That each might in moderate manner be at ease.

    In His kindness He commanded three things common
       to all; 20
None but these is needful, and I mean to name them,
Reckoning them by reason; and you shall repeat them.
First there is clothing, to keep you from cold;
Then food to furnish your meals, and keep you from
       discomfort;
And drink for when you are dry: but drink within reason;
Beware of being the worse for it when you should work.
For Lot, when he was alive, from his love of drink
Did things to his daughters that pleased the Devil.
He delighted in drink, as the Devil would have wished,
And lechery laid hold on him, and he lay with them both; 30
And wine it was he must blame for the wicked deeds:
    Inebriamus eum vino, dormiamusque cum eo,

ut servare possimus ex patre nostro semen.
(The first-born said to the younger, Come, let us make
    our father drink wine, and we will lie with him, that
    we may preserve seed of our father.)[1]
Thus by wine and by women was Lot overwhelmed,
And begat there in gluttony ungracious sons.
Dread, therefore, delectable drink; you will do better to;
Moderation is medicinal, however much you yearn.
Not all that the stomach beseeches is good for the soul,
Nor food for the flesh all that the soul finds pleasing.
Put no faith in your flesh, for a liar instructs it –
Namely, the wicked World, with its wish to betray you;
For the Fiend and the Flesh are fellow-hunters,[2]   40
Each pursuing your soul, speaking sin to your heart.
I tell this by way of warning, so that you shall beware.'
  'My thanks to you, madame,' said I. 'Your words please
    me well.
But the wealth of this world, that men so watchfully cling to:
Tell me to whom, madame, this money belongs?'
  Said she, 'Go to the Gospel, and read God's own word,
At the question put Him with a penny, by people in
    the temple,
To pay or not to pay to Tiberius Caesar.
And Christ asked whose inscription was upon the coin,
And whose the likeness lying within the lettering.   50
"Caesar's," they said, "as we all plainly see."
"Give unto Caesar," said Christ, "the things that are Caesar's;
And unto God, God's things; you go astray else."[3]
I say, it is Rightful Reason that should rule you all,
With Mother Wit[4] as the warden that holds your wealth,
The guardian of your gold, who gives you it as needed:
Good Management and these two go hand in hand together.'
Then earnestly I asked her, in Our Maker's Name,
'That dungeon in the dale, so dreadful to look at,
What may its meaning be, madame, I beseech you?'   60
  'That is the Castle of Care; and whoever comes there
Indeed may curse the day that his body and soul were
    conceived.

A creature dwells in the Castle, and is called Wrong.
He first founded the dungeon, and is father of Falsehood.
Adam and Eve he egged on to evil,
He counselled Cain to kill his own brother;
Judas he be-japed with Jewish silver,
And high on an elder-tree he afterwards hanged him.[5]
He sets leashes on love, and he lies to all men;
Those who trust in his treasure, he betrays the soonest.'   70
Then I wondered within me who this woman could be,
Who spoke with such wisdom the words of Holy Scripture.
I asked her, 'In the Name of the Highest, before you go hence,
Who are you, truly, that so tenderly teach me?'
    Said she, 'I am Holy Church. It behoves you to know me;
I first received you, and first taught you the Faith;
You brought me at baptism sureties of obedience,
Loyally to love me while your life should last.'
    On bended knees I begged her then to be merciful,
And in pity to pray for the pardon of my sins;   80
Also to acquaint me clearly with true belief in Christ,
That I might keep the commands of Him Who created me.
'Teach not of earthly treasure,' I cried, 'tell me this only:
How may I save my soul, oh sanctified Lady?'
    Said she, 'When all treasures are tested, Truth is the best;
And the text "God is Love"[6] I take as my attestor.
Truth is a leman as loveable as the dear Lord Himself.
    Whoever is truthful of tongue, and tells no lies,
And is faithful in works as in words, and wishes no man evil,
He is godlike, says the Gospel, both here and on high,   90
And is like Our Lord Himself, as St Luke says.[7]
    Men well taught in this truth should tell it around,
Christians and unChristians too are clamouring for it.
Kings and their cohorts should by rights be its keepers,
Riding forth to repress wrong throughout their realms,
Trapping transgressors and tying them tightly
Until Truth has determined the extent of their trespasses.
That is the profession plainly proper for knights –
Not just to fast on one Friday in five-score winters,
But to stand by him and by her who would uphold Truth,   100

And leave them neither for love nor for latching on to money.
 King David in his day was a dubber of knights,[8]
And made them swear on their swords to serve Truth always;
And apostate from that Order was any who broke that oath.
 But Christ, who is King of Kings, founded *ten* knightly
  Orders
(Seraphim and Cherubim, seven lower, and last of all, Satan's),[9]
Deputing them power from His might – and the prouder
  they were for it –
And over His lesser lieges made them Archangels,
And taught them to know Truth by virtue of the Trinity,
Obedient when He bade them; He asked nothing besides. 110
 Lucifer and his legions also learned this in Heaven,
But for breach of obedience lost Heaven's bliss
And fell from that fellowship in the forms of fiends,
Into deep dark Hell, there to dwell for ever.
Many more thousands than a man could count
Leapt out with Lucifer, in loathsome shapes,
For they believed in him though he lied in these words,
  "Ponam pedem in aquilone, et similis ero altissimo."'
  (My foot shall I set upon the North Wind, and be like
   unto the Most High.)[10]
All who hoped it might be so, Heaven could not hold them;
Out they fell, in fiends' forms, for nine whole days.
Till God in His goodness stemmed and staunched
  that gushing, 120
Fixing the firmament close, to stand fast and quiet.
 When these wicked ones fell, it was in a strange way,
Some into air, some to earth, some deep into Hell.
But Lucifer lies the lowest of them all:
For the pride that he displayed, his pains are endless;
And all evildoers shall go down and dwell,
After the day of their death, with that same devil.
But they who wrought righteousness, as Holy Writ shows,
And whose end is in that Truth I have said is best,
Certain are they that their souls shall ascend to Heaven: 130
The threefold God's is their truth, and He shall
  enthrone them.

Therefore I tell you again, and have proved by my texts,
When all treasures are tested, the best is Truth.
Let unlearned men hear this, for the lettered know it:
The treasure of treasures upon Earth, is Truth.'
    'I do not know Truth by nature; you must teach me better
By what faculty it enters my flesh, and where it is found.'
    Said the Lady, 'You doltish dullard, dim are your wits!
Too little Latin, my friend, you learned in your youth!'
        Heu mihi, quod sterilem duxi vitam juvenilem!
        (Woe's me! How barren, in truth, was the life I led
            in my youth!)
    'In your heart you know by nature the need you have   140
To love your Lord better than your own life,
And commit no mortal sin though death might befall you.
Trust me, that is truth; if any can teach you better,
Be sure to listen, and let him speak, and so learn from him.
    Thus witnesses God's word – let your works conform:
Truth will tell you that Love is the tried elixir of Heaven;
They suffer from no sin, who use *that* sovereign balm;
God worked, as He willed, by Love, when framing the world,
And Moses learned from Him that Love is likest to Heaven.[11]
It is the Plant of Peace,[12] and most precious of virtues.   150
    For Heaven could not hold it, it was so heavy in itself,
Till it had eaten all it could of the Earth;
And when it had upon Earth assumed flesh and blood,[13]
Thereafter it was lighter than a leaf on a linden-tree,
And nimble and keen as the point of a needle;
No armour could resist it, nor high ramparts bar it.
    Therefore Love is leader of Our Lord's folk in Heaven,
Our mediator, as mayors are between king and people.
Just so is Love a leader, and a framer of laws;
Its amercement on man for misdeeds is mercy.   160
To know it by nature needs the power of God
At work in the heart, where its fount and high well-spring lie.
For natural knowledge in the heart, a power is needed,
That comes forth and from the Father Who formed us all,
And Who looked on us with love, and let His Son die
Meekly for our misdeeds, to amend us all.

And He called down no curse upon his crucifiers:
Mildly did His mouth beseech God's mercy
And pity on those people, in His pain and death.
 You have an example here, in His own self: 170
He was mighty but meek, and He granted mercy
To them that hung Him high, and pierced His heart.
 Rich people, have pity, I counsel you, for the poor;
Though mighty to command them, let your acts be mild.
For "with what measure ye mete",[14] amiss or truly,
You shall be weighed therewith when you leave this world.
Eadem mensura qua mensi fueritis, remetietur vobis.
For though your tongue be truthful, and you trade honestly,
Though you be chaste as a child that weeps at its churching,
Unless you love Man loyally, and relieve the poor,
Sharing the gifts God sent you, in goodly bounty,   180
You will get no more merit from your Masses and your prayers
Than Molly the Slut from her maidenhead – which no man
  has tried for.
As noble St James says in his Epistle,
  Fides sine operibus mortua est:
Faith without Works has no worth at all,[15]
As dead as a door-post unless deeds confirm it.
So, chastity without charity shall be chained in Hell;
It has less value than an unlit lamp.
 Many chaplains are chaste, but lacking in charity:
Are any men more greedy than these, once promoted?
Unkind to their kin and to all fellow-Christians?   190
They gulp down all gifts, and grumble for more:
Such chastity lacking charity shall be chained in Hell.
 Parish priests in plenty are bodily pure,
Yet encumbered by covetousness – and cannot get rid of it,
It is hammered hard into them, like a hinge to a door.
This is not the Truth of the Trinity, but the treachery of Hell;
And laymen learn from it to give less readily.
Wisely, then – by Our Lord – were these words said:
"Give and it shall be given unto you; for *I* gave you my all.
This is the latch of love, that releases my grace   200
To comfort the comfortless encumbered with sin."

Love is the healer of life, that stands next to Our Lord,
And the road that leads directly to the realm of Heaven.
   I tell you again what I took from those texts:
When all treasures are tested, Truth is the best.
   Now I have told you what Truth is – that no treasure
     is better:
I may linger with you no longer. May Our Lord preserve you!'

PASSUS 2

Again I besought a boon, on my bended knees,
And said, 'Your mercy, madame, for the love of Mary
    in Heaven
That bore the blessed child who brought our salvation,
Let me now learn some way to distinguish lying.'
  'Look to your left side: lo! there they stand –
Falsehood and Fauvel[1] together, and their many friends!'
  I looked to my left, as the Lady had bidden me,
And grew aware of a woman with splendid clothing
Fringed with rich fur, the finest in the world.
She was crowned with a coronet as good as the king's.   10
Daintily were her fingers adorned with spun gold
In rings, with rubies on them like red-hot embers,
And diamonds of the dearest, and sapphires both deep
    blue and light,
And orient pearls, and iolites as antidotes to poison.
Her robe was very rich, a fast-dyed red scarlet,
With rows of red gold and of radiant jewels.
I was ravished by her array; such riches were new to me;
I wondered who she was, and whose wife she might be.
  'Who is this woman,' I asked, 'so wonderfully dressed?'
'That is Meed[2] the Maiden,' said she, 'who has many
    times harmed me,   20
And slandered my sweet friend who is called Straight-Dealing,
And lied about her to the lords in the law-courts.
In the palace of the Pope she is as privileged as I –
Though Truth is bemocked by it, for Meed is a by-blow.
Her father was Fraud, of the faithless tongue,
Who never spoke sincerely since he came to Earth;
And Meed is modelled upon him, as is Nature's manner:
    Qualis pater, talis filius; bona arbor bonum fructum facit.
  (Like father, like son; a good tree bears good fruit.)[3]
I ought to be honoured above her; my lineage is higher:
My Father is great God, the ground of all graces,

One God, Who had no beginning; and I am His good
    daughter,   30
And He gave Mercy to me, to be my marriage-portion.
Whatever man shews Mercy, and loves me loyally,
Shall be my lord, and I his beloved, in Heaven above.
But whatever man takes Meed – I wager my head –
He will lose for love of her his heirloom of Charity.

    What King David conveys, about men who take Meed,
And of others who go among us maintaining Truth,
And how one may save oneself, the Psalter bears witness:
    Domine, quis habitabit in tabernaculo tuo?
    (Lord, who shall abide in thy tabernacle? or who shall
        dwell in thy holy hill?
    He that taketh not reward against the innocent.)[4]
    And now Meed the Maid is to marry an excommunicate
      villain,
Fraud Faithless-Tongue,[5] offspring of the Fiend;   40
Fauvel first, with fair speech, enchanted these folk;
But Liar was chief match-maker for the wedding of Meed.

    Tomorrow, then, shall this maiden's marriage feast be held;
And there you might learn, if you wished, who the others are,
Both little and great, who belong in their lordships' train.
Contrive, if you can, to know them; but keep your
      tongue quiet;
Do not abuse them, let them be, till Straight-Dealing becomes
A Justice with power to punish them: put your case *then*.
    Now I commend you to Christ and His immaculate
      Mother.
Never encumber your conscience by coveting Meed.'   50
    Thus the Lady left me lying asleep;
And how Meed was married, I imagined in my dream.
All the rich retinue that were retainers of Fraud
Were bidden to the bridal by the kin of both sides:
All manner of men, the humble and the mighty,
To see this maiden's marriage, were assembled in multitudes.
Clergy and knights had come; and, of the common people,
Assize-jurors, summoners, and sheriffs and their clerks,
Beadles and bailiffs and bargainers and brokers,

Pre-emptors and provisioners, and advocates of the
    Arches Court[6] –   60
I cannot recall or count all who came to see Meed.
But Simony and Civil Law and the Assize-Court jurymen
Were of all men, I thought, the most familiar with Meed.
Fauvel went first to fetch her from her boudoir,
And as marriage-broker brought her to be joined with Fraud.
When Simony and Civil Law understood what was wanted,
They assented, for a small fee, to say whatever they
    were asked.
Then Liar lunged forward, saying, 'Look! A deed of
    conveyance
That Guile, with his great oaths, has given to the couple!'
And he begged Civil Law to scan it, and Simony to read it.   70
Then Simony and Civil Law both stood up,
And unfolded the feoffment drawn-up by Fraud.[7]
Then Simony started singing-out at the top of his voice,
    '*Sciant praesentes et futuri*' ...
    (Be it known to all present and to come ...)
   'Be it witnessed and warranted by all the world
That Meed has been married more for her money
Than for any quality or comeliness or native kindness.
Fraud is fond of her, for he knows her wealth;
And Fauvel with his faithless tongue empowers them by
    this feoffment
To live proudly as princes, and despise the poor;
To backbite and to boast and to bear false witness;   80
To be scornful and scurrilous, and to spread scandal;
To be bold and disobedient in breaking the Ten
    Commandments.
   And the Earldoms of Envy and of Ire, conjoined,
And the Castles of Contention and of Chattering Claptrap,
The County of Covetousness, and the communes adjoining,
To wit, Usury and Avarice: I grant all these,
With their backdoor deals and brokery, plus the Borough
    of Theft,
And the Lordship of Lechery in all its length and breadth,
As well in words and in deeds as in wanton ogling,

As well in clothes and concupiscence as in fond conceits   90
That endure in the desire though the doing fails.'
   He gave them Gluttony too, and Great Oaths, its twin,
And the right to drink all day at a dozen taverns,
To jabber there, and joke, and judge their fellow-Christians,
And on fast-days to feast themselves before noon
– And then to sit and surfeit until sleep assailed them;
To breed like boars in town-gutters, and bed in luxury
Till Sloth and sleep had sleekened their sides.
In despair they should wake then, but without repentance,
And in their last agonies believe themselves lost.   100
   'To have and to hold, I give them and their inheritors
A dwelling with the Devil, and eternal damnation,
With the purlieus of Purgatory and the pains of Hell:
They in return to yield, at one year's end,
Their souls to Satan, with him to suffer torment
And with him to dwell in woe so long as God is in Heaven.'
   Of the witnesses of which deed, the first was Wrong
     himself,
Then Pete the Pardoner with his Pauline doctrine;[8]
Bartie the beadle of Buckinghamshire;
Reynold the reeve of the Soke of Rutland;   110
Munday the Miller, and many more such others.
'On Devilsday do I set my hand to this Deed,
With Sir Simony as witness, by right of Civil Law.'
   Now Theology lost his temper at that loud proclamation,
And said to Civil Law, 'Now, sorrow be upon you,
To manoeuvre such marriages in mockery of Truth![9]
You'll be sorry before you see the end of the ceremony!
   For Meed was of honest birth, engendered upon Amends,
And God has already given Good Work His promise of her.
You have given her to a guileful rogue, God damn you!   120
Is *this* how you interpret the text, that is Truth's own words?
    Dignus est enim operarius mercede sua.
    (For the labourer is worthy of his hire.)[10]
And you have handfast Meed to Fraud! A fig for your law!
For you live by lying and by lecherous business.
Simony and yourself are spoilers of Holy Church;

You and your notaries are a nuisance to the nation.
By the God who made me, you shall both buy this dearly!
Well do you know, double-faced ones, unless you are doited,
That Fraud is faithless and treacherous in all his affairs,
And was born in bastardy, Beelzebub's kinsman.   130
But Meed is a maiden well-born of Amends,
Who might kiss the king as her cousin if the fancy took her.
    Then use what wits you have; and if you are wise
You will lead her up to London, where the Laws are declared,
And find if any law will let these two lie together.
Even should the Justices judge her joinable with Fraud,
Still beware of that wedding; for Truth has His wits
        about him,
And Conscience is His counsellor, who knows you both
        quite well:
Should he find you at fault, and siding with Fraud,
Your souls shall both rue it bitterly, at the Bar of Heaven!'   140
Civil Law assented to this; but Simony refused
Until he had silver for his services, and so did the notaries.
    Then Fauvel fetched out a quantity of florins,
And told Guile to give the gold out all round –
To the notaries in particular, so that none should fail them
        at need.
He gave many florins to False-Witness, as a retaining fee,
For he could well manage Meed, and make her obedient.
With all this gold gathered in, there was great thanksgiving
To Fraud and Fauvel for their fine gifts,
And many came to comfort Fraud in his quandary,   150
Saying, 'Be sure, sir, we shall never slacken
Till Meed is your wedded wife by the work of our wits.
We have overmastered Meed with mild persuasion;
And she has agreed, good-humouredly, to go with us
To London, and look into whether the Law
Will judge you both rightly to be joined in lasting joy.'
    Fraud, at this, felt much happier, and so did Fauvel;
They summoned all and sundry from the surrounding shires,
And bade them, beggars included, be ready
To go with them to Westminster Court as witnesses.   160

They must cast-about, now, for caples to carry them there,
So Fauvel's men led forth mounts enough for them all.
Meed the Maiden they shoved upon a Sheriff newly-shod;
Fraud sat on an Assize-juror, who trotted softly;
Fauvel's own mount was a flatterer, finely harnessed.
    But the notaries had no horses, and were annoyed
That Simony and Civil Law must slog-it on foot.
Civil Law and Simony both swore
That the summoners should be saddled and serve
      to bear them.
'And let Pope's-priests[11] be apparelled as if they were
      palfreys;   170
Sir Simony himself shall sit on their backs.
You deans and sub-deans, let all draw together,
Bishops' officers and archdeacons, and all your registrars:
Have them saddled with silver to excuse our sins –
Our divorces and adulteries and undiscovered usuries.
And let them bear bishops about, on visitations.
    Paulines, as privies to the action, shall plead in
      the Consistory,
Serving myself: who am named Civil Law.
Cart-saddle the Commissary:[12] he shall draw our carriage,
And with fines from fornicators shall feed us all.   180
Tie Liar to a long cart, and let him lug all the remainder,
Such as friars and fakers, who are still on foot.'
    Thus Fraud and Fauvel set forth together,
With Meed in the middle, and all those men following.
I have no time to tell you all who trailed behind,
Of so many kinds of men who live in Middle Earth;
But going ahead of them was Guile, who guided them all.
    Straight-Dealing, though, understood him and, although
      saying little,
Spurred-up her palfrey and passed the whole troop,
And came to the King's Court, and told the news
      to Conscience;   190
And Conscience carried the story to the King.
    The King said, 'Now, by Christ, could I only catch
Fraud or Fauvel, or any of their followers,

I would have my revenge on those wretches who
    rouse-up trouble!
I would have them hanged by the neck, and their whole
    horde with them!
Not even the least shall go loose, on bail or licence:
Let the full force of the Law fall on them all.'
And he called for a Constable, who came forthwith,
And ordered them arrested: 'At all costs, I say!
And put that felon Fraud in fetters, refusing all bribes;   200
And get the head off Guile, before he goes further;
And if you lay hands on Liar, do not let him escape,
But put him in the pillory, however hard he pleads.
And bring Meed the Maid before me, no matter what!'
    Sir Dread was standing by the door, and heard
      these decrees;
How the King was commanding Constables and Sergeants
To bind and fetter Fraud and all his fellowship.
So he went away quickly, and gave warning to Fraud,
Bidding him flee for fear, and his followers with him.
And Fraud, being truly afraid, took refuge with the friars;   210
And Guile, aghast at his danger, did not know where to go,
Till certain merchants met him, and made him go with them
To be shut-up in their shop, and show their goods to buyers,
And wear an apprentice's apparel, and serve the public.
    As for Liar, he leapt lithely away
To lurk in the city lanes, and be lugged-about by everyone,
Nowhere welcome, despite his wealth of stories.
Everywhere hooted at and told to 'sling his hook';
Till the pardoners at last had pity, and pulled him indoors.
They washed him and wiped him, and wound him about
    with napkins,   220
And sent him on Sundays to the Church, with seals,
Giving pennyworths of pardons for a pound here and there.
The physicians began to frown, and sent off a letter
Inviting him to join them and inspect people's urine.
Spicemongers bespoke him to inspect their goods
(For he knew the tricks of their trade, and their
    merchandise too).

Then some minstrels and messengers happened to meet him,
And held on to him half a year and eleven days more.
Fair-spoken friars fetched him away,
And clad him in their clothes to conceal him from visitors;   230
But they let him leave and return whenever he likes,
And he is always welcome among them, and stays with
    them often.
  Thus all Fraud's rout fled in fear, and took refuge
    in corners;
Only Meed the Maiden dared to remain.
Even so, to tell the truth, she trembled with terror,
And sorrowed, and wrung her hands when they came
    to arrest her.

PASSUS 3

So, then, Meed the Maiden, and no more of the band,
Was brought before the King by beadles and bailiffs.
The King called for a clerk (I cannot tell you his name)
To take charge of Meed the Maiden and make her comfortable:
'I shall examine her in person, and ask her directly
Which man in all the world she would rather wed.
If she conforms to my counsel, and obeys my commands,
I will forgive all her guilt, God helping me.'
  Courteously, then, this clerk (as the King commanded),
With his arm round her waist, took Meed away to
      her room,   10
Where musicians and minstrels were ready to amuse her.
  All who dwelt in Westminster were respectful to her.
Some law-lords got themselves up with gallantry and
      good humour,
And bustled along to her boudoir to befriend her
And comfort her kindly. And thus they commenced:
'Do not mourn, Meed, nor make yourself afraid;
Soon we shall speak to the king, and smooth your path for you
To be wedded to whom you wish, and where you please,
Despite the cunning of Conscience, forsooth, and his
      crafty tricks.'
  Graciously Meed the Maiden spoke of her gratitude   20
For their great goodness; and to each one she gave
Goblets of pure gold, and great silver cups,
And ruby rings, and many other riches;
And even for the lowest of the lackeys, a large coin.
Then lightly did these lords take leave of Meed,
And up came the clergy, to comfort her likewise.
  They told her, 'Take heart! We will serve you truly;
As long as you last, you shall live as you please.'
Courteously, to the clergy, Meed returned the compliment.
'Loyally shall I love you, and make each of you
      Lord Bishop,   30

Or at least have your names called to Consistory Courts.
Lack of learning shall not hold back the man that I love
From early advancement: I am very well known
Where clever clergy must crawl in the back ranks.'
    Then there came a Confessor in a friar's cope.
To Meed the Maiden he murmured this speech
Mellowly and mildly, as to one making a confession.
'Though men both lay and learned might have lain with you,
And Falsehood have been your familiar these last fifty winters,
For a horse-load of wheat you should have absolution;   40
I will be your beadsman, and spread abroad your gospel
Among cavaliers and clergy, to the ruin of Conscience.'
    Then for all her misdeeds, Meed knelt, and by that man
Had her sins shriven in short order – and without shame,
        believe me:
She told him the tale, and then tipped him a gold noble
To be her beadsman and her go-between.
    He gave her swift absolution; and then he said,
'We are having a stained-glass window made for us,
        that's working-out dear.
Were you to give us the glass, and have your name
        engraved there,
You could safely count on your soul's sitting in Heaven.'   50
Said the woman, 'Were I sure of that, I would spend freely
To be your friend, my dear friar, and never fail you
While you gave licence to lords who follow lechery,
And did not lash those ladies who love it as well.
It's a frailty of the flesh, as one finds in all the books,
An inborn attraction – from which we all originate.
If one escapes a scandal, there's scarcely any harm in it;
Of all the seven great sins, it's the soonest absolved.
If you're friendly, therefore, to folk who enjoy it,
I'll buy coping for your kirk, I'll build you a cloister,   60
Whitewash your walls, and glaze your windows
With pictures, and with portraits of *me*, and pay for the lot,
So that everyone will say I'm one of your Lay Sisters.'[1]
    God forbids all such emblazoning by good people;
Such advertised virtuous deeds may peradventure

Be the paintings of Pride and of worldly pomp.
Christ knows our consciences and our native corruption;
All our costs and covetousness, and to whom the cash belongs.
Therefore my lesson is, all you lords, leave off such boasts
As engraving on window glass all your good deeds,   70
Asking the clergy's attention when you give alms,[2]
Lest you have your reward here on Earth, but not in Heaven:
> *Nesciat sinistra tua quid faciat dextera tua*:
Let not thy left hand either early or late
Have reason to know what is wrought by thy right.
That is God's command in the Gospel for them who give alms.
All you mayors and magistrates, that are mediators
Between the King and the commoners, in the keeping of laws,
To punish folk on pillories or on penal stools:[3]
Look to brewing-wives and bakeresses and cooks and butchers.
Of all men and women in the world, they work most harm   80
Upon poor people who must buy small portions.
For they poison these people, often but unpublished:
Dishonest retailers grow rich, and become great rentiers
From food that poor people should be putting in their bellies.
Were they truthful traders, they could not build
> such tall houses,
Nor batten on tenements, be sure of that.
   But Meed the Maiden has begged all mayors
To accept from such sellers whatever silver they offer –
Or presents other than specie, such as plate silver,
Rings, or other rich gifts – to ignore retailers.   90
Said the maiden: 'If you love me, then love all of *them*:
Let them profit just a penny or two more than is proper.'
   Solomon the great Sage wrote a sermon
For the amendment of all mayors and law-keeping men,
And took as his text this that I shall tell you:
> *Ignis devorabit tabernacula eorum, qui munera*
> *libenter accipiunt.*[4]
For lettered and learned people, this Latin means
That fire shall come from Heaven and burn to fine
> blue ashes
The houses or homes of all those that are hungry

For the annual gift or the odd gift, on account of their offices.
   Well, the King came from his Council, and called
      for Meed,   100
Sending many servants to escort her forthwith
To his private apartments, in the pleasantest of spirits.
   The King then courteously began the conference,
And explained to Meed the Maiden his full meaning.
'Often enough, my lady, have you acted unwisely;
But never, forsooth, with more folly than when you
      accepted Fraud.
That guilt, though, I forgive, and grant you my mercy.
But from now till your dying day, never do so again!
   A knight of mine, called Conscience, lately came
      from abroad:
If *he* wants you for his wife, are you willing to take him?'   110
'Indeed yes, my liege; Lord forbid but that I allowed it;
Hang me at once unless I heed your slightest behest!'
   So they called Sir Conscience to come and present himself
Before the King in Council, both clergy and laymen.
He bowed low in obeisance, then on bended knee
Waited to hear the King's will, and what he should do.
   'Would you wed this woman,' said the King,
      'were I to consent?
She is eager for the alliance, and to be your spouse.'
   Said Conscience to the King, 'Now, Christ forbid!
To wed such a wife? I would sooner be damned!   120
Her faithfulness is frail, and her speech fallacious;
She has made men scores of times commit misdeeds;
To wives and widows she teaches wantonness,
They are lured to lechery by love of her gifts;
But trust in her treasures has betrayed countless people:
She felled your own father with false promises.[5]
She has poisoned popes, and impaired Holy Church.[6]
There is no bawdier bitch, by God Who made me,
Between Heaven and Hell, though one searched
      the whole Earth.
She has a teetotum twat and a tale-bearing tongue;   130
She's as common as a cart-track to every crook on two feet –

To monks, to minstrels, to mumping lepers under hedges.
Summoners and assize-jurors – such men prize her;
Sheriffs could shut up shop but for her,
For she makes men lose their land and their lives alike;
She pays to let prisoners loose, to parade at large,
Giving their jailers groats or gold all round
To unfetter felons who are then free of the country;
But the innocent she arrests and securely imprisons,
And hangs for pure hatred those who have done no harm.   140

    To be cursed in the Consistory she considers no risk,
For she keeps the Commissary in copes, and clerks in coats;
She gets absolution as soon as she herself likes,
And with her money does almost as much in a month
As your Privy Seal[7] in six score days.
She has the Pope's private ear – provisors know that –
For she and Sir Simony seal their certificates.

    She bestows on men bishoprics, though they be unlettered,
Gives prebends to parsons, and enables priests
To use courtesans and concubines all their lives long   150
Who bear the priests' babies though God's law forbids it.
Woe to that kingdom where the king thinks well of her,
For she favours falsehood and befouls the truth.

    By Jesus, her jewels corrupt even your Justices
To lie against the Law, and delay its course;
Her florins fly so thickly, the truth is forestalled.
The law is dragged on her leash, and she picks her own
      love-days;[8]
For love of her, men lose what good law might have won them.
The poor might plead here for ever, and gain only perplexity;
So lofty is the law, and so loth to end a case,   160
Without presents or pence, it will please very few.

    Barons and burgesses Meed brings to grief,
And calamity to common folk who care about honesty;
For clerkship and covetousness she couples together.
Such is the life of this "lady" – may Our Lord bring her low!
And all who maintain her men, may misfortune undo them!
Poor men, because of her, have no power to complain
      of their wrongs,

Such mastery has Meed over men of property.'
  Then Meed looked mournful, and asked the king meekly
For permission to put in her defence and plea;   170
And her wish was granted by him very willingly:
  'Excuse yourself if you can; I keep myself neutral;
For Conscience's case, if just, condemns you to exile.'
'No, lord,' said that Lady, 'no longer will you believe him
When you know the facts fully, and where the fault lies.
In moments of misfortune, Meed may help most.
You know quite well, Conscience, I am not here to quarrel,
Nor to disparage your person with a proud heart.
You are well aware, you weasel – unless willing to lie –
That you have hung about my neck half-a-million times,   180
And grabbed at my gold, and given it where you pleased;
So why you wax wroth just *now*, is a wonder to me!
I could honour you now, as always, with awards,
And do more for your dignity than you deem fit to think.
  But you have defamed me foully before the king:
I never killed a king, nor ever conspired to,
Nor anything that you think I did, by the throne I swear it!
  In Normandy⁹ I was in no way a nuisance to the king;
But you, Conscience, a dozen times did him dishonour,
Huddling in hovels to heat your finger-nails,   190
Wondering if that winter would last for ever,
And dreading that a storm-cloud meant your death
And then hastening home because your belly was hungry!
  You pillager! Without pity you have robbed poor men,
And carried off their copper-work on your back, to sell
    in Calais.
But *I* lingered with my lord, to preserve his life,
And make his men merry, and relieve their misery.
I clapped them on the back, and kept up their courage,
Till they jigged for the joy of judging me their own.
Had I been Marshal of the King's Men, then by
    Holy Mary   200
I would have laid my life (no less a wager)
He'd have been lord of the length and breadth of that land –
And King, too, of that country, to promote his own kinsmen,

The lowest brat of his blood a baron's equal!
But you, Conscience, you coward, counselled withdrawal!
For a little silver, to let go of that lordship,
The richest realm that ever lay beneath rain-clouds!
  It is becoming in a king, the guardian of his country,
To give *meed* to those men that meekly serve him –
As to aliens, and to all men, and honour them with
      presents!   210
Meed makes men love him, and respect his manhood.
Emperors and earls and every kind of noble,
By *meed* retain young men to ride and run for them;
The Pope and all his prelates do not scorn presents,
And themselves give meed to the men who maintain
      their laws.
Servants are paid for their service, as is plain to see:
They take such *meed* from their masters as may be agreed
      between them.
Paupers promise their prayers in return for *meed*;
Minstrels demand *meed* for the music they make;
The king takes *meed* from his men, for maintaining
      the peace;   220
Teachers of children all ask *meed* from their charges;
Priests who preach virtue to the people, ask for *meed*
In the form of Mass-fees or their food at mealtimes.
Masters of all kinds of crafts call for *meed* from their
      'prentices;
Merchants and *meed* needs must go together:
I am sure no man under the moon can live without *meed*!'
  Said the King to Conscience, 'By Christ, I believe
That Meed has most soundly overmastered your speech!'
  But Conscience cried out, as he knelt to the King:
'By your leave, my lord, there are two kinds of "meed".   230
The one is granted, of His grace, by God in Heaven,
To those who do their duty well, down here on Earth.
The Prophet preached of this, and it has its place in
      the Psalms:
      Domine, quis habitabit in tabernaculo tuo?[10]
Who shall abide in Thy abode, beside Thy holy saints,

Or rest on Thy Holy Hills?, is how David assesses it;
And David himself gives the answer, as we see in the Psalter:

> *Qui ingreditur sine macula, et operatur justitiam.*

> (He that walketh uprightly, and worketh righteousness.)

He, that is to say, who is spotless and of steady mind,
Who has ruled his deeds by reason and by rightful dealing;
Who has never lived usuriously, but has ever
Improved the minds of the poor, and pursued the truth: 240

> *Qui pecuniam suam non dedit ad usuram, et munera
> super innocentem.*

> (Who putteth not out his money to usury, nor taketh
> reward against the innocent.)

All who help the innocent and hold by the righteous,
Maintaining truth *without* meed, but for mercy only:
Such are the men, my lord, who receive that meed
From God, in the great need of their going hence.

But there is another *measureless* meed that the
master-classes covet:[11]

The meed that they take for the maintenance of misdoers.
And the Psalter speaks of that, too, at the end of a Psalm:

> *In quorum manibus iniquitates sunt, dextera eorum repleta
> est muneribus.*

> (In whose hands is mischief, and their right hand is
> full of bribes.)[12]

He who grabs at their gold, so help me God,
Shall make a bitter bargain, unless the Bible lies.

The priests and parsons who seek their own pleasure,   250
Taking meed of money for the Masses they sing,
Have *human* meed only, as Matthew teaches:

> *Amen, amen, receperunt mercedem suam.*

> *(Verily I say unto you, they have their reward.)*[13]

What labourers and lowly folk are allotted by their masters
Is by no means *meed*, but a *measured* reward;
Nor is there any meed, I may say, in the deals of merchants:
Obviously, that is only exchange – one penny's worth
for another.

Have you never read the record, you recreant madam,
Of why vengeance was sent down upon Saul and his children?

God sent to Saul, by the mouth of His prophet Samuel,
Word that Agag of the Amalekites, and all his people
    after him,   260
Must die for a deed that their ancestors had done.
   "Therefore," said Samuel to Saul, "God Himself orders
That you be obedient, and act as He bids you.
Go to Amalek with your army; and all that you find
    there, slay:
Be they men or beasts, burn them to death;
Widows or wives, the women and their children;
Their possessions and plantations, all the property you
    may find,
Burn it, bearing nothing away with you, be it never
    so costly,
Neither for meed nor for money: make no exception.
Ruthlessly wreck it – or you shall rue the day."[14]   270
   But because he coveted the booty, King Saul forbore;
He spared both him and his herds, as we hear in the Bible,
Quite otherwise than he was warned by the prophet.
And God said to Samuel that Saul should die;
And for that sin, all the seed of Saul end shamefully.
These were the mischiefs you, Meed, made for Saul,
So that God hated him for ever, and his heirs after him.
My conclusions from that case, I will keep to myself,
And for fear of offending royalty, will find no moral:
For such is the way of this world, with those who
    have power,   280
That whoever tells them the truth, is the first to find trouble.
   Mother Wit was my teacher, so that *one* thing I know:
That one day Reason shall reign over all Earth's realms,
And we shall find the fate of Agag befalling others:[15]
Again shall Samuel slay him, Saul be accursed,
David assume his diadem and subdue all nations;
And one Christian King shall have care of them all.
   Meed shall no more have mastery, as now;
But love, and lowliness of heart, and loyalty,
Together shall take mastery of the world, and be saviours
    of truth.   290

Whoever shall trespass against Truth, or take bribes to
    subvert it,
Loyalty shall bring him to law, and no-one else living.
No Serjeant-at-Law, for his services, shall wear a silken coif,
No fur to fringe his gown, bought with fees for pleading
    in Court.
Meed makes law-lords of many malefactors,
Then over-rules those lords' laws, herself to reign in the realm;
But Natural Love shall come, as my – Conscience's –
    companion,
And make Law an honest labourer; and such love shall arise,
Such peace among the people, and such perfect honesty,
That the Jews shall rejoice because in their judgment   300
Moses has returned, or the Messiah come among men;
And wonder shall hold their hearts, at the truthfulness
    of humanity.
    Whoever bears a bayonet, a broadsword, a lance,
A hatchet or axe or any other weapon,
Shall be doomed to die, unless the smith do it over
Into a sickle or scythe, a ploughshare, or its coulter:
    Conflabunt gladios suos in vomeres.
      (They shall beat their swords into ploughshares, and
        their spears into pruning hooks.) [16]
Every man shall ply a plough or a spade or a pick-axe,
Or spin, or spread dung – or else be ruined by Sloth.
    Fox-hunting priests and parsons will then pursue
      God's pleasure,
And study away at the Psalms from dawn till sunset.   310
If hunting or hawking is a habit with such men,
Their boasted benefice shall belong to them no more.
Neither king nor cavalier, neither mayor nor constable,
Shall put-upon the people, or drag them into courts,
Nor jury-empanel them, nor press them to swear upon oath;
The criminal once convicted, one decree shall suffice:
A mild sentence or a severe one, as Truth shall decide.
King's Bench and Common Pleas, Church Court and
    Chapter,
Shall all be but *one* Court, with one Law-Baron as Judge:

And he shall be True-Tongue, an exact man who has
    never troubled me.   320
There shall be no more battles or bearers of weapons,
And the smith who smithies a weapon shall be smitten
    to death with it:
    Non levabit gens contra gentem gladium.
    (Nation shall not lift up sword against nation, neither
        shall they learn war any more.)[17]
But before this good fortune befalls us, men shall find
    foul omens,[18]
Such as six suns in the sky, with a ship and half a sheaf
    of arrows;
At a Paschal plenilune shall the Jews repent;
And Saracens, at such visions, shall sing *Gloria in Excelsis*:
For both Meed and Mohammed shall fare amiss in those days.
    Melius est nomen bonum quam divitiae multae.'
    (A good name is rather to be chosen than great riches.)[19]
 And now Meed grew gustier than a March gale.
'I am not learned in Latin,' she said, 'I leave that to
    book worms.
But see what Solomon, in his Book of Wisdom, says: 330
    Honorem acquiret qui dat munera:[20]
He that giveth gifts shall gain the victory,
And have high honour as well – that is Holy Writ.'
'I well believe, lady,' said Conscience, 'that your Latin
    is correct.
But you are like that lady who, reading *Thessalonians*,[21]
Found the phrase "prove all things", and was well satisfied.
But those were the last words of a line at the bottom of
    the leaf:
If she had turned the page, to see the rest of the text,
She would have found not a few words following after –
"Hold fast that which is good"; and the *whole* text is *God's*.
    You have made the same error, madame; you could
    find no more   340
Even were you to sweat from your study of Solomon.
The text that you have told us would tickle potentates,
But you lacked someone learned to turn the leaf for you.

Study your Solomon again, and see what comes after –
A very troublesome text for those who love Meed:
>   *Animam autem aufert accipientium.*
>   (But he beareth away the soul of the taker.)[22]
That is the true end of the text you trotted out:
Although we win honour and victory through you, Meed,
The soul of the receiver is ensnared by what he accepts!'

Said the King then, 'Cease! I will sanction no more.
You shall be reconciled, I swear it, and both shall serve me.
Kiss her, Conscience, for I command it.'
　'By Christ I will not,' said Conscience, 'though my
　　banishment be for ever!
Unless Reason says it is right, I would rather die!'
So the King said to Conscience: 'Then I command you
To be ready at once to ride, and bring Reason back.
Command him to come here to my Council;
For he shall rule my realm with correct advice,
And discuss with you, Conscience, as Christ is my witness,　10
How you instruct my people, either clergy or laymen.'
　'I gladly agree,' said the good man.
He rode off directly, to whisper in Reason's ear,
And told him the King's tidings, and began to take his leave.
But Reason said, 'I shall make ready to ride, so rest a while.'
Then Reason called Cato,[1] his servant (so courteous of speech),
And also Tom True-tongue-tell-me-no-tattle-
Nor-lying-tales-to-laugh-at-for-I-never-liked-them.
'Saddle my steed called Stay-till-I-see-my-Chance,
And gird him well with the girths of Witty-Words,　20
And harness him with a heavy bridle, to keep his head low,
For he will whinny twice at least on the way.'
　Then Conscience mounted his courser, and quickly made off;
Reason riding along with him, secretly conferring
About Meed the Maiden and her doings among men.
　A certain Warren Wisdom, and Witty his friend,[2]
Followed them fast, for they had certain affairs
To clear-up in the Court of the Exchequer, and in Chancery.
They rode hard in hope of having Reason's advice
To save them, for a consideration, from serious trouble.　30
Conscience knew this couple well, and their covetousness;
He told Reason to ride faster, recking nothing of either.
'For their words are wily, and they dwell with Meed,

Where rage and wrangling are – their sources of silver.
For where there is love and loyalty, they leave.

    Contritio et infelicitas in viis eorum.

   (Destruction and misery are in their ways, and the
     way of peace they have not known.)[3]

For God, they would not give a goose's wing:

    Non est timor Dei ante oculos eorum.

   (There is no fear of God before their eyes.)[4]

For, God is my witness, they would do more for a dozen hens,
Or an even number of capons, or a horse-load of oats,
Than for love of Our Lord, or all his blessèd saints.
So, Reason, let them ride by themselves, rich as they are.   40
Conscience accounts them worthless and so does Christ,
    I think.'
Then Reason rode faster along the straight high-road,
With Conscience his convoy to the King's presence.
The King came himself to receive Reason courteously,
   And gave him a seat on the King's bench, between himself
    and his son;
And they exchanged words together for a long time.
   Now Peace came to Parliament, and presented a petition:
How against all righteousness, Wrong[5] had run off with
    his wife;
And ravished Rose, the sweetheart of Reginald;
And had taken Margaret's maidenhead, maulgre her
    struggles.   50
'My geese, and my grunters too, were grabbed by his
    blackguards,
But for fear of him I dare not fight or complain.
He borrowed my horse Bayard, and never brought him back,
And Wrong paid not a farthing for it, though I followed him,
    begging.
He permits his men to murder my servants,
Forestalls my goods from fairs, and fights for them at market;
He breaks down my barn doors, and bags all my wheat,
And all I get is a token[6] for ten quarters of oats.
In addition to all this, he drubs me – and beds with
    my daughter.

But I have hardly the courage to look him in the eye.'   60
   The King could well believe all this; Conscience had
     told him
That Wrong was a wicked wretch, wreaking widespread
     sorrow.
   Wrong now grew worried, and asked Warren Wisdom
To buy-off Peace with pence – and he proffered many,
And said, 'If my lord the King only liked me, little I'd care
Though Peace and his party should complain for ever.'
Then Wisdom and his friend Witty were of opinion
That since Wrong had wrought so many kinds of ruin
They should warn him, before they worked, with some
     wise words.
'If men do as they please, upon impulse, they will make
     people angry;   70
And soon you shall see that this applies to yourself –
Unless Meed makes things easier, your undoing is imminent,
For both your life and your land lie at the King's mercy.'[7]
   Wrong wooed Wisdom with all his might,
And played handy-dandy with his pence for procuring
     acquittal.
So Wisdom and Witty went off together,
Taking Meed the Maiden with them, to buy mercy for him.
   Peace poked forward his head, with its bloodstained pate:
'For no guilt at all, God knows, I got this wound,
As Conscience will confirm, and all my community.'   80
   But Wisdom and Witty went quickly to work
On the King, to convince him by the power of cash.
   Still the King swore, by Christ and by his crown,
That the crimes committed by Wrong deserved condign
     punishment.
He commanded a constable to cast the fellow into irons –
'So heavy, he shall not see his feet for seven years!'
   But Wisdom said, 'By God, that is not the best course.
Were he to make amends, might not Mainprise release him,
And be bailsman for him, so buying him freedom,
Restoring all that Wrong ravaged, and setting all right?'   90
   Witty was well in agreement, and said the same.

'It was better that bail should bring benefit with it,
Than that bail be denied and there be no benefit.'
    Then Meed had to meddle, and also asked for mercy,
And offered Peace a present of purest gold:
'Have this from me, my good man, to mend your wound;
Never again, I guarantee, shall Wrong be so guilty.'
    Then Peace himself took pity, and prayed the King
To have mercy on the man who had misused him so often:
'He has given me guarantees, as Sir Wisdom engaged,   100
And I forgive him his guilt, with a good will –
So long as the King assents. I can see nothing better:
Meed has made me amends; I have no more to ask.'
    Said the King, 'No! Not so, as Christ is my Saviour!
Wrong shall not wriggle away until I learn more.
If he escaped so easily, he would only laugh,
And be all the more bold to abuse my servants.
Unless Reason reprieves him, he shall rot in the stocks
As long as he lives, or till his true repentance.'
    Some reckoned that Reason should have pardoned
        the wretch,   110
And have counselled the King, and Conscience as well,
That Meed by rights must be his mainpernor.
    But Reason said: 'No more advice to *me* about having mercy,
Till every lord and lady learns to love Truth
And hate all harlotry, whether of speech or of hearing;
Till Petronella Peacock[8] puts her furs back in the press;
Till parents cherish children with chastisement;
Till harlots' false holiness be held a shame;
Till the covetousness of the clergy be to feed and clothe
        the poor,
And religious ramblers[9] sing remembrance Masses
        in cloisters –   120
As St Benedict bade them, and St Bernard and St Francis;
Till prelates practise in their own lives what they preach;
Till the King's Council be for common good;
Till bishops sell their stables to give poor folk asylum,
And their hawks and their hounds for the help of poor clergy;
Till St James be sought where *I* shall assign,

And no man go on pilgrimage to Galicia, unless for good;
Till all who run off to Rome and the robbers of Europe[10]
Take overseas no silver of the King's sterling,
Nor gold neither, engraved or not engraved,   130
On pain of forfeiting the same to any who find it at Dover,
Unless carried by a merchant or his men, or messengers
    with letters,
Or a priest or provisour,[11] or a penitent pilgrim.
  Yet still I shall harden my heart, by the Holy Cross,
While Meed has any mastery in this Moot-Hall.
I could cite you examples that I have seen many times.
I say for myself, that if it so were
That I were crowned king and keeper of this realm,
There should be no crime in this kingdom (that came
    to my notice)
But within my powers I should punish it, on peril of
    my soul!   140
Nor should gifts win my good will, God bless us all!
Nor should Meed buy my mercy, but Meekness only.
  For a man named *Nullum Malum* met with one *Impunitum*,
And he bade *Nullum Bonum* be *Irremuneratum*.[12]
Let your confessor, Lord King, construe this riddle plainly;
And if you act accordingly, I will bet my ears
That lawyers become labourers laying dung on the fields.
And love shall rule the land as you, lord, would wish.'
  Then the Court confessors went into conclave,
To construe that couplet for the King's profit –   150
Not for the King's soul, nor the comfort of the common weal.
  I saw Meed in that Moot-Hall wink at the law-men,
And many joined her joyfully, rejecting Reason.
Warren Wisdom winked back at Meed,
And said, 'Madam, I am your man, never mind how I sound:
Fed with florins, I fall about, and my mouth fails me!'
  All upright men agreed that Reason was right;
Even Witty was in accord, and commended his judgment;
And most of the men in that hall, with many of the law-lords,
Thought Meekness a master, Meed a curst vixen.   160
  Love thought little of her, and Honesty still less –

Who said, speaking high so that the whole Court heard:
'Whoever wants her as wife because of her goods and wealth
Will of course be cuckolded, cut off my nose else!'
　　Meed now grew melancholy, and her face mournful,
Three quarters of that Court having called her a whore.
But an assize-juror and a summoner still paid suit to her,
And a sheriff's clerk beshrewed the whole company:
'Have I not often helped you at the Bar?
And when have I had from you so much as a halfpenny?'　　170
　　The King called Reason and Conscience to his side,
And ratified that Reason had argued rightly;
He looked with menace at Meed, and with more at Law
That man whom Meed had almost undone.
'It is your fault, Law, I believe, that I lose so many escheats;
Meed overmasters you, Law, and so makes justice slow.
But you shall have Reason to reckon with, if I rule
　　a while more;
And, for your deeds today, you'll get what you deserve.
Meed shall not mainprise *you*, by St Mary in Heaven!
I will have my lawyers loyal, so leave off your jabbering.　　180
And since most have said he is guilty, Wrong shall
　　be sentenced.'
　　Said Conscience to the King, 'Without consent of the
　　common folk,
You will find it hard, by my head, to uphold all that,
And so righteously rule your whole realm.'
Said Reason to the King, 'By Christ who lay on the Cross,
If I otherwise ruled this realm, wrench out my ribs!
But always bid Obedience be by my side.'
　　Said the King, 'I shall assent, by Our Lady St Mary,
When my Council of Clergy and Lords comes together.
And not readily, Reason, shall I let you ride from me;　　190
For as long as I live, I shall not let you go.'
　　Said Reason, 'I am ready to remain with you always,
If Conscience will be our counsellor – I can think of
　　none better.'
Said the King, 'I agree; God grant that we succeed!
As long as our lives last, let us live together!'

PASSUS 5

The King, and the knights of his household, now hied
    them to church,
Every man to hear the day's Matins, and then the Mass.
Now I woke from my forty winks, and was very grieved
That I had not slept more soundly, and seen more.
But before I had walked a furlong, I was seized by faintness;
My feet would carry me no farther, I felt so sleepy;
So I simply sat down and said my Creed.
While I mumbled over my Rosary, I once more fell asleep.
    Then I saw much more than had met my eyes before.
Now I saw that pleasant plain full of people, that I spoke
    of earlier,   10
And Reason preparing to preach to the whole realm,
Carrying a cross in his hand, in front of the king.
    He preached that their pestilences were punishments
    for sin,
And that South-West wind on a Saturday evening
Was plainly a punishment for Pride, and nothing else.[1]
Their pear-trees and plum-trees were blown prostrate
As a warning, he went on, to amend their ways.
The beeches and burly oaks were blown to the ground,
And turned topsy-turvy, to put them in terror
That Deadly Sins would on Doomsday undo them all.   20
    (On this matter, I myself could muse at length,
But shall say only what I saw, so help me God,
And how plainly Reason preached before the people.)
    He told Waster to go work at whatever he knew best,
And so recover what he had squandered, by some kind
    of trade.
    He implored Petronella to put away her fur-pieces,
And keep them in her coffer in case of hard times.[2]
Tom Stowe he told to take a couple of sticks
And fetch Felicity home from the fate of the scold.[3]
He warned Walter that his wife was at fault,   30

With a half-mark head-dress,[4] and his own hood not
    worth fourpence.
He bade Betts to cut himself a few swishy branches,
And beat his Betty with them if she stayed bone-idle.
He charged all merchants to chastise their children:
'However much money you make, do not molly-coddle
    your young,
Nor over-pamper them, though the Plague were at its peak.
  My father used to say this, and so did my mother:
"The dearer you hold son or daughter, the harder your
    discipline."
 And Solomon said the same, in his Book of Proverbs:
    Qui parcit virgae, odit filium suum.
    (He that spareth his rod hateth his son.)[5]
That is the English of the Latin, if you care to know;   40
Or, "He that stints the switch spoils his children."'
  Then he begged the beneficed clergy and bishops:
'That which you preach to the people, practise yourselves –
It will bring blessing to you, if you do as you bid;
And if you live as you lecture, we shall believe you better.'
  Then he told the Regular clergy to respect their Rule:
'Lest the King and his Council cut down your endowments,
And are stewards of your estates till you keep your own
    statutes.'
  Then he counselled the King to love his common people:
'They are your true treasure in peacetime, and your balm
    in times of trouble.'   50
Then he prayed the pope to have pity on Holy Church,
And before granting others forgiveness, first govern himself.
'And all you who look to the laws, covet only the truth,
Not gold or gifts, if you wish to please God:
For they that turn against Truth, as the Gospel tells,
Are no longer known to God, nor to any saint in Heaven:
    Amen dico vobis, nescio vos.
    (Verily I say unto you, I know you not.)[6]
  And you who seek St James, and the saints in Rome,
Seek rather, St Truth[7] – for He can save you all,
    Qui cum Patre et cum Filio . . .

Who dwells with the Father and the Son, and whose
    blessing be on those
Who respond to my sermon.' So Reason fell silent.   60
    Then Repentance ran in, and recited his text
Till I, William, wept my eyes full of water.

    Petronella Proud-heart[8] threw herself prostrate,
And lay long on the ground ere she looked up and cried:
    'Lord have mercy!'
She made a vow to the Maker of all mankind
That she would unsew her shift and wear a hair-shirt inside,
To mortify her flesh and its fierceness of sin:
'Never more shall a high heart hold me, but humility;
Yes, even to endure insults – as I never used to.
I will make myself meek, now, and pray for mercy,   70
Since beforehand I hated such things with all my heart.'

    Then Lechery cried 'Alas!', and called upon Our Lady
To pray mercy for his misdeeds, as his soul's intermediary
    with God.
And he swore that every Saturday for seven years thence
He would drink only what ducks drink, and dine only once.

    Envy with heavy heart asked for *his* shriving.
In sorrow he began to say his *I have sinned.*
He was pale as a sheep's pelt, and shook as if with palsy,
And was clothed in such coarse stuff that I cannot
    describe it –
In a kirtle and a cutty coat, a knife by his side.   80
He had cut his foresleeves from a friar's habit;[9]
And like a leek that has lain too long in the sun,
So did *he* look, with his lean cheeks and ugly louring.
    His body was bursting with rage, he bit his lips for it,
Writhing his fingers around while he waited to wreak
    vengeance
In word or in deed whenever he might see his chance.
He uttered never a word but with an adder's tongue;
Quarrels and complaints were his usual conduct,

And backbiting and besmirching and bearing false witness:
These were all his courtesy in whatever company.   90
    This shit said, 'I *would* be shriven but for shame
      I dare not.
I would be gladder, by God, to see old Gilbert ruined,
Than to win this very week a waggon-full of Essex cheese.
    I've a near-by neighbour to whom I'm a constant nuisance.
I've lied about him to the law-lords, and so lost him money,
And turned his friends into foes with all my falsehoods;
Any good luck or grant he may get, grieves me horribly.
Between this man and his minions I make such quarrels
That lives and limbs are lost because of me.
Yet when I meet him in the market-place, this man
      I hate most,   100
I give him a hearty hullo, as if I were his friend –
For he's beefier and braver than I am; I dare not beard him.
But oh, if I had him at my mercy, God knows what
      I mightn't do!
    When I arrive in church, and should with reverence
      kneel to the reredos,
And pray for such people as the priest directs –
Pilgrims and palmers, and people who've paid for Masses –
I crouch on my knees and I call on Christ to curse those
Who buggered off with my shaving-bowl and my torn
      bed-sheet.
    I turn my eyes away from the altar
To see how Helen has got a new coat;   110
And I wish it were mine, and the whole web it came from.
I love other men's losses – they delight my heart –
But weep and wail if I see them faring well;
    And my own "fair dealing" is "dirty work" if they do it.
Take me to task for this, and I'll hate you eternally.
I wish all men and women I meet were my serfs,
For it angers me if anyone has more than I have.
And so I live unloved, like a surly dog,
My body swollen and bubbling with my bitterness.
    It's years since I was able to eat like anyone else: 120
Envy and ill will are not easy to digest.

Have you no sugar or sweet syrup to assuage my swelling,
No twisted canes of candy to clear my heart,[10]
No shame or shriving, but only to shred-out my belly?'
   'Readily!' said Repentance, giving first-rate advice.
'Sorrow for sins is the salvation of souls.'
   '*Sorry?*' said Envy, 'I am seldom anything else!
What else do you think makes me thin, but thoughts of
     missed vengeance?
But when I was in business among the burghers of London,
I paid Slander as my secret agent to slate their goods.   130
When my neighbour's sold well, and mine did not,
     I made myself ready
To sniff and sneer at their stock, and spoil their trade.
Still, if I may, I will make amends through Almighty God.'

Wrath roused himself now, eyes rolling to show their whites;
He breathed noisily through his nose, and his neck
     hung awry.
   First, 'I am Wrath!'[11] said he. 'I'm a former friar.
I began as the Friary gardener, grafting shoots.
What I grafted on the Limiters and Lectors[12] were lies,
Till they burst into foliage of flattery for the pleasure of lords,
And blossomed abroad with mild shrifts in ladies'
     boudoirs.   140
Now the fruit has come to full ripeness, and folk would
     much rather
Confess to a friar than to a parish priest.
   And now that parsons perceive they must share their
     profits,
These possessors of preferments preach against friars;
And the friars pick faults in *them*; and everyone finds,
When friars go preaching in public from place to place,
That I, Wrath, go the rounds with them, teaching *my*
     Holy Writ.
Both sorts speak of their "spiritualty", each despises the other,
Till both are beggars with nothing to live by but me
(Unless both become rich, and career around upon
     horseback).   150

So I, Wrath, never rest, but must run after
These wicked folk – for such are my fate and my "grace".
   I have an aunt who is a nun – in fact an Abbess –
Who would sooner swoon, or succumb, than suffer pain.
I was once a cook in her kitchen,[13] and served the convent
For many months, as well as the monastery.
I was pottinger to the Prioress and the other "poor ladies",
So I served them up stews of slanders: Sister Joan was
      a bastard;
Clarice indeed a cavalier's daughter, but her father a cuckold;
Sister Parnel, a priest's whore – "*She'll* never be Prioress;   160
She bore a child in cherry-time, as the whole Chapter
      knows."
   I, Wrath, seasoned their soup with such wicked words
That "You liar!" and "You liar!" two nuns would squeal
      out together,
And each of them slap the other across the chops:
Had they had knives, by Christ they'd have slain each other!
St Gregory[14] was a good pope, and had great foresight:
For this cause he ordained that no abbess should ever
      play priest;
Women cannot keep secrets – in one day the whole
      convent would be defamed.
   I *might* be found among monks, but I mostly avoid them:
There are too many tough men spying for my type –   170
Priors and sub-priors, and the Father Abbot in person;
And if I tell any of my tales, they hold council together,
And make me fast every Friday on bread and water;
Or I am chidden in the Chapter-house as if I were a child,
And beaten with my breeches down, on my bare arse.
So I do not like living among such lads!
Their food is third-rate fish and feeble ale;
But at times when there *is* wine, and when I have some
      at night,
I talk a flood of filth for five days afterwards.
All the evil that I know of any of our brethren,   180
I recount in the cloisters till the whole convent knows it.'
   Said Repentance, 'Repent, then, and never again repeat

Any confidences you collect either casually or by right.
Do not drink too daintily, nor too deeply either,
For fear your intentions may turn once more towards malice.
Be sober! [15] he said, and then gave absolution,
And told Wrath to weep for his wickedness, and amend
     his ways.

   Then Covetousness came; and him I cannot describe,
So hungry and so hollow the old hunks looked.
He was beetle-browed, and blubber-lipped as well,   190
Both eyes as bleary as a blind hag's;
Like a leather purse his cheeks lapped down,
And far below his chin they shivered in senility.
His beard was beslobbered like a bondsman's with bacon-fat.
A hood was on his head, and a lousy hat on top of it;
And his turd-brown surtout had seen twelve winters,
All tattered and filthy, and alive with lice.
(Though if only the lice could have found a better lodging
They would not have walked that Welsh flannel, it was
     so threadbare.)
'I have been avaricious,' [16] said that wretch, 'and I admit
     it here.   200
For some time I served under Simon Stiles,
As his apprentice, pledged to take care of his profit.
First I learned to lie by the thickness of a leaf or so,
And the first wickedness I knew was using false weights.
To Weyhill and Winchester I went, on fair-days,
With all kinds of commodities, as commanded by my master;
And but for the grace that Guile gave, in amongst them,
They would not have sold in seven years, so help me God!
   Then I was drawn among drapers, to drink in the
     rudiments,
And so learned how to stretch the selvedge, making cloth
     look longer.   210
I memorised how, handling heavy striped scarlet,
To sew strips with strong needles, seaming them together,
And putting them into a press, pinned closely,
Till ten or twelve yards stretched out to thirteen.

My wife was a weaver of woollen cloth;
She spoke to the spinsters, and they spun the yarn loosely;[17]
She paid them by the pound, but employed a twenty-ounce
    weight,
As I tested by my own steelyard, which *did* weigh true.
    I bought her some barley-malt, and she took to brewing;
But penny-ale and pudding-ale[18] she poured together,   220
And laid it aside for labourers and the lower classes.
The best ale was kept in the back room, or my bed-chamber;
And anyone having a nip of *that*, paid through the nose –
No less than a groat a gallon, as God's my witness;[19]
And it came by the cupful, she was so crafty!
She was known as Rose the Retailer[20] – and rightly,
For she'd been at her spivvery ever since she could speak.
    But I swear now, so I do, I will stop sinning,
And never short-weight anyone, or wangle bargains,
But make my way to Walsingham, and my wife with me,   230
And pray to the Relic at Bromholm[21] to remit my penance.'
    'Did you never repent?' asked Repentance, 'or make
    restitution?'
    'Yes, once,' said he, 'I lodged at a pub with a party
    of pedlars,
And I rose when they were at rest, and rifled their baggage.'
    'That was no restitution, but rank robbery!
You more deserve hanging for having done that
Than for all the rest that you have told me yet.'
I thought "restitution" *meant* robbery; I never learned to read;
And, faith, I know no French but that of the far side of
    Norfolk.'[22]
    'Were you ever in your life guilty of usury?'   240
    'Certainly not, except perhaps in my youth.
I learned from Lombards and Jews[23] a lesson or two,
Such as clipping coins I had discovered were heaviest,
Then lending them, for love of the cross,[24] on pledges
    I knew were lost.
Such documents did I draw-up, in case the debt fell in arrears,
That more manors became mine that way than by merciful
    dealing.

To lords and ladies I have lent goods in place of money,
And redeemed the goods afterwards for almost nothing;
My commerce is chiefly in such contracts and exchanges,
And the people I lend to lose a lot on every deal.   250
By carrying Lombards' letters, I've leaked gold to Rome,
Giving less gold there than I gave tokens for, here.'
'Have you lent money to lords to protect you from the law?'
'Indeed I have lent to lords, but they liked me none
    the better!
I have made many a knight my mercer or draper,
Who paid for his apprenticeship not so much as a pair
    of gloves.'
'Have you pity upon poor men who borrow under pressure?'
'I pity poor men as much as a pedlar pities cats –
He'd kill them, if he could catch them, for the sake of
    their skins!'
'Do you make free among your neighbours with your
    meat and drink?'   260
'They think of me as kindly as of a cur in their kitchen;
And the nearer my neighbours, the worse my name is.'
   'Now God forbid but you repent before long!
Else, may you never on this earth use your wealth well,
Nor your issue after you enjoy your earnings,
Nor your executors invest your money advisedly;
And wicked men waste all that you won by wickedness!
If I were a friar, in a House full of good faith and charity,
I could not spend *your* cash on our clothes and repairs,
Nor accept a penny from *you*, by my soul, as part of
    my pittance –   270
Not for the best book on our shelves, with burnished-gold
    leaves;
Not if I were certain you were such as you say,
Or if I could come by proof of any kind.
     Servus es alterius cum fercula pinguia queris;
     Pane tuo potius vescere, liber eris.[25]
     (Another man's slave must you be,
     If juicy dishes entice you;
     Would you rather call yourself free,

Let your own plain bread suffice you.)
You are not a natural creature; I can never absolve you
Till you reckon-up all your robberies, and make restitution;
Until Reason has enrolled it upon the register of Heaven
That you have made full amends, I *must* not absolve you:

Non dimittitur peccatum, donec restituatur ablatum.

(The sin is not remitted until that which was taken
be restored.)[26]

And all who have had any part of your wealth, I have God
as my witness,   280
Are required by the High Court of Heaven to help you
restore it.
If you think this is not so, see the gloss on Psalm Fifty-one,
Have mercy on me, O God – I mean the verse about Truth:

Ecce enim veritatem dilexisti.

(Behold, thou desirest truth in the inward parts.)[27]

No man or woman in the world can thrive on what you
acquire:
Cum sancto sanctus eris – or, construing that into English,
With the merciful thou wilt show thyself merciful;
With an upright man thou wilt show thyself upright;
With the froward thou wilt show thyself froward.'[28]

Then the old hunks lost all hope, and would have
hanged himself,
Had not Repentance recalled him rather to comfort.
'Turn your mind towards mercy, and your mouth to
praying for it;

Miserationes ejus super omnia opera.

(The Lord's tender mercies are over all his works.)[29]

All the wickedness that might be thought or worked
in this world,   290
Is no more to God's mercy than a little flame in the sea:

Omnis iniquitas quantum ad misericordiam Dei,
est quasi scintilla in medio maris.[30]

Turn your mind, then, to mercy; and give up your
merchantry:
It gives you no grounds to buy yourself good bread –
Only if you earn with your own hands, or will beg.

For all the goods you have gained began in falsehood,
And to live by them is not to buy, but to borrow.
   If you have no means to restore the money to
      the right man,
Carry it to the Bishop and ask him, of his kindness,
To dispose of it himself as will do your soul most good.
Then he shall answer for it at Heaven's High Court –   300
Both for you and for many more, shall that man
      make account;
What you learned from him in Lent, do not cease to believe,
Nor what he lent you from Our Lord's wealth, to lead
      you from sin.'

   Now Gluttony at least *began* to go to his shriving,
And went casually kirkwards to confess his sins.
   But Betty the Brewster bade him good morning,
And with that asked him whither he was going.
   'To Holy Church,' said he, 'to hear Mass,
And so to get my shrift, and sin no more.
   'I have good ale here, gossip. Won't you try some,
      Gluttony?'   310
'Have you anything in your handbag – any hot spices?'
   'I have pepper and peony-seeds and a pound of garlic;
Or a farthing's-worth of fennel, since it's a fast-day.'[31]
   So in goes Gluttony, and Great Oaths follows him.
There Cicely the shoemaker sat on the bench,
With Walt the Warrener, and also his wife,
Timmy the Tinker, and two of his 'prentices,
Hicks who hired-out horses, and Hugh the needlemaker,
Clarice the Cock Lane Whore, and the clerk of the parish,
David the Ditcher, and a dozen others –   320
A fiddler, a rat-finder, and a Cheapside filth-raker,
Piers the Prelate and his Flemish popsy Parnel,
A rope-maker, a rider, and Rose the dish-seller,
Godfrey of Garlickhithe, and Griffith the Welshman,
And a rabble of rag-sellers. Early in the morning
All welcomed Gluttony gladly, with a gift of good ale.
   Clement the Cobbler threw off his cloak,

And offered it as his forfeit in a game of New Fair;[32]
Hicks the Hackneyman hurled his hood after it,
And asked Betts the Butcher to be his agent.   330
Then they chose chapmen to value the exchange,
How much extra should be had by him who owned the cloak.
  The two hawkers hurried to have the game over
And, whispering in private, they priced the poor pennorths,
But declared that they could not, on their consciences,
        agree . . .
So they asked Robin the Ropemaker into the ring,
Enlisting him as their umpire, to avoid strife;
And between the three of them the business was
        by-and-by settled.
  Hicks the Hostler was to have the cloak
On condition that Clement should stand him a cupful;   340
And have Hicks's hood, and shake hands on the deal;
And the first who renegued on the arrangement was required
To give old Gluttony a gallon of ale.
  So they laughed and they lowered and yelled,
        'Let's have a drink'
And sat there till Evensong, singing now and then,
Till Gluttony had golloped a gallon or more
And his guts began grumbling like two greedy sows.
He pissed four pints in the space of a Pater-noster,
And blew the round bugle at his backbone's end
So that all who heard that horn held their noses,   350
And wished he had bunged it with a bunch of whins.
He could neither stir nor stand without his stick,
And then walked no better than a bar-fiddler's bitch,
Sometimes sideways and sometimes backwards,
His course criss-crossing like a man laying bird-nets.
  And when he drew near the door, his eyes grew dim;
He thrumbled on the threshold, and was thrown to earth.
Clement the Cobbler caught him round the waist
To lift him a little, at least to his knees;
But Gluttony was a burly brute, and a bastard to lift;   360
And he coughed-up such a caudle into Clement's lap
There is no hound so hungry in the whole of Hertfordshire

He'd have lapped-up those leavings, so unlovely they smelt.
    At last, with a world of trouble, his wife and his wench
Brought him back home and put him to bed.
There, after all his excesses, he became unconscious,
And slept all Saturday, and all Sunday till sunset.
Then he came out of his coma, and wiped his eyes clean;
And the first words from his tongue were, 'Who's taken
        my tankard?'
His wife began to upbraid him for his beastly ways,   370
And Repentance was there also to rebuke him.
    'Evil in word and deed alike has your life been;
Be ashamed of yourself, show it in your speech, and be shriven.'
    'Guilty I am,' said Gluttony, 'I grant it freely.
I've transgressed with my tongue I cannot tell how often,
Swearing "by God's soul" and "So help me God and
        the saints",
Nine hundred times, when there wasn't any need for it.
I've stuffed myself so at supper, and sometimes at noonday,
That I've spewed it all up along the space of a mile,
Wasting what might have been saved for those in want.   380
On fast-days I've both drunk and eaten delicacies,
And sometimes been so long at the table that I slept
        while I ate,
Or have taken my meals in taverns, to continue talking
        and tippling;
And even on fast-days have been off to my food before noon.'
    'So full a confession cannot fail to win you merit.'
    Then Gluttony began to weep and be in great grief
For the loose life that he had been living;
And he made a vow: 'Every Friday henceforward for ever,
Whatever hunger and thirst I may have,
Not even of fish shall my bowels have knowledge
Till my Auntie Abstinence gives her authority –   390
She whom till now I've hated all my life!'

Then came Sloth, all slobbery, with slimy eyes.
'I must sit down,' said the sluggard, 'or I'll fall asleep;
I cannot stand, nor stoop, nor kneel without a stool.

Were I back in bed, you might ring all your bells,
And I'd not rise till ready for dinner, unless my rear
    made me.'
He began his 'Bless me, father', then belched, then beat
    his breast,
Then stretched himself with a groan, and finally snored.
'How's this? Wake up, wretch!' cried Repentance. 'Make
    haste with your shrift!'
  'Were I to die today, I'm too weary to wake   400
Nor am I perfect in my Pater-noster – not as a priest
    should sing it –
Though I do know rhymes of Robin Hood, and
    Randolph Earl of Chester;[33]
But not the least that was ever made of Our Lord
    or Our Lady.
  Many a time I've made vows, and forgotten them in
    the morning;
I have never performed the penances that the priest
    laid on me,
Nor been seriously sorry for my sins.
If I ever utter a prayer, unless in a temper,
My tongue is two miles from what my heart intends.
Every day, whether holy or not, I employ
In idle chat over ale (or even in church).   410
The Passion of Christ, though – I seldom think of *that*.
  I have never been a visitor of sickbeds, or of folk chained
    in bridewells;
I would rather listen to lewdness, or a cobblers' holiday-play,
Or some dirty jokes, or detraction of my neighbour,
Than everything Mark or Luke wrote, or Matthew –
    not to mention John.
As for vigils or fast-days, I've bidden them farewell;
I lie in bed all through Lent with my lady-love in my arms,
Till Matins and Mass are ended, then make do at the Friary.
If I'm in time for the *Ite, missa est*, it's enough for me.[34]
I've kept away from confession, unless being ill scared me; 420
Not twice in two years do I tell my sins – and then by
    guesswork.

I have been priest and parson these thirty years past,
Yet cannot sol-fa, say Mass, or read the Lives of the Saints;
But I can find a hare in a furrowed field
Better than construe for my congregation a catchphrase
    of Latin
Such as *Blessed is the Man*, maybe, or *Blessed is everyone*.[35]
I can hold love-days, and hear a reeve's reckoning,
But of Canon Law or the Decretals I cannot read a line.
  If I borrow, or buy on credit, unless a book is kept
I forget it forthwith; and if I am asked for it,   430
Six or seven times I swear it is not so;
And thus I have troubled honest men ten thousand times.
Sometimes my servants' salaries are in arrears,
And a rueful reckoning I find it, when the accounts are
    read out;
It's only with ill-will and anger that I pay my workers.
  If anyone does me a good deed, or lends me a hand
    when I'm down,
I requite him unkindly: I cannot understand courtesy;
For I have, and always had, something like a hawk's manners:
I am not to be lured with love, but with what lies under
    the thumb.
  The kindness my fellow-Christians formerly conferred   440
Scores of times, on myself, I have slothfully forgotten,
Or by silence or by sour speech have spoiled many gifts
Of fish or flesh or other sorts of foodstuff;
But bread and ale alike, and milk and cheese and butter,
I have left lying about until they were useless.
  I ran around in my youth, and neglected my reading,
And ever since have been beggarly, because of my filthy sloth:
    Heu mihi, quod sterilem vitam duxi juvenilem!
    (Woe's me! How barren, in truth,
    Was the life I led in my youth!)'
  'Do you not repent?' asked Repentance. But that
    wretch was asleep again,
Till Vigilant Leveilleur[36] threw water over his face,   450
Splashing it into his eyes, and shouting to shift him:
'You're in danger of despair, and that would be your undoing!

Say to yourself "I am sorry for my sins";
Beat yourself on the breast, and beseech God for grace;
No earthly guilt is so great but His goodness is greater.'
   Then Sloth sat up and crossed himself speedily,
And made oath before God to overcome his acedia:
'Every Sunday for seven years (unless sickness prevents me)
I shall hie to Holy Church before the sun has risen,
And hear Matins and Mass as if I were a monk;   460
Nor shall after-dinner ale keep me out of it,
Till I have heard Evensong: by the Holy Rood I swear this!
I promise to repay – if I have pounds enough –
All the wealth I have wickedly gained since I first walked,
   Even though this may leave me too little to live on.
Each must have his own, ere I join the hereafter;
And if any remains, with the rest, by the Rood of Chester,
I shall turn pilgrim towards Truth, rather than seek Rome.'
   Robert the Robber remembered the text in *Romans*:
      Reddite ergo omnibus debita.
      (Render therefore to all their dues.)[37]
He began weeping bitterly, because he had nothing.   470
But the sinful wretch was saying to himself:
'Oh Christ who died on the Cross at Calvary,
Beside Dysmas[38] my brother, who besought you for grace,
And you had mercy on that man because he said,
      "Remember me, Lord":
Reprieve now *this* robber, who *cannot* repay,
Nor has any art by which to earn what he owes.
By your great mercy, mitigate my punishment,
Let me not be damned on Doomsday for doing such evil.'
   What became of this criminal I cannot rightly say;
But I well know that water went streaming from his eyes,   480
And to Christ again and again he acknowledged his guilt,
And swore to polish anew his pikestaff of penitence,
And walk the world with it while his life should last:
For he had lain with Latro,[39] Lucifer's aunt.

Then Repentance took pity on the penitents, and bade
      them kneel:

'For I shall seek from Our Saviour His grace to all sinners,
That he amend our misdoing and have mercy upon us all.

Oh God, who of Your goodness began this world,
Making all out of nothing, and Man most like Yourself:
Yet allowed Adam to sin, and bring sickness upon us all –   490
Which was all for the best, I believe, whatever the Bible says:

> *O felix culpa! O necessarium peccatum Adae!*
> (O happy fault! O necessary sin of Adam, that merited
> such a Redeemer!)

For through that sin, Thy Son was sent to this earth,
And became a man, born of a maiden, to save Mankind,
And make Yourself and Your Son like us sinful men:

> *Faciamus hominem ad imaginem et similitudinem nostram.*
> (Let us make man in our image, after our likeness.)[40]

And elsewhere it is written:

> *Qui manet in caritate, in Deo manet.*
> (He that dwelleth in love dwelleth in God.)[41]

Since You Yourself appeared in our fleshly suit, and died
For Man's sake on Good Friday, at full noonday,
Though neither Father nor Son felt sorrow in the fact
of death,
Except only in the suit of Man's flesh, and Your Son
overcame that:

> *Captivam duxit captivitutem.*
> (He led captivity captive.)

Still, in the sorrow of that, Your Son lost the light
for a space,
At the middle of the day, then most bright, and the
mealtime of the saints,   500
For then with Your fresh blood You fed our forefathers
in their darkness:

> *Populus, qui ambulabat in tenebris, vidit lucem magnam.*
> (The people that walked in darkness have seen a
> great light.)[42]

By the light that then leapt from You, was Lucifer blinded,
And Your last breath blew the blessèd into Heaven's bliss.

And three days after, again You were clad in our flesh,
And a sinful Mary saw You before St Mary Our Lady;[43]

And for the solace of sinners You let this be so –
    Non enim veni vocare justos, sed peccatores.
      (For I am not come to call the righteous, but sinners
        to repentance.)[44]
  And your mightiest deeds, told by Mark, or John or
    Luke or Matthew,
Were done in the armour of our human flesh:
    Verbum caro factum est, et habitavit in nobis.
    (The word was made flesh, and dwelt among us.)[45]
And by so much the more, I believe, may we be sure
In begging and beseeching You (if it be Your will,   510
Who are our brother and our father) to have mercy here
On this rabble of wretches who so sorely repent
That they ever in this world offended you by thought,
    word, or deed.'
Then Hope set his hands upon the horn of
    Deus, tu conversus vivificasti me
    (Yet didst thou turn and refresh me),[46]
And he blew it with '*Beati quorum remissae sunt iniquitates*'
(Blessed is he whose transgression is forgiven).[47]
And all the saints in Heaven sang with one voice:
    '*Homines et jumenta salvabis, Domine; quemadmodum*
      multiplicasti misericordiam tuam, Deus.'
    (O Lord, thou preservest man and beast. How excellent is
      thy loving-kindness, O God! Therefore the children of
      men put their trust under the shadow of thy wings.)[48]
Then a thousand men thronged together,
Crying up to Christ and His immaculate Mother
That grace might go with them in their pilgrimage to Truth.
  But no one there was wise enough to know the way.   520
They blundered out like beasts over the banks and hills.
They had wandered long, and it was late, before finding
    a leader,
A man in pagan apparel, as pilgrims may be.
He bore double staves, and a broad strip to bind them
Wound spirally all the way round, like a withy.
By his side he had a bag and a begging-bowl,
And on his hat he had a hundred little bottles,

And souvenirs of Sinai, and Galician scallop-shells,
And many a cross on his cloak, and the Roman cross-keys,
And a vernicle-badge[49] worn before them: all to bear
    witness   530
And be signs to let men know what shrines he had sought.
    And all the folk asked him first where he had come from.
He said, 'From Sinai, and from Our Lord's sepulchre;
I have been both in Bethlehem and in Babylon;
In Armenia, Alexandria, and other such places.
You may see by the signs that are set on my hat
That I have walked far and wide, in wet and in dry,
Seeking the saints of God for the good of my soul.'
'Can you tell us at all about a saint called Truth?
Can you tell us where he dwells, and the best way there?'   540
Said the stranger, 'So God help me, no.
I never saw a palmer, with staff and scrip,
Who asked after Truth, until here and now.'
'By St Peter!' said a Ploughman, as he pushed through
    a hedge,
'I'm as close-acquainted with Truth as a clerk with his books;
Conscience and Mother Wit made me come to his country,
And made me swear solemnly to serve him for ever,
To sow and plant his seed so long as I had strength.
I have been his follower for forty winters,
And have sown his seed and seen to his beasts,   550
And indoors and out have had an eye to his profit.
I dig and I ditch, and do all that Truth commands;
Sometimes I sow, and sometimes I thresh;
I work as a tailor or a tinker, as Truth may require,
I weave, I wind yarn – whatever Truth commands.
    And though I say it myself, he is pleased with my service:
He gives me good wages, and a gratuity sometimes,
And is the promptest payer a poor man could find:
He never withholds from a henchman his full hire at
    day's-end;
He is lowly as a lamb, and of loving speech.   560
And if you would like to learn where Truth lives,
I will tell you truly the way to his dwelling.'

'If you please, good Piers,' said the pilgrims, and offered to
    pay him
If he would go with them and show them Truth's dwelling.
'Not so, by my soul's health,' swore Piers,
'I wouldn't finger a farthing, not for St Thomas's shrine![50]
Truth would love me the less for it, a long time after!
But if what you want is the right way to go,
Then certainly I will describe it, and set you on your path.
    You must start by way of Meekness, men and
      women alike,   570
Till you come to Conscience – and by then Christ
    will know
That you love Our Lord God above all else;
And next to Him, your neighbour, whom you will never use
Otherwise than you would wish that he used you.
Turn beside a brook called Be-gentle-of-speech,
Till you find the ford called Honour-your-father-and-
    your-mother.
    Honora Patrem et matrem ...[51]
Wade into that water, and wash yourselves well,
And you will leap the lightlier for it all your lives.
    Then you will see a place called Swear-not-needlessly-
      and-especially-take-not-in-vain-the-name-of-
      Almighty-God.   580
Next you will come to a croft: keep away from it,
For the name of that croft is Covet-not-thy-neighbour's-
    cattle-nor-his-wife-nor-his-servants-lest-you-do-
    him-an-injury.
See that you break no branches there, unless they belong
    to you.
Two tree-stumps stand near-by; but do not stop there,
For they are called Steal-not and Slay-not: go straight
    past them,
Leaving them on your left hand, and do not look back.
Hold well to the high-road of observing Holy Days.
Carry on till you come to a hill called Bear-no-false-witness;
It is forested with florins and fenced with fees: 590
See that you pluck no plant there, on peril of your souls.

Next you will see Speak-truth-and-act-as-you-say-
  and-abide-by-it-always-no-matter-who-bids-you-
  otherwise.
Then soon you will see a Castle[52] as bright as the sun.
The moat around this manor is called Mercy,
And its walls are of wisdom, to keep out self-will
Crenellated with Christendom, to preserve Mankind,
And buttressed with Believe-or-you-cannot-be-saved.
  All the out-houses, halls, and chambers, have been roofed
Not with lead but with love and with Lowly-speech-
  of-brethren.   600
The drawbridge is Beseech-well-and-it-shall-be-given-you;
Each pillar is made of penance, and of prayers to saints;
And the gates are hung on hinges of gifts of alms.
  The gatekeeper is Grace, a good person;
And his man is called Amend-your-life, well known to many.
That Truth may know he can trust you, tell the porter
  this password:
I performed the penance that the priest laid on me;
I am indeed sorry for my sins, and shall always be so
Whenever I think of them, even though I were to be Pope!
  Ask Amend-your-life to approach his master humbly   610
For leave to throw wide the Wicket-gate that the
  woman closed
When Adam and Eve ate unroasted apples:
      Per Evam cunctis clausa est, et per Mariam virginem iterum
        patefacta est.
      (Through Eve it was closed to all men; through the
        Virgin Mary it was once more thrown open.)[53]
For she has the key and the door-catch, even though
  the King sleep.
If Grace gives you leave to go in by that gate,
Then you shall see Truth enthroned in your hearts,
Wearing the chain of charity. As if you were children,
Submit yourselves to him; say nothing against your sire's will.
  But beware then of Wroth-waxing, who is a wicked wretch,
And envious of him who is enthroned in your hearts.
He will push Pride into your path, and Self-praise;   620

And the brightness of your benevolences will make you blind:
You will be as the early dew[54] – driven out, and the door closed
And latched and locked behind you; and you may linger
Outside perhaps for a century,[55] before your second chance.
Thus you may lose his love by loving yourself too well,
And perhaps have no second chance, unless helped
    by his grace.

    Even so, there are seven sisters that serve Truth forever;
They are protectresses of the postern-gate of that palace.[56]
And one is called Abstinence, and Humility another;
Chastity and Charity are his chief maidens,   630
With Patience and Peace, who help many people,
And the Lady Largesse, who has let many enter:
She has plucked many thousands from Apollyon's pinfold.

    Any kinsman of this company, so help me Christ,
Is wonderfully welcomed by them, and warmly received;
But someone who is no kin to any of the seven
Will find it hard, by my head, to have hope
Of getting in at any gate, unless by God's grace.

    'Oh Christ!' said a cutpurse, 'I've no kinsfolk there!'
'Nor I,' said an ape-leader, 'for all I know.'   640
'I call God to witness,' a confectioner said. 'Could I be
    sure of all this,
I'd not put one foot in front of the other, for any friar-talk.'
    But Piers said, 'Please listen!' And he prodded them
    onwards.
'Mercy herself is a maid there, and commands the others:
She and her son are akin to all sinners.
Through the help of these two – do not hope there are others –
You may be given grace there. Only – go quickly!'

    Said a pardoner, 'By St Paul, perhaps I'm unknown there!
I must get my box of briefs and of bishops' bulls!'[57]
And his concubine cried, 'By Christ, and I'll come with you!
You can say I'm your sister.'

    So I saw no more of them.   651

'The way you describe would be hard, without a guide
For every foot of the way.' So said the folk.
But Piers the Ploughman said: 'By St Peter of Rome,
I have half an acre to plough, beside the highway;
Had I ploughed this half-acre, and had I sown it,
I would willingly come with you and show you the way.'

   'That would be a long while to wait,' said a lady in a veil.
'What would we women be doing meanwhile?'

   'Some could sew-up sacks to keep the wheat from spilling;
And all you lovely ladies with your long fingers,   10
Take silks and satins to sew at your leisure
Into chasubles for chaplains, and the Church's honour.
Wives and widows may spin wool and flax.
And turn them into cloth, and teach their daughters how to;
Note then how the needy and the naked fare,
And carry clothes to them, as Truth commands.
I shall furnish their food, unless my field runs barren;
And so long as I live, for love of Our Lord in Heaven,
Both to rich and poor I shall bring meat and bread.

   Come, now, all manner of men who live by meat
     and drink,   20
Help speed the labours of him who provides your food!'
Said a cavalier then, 'By Christ, he counsels well!
But, truly, I was never taught how to manage a plough-team.
Still – teach me how to, and by Christ I will try!'

   'By St Paul!' said Piers, 'That's so generous a proposal,
That I myself will sweat and toil and sow for us both,
And will gladly do all such work, life-long, as you may want.
You must promise, for your part, to protect Holy Church
     and me

   From the wasters and the wicked who despoil the world;
And be hot in your hunting of hares and foxes,   30
Of boars and badgers that break down my hedges;
And train falcons for yourself to kill the wild-fowl

That come to my croft and crop my wheat.'
    The cavalier's comment was truly courteous.
'By my purview, Piers, I give you my promise
To abide by this bargain to the point of battle;
So long as I live, look to me for protection.
    Said Piers, 'Well, but one more point I must put to you:
Never ill-treat your tenants, unless Truth gives warrant;
And if you must amerce them, let Mercy be your assessor,   40
And Mildness your master, for all Meed's allurements.
And if poor men approach you with presents or offerings,
Accept nothing, ever, in case it exceeds your deserts,
And at one year's end or another you must yield it back
In a truly perilous place – called Purgatory!
    Do not misuse your serfs – you will profit, so:
Though *here* they are your underlings, it may well happen
        in Heaven
That the serf sits higher than you, and receives more bliss,
Unless yours was the worthier life; for Our Lord said,
        Amice, ascende superius.
        (When thou art bidden, go and sit down in the lowest
            room; that when he that bade thee cometh, he may
            say unto thee, Friend, go up higher.)[1]
In the church charnel-house, it is hard to tell churls   50
Or serfs from their seigneur; so have that at heart.
Let your tongue be truthful, and hate all tales
But those that are wise and worthy, for correcting your
        workers.
Licence no jesters, nor listen to their lewdnesses,
And avoid such men above all when you sit at meals:
They are the Devil's discoursers, I do assure you.'
    'I swear by St James,' said the knight in reply,
'To act on your advice as long as I live.'
    Said Piers, 'I shall put on, then, a pilgrim's dress,
And take you all with me until we find Truth.   60
I shall put on my poor clothes, all ragged and patched,
My gaiters, and my gloves to get warmth in my fingers,
Sling my seed-bag round my neck instead of a scrip,
And bring along in it a bushel of bread-corn.

This I myself will sow, and then soon after
Will pilgrim-it like a palmer, in search of pardon.
　　And whosoever will help me beforehand to plough or sow,
Shall have leave, by Our Lord, to glean here at harvest,
And make merry with their takings, no matter who grumbles.
And for all kinds of craftsmen, of Christian life,[2]　　　　70
I shall find food if they are faithful and honest.
But Jack the Jester and Jenny from the whorehouse,
Dan the Dicer and Denise the Bawd,
And Friar Faker and his fellow brothers,
And Robin the Ribald with his ruttish jokes:
Truth once told me, and bade me tell it to others,
Have no dealings with them: *deleantur de libro viventium.*
　　　(Let them be blotted out of the book of the living.)[3]
For Holy Church has been told not even to take tithes
　　　from them,
　　　　Quia cum justis non scribantur.
　　　(For let them not be written with the righteous.)[4]
They have had good luck to get away with it, may God
　　　make them better.'
　　Now, the wife of Piers was called Dame Work-when-
　　　you-can;　　　　　　　　　　　　　　　　　　　　　　80
His daughter was called Do-your-duty-or-get-a-beating;
His son was Be-sure-your-betters-are-obeyed-
　　　and-do-not-dispute-with-them-or-you'll-pay
　　　dearly-for-it.
'May God be with you all, as His word teaches;
For now that I am old and grey, and own a little property,
I propose as a penance to be a pilgrim with these people.
And I wish, before I go, to have my will drawn up well.
In the name of God, Amen. I myself make this Will.
He shall have my soul who has best deserved it,
And shall defend it from the Fiend (for so I believe)　　　90
Till I come to Accounts-Day, as my Creed tells me,
Then to have release and remission from all my back rent.
　　The Kirk shall have my carcass and the keeping
　　　of my bones:
From my harvest and my havings it would have its tithes,

Which I paid promptly, to save my soul from peril;
It must therefore, I hope, remember me in Masses,
And have me in mind among all other Christians.

    What I honestly earned, and no more, I leave to my wife,
To distribute among herself and my dear children;
For though I should die today, my debts are all paid,   100
Because I always gave back before bedtime whatever
    I borrowed.[5]

    And any residue or remnant, by the Rood of Lucca,[6]
I will worship Truth with, all my life,
And behind the plough be his pilgrim, for the sake
    of poor men:
My pilgrim-staff my plough-staff; to cut roots apart,
And help my coulter to carve and cleanse the furrows.'

    Now Piers and the pilgrims have gone to plough,
And many are helping him to ear his half-acre.
Ditchers and delvers dug up the ridges
(Which pleased Piers greatly, and he praised them well).   110
But others also were working eagerly,
Every man in some manner making himself useful –
Such as hoeing out weeds, perhaps, which also pleased Piers.

    But promptly at nine o'clock Piers stopped his plough,
To oversee his helpers; for those who worked best
He would hire at highest wages when harvest-time came.
And some were sitting and singing over their ale –
Helping him 'plough his half-acre', forsooth, with *Hey,*
    nonny nonny!

    'Now, by my soul's peril,' cried Piers, in pure rage,
'Unless you're on your feet fast, and flying to work,   120
Not one grain that I grow shall you get when you need it;
And though you die of dearth, devil take me if I care!'
Then the slackers grew scared. Some claimed to be blind,
Or flexed their legs all awry, as such losels know how.
And plaintively whined at Piers, and begged him to pity them.
'We have no limbs to labour with, Lord save you, master!
But we pray for you, Piers, and for your plough as well,
And that by God's grace your grain shall multiply
And yield you a return for the alms you give us here:

For so grave are our afflictions, we are utterly useless.'   130
    Said Piers: 'If that were so, I should soon perceive it.
Well I know you are wasters, and so is Truth aware of it;
I am his oldest hired-man, and promised to warn him
Who they were in this world that injured his workers.
You waste what other men earn with toil and worry:
But Truth shall teach you in time how to drive his ox-team,
Or your food shall be barley-bread and the brooks your drink!
The truly blind or disabled, or with legs braced in irons,
He shall eat wheaten bread; and he shall drink at my table
Till God in His goodness gives him a remedy.   140
But you *could* work as Truth wishes, for food and wages,
By keeping the beasts from the corn, or by herding cattle,
Or ditching or digging, or drubbing away at sheaves,
Or helping mix mortar, or carrying muck afield.
    But you live in lechery, and in slander and sloth;
And by God's long-suffering alone are you saved from
      His vengeance.
    Anchorites and hermits who eat only at noon,
And no more till the morrow – they shall have my alms
To clothe them; and so shall the keepers of cloisters
      and churches;
But Robin Runaround[7] shall receive nothing of mine,   150
Nor any scripture-expounders but preachers with
      episcopal licence:
I'll give *them* their bread and soup, and seat them in comfort,
For even the religious must by reason be sure of their keep.'
    One waster grew angry, and wanted to fight;
He challenged Piers Ploughman by proffering his glove.
And a braggartly Breton[8] also blustered at Piers:
'Go and piss on your plough, you pitiful bastard!
We'll do what we want, whether *you* like it or not,
And we'll fetch away your flour and your food when we please,
And make good and merry with them, for all your
      maundering!'   160
    Then Piers the Ploughman appealed to the knight
To preserve him, as he promised, from these cursèd reprobates,
Those wolvish wasters who make the world dangerous.

'They use up all, earn nothing; and, in the meanwhile,
The people will never have plenty if my plough stands idle.'
The knight, with urbanity that was his by nature,
Then warned the wasters against evil ways –
'Or you shall be brought to justice, by my Order of
    Knighthood!'
  'I was never used to work, and I won't begin now!'
Said the waster, and scoffed at the law and scorned
    the knight,   170
And said Piers and his plough were neither worth a pea-pod,
And menaced Piers and his men should they soon meet again.
  'By the peril of my soul!' cried Piers, 'You shall pay for this!'
And he cried 'come hither' to Hunger, who heard him at once.
'Work vengeance on these wasters who ruin the world!'
  And Hunger took hold of the waster by his belly,
And wrung him so by his innards that his eyes ran water;
And he so buffeted the Breton about his cheeks
That he looked like a lantern all the rest of his life.
He so battered them both, he nearly burst their guts.   180
Had not Piers with a pease-loaf persuaded Hunger to stop,
They would both have needed burying, don't believe
    otherwise.
'Allow them to live, but let them eat with the pigs,
On bean-and-bran mash; or else be reduced
To skimmed milk and small ale.' Thus Piers prayed for
    these men.
  In utter fear, these fakers fled off to the barns
And flogged away with their flails from morn till eve,
So that Hunger had not the courage to harm them,
Because Piers had prepared them a potful of peas.
A horde of hermits got hold of spades,   190
And cut up their copes to make short coats,
And went out as workmen with spades and shovels,
And ditched and delved to drive away Hunger.
  Thousands of the 'blind' and 'bedridden' grew
    suddenly better;
Those who had sat and begged for silver were swiftly healed.
Food baked for Bayard[9] was brought many starving,

And many a beggar, for a few beans, turned biddable
     workman;
And many a poor man was pleased to have peas for his wages.
They pounced on the work Piers gave them, as promptly
     as sparrow-hawks.
Piers was proud of all this, and put them to work,   200
And gave them what food he could afford, and fair wages.
   Then Piers had pity, and pressed Hunger to go
Back to his homeland, and keep himself there:
'I am well avenged now on those vagabonds, thanks to
     your vigour;
But I pray you, before you depart,' said Piers to Hunger,
'What is best to be done with beggars and cadgers?
For I know well, once you're gone they'll again work badly.
It is only their misery that makes them so meek now,
Only for want of food do these folk obey me;
Yet they are my blood-brothers, for God bought us all,   210
And Truth taught me once to love every one of them,
And assist them in all things, as their need might be.
So now I would learn from you what the best way is
To make myself their master, and them to work.'
   Said Hunger, 'Hear me, now, and hold on to my words.
The big burly beggars who could labour for their bread,
Give them horse-feed or hounds'-food to keep their
     hearts high;
Or abase their bodies with a diet of beans.
If they begin to grumble, just say "Go and work":
Their suppers will be more savoury if earned with sweat.   220
   But if you find a fellow truly ill-used by Fortune,
Or by vile men's villainy, learn to know such victims,
And comfort them as you can, for the love of Christ in
     Heaven;
Love and relieve them, as God's law teaches:
    Alter alterius onera portate.
    (Bear ye one another's burdens.)[10]
And all manner of men whom you may come across,
Who have nothing, or are needy – let your own goods
     help them.

Give them charity without chiding – leave their
    chastisement to God;
If they have done evil, vengeance is His.
    Mihi vindicta, et ego retribuam.
    (Vengeance belongeth to me; I will recompense, saith
      the Lord.)[11]
If you wish for God's grace, obey the Gospel,
And make yourself loved by the lowly; thus you lay hands
    on grace: 230
    Facite vobis amicos de Mammona iniquitatibus.'
    (Make to yourselves friends of the mammon of
      unrighteousness.)[12]
'I would not grieve God for all the wealth in the world;
Is it possible to do as you say, and commit no sin?'
'It is, I assure you, or else the Bible is lying.
Look at the giant *Genesis*, that engendered us all:
"In the sweat of thy face shalt thou eat bread."[13]
"Thou shalt labour for thy living" – so our Lord said.
And Solomon says the same – I saw it in the Bible:
    "The sluggard will not plough, by reason of the cold."[14]
Hence, he shall beg at harvest-time, and have nothing.
    Matthew of the Man's Face mouthed these words:[15]   240
The worthless servant would not set his one talent to work,
And lost the esteem of his master for evermore;
And his master took that one talent away from him
And gave it to the servant who had gained ten talents;[16]
And let Holy Church hear what he said at that time:
"He that hath shall have, and help at need;
He that hath not shall have nothing, and no man shall
    help him;
And from him who thinks he has something, I shall
    withhold even that."[17]
    Mother Wit would teach us that all men should work
In ditching or delving, or in drudging at prayers –   250
The contemplative life or the active – as Christ commands.
And the Psalter says, in the Psalm *Blessèd is every one*,
That the fellow who feeds himself by straightforward labour
Is blessèd (so says the Book) in body and soul:

Labores manuum tuarum.'
    (Thou shalt eat the labour of thine hands: happy shalt
      thou be, and it shall be well with thee.)[18]
  'If you please, there is one more point,' said Piers.
    'If perhaps you have
Any morsel of medical knowledge, teach it *me*, dear friend:
For some of my servants – and myself too –
Have not worked for a week, we have such belly-aches.'
  'I know all too well,' said Hunger, 'what your sickness is.
You have all been guzzling too much – that's what gives
    you such gripes.   260
Here is my advice: if you hope to stay healthy,
Drink nothing, any day, until you have dined a little;
Have nothing to eat until true hunger
Has sent the savour of its sauce to your lips;
Save some of that sauce for supper, and don't sit there
    too long –
Be up and away before Appetite has eaten his fill.
Never let Sir Surfeit sit at your table;
Have no faith in him, for he is lecherous, and a fastidious
    eater,
And his guts are always greedy for gourmet dishes.
Make this your daily diet, and I'll wager my ears   270
Dr Physic's furred hoods will be sold to buy food,
And his cloak of Calabrian fur, with all its clasps of gold;[19]
And he'll be glad, by God, to give up medicine,
And learn to labour on the land, for sweet life's sake:
For many such quacks are murderers, may God forgive them.
Their drinks make men die much sooner than Destiny does!'
  Said Piers, 'By St Paul, these are profitable words!
But away with you now, if you wish, and the best of luck
    with you.
You have read us a lovely lesson, may the Lord reward you!'
  'Good God be my witness,' said Hunger, 'I'm not
    going yet –   280
Not till I've had today's dinner, and some drink as well!'
  'I've not so much as a penny to purchase you pullets,
Nor geese nor grunters; I have only two green cheeses,

A few curds, and some cream, and an oaten cake,
And two bean-and-bran loaves that I baked for my children.
And I swear by my soul, I have no salt bacon,
Or eggs, by Christ, to cook-up for you into collops.
I have parsley, and pot-herbs, and plenty of greens,
A cow and a calf, and a cart-mare
To drag my dung afield while the drought lasts.   290
That is all I have to live on, until Lammas-time;
Though by then, I hope, I shall have my field's harvest in;
And then I'll dish up such a dinner as I'd dearly like to.'
Then all the poor people came with peasecods,
And brought beans in their laps, and baked apples,
And chibols, and chervil, and loads of ripe cherries,
And presented them to Piers for Hunger's placation.
    And Hunger ate all up fast, and asked for more.
Then the poor folk were afraid, and fed Hunger faster,
With plenty of green leeks and peas, in hope to polish
        him off.   300
By now it was nearly harvest-time, and new corn came
        to market;
So the folk were happier, and fed Hunger finely,
And gave him good ale such as Glutton loved, until Hunger
        grew sleepy.
    Then Waster would work no longer, but went
        wandering off;
And the beggars refused any bread that had bean-flour in it;
They called for high-class wheat of one kind or another,
And could not be persuaded to sample small beer,
But only the best and the brownest in the borough.
    Landless labourers who must live by their hands
Would not deign to dine on day-old greens;   310
No penny-ale would please them, nor a piece of bacon,
But only fresh meat or fish, either baked or fried –
And steaming hot, at that, lest a chill harm their stomachs.
And without the highest of wages they would all grumble,
Bewailing the day whereon they were born to be workmen,
Coming at last to cry out against Cato's advice:
        Paupertatis onus patienter ferre memento.

(Remember to bear with forbearance the burden of
    your poverty.)[20]
They grew angry with God, and grumbled at Reason,
And cursed the King and his Council too,
For laying down laws that harassed labourers.[21]
Yet when Hunger had the upper hand, *he* kept them quiet;   320
They made no strife with *his* statutes – his looks were
    too stern!
   But I warn all you workmen – earn while you may,
For Hunger is making haste, and will soon be here.
He shall awaken with the waters, for chastening wasters.[22]
Before five years have passed, there shall be a great famine,
Through floods and foul weather the fruits of the earth
    shall fail.
For so Saturn has foreseen, and sent you this warning:
When you see the Sun stand awry, and two monks' heads
    beside him,
And a maiden has mastery, multiplied by eight,
Then Death shall withdraw, and Dearth be your judge,   330
And Dawes the Ditcher shall die of hunger
Unless God in His great goodness grants us a truce.

Truth heard tell of all this, and he sent word to Piers
To go back to his ox-team, and till the soil;
And he granted Piers a pardon from both punishment
    and guilt,[1]
For him and for his heirs for ever more,
So long as he stayed at home and ploughed his soil.
And whoever might help him to plough, or to sow or
    to plant,
Or in any other activity useful to Piers,
Truth granted him too a pardon like that for the ploughman.
    The kings and cavaliers who took care of Holy Church,
And righteously ruled the people in their realms,   10
Had pardon enough to pass easily through Purgatory,
And be with patriarchs and prophets in Paradise.
    Truly blessèd bishops, who lived by their duty,
Learnèd in both kinds of law,[2] and preaching them to laymen,
And who did as much as they might to amend all sinners,
Were peers of the Apostles (so Piers's pardon showed),
And on Doomsday should sit upon God's high dais.
    Merchants were granted marginally many years' indulgence,
But none from both guilt *and* punishment – that, no Pope
    could provide:
Because they do not hold by Holy Days, as Holy Church
    teaches,   20
And because they swear 'By my soul' and 'So help me God',
Oaths taken against their conscience, only to sell their goods.
    Still, under his personal signet, Truth sent them a letter
Telling them to buy up boldly what goods they found best:
Then sell all the stuff again, and save the profit
To endow hospitals, and help the poor in health,
And promptly to put right all unrepaired roadways
And to rebuild all broken-down bridges,
And give poor men's daughters their dowries or their
    convent dues,

For paupers and prisoners to provide food,   30
And give scholars their schooling, or set them to a trade,
And assist and endow the Religious Orders.
'Then I myself shall send you St Michael, my Archangel,
That no devil, when you die, shall bring you dread or harm;
Do this, and he shall save you from all despair,
And bring your souls in safety to my saints in bliss.'
    This made the merchants happy – many wept for joy,
And praised Piers Ploughman for procuring this Bull.
    The lawyers had least indulgence, who make pleas for
        Meed the Maiden;
For the Psalter offers no salvation to such as take bribes,   40
Especially against the innocent and inexperienced:
        Munera super innocentem non accipies.
        (Thou shalt not take reward against the innocent.)[3]
The pleaders should take pains with their pleas for such
        people,
And princes and prelates should pay them for their trouble:
        A regibus et principibus erit merces eorum.
        (From princes and prelates shall their payment be.)[4]
But many a judge or juror would do more for Old Jack
Than they would do for love of God – and do not you
        doubt it!
But the speaker who speaks unsparingly on behalf of the
        poor man
Who is innocent, or of the needy, and oppresses no one,
But comforts them in calamity, without coveting gifts,
And explains for love of Our Lord the law he has learned:
No devil shall do him a jot of harm on his death-bed,   50
But he and his soul shall be safe, as the Psalter bears witness:
        Qui facit haec, non movebitur in aeternum.
        (He that doth these things shall never be moved.)[5]
    One cannot buy water or wind, or wisdom, or fire;
These four the Father of Heaven gave in common to all
        earthly folk;
They are Truth's treasures, intended for all honest men,
And cannot wax or wane without God's own will.
    When lawyers draw near their deaths, and want indulgences,

Très petit[6] is their pardon, before their departure,
If they ever took pay from poor men for their pleading.
All you legists and lawyers, learn this true lesson
(Or if it is false, the fault is St Matthew's, not mine,   60
For I have it on his authority, and the proverb is his):

> *Quaecumque vultis ut faciant vobis homines, et vos*
>   *facite eis.*

> (All things whatsoever ye would that men should do
>   to you, do ye even so to them.)[7]

But all labourers alive, who live by their hands,
And have honestly earned whatever they receive,
And who live in love, and lawfully, with lowly hearts,
Theirs is the same absolution that I send to Piers.

   But cadgers and beggars have no part in my Bull,
Unless the cause was honest that induced them to beg.
For they who beg and beseech without being in need,
Are as false as the Fiend, and defraud the true poor,
And also beguile one to give against his will: 70
For if he knew they were not in need, he would give
      to others
Who were in real hardship, and so lend help to the poorest.
Cato, and the Clerk of the Stories,[8] both inculcate this:
Cui des, videto, 'Take care whom you give to,' says Cato;
And the Stories also teach us the bestowing of alms:

> *Sit eleemosyna tua in manu tua, donec studes cui des.*

> (Let your alms remain in your hand till you know who
>   receives them.)

   But St Gregory was a good man, and he bade us give
Alms to any that asked, for love of Him who gives all:

> *Non eligas cui misererais, ne forte praetereas illum*
>   *qui meretur accipere. Quia incertum est pro quo*
>   *Deo magis placeas.*

> (Do not choose upon whom you will have compassion,
>   lest perhaps you pass over the man who really
>   deserves your gift. For it is uncertain on whose behalf
>   you will better please God.)[9]

   One never knows who is worthy, but God always knows
      who is needy;

The treachery is the taker's, if there *is* betrayal afoot;
To give is to repay God and prepare for one's grave,   80
But he who begs is a borrower, and brings debts on himself:
Beggars, I say, are all borrowers, and their bailsman is
    God Almighty,
Who alone can repay the debt, with interest added.
    Quare non dedisti pecuniam meam ad mensam, ut ego
        veniens cum usuris utique exegissem illam?
    (Wherefore then gavest not thou my money into the
        bank, that at my coming I might have required my
        own with usury?)[10]
  Therefore beseech not, you beggars, unless in utter
    abjection;
For whoever has enough to buy bread, as the Bible bears
    witness,
Even if that is all he has, has riches enough –
    Satis dives est qui non indiget pane.
    (He is rich enough who is not poor in bread.)[11]
  Let your solace be the steadfast reading of saints' lives,
Since the Book forbids begging, and blames it thus:
    Junior fui, etenim senui; et non vidi justum derelictum,
        nec semen ejus quaerens panem.
    (I have been young, and now am old; yet have I not seen
        the righteous forsaken, nor his seed begging bread.)[12]
  You beggars live in no love, and keep no law:
Many of you do not marry the women who are your mates,   90
But whinny like wild horses, and mount, and set to work;
And the babies that are born are flagrant bastards.
Then you break their bones or their backs, in childhood,
And falsely beg with your offspring for ever after.
There are more mis-shapen folk among you beggars
Than among any other sort of men that walk Middle Earth;
And those who lead this kind of life shall loathe the day
They were ever made man, when the time of their death
    is come.
  But old grey-haired grandads, grown weak or disabled,
Or women who are with child, and cannot work,   100
And the blind, the bedridden, or the broken-limbed,

Or lepers or the like: if they lowlily bear their afflictions,
They have pardons as plenary as the Ploughman himself
For love of their lowly hearts, their Lord has granted them
Their penance and their purgatory here upon Earth.
   Then a priest said, 'Piers, let me read your pardon;
I will construe its clauses into clear English.'
And Piers, at the priest's request, unfolded his pardon;
And I, behind them both, could read the whole Bull.
It was all in only two lines, not a letter more.   110
And the two lines read thus, with Truth's attestation:
      Et qui bona egerunt, ibunt in vitam aeternam;
          Qui vero mala, in ignem aeternum.
      (The righteous shall go into life eternal,
          But the unrighteous into everlasting fire.)[13]
   Said the priest, then, 'By St Peter! I can find no pardon
      here,
But only, "Do well, and deserve well, and God will save
      your soul;
Do evil, and deserve evil, and dare hope no other
Than that after your death-day the Devil shall have it."'
   And Piers, in pure fury, tore the pardon in two,
      And said: '*Si ambulavero in medio umbrae mortis,*
          Non timebo mala; quoniam tu mecum es.
      (Yea, though I walk through the valley of the shadow
          of death,
      I will fear no evil, for thou art with me.)[14]
I shall cease from my sowing, and toil and sweat no more,
And nevermore be so busy about the joy of my belly.
Prayers and penitence shall henceforth replace my plough;
I will weep instead of sleeping. And what though I lack
      wheaten bread?   120
King David ate his bread in dolour and penance,
By what the Psalter says; and so did many others.
Love God loyally, and your livelihood will not lack:
      Fuerunt mihi lacrymae meae panes die et nocte.
      (My tears have been my meat day and night.)[15]
   And unless St Luke is a liar, we are to live like birds,
And not be so busy about this world's pleasures:

Ne soliciti sitis, he says in his Gospel,
    (Be not solicitous, saying what shall we drink?)[16]
And he teaches us by examples to instruct ourselves.
The wildfowl in the fields – who feeds them in winter?
They have no granaries to go to, yet God feeds them all.'
    The priest said to Piers, 'Why, Peter, it seems to me   130
You are not wholly illiterate. Where did you learn to read?'
    'Abstinence the Abbess taught me my ABC,
And Conscience came later, and schooled me in much more.
    'Were you a priest, Piers, you might preach if you chose
Like a Doctor of Divinity with "The fool has said" as
      your text.'[17]
    'You graceless good-for-nothing! A great deal *you* know
    of the Bible.
You have seldom looked, it would seem, at Solomon's proverbs
    Ejice derisorem, et exibit cum eo jurgium.'
    (Cast out the scorner, and contention shall go out.)[18]
    Then Piers and the priest disputed with each other
Till the noise of their words awoke me. So I looked about,
And saw that the sun was now standing in the South,   140
And I, without meal or money, on the Malvern Hills.
Thus, wondering at my dream, I went on my way.
    This dream has made me ponder many times
Whether what I saw while sleeping might be truly so;
I have been inwardly pensive about Piers the Ploughman,
And what kind of pardon Piers had, that comforted people,
And how the priest impugned it with a pair of neat phrases.
But I have no relish for dream-reading – it is rarely true.
Cato and the Canon Lawyers counsel *Somnia ne cures*:
'Do not put faith in dreams, or in dream-divination.'   150
    Yet a certain book of the Bible bears witness
How Daniel divined the dreams of a king
Whom clerks and scholars call Nebuchadnezzar.[19]
Daniel said, 'Sire, your dream signifies
That paladins of Media and Persia shall come to split
    your kingdom,
And lesser lordlings partition the land among them.'
And as Daniel divined, so indeed it befell –

The king lost his kingdom, and lesser lords took it.
  And Joseph dreamed a marvel – how the moon and
    the sun
And the eleven stars all made obeisance to him.   160
Jacob gave this judgment of Joseph's dream:
'Fair son,' said his father, 'this means that in time of famine,
I myself, and my other sons, will seek your help.'
  It befell as his father said, in the days of Pharaoh,
When Joseph was Justice over the land of Egypt,
That indeed his father and family came to him for aid.[20]
  All this makes me more thoughtful about my dream,
And the priest's proof that no pardon could match Do-Well,
His decision that Do-Well surpassed indulgences,
Biennial or triennial Masses, or Bishops' Bulls,[21]   170
And how Do-Well on Doomsday will be honoured
    with dignity
Surpassing all the pardons of St Peter's Church.
  Now, the Pope has power to grant people
Pardon, to pass into Heaven without doing penance;
This is our belief, and all learned men teach it:
    Quodcumque ligaveris super terram, erit ligatum et in coelis.
    (Whatsoever thou shalt bind on earth shall be bound
      in heaven.)[22]
So I loyally believe (the Lord forbid otherwise!)
That pardons and penances and prayers do save
Even souls that have sinned in seven deadly ways.
But to trust those triennials, I truly think,
Is certainly not so safe for the soul as Do-Well is.   180
Therefore I recommend to all you with riches on Earth,
Who trust in your treasure and the buying of triennials:
Do not be any bolder to break the Ten Commandments.
In especial, you masters of men, and mayors and judges,
Who hold this world's wealth and are thought to be wise,
And can purchase your pardons and Papal Bulls:
On that dreadful Doomsday when the dead shall rise up
And all come before Christ to render their accounts,
Your doom will depend on what you did day by day –
How you lived your life on Earth, and kept God's laws.   190

Then a pack full of pardons and Provincial's letters
Affirming you confrater in all the Four Orders,[23]
And your double indulgences – unless Do-Well stands
    by you,
I value your patents and pardons at a dried pea-pod.
  All Christians, therefore, I counsel: Pray to Christ
And to Mary His Mother as our mediator,
That God shall give us grace, before we go hence,
To do such deeds while we are down on Earth
That after our dying day Do-Well shall declare
On the Day of Doom, that we did as he ordained.   200

PASSUS 8

Thus robed in my russet I roamed about
All that summer season, seeking Do-Well;
And often I would ask of the folk I met
If anyone knew where Do-Well's lodging was,
And asked many more what sort of man he might be.
But wherever I went, not one could tell me –
Low and high alike – where the fellow lived . . .
   It fell out, one Friday, that I met two friars,
Masters of the Minorites,[1] and men of great intellect.
I gave them courteous greetings, as good manners teach,   10
And begged them, by God's mercy, before they proceeded,
If they had come across, in their travels, any country
    or quarter
Where Do-Well was dwelling, would they divulge it.
For they, of all walkers on Earth, are the most widely
    travelled,
Knowing countries and courts and all kinds of places,
From the palaces of princes to poor men's cottages,
And should know where Do-Well – and Do-Evil –
    both dwell.
   Said the Minorites, 'Why, that man dwells among us;
And he always has done, and I hope always will.'
   '*Contra!*'[2] said I, like a clerk, and commenced my
    disputation.   20
'The Scriptures say *septies in die cadit justus*:[3]
Seven times in a day the righteous man sins.
And whosoever sins,' I said, 'does evil, it seems to me;
But Do-Well and Do-Evil cannot dwell together.
Ergo, Do-Well is not always among you friars;
He must at times be elsewhere, as the people's teacher.'
   Said the friar, 'My son, I shall explain to you
The sinning of a just man seven times a day.
I shall expound it plainly, by means of a parable.
Imagine a man in a boat, amidst open water: 30

The wind, and the waves, and the boat swaying,
May make the man fall, and get up again, many times;
For however strongly he stands, a move makes him stumble.
And yet he is safe and sound, and so he needs to be:
For unless he stood up soon, and snatched the helm,
The boat would be overturned by the wind and water,
And his life be lost by his own laziness.
　　Even so it is with all men on Earth:
The water, which dips and swells, is like this world;
The wealth of this world is like the great waves   40
That wallow about with the winds and weathers.
The boat is like our body, by nature so frail
That by force of the fickle world, the flesh, and the Devil,
The righteous man himself sins seven times a day.
　　Yet his sins are not deadly; he is defended by Do-Well –
That is, by charity, our chief champion against sin;
He gives man strength to stand, and steers man's soul,
So that though your body may bow like a boat on the water,
Your soul is safe – unless of your own free will
You do fall to deadly sin, and so drown your soul: 50
God will not save your soul if you squander it.
For He gives you a constant gift by which to guard
　　yourself –
Wisdom and Free-Will – in which all creatures share,
Though they be birds of the air, or beasts or fishes.
But since man has most of these, then he is most
To blame if he makes bad use of them, and disobeys
　　Do-Well.'
　　'I am too stupid,' said I, 'to understand your meaning;
But if I may live and reflect, I shall learn better.'
'I commend you, then, to Christ, who died on the Cross.'
'And may the same,' said I, 'save *you* from misfortune,   60
And give you grace in this world to be good men.'
　　So I wandered widely, always walking alone,
And came to a wild waste-land beside a wood.
The blissful songs of the birds made me bide there;
So I lingered a little under a lime-tree in a glade,
To listen to the lyrics of the lovesome birds;

And the minstrelsy from their mouths made me fall asleep,
And there came to me then the most marvellous dream
That ever was dreamed by anyone, I think, in this world.
    It seemed that a tall man, one very much like myself   70
Came and called me by my Christian name.
'Who are you?' I asked him, 'How do you know my name?'
    'You are well aware of that, and no one better!'
'I really ought to know you?' 'I am Thought,
Who has followed you for years. Have you never seen
    me before?'
'It is likely, if you are Thought, you could let me know
Where Do-Well's dwelling is, and describe it to me.'
    'Do-Well, Do-Better, and a third called Do-Best,
Are three fair virtues, to be found not far away.
Whoever is trustworthy of tongue and of his two hands,   80
Earning his living from his own land or labour,
Whose tally is trustworthy, and who takes only his due,
Who is not drunken or disdainful: *he* knows Do-Well.
Do-Better does all this, but he does much more:
He is lowly as a lamb, and of likeable speech,
And assists all men according to their needs;
He has burst all the money-bags and boundaries
That once belonged to Earl Avarice and his heirs,
Has made himself friends with the money of Mammon;[4]
Has enrolled as a Religious, and re-translated the Bible,   90
And preaches now to the people on the words of St Paul:
    Libenter enim suffertis insipientes; cum sitis ipsi sapientes.
    (Ye suffer fools gladly, seeing ye yourselves are wise.)[5]
Allow those of little wisdom to live among you,
And gladly do them good, since God so commands.
    Do-Best is placed above both, and bears a bishop's crozier,
With a hook on one end to haul men out of Hell,
And a spike at the staff's other end, to strike down the wicked
Who lie in wait to work evil upon Do-Well.
Do-Well and Do-Better have determined between them
To crown a man to be king and control them both,
So that if Do-Well or Do-Better should injure Do-Best,   100
That King shall come and cast him into irons;

And unless Do-Best begs him off, he shall lie there forever.
  Thus Do-Well and Do-Better, and Do-Best for a third,
Have crowned a man to be King and protect *them all*,
And rule the realm by their threefold reason,
And only accordingly as these three shall advise.'
  I thanked Thought then for teaching me all this.
'But your lesson leaves me unsatisfied; I long to learn
How Do-Well, Do-Better, and Do-Best may act
        among men.'
'Only Reason[6] can instruct you where those three are.   110
I know of nobody else among those now living.'
  Thus for three days, Thought and I went on together,
Discussing Do-Well one day after another;
Till we ran quite unawares across Reason.
He was long and lean, and like no other man;
Neither pride nor poverty showed in his apparel;
So grave his manner, and so sweet his countenance,
I dared not moot any matter to move him to argument,
But begged Thought to be my go-between
And introduce the topic that might test his wits –   120
The difference, namely, between Do-Well, Do-Better
        and Do-Best.
  With this intention, then, Thought spoke these words:
'Here is Long Will who, if you could tell him, would ask
Where in this country are Do-Well, Do-Better and Do-Best;
He would also learn whether they are men or women:
For his desire is to do as these three direct.'

Said Reason, 'Sir Do-Well's dwelling is not a day's
    journey hence,
In a castle constructed by Nature[1] from four kinds of thing:
It is made of earth intermingled with air,
And with fire and water wondrously conjoined.[2]
And Nature has cunningly enclosed within this castle
A leman whom he loves no less than himself.
Anima[3] is her name, and Envy abhors her:
He's a proud prancer from France, called the Prince of
    this World,[4]
And would lure her away to him with his wiles, if he could.
  Nature of course knows this well, and keeps her the
    closer,   10
Defended by Sir Do-Well, who is Duke of the Marches.[5]
Do-Better is her damsel, Sir Do-Well's daughter,
Who serves the lady loyally both early and late.
Do-Best is above them both, and ranks with bishops;
His commands are unquestioned, and he rules the whole castle;
Lady Anima too is controlled by his teaching.
  Now, the Constable of the castle, and Captain of the
    Watch,
Is called Sir Insight,[6] a wise knight certainly.
He has five fine sons by his first wife:
Sir See-Well and Sir Say-Well and Sir Hear-Well the
    Courteous,   20
With Sir Work-Well-with-your-Hands (a strong,
    active man)
And Sir Godfrey Go-Well – all very great lords.
So these five are assigned to safeguard Lady Anima
Until Nature comes or sends for her to keep her safe for ever.'
  'What kind of character is this Nature? Can you tell me?'
'A conceiver and creator of all kinds of things;
The father and fashioner of all that was ever formed.
For he is the great God that had no beginning,

The Lord of life and light as of bliss and pain.
The angels, and all that live, are at his command;   30
But Man is the creature most like him, in image and quality.
It was at Nature's word that the animals issued forth:
> *Dixit, et facta sunt.*
> (He commanded, and they were created.)[7]
But when he made Man, in his own image,
And Eve out of Adam's rib, the act was "immediate";[8]
For, though singular himself he said "Let us make",
As who would say, "More must be used than my word alone;
My might must help, and not my speech merely."

If a lord must write letters, but lacks parchment,
Or, however fine his hand, if he has no pen:
For all his lordship, his letter, I believe, will go unwritten.   40
And it seems that God is the same, as we see in the Bible;
For where it says *Dixit, et facta sunt*,
He must work through His Word, and reveal His wisdom;
And in this manner Man was made, through power of
> Almighty God,
By His word and by His handiwork, for life everlasting.
For He gave him a soul from the Holy Spirit in Heaven,
And of His great grace granted bliss to him.
In life everlasting, and to his lineage after him.

This castle that Nature created is called Flesh;
And the meaning of that is Man made with a soul
By the word and the workmanship, acting as one,   50
And by the might, of God's majesty. Thus was Man made.
Conscience,[9] and *all* mental qualities, are enclosed
> in this castle,
For love of Lady Anima, whose name is Life;
She may move as she likes throughout all Man's body,
But her home is the heart, her haven of rest.
The home of Insight is the head, but he rules the heart:
What Anima likes or loathes, he allows – or not –
For, next to God's grace, her greatest friend is Insight.

Much misery will befall the man who misuses Insight,
As it might be those gluttonous gobblers whose god is
> their belly: 60

Quorum deus venter est.[10]

Because they serve Satan, he shall have their souls,

For those who lead sinful lives have souls like his;

And all who lead good lives are like God Almighty.

Qui manet in caritate in Deo manet.

(He that dwelleth in love dwelleth in God and God
in him.)[11]

Alas, that drink should undo those whom God bought
so dearly,

And force Him to forsake those whom He framed in His
likeness!

Amen dico vobis, nescio vos.

(Verily I say unto you, I know you not.)

Et alibi: et dimisi eos secundum desideria eorum.

(And elsewhere it is written, So I gave them up unto
their own hearts' lust.)[12]

But fools whose insight fails them ... I feel that Holy Church

Should furnish the needs of such fools, and of fatherless
children,

And of widows without skill wherewith to earn a living,

And mad men, and young girls who maybe are helpless:

All these lack insight, and are in need of instruction.   70

I might make a long speech about this matter,

And find a flock of proofs in the Four Doctors;[13]

And that I do not lie in my allegations, St Luke bears
witness.[14]

Godfathers and godmothers who see their godchildren

In misery or misfortune, and have means to relieve them,

Shall do penance in Purgatory if they provide no help:

They owe more to the infant still unlearned in God's Law

Than giving him a name, of which he knows nothing!

No Christian creature need ever cry at men's gates,

Nor lack bread or bouillon, if priests behaved as they
should.   80

No Jew would let another Jew be a jabbering beggar,

Not for all the wealth in the world, were he able to help him.

Alas that one Christian creature should be unkind
to another,

When Jews – whom we judge to be just like Judas –
Will all help each other if need arises!
Why will not we Christians as kindly share Christ's goodness
As Jews? – who are thus our exemplars; shame to us all!
I fear all Christians in common shall pay for such unkindness.
Then the bishops will be blamed for the beggars' plight:
It's to act worse than Judas, to give money to a jester   90
And bid the beggar be off because his clothes are tattered.

> *Proditor est prelatus cum Juda, qui patrimonium Christi*
>   *minus distribuit.*

> (That prelate who distributes too little of Christ's
>   patrimony, is a traitor like Judas.)

> *Et alibi: Perniciosus dispensator est, qui res pauperum*
>   *Christi inutiliter consumit.*

> (And elsewhere it is written, He is an evil bursar, who
>   unprofitably scatters the property of Christ's poor.)[15]

Such a man does not do well, nor dreads God Almighty,
Nor savours the proverbs of Solomon, who says in his
    wisdom,

> *Initium sapientiae timor Domini.*

> (The fear of the Lord is the beginning of wisdom.)[16]

 He who dreads God, does well; he who dreads Him
    from love,
And not for fear of punishment, therefore does better;
 And he does best who withdraws, by night and day,
 From needlessly spending speech or expending time:

> *Qui offendit in uno, in omnibus est reus.*

> (For whosoever shall keep the whole Law,
>   and yet offend in one point, he is guilty of all.) [17]

 Waste of time (God knows this is true)
Is that thing on Earth most hated by those in Heaven;
And second is waste of speech, that sprouting of
    God's grace,   100
God's gleeman, and a game played in Heaven.
Our faithful Father could not wish His fiddle untuned,
Nor his gleeman a good-for-nothing who goes round
    the taverns!
 All honest, exact men who are eager to work,

Our Lord will love – and allow them (come hell or high water)
 Grace to go labour and gain their livings:

> *Inquirentes autem dominum non minuentur omni bono.*
> (They that seek the Lord shall not want any good
>   thing.)[18]

 To live truly wedded in this world is Do-Well also,
For the married must work and earn wages and keep the
    world alive.
From this kind of folk come all who are called
    Confessors –
And kings and cavaliers and Kaisers and countrymen,   110
And maidens and martyrs: all descended from one man
Whose wife was made as a means to help his work.
So wedlock was established with common people,
First by the father's will and the advice of friends,
Then by the assent of the two spouses themselves.
Such was wedlock's foundation, and God Himself was
    its founder,
And its Heaven is here on Earth, with Himself as its
    witness.[19]
But all false faithless folk such as thieves and liars,
The wasters and the wicked – out of wedlock, I think,
They were conceived, in a cursed time, as Cain was
    by Eve.[20]   120
 Of such sinful wretches the Psalter makes mention:

> *Ecce parturit injustitiam: concepit dolorem, et peperit
>   iniquitatem.*
> (Behold, he travaileth with iniquity, and hath
>   conceived mischief and brought forth falsehood.)[21]

And all who are counted Cain's offspring come to evil ends;
 For God sent a message to Seth by an angel, and said,
"My will is that your issue wed with your issue only,
And that your kin shall not couple nor marry with those
    of Cain."[22]
 Yet some, against that speech from our Saviour in Heaven,
Did couple Cain's offspring with the kin of Seth,
Till God grew angry at their deeds, and gave this judgment:
"That I ever made Man, now makes Me sorry" –

Delebo, inquit, hominem ... poenitet enim me fecisse eos.
(The Lord said, I will destroy men ... for it repenteth
   Me that I have made them.)[23]

  So anon He came to Noah, and bade him not delay: 130
"Go now, and build a boat of boards and timbers.
Yourself and your three sons, and your wives also,
Must hasten aboard that boat, and abide in it
For a full forty days, when the Flood will have washed
Clean away the accursed blood that Cain has begotten.
And animals now alive shall also damn the day
That ever the accursed Cain came to this earth,
And shall die for his misdeeds, by dale and hill,
Even the flying wildfowl, like all other flesh –
Except only a couple of each kind of creature   140
That shall be saved in the shelter of your shingled ship."[24]

  Thus was ancestral sin paid-for by Cain's descendants;
And, for their forefather's sake, those folk must suffer.
In one regard, I find, the Gospel goes against this:
    Filius non portabit iniquitatem patris, et pater non portabit
      iniquitatem filii.
    (The son shall not bear the iniquity of the father, neither
      shall the father bear the iniquity of the son.)[25]
But I feel that if the father is a fraud and a villain,
The son will to some extent inherit his father's stain.
Graft an apple on an elder-tree, and if your apple grows sweet
I shall marvel very much – and far more if a scoundrel
 Can beget any boy but will grow up like him
And have some smack of his father. One seldom sees
    otherwise: 150
    Numquid colligunt de spinis uvas, aut de tribulis ficus?
    (Do men gather grapes of thorns, or figs of thistles?)[26]
And thus, through accursed Cain, sorrow first came
    upon Earth –
And all because they wedded in ways God's will forbade.
Misery follows the marriage if children are thus married-off;
Yet nowadays I see some, to speak the truth,
Who marry thus monstrously for lust of money;
But the progeny of such pairings inherit as much pain

As the folk who died in the Flood, as I told you before.
Good men should marry good women, even if they lack
    goods:
Ego sum via et veritas,[27] says Christ, "and can advance
    anyone".
   What an uncomely coupling – or so, by Christ,
     I think –   160
It is, if a young girl is given to a feeble greybeard;
Or the wedding of a widow for her wealth's sake,
A woman too old to bear babies – except in her arms!
Since the pestilence, many a pair have been plighted together
Whose only offspring have been oaths and abuse,
Living joylessly in jealousy, and jangling in bed,
Breeding no babies but abuse and nagging.
If they did go off to Dunmow, they'd need the Devil's help
To afford them the flitch,[28] or they'd never fetch it home;
And unless they both swore lies, they would lose
    the bacon.   170
   Therefore I counsel all Christians: take no account
    of marrying
From the wish of wealth, or for well-off kindred.
Maidens and unmarried men should match themselves off,
And widows marry widowers in the same way.
Look to be wedded for love, and not for lands;
Then you will earn God's grace – and enough goods to live-on.
And every layman who lacks the power to live chastely,
Will be wise to wed, and avoid wickedness;
For lecherous delights are the lime-twigs of hell.
While you are young, and your weapon is eager,   180
Work it off within wedlock if you want an excuse:
     Dum sis vir fortis, ne des tua robora scortis;
     Scribitur in portis, meretrix est janua mortis.
     (While you are still a strong man, give not your strength
       to the whore;
     It is written upon the gates, *The harlot is Death's
       front door.*)[29]
   When you have wedded, beware to use the right days only,
Unlike Adam and Eve when Cain was engendered.

For truly, at forbidden times,[30] between man and woman
There should be no sport in bed; and unless both are pure,
In life and in soul, and alike in perfect charity,
That same clandestine deed should be done by no one.
If they lead their lives thus, our Almighty Lord is pleased;   190
For he first created marriage, and He Himself ordained,

> *Propter fornicationem autem unusquisque suam uxorem*
> *habeat, et unaquaeque suum virum habeat.*

> (Nevertheless, to avoid fornication, let every man have
> his own wife, and let every woman have her own
> husband.)[31]

And those born of base unions will be mostly vagrants,
Fraudulent folk, foundlings, fakers and liars;
Graceless to get their living, or people's love,
They wander about, and waste whatever they can snatch.
In Do-Well's despite, they do evil, and serve the Devil;
And after their death-day they will dwell with him
Unless first God's grace is given them, to amend.

Do-Well, my friend, is to do as the Law demands;
Do-Better is to love both friend and foe, believe me;   200
But charity and cherishing to all, young or old,
To heal them and help, is Do-Best of all.
Do-Well is to fear God, and Do-Better is to suffer;
And, beyond both, Do-Best, who subdues rebellion
And that wicked self-will which spoils many good works
By driving Do-Well away through deadly sins.'

Now, Reason was wedded to one Dame Study,
A lady as lean in the face as in limbs and figure.
She was really enraged by what Reason had taught me;
Eyes wide with anger, she admonished him sternly.
'What a wise man you are, to speak words of wisdom
To flatterers and fools who are not fully sane!'
She condemned him and cursed him and told him
      to keep quiet
Rather than waste wise words upon the witless.
'In St Matthew it is said, "Do not scatter your pearls
Before swine"[1] – or such hogs as have haws to eat in plenty,   10
And only dribble on jewels: they would rather have draff
Than all the precious pierreries that grow in Paradise.[2]
And when I say "swine",' said she, 'I mean such as show
      by their acts
That they better love land and earthly lordship,
Or riches and rents, and repose when they please,
Than all the sage precepts that Solomon ever spoke.

    Insight and intelligence today are not worth a cress-leaf
Unless carded with covetousness, as clothiers comb wool.
Whoever can contrive deceits, and conspire to do wrong,
And lay snares for truth, from his seat on Settlement Days – [3]
Such crafty men are called into solemn councils,   20
And mislead lords with their lies, and blacken truth.

    The blameless Job bears witness in his book
That wicked men wield all the wealth of this world;
They are lords in every land, who live outside the law:

> *Quare ergo impii vivunt? ... bene est omnibus,*
> *qui praevaricantur, et inique agunt?*
> (Wherefore do the wicked live? ... Wherefore are all
>   they happy that deal very treacherously?)[4]

And the Psalter says the same of such as do evil:

> *Ecce ipsi peccatores, et abundantes in saeculo, obtinuerunt*
> *divitias.*

(Behold, these are the ungodly, who prosper in this
     world; they increase in riches.)[5]
"Lo!" says this holy literature, "what lords these villains are!"
That man to whom God gives most, distributes least goods
     to others;
And the most unkind to common folk are those who
     command most wealth:
    Quoniam quae perfecisti, destruxerunt: justus autem
      quid fecit?
    (For what thou hast accomplished, they have destroyed;
     and what hath the righteous done?)[6]
Harlots may have payment for their harlotry,   30
And jesters and jugglers and the jabberers of ballads;
  But he in whose mouth Holy Writ comes always,
He who can talk of Tobit and the Twelve Apostles,
Or preach about the pains that Pilate inflicted
On gentle Jesus Whom the Jews destroyed –
Little is he loved, who teaches such lessons;
He is daunted or disregarded, I declare by God Himself!
  And those who feign themselves fools, and live by
     false pretences –
Against the law of Our Land – and lie about themselves,
And spit and spew out the words of their foul speech,   40
And drink and drivel till the audience gapes at them,
And mock men, and make up tales about those who refuse
     them money,
And know no more of minstrelsy, or of music to give
     men pleasure,
Than Munday the Miller[7] knows of the Nine Muses:
But for their vile ribaldry, may God be my witness,
Never king or cavalier nor Canon of St Paul's
Would give them as gratuity or stipend even a groat!
  But merriment and ministrelsy among men are now
Mere bawdry, backbiting, and beastly stories;
Gluttony and Great Oaths adore such glee.   50
And if these clerks and laymen do discuss Christ,
When at table amid such amusements, when the minstrels
     have paused,

It is only to tell a jest or two about the Trinity,
Or to bring out some bald opinion, with St Bernard as
    their source,
And prove their point with a *petitio principii*.
Thus they drivel at High Table about the Deity,
And gorge on God with their tongues, when their guts
    are full.
  The poor man may meanwhile call and lament at
    their gates,
Half dead from hunger or drought, or ashiver with cold;
No one asks him inside, to ease his pain;   60
He is howled at like a hound, and hurried away.
How little they love the Lord who allowed them their luxury,
If this is their way of sharing it with the needy:
If the humble had no more mercy than the rich have,
Every beggar would go to bed with an empty belly!
"God" is much in the gullets of such great masters,
But among humble men are His mercy and His works;
And so the Psalter says, as I have seen often:
    "*Ecce audivimus eam in Ephrata: invenimus eam in
      campis silvae.*"
    (Lo, we heard of it at Ephratah; we found it in the
      fields of the wood.)[8]
The clergy, and men akin to them, converse easily about God,
And have Him much in their mouths: He is in common
    men's hearts.   70
  Friars and frauds have faked-up such questions
For the pleasure of proud men, since the time of the
    pestilence,
And preach at St Paul's[9] from pure envy of the clergy,
So that folk are neither confirmed in faith nor free in charity;
Nor are they sorry for their sins. So great has pride grown
Among the Religious, and in all the realm, both rich
    and poor,
That prayers have no power to halt the pestilence.
Yet not one of these worldly villains takes warning from
    others;
No dread of death reduces their pride,

Nor makes them profuse to the poor, as pure charity asks: 80
In gaiety and gluttony they themselves gulp down their
    wealth,
Breaking no bread for the beggar, as the Good Book teaches:
    Frange esurienti panem tuum.
      (Deal thy bread to the hungry, and ... bring the poor
        that are cast out to thy house.)[10]
And the more they acquire and control, of capital and goods,
And gain the lordship of lands, the less they give away.
   Tobit tells us quite otherwise: take heed, you rich men,
How that book of the Bible bears witness of his words:
    Si tibi sit copia, abundanter tribue; si autem exiguum,
      illud impertiri stude libenter.
      (If thou hast abundance, give alms accordingly: if thou
        have but a little, be not afraid to give according to
        that little.)[11]
Tobit means: if you have much, spend manfully;
If you cannot manage much, make that your guide;
For we have no letters-patent for how long we shall live.
Lords should love to hear such lessons as this,   90
And how they might maintain the greatest household
    magnificently.
Not in the fashion of fiddlers and friars, who hunt-up feasts,
Making other men's houses theirs, and hating their own:
Unhappy is the hall when every day in the week
The lord and the lady like to eat elsewhere.
The rule is, today, for rich men to regale themselves alone,
In a private parlour (so escaping the poor),
Or in a chamber with a chimney – avoiding the chief hall
That was made for men to eat their meals in.
And all to spare the expending of what will be squandered
    by an heir!   100
   I have heard men of high rank, who were eating at table,
Conversing as if they were clergy, about Christ and His
    powers,
And finding faults in the Father Who framed us all,
And complaining crabbedly against the clergy:
"Why should our Saviour suffer the Serpent to enter Eden,

There to beguile first Eve and afterwards Adam,
So that through his wily words they went to Hell,
And their seed, for their sin, must endure the same death?"
Your lore is fallacious here, such lords will argue,
"For by what you clergy can tell us of Christ's words in
    the Gospels,   110
    Filius non portabit iniquitatem patris.
    (The son shall not bear the iniquity of the father.)* [12]
So why should we, living now, because of what Adam did,
Be so rotted and ruined? Reason is against it –
    Unusquisque enim onus suum portabit.
    (For every man shall bear his own burden.)" [13]
Such are the motions moved by these masters in their glory,
So that men who muse much about them turn misbelievers.
  But Imagination hereafter shall answer them to good
    purpose.
In answer to such arguers, Augustine quotes this text:
    Non plus sapere quam oportet sapere.
    (Not to think of himself more highly than he ought
      to think.) [14]
Never, then, ask to know why God in His wisdom
Would allow the Devil to deceive His children;
But loyally believe in the lore of Holy Church,
Pray to God for pardon and the gift of repentance in
    this life,   120
And that by His mighty mercy you may cleanse your
    souls *here*.
All such who would learn the ways of the Lord Almighty,
I wish their eyes in their arse, and their finger in both!
I mean such men as wish to know what God's motive was,
In suffering Satan to lead His children astray,
Or Judas to betray Jesus to the Jews.
All was according to Thy will, O Lord, and worshipped
    be Thou,
And all shall be as Thou wilt, however we argue!
  And whoever has recourse to such quibblings, to cloud
    men's minds,
About Do-Well and Do-Better, he deserves to go deaf.   130

Does this long lout really want to learn which is which,
Or lead the kind of life that belongs to Do-Well?
I will boldly go bail that *he* will never do better,
Even if Do-Best drags him on day after day.'

   When Reason understood the import of this oration,
He became so confused that he could not face her,
And withdrew to the room's end, as dumb as death:
Nor afterwards, for all my asking, and even kneeling
      before him,
Could I get from him one grain of his great wisdom.
He gave a little laugh, and looked with a bow
      towards Study,   140
As a sign that first I must ask for her forgiveness.

   So when I saw what he meant, I bowed to his wife,
And said, 'Madame, I ask mercy; I will be your man
So long as I live, to serve you early and late;
And I shall do all you wish, while my life endures,
If you will tell me truly what is Do-Well.'

   'Because of your meekness, my man,' said she, 'and your
      mild speech,
I will acquaint you with my cousin, whose name is Clerisy.[15]
He wedded a wife within these last six months;
She is called Scripture, and is kin to the Seven Arts.[16]   150
The two of them, I trust, since I myself taught them,
Will direct you to Do-Well; I dare promise you that.'

   Then my heart grew light as a lark's on a lovely morning;
I was merrier than a minstrel with money in his purse;
I enquired the quickest way to Clerisy's home,
And, since it was time I went, to be told some token.

   'Ask for the highway from here to the hamlet of Suffer-
Both-Weal-and-Woe, if you are willing to learn that;
Then ride on past Riches, and take no rest in that region,
For if it attracts you, you will never advance to Clerisy.   160
There is also a lovely lea-land called Lechery:
Leave it on your left side, by a mile or longer,
Till you come to a castle called Keep-your-mouth-clear
of-lying-and-loathsome-speech-and-lubricious-drinks.
There you will see Sobriety and Simplicity-of-Speech,

With whom all men are eager to display their wisdom;
And so you will come to Clerisy and his many skills.
Speak to him this password: that *I* first set him to school;
And I greet his wife warmly, since I wrote many works for her,
And set her to Solomon's proverbs, and the Gloss on
    the Psalms.   170
I left her skilled in Logic and in much other learning,
And in all the modes of Music I made her expert.
    It was I who first put Plato the poet to his book,
And first taught Aristotle and many others to argue.
I first got a grammar-book written for girls and boys,
And had them beaten with birches if they baulked at learning.
I contrived the tools for all kinds of crafts,
Such as carpenters and sculptors; I taught masons their
    compasses,
And the use of line and level, though now I see less clearly.
    Theology, though, has troubled me ten thousand times;   180
The more I muse upon it, the mistier it grows;
And the deeper I dare guess, the darker it seems:
It is certainly no science in which to play with subtleties,
And, if love were lacking, would be loathsome indeed.
But I love it the better because it sets love before all else;
And where love is the leader, grace is never lacking.
First learn to be loyal in love, if you look to Do-Well;
For Do-Better and Do-Best are both love's kinsfolk.
    In every other science, as I saw in Cato,
      Qui simulat verbis, nec corde est fidus amicus,   190
      Tu quoque fac simile, sic ars deluditur arte.
      (If a man speaks false but fair, and is no true friend
        in his heart,
    Do the same back to him – so art is deceived by art.)[17]
When flattered by some deceiver, do the same to him,
So false untruthful folk shall be fooled by you:
Such is the counsel that Cato teaches to clerks.
But theology, if you think, teaches otherwise;
Its counsel is contrary to Cato's words,
For it orders us to live as brothers, and pray for our enemies,
And love those who tell lies about us, and relieve their wants;

And to give back good for evil is God's own commandment:

> *Dum tempus habemus, operemur bonum ad omnes, maxime*
> *autem ad domesticos fidei.*
>> (As we have therefore opportunity, let us do good
>> unto all men, especially unto them who are of the
>> household of faith.)[18]

  Thus Paul preached to the people, he who loved
    perfection: 200
To do good for the love of God, and give to whoever asked,
But especially to such as accept our own faith.
And Our Lord teaches us to love all who malign us or
    slander us;
And God has forbidden us to injure those who injure us:

> *Mihi vindicta: ego retribuam.*
>> (Vengeance is mine; I will repay, saith the Lord.)[19]

Therefore, so long as you live, see that you love,
For no science under the sun can so heal the soul.
  Now, astronomy is a difficult discipline, and the devil
    to learn;
And geometry and geomancy have confusing terminology:
If you wish to work in these two, you will not succeed
    quickly,
For sorcery is the chief study that these sciences entail.   210
  There are many men, also, who make use of strange devices,
Alchemical experiments for the deception of others:
If you desire to do well, have no dealings with these.
I myself conceived and set-out these sciences,
And was their first founder, in order to lead folk astray.
  These things are all tokens that you must tell to Clerisy
    and Scripture;
They will gladly teach you then the meaning of Do-Well.'
I said, 'Many thanks, madame,' and meekly took my leave,
And went at once on my way, with no more ado,
And could not rest until I came into Clerisy's presence.   220
I greeted that good man, as guided by Study,
And afterwards his wife, and was respectful to them,
And told them the tokens that I had been taught.
No man beneath the moon, since God made the world,

Was ever more friendlily welcomed and made warmly at ease,
Than certainly I myself was, as soon as Clerisy learned
How I had come from the house of Reason and of his wife
    Dame Study.
I told them truthfully that I had been sent to them
To learn about Do-Well, Do-Better, and Do-Best.
   'Do-Well,' said Clerisy, 'is a life among laymen, believing
    in Holy Church   230
And in all the articles of faith that are to be known.
That is, learned and unlearned alike must loyally believe
In that great God who was without beginning,
And in His steadfast Son Who saved mankind
From death and damnation and the Devil's power,
By the help of the Holy Ghost that proceeds from them both:
Three separate Persons, yet not plural in number,
For all are only one God, and each is Himself God:
    Deus Pater, Deus Filius, Deus Spiritus Sanctus:
God the Father; God the Son, God the Holy Ghost
    proceeding from both,
The Maker of mankind and of dumb animals.[20]   240
   St Augustine of old wrote books about this doctrine;
He first gave it form, to make us firm in faith.
On whose authority? That of all four Evangelists,
Who all confirm that Christ called Himself God:
    Qui videt me, videt et Patrem ... Ego in Patre et Pater
      in me est.
    (He that hath seen me hath seen the Father ... I am in
      the Father, and the Father in me.)[21]
No clerk who followed Christ could ever explain this,
But thus the unlettered must believe if they long to do well;
For if no men had minds fine enough to question the Faith,
Or if it might be proved, no man would gain merit
    from believing it:
    Fides non habet meritum, ubi humana ratio praebet
      experimentum.
    (Faith has no merit where human reason affords
      adequate proof.)[22]
   So Do-Better is to suffer for your soul's health

All that the Bible bids, and is taught by Holy Church;   250
Which is, "Man, be mighty, for the sake of mercy,
To put into practice all that your words profess:
    Appare quod es, vel esto quod appares:
As you seem in men's sight, so be in yourself.[23]
Let nobody be beguiled by your outward bearing,
But be in your soul the same as you show yourself."
    Do-Best is to be bold to blame the guilty,
So long as you see *yourself* to be clean of soul;
But blame nobody, ever, if you are blameworthy yourself:
    Si culpare velis, culpabilis esse cavebis;
    Dogma tuum sordet cum te tua culpa remordet.   260
    (If others you wish to blame,
    Take care *you* have no cause for shame;
    Your dogmas are filthy and thin
    If your own crimes gnaw you within.)[24]
God in the Gospels grimly reproves
Those who find fault in others but do not feel their own:
    Quid autem vides festucam in oculo fratris tui; et trabem
       in oculo tuo non vides?
    (Why are you moved to condemn a mote in your
       brother's eye, since you are blind to the beam that
       is in your own?)[25]
    Ejice primum trabem de oculo tuo.
    (Thou hypocrite, first cast out the beam out of thine
       own eye.)[26]
For that stops you from seeing either great things or small.
    I advise every blind buzzard to better his soul:
Abbots, I mean, and priors, and all kinds of prelate,
And parsons, and parish priests, who should preach
    and instruct
All men to amend themselves with all their might:
All of you take this text as a warning; before you teach,   270
Be such as you say others must if they hope to be saved.
For *your* loss would not lose God's word; *that* works eternally,
And even if useless to others, might be useful to you.
    But it certainly seems today, from a worldly standpoint,
That God's word is *not* at work, among learned or unlettered,

Unless in the manner that Mark has mentioned in his gospel:

> *Caecus autem si caeco ducatum praestet, ambo in*
> *foveam cadunt.*
> (If the blind lead the blind, both shall fall into
> the ditch.)[27]

Unlearned men may allege of you that the beam lies in
your eyes,
And the mote of filth has fallen, by your fault, mainly,
Into all manner of men's eyes, you maledict priests.
The Bible bears witness what the Israelites had to bear,   280
Most bitterly buying the guilt of two bad priests,
Hophni and Phineas: for their avarice,
The Ark of the Covenant was miscarried, and Eli broke
his neck.[28]

Therefore, you "correctors", claw *this* in: correct
yourselves first;
And then you may safely say, as David says in the Psalter,

> *Existimasti inique quod ero tui similis: arguam te,*
> *et statuam contra faciem tuam.*
> (Thou thoughtest wickedly that I am even such
> a one as thyself: but I will reprove thee, and set
> before thee the things that thou hast done.)[29]

Then such homespun scholars shall be ashamed to disparage
or grieve you,
Or carp as they carp now, calling you dumb dogs;

> *Canes muti non valentes latrare.*
> (They are all ignorant, they are all dumb dogs, they
> cannot bark.)[30]

They'll be anxious not to anger you by a word, or hinder
your activity;
They'll appear faster for your praying than for a pound
in gold nobles –
And all because of your holiness: hold *that* in your hearts.   290
Among upright religious, this rule should be upheld.
St Gregory, that great scholar and good Pope,
Rehearses in his *Moralia* the rules for all religious orders,
And says, as a case in point, for them to follow suit,
"When the flood or the fresh water fail the fish,

They die of drought, lying upon dry land.
Just so," said Gregory, "a religious is spoiled,[31]
And suffocates and stinks, and steals alms from lords,
Who covets a life outside cloister or convent."
For if Heaven exists on earth, and ease for any soul,   300
For many causes I think it is in cloisters or convent schools.
No man comes into cloisters to quarrel or fight;
All is obedience there, and books, and imbibing of learning.

He is scorned in school, if a scholar cannot learn;
Else, all is delight and love, and love of one another.
But the religious today is a rider, a roamer of streets,
The leading man on love-days, and a land-buyer,
A hustler on horseback from manor to manor,
An army of hounds at his arse, like an aristocrat.
And unless his lackey kneels when bringing his liquor,   310
He frowns at him, and asks him who taught him
        his manners.
The lords are ill-advised to shift land from their heirs
To religious who would not care if it rained on their altars!

In many places they rule parishes, and are perfectly at ease,
But are pitiless to the poor; and pass that off as "charity".
They believe themselves barons, so broad are their lands.

But a king shall arise and reform you Religious Orders,
And beat you – like Christ in the Bible – for breaking
        your Rule;[32]
And amend all ancresses and abbots and canons,
And put them to penance till their pristine state return.   320
And barons and earls shall beat them with "Blessed the
        man that walketh not in the counsel of the ungodly."[33]
And their children shall shout at them and deride
        them shamefully
        Hi in curribus, et hi in equis.
        (Some trust in chariots, and some in horses, but we
            will remember the name of the Lord our God.
        They are brought down and fallen, but we are risen and
            stand upright.)[34]
    The friars in their fraters will find a key
To Constantine's coffers, which conceal the wealth

That Gregory's god-children have let go to waste.[35]
Then the Abbot of Abingdon,[36] and all his issue for ever,
Shall catch from that King's clout an incurable wound.
    That this will be so, search out – you who often study
the Bible –

> *Quomodo cessavit exactor, quievit tributum? Contrivit*
>   *Dominus baculum impiorum, virgam dominantium.*
> (How hath the oppressor ceased! The exactress of gold
>   has ceased! The Lord hath broken the staff of the
>   wicked, and the sceptre of the rulers.)[37]

But before that king shall come, Cain[38] shall awake,
And Do-Well shall strike him down, and destroy
    his power!'   330
'Then Do-Well and Do-Better,' said I, 'are knighthood
    and kingship?'
Said Scripture, 'I do not scoff; but unless scriveners lie,
Neither knighthood nor kingship, by any text I know,
Has ever got one hair's-breadth nearer Heaven –
Nor, indeed, riches, nor the rule of lords.
St Paul proves it impossible for the rich to reach Heaven,[39]
And Solomon says that silver is the worst thing to love:

> *Nihil iniquius quam amare pecuniam.*[40]

Cato tells us not to covet more than our state requires:

> *Dilige denarium, sed parce dilige formam!*
> (Know the value of money, but value it little for
>   itself.)[41]

Patriarchs and prophets and poets alike   340
Have warned us in their works not to wish for wealth,
And all praise poverty patiently borne. The Apostles
    bear witness
That the poor have by true right their heritage in Heaven,
Where rich men may claim *no* right but by grace and
    favour.'[42]
    '*Contra!*'[43] cried I. 'By Christ, I can rebut that
And prove you wrong by St Peter and St Paul.
The baptised shall be saved, both rich and poor.'[44]
    'Only if they are heathen, and at the point of death.
They may be saved thus, and that is part of our faith –

That even a non-Christian may in such cases
    christen heathens   350
Who, for their true belief when they take leave of life,
Shall inherit Heaven as surely as if they *had* been Christian.
But Christians cannot reach Heaven by Christianity alone,
For Christ confirmed the Law, by dying for Christians,
That whoever wishes and wills to rise up with Christ,
Should believe, and love, and fulfil the Law.
    Si cum Christo surrexistis.
    (If ye then be risen with Christ, seek those things
       which are above.)[45]
That is, Thou shalt love the Lord God above all,
And then all Christian creatures in common, each one another.
So, lacking love, do not believe yourself saved.
And unless we do love indeed, before Doomsday comes,   360
Bitter burdens shall be our hoards of silver,
Our mantles left for the moths while poor men went naked,
Our delight in wine and in wildfowl, while others went hungry.
For all Christian creatures should show kindness to
    each other –
And help the heathen too, in hope of their conversion.
God has told both high and low that no man must harm
    another;
He says, "You shall kill no creature created in My image,
Unless I send you a sign." That is, *non occides* –
Thou shalt not slay[46] – but suffer; and so all shall be well.
For "*Mihi vindicta; ego retribuam, dicit Dominus.*
    (Vengeance is mine; I will repay, saith the Lord.)[47]
"I shall punish in Purgatory or in the pits of Hell,   370
All Men's misdeeds, unless mercy restrains Me."'
  'This is a long lesson,' said I, 'but I am little the wiser;
Where Do-Well or Do-Better may be, you explain only
    darkly;
And you tell me many tales of what Theology teaches.
But that I was made a man, and my name entered
In the log-book of life[48] long before I was born,
Or else left unwritten for some sin, as the Scriptures
    bear witness –

Nemo ascendit in coelum nisi qui descendit de coelo.
(No man hath ascended up to heaven, but he that came
    down from heaven) [49] –
I believe this well,' said I, 'on Our Lord's word (no lecturer
    better).
For the sage Solomon, who taught sagacity,
Was given by God the grace of wisdom, and great
    wealth too,   380
To rule his realm and increase his riches.
He judged well and wisely, as is witnessed by the Scriptures.
Aristotle and he – who ever taught men better?
Masters who speak of God's mercy, when they teach men
    or preach to them,
Will use the words of these two, the wisest of their times:
Yet all Holy Church holds that both are in Hell! [50]
    So if I should act as they did, in order to reach Heaven,
They who for all their wisdom and works now dwell
    in damnation,
I should act most unwisely, despite all that you preach.
But, for many clever men, I do not marvel, truly,   390
If their souls are unacceptable and unpleasing to God.
For many men in this world have more set their hearts
Upon goods than on God; and they lack grace, therefore,
In their direst disaster, when death comes to them –
Like Solomon, and many such, who had great sagacity
But always acted unwisely, as Holy Writ proves.
So clever and sagacious men, and well-read scholars,
Themselves admit that their actions rarely accord with
    their knowledge:
    Super cathedram Moysi sederunt Scribae et Pharisaei.
    (The scribes and the Pharisees sit in Moses' seat.) [51]
    I believe it will be, for many, as bad as in Noah's day,
When he built his boat out of boards and timbers: 400
Not one of the carpenters and workmen who toiled on it
    was saved,
Only the birds and beasts and the blessèd Noah himself,
With his wife and sons, and with their wives too;
Not one was saved, of all the workmen who toiled there.

God grant that things go otherwise for those who teach
    the Gospels
And the faith of Holy Church, our harbour and God's house
    of refuge,
In which we are shielded from shame, like the beasts in
    Noah's ship,
Though all the men who made it were drowned amid
    the Flood.
The class this comment is aimed at are the priests with
    Cure of Souls,
The carpenters that build Holy Church for Christ's own
    creatures: 410
    Homines, et jumenta salvabis, Domine:
    (O Lord, thou preservest man and beast.)[52]
On Doomsday shall come a deluge of death and fire
    together;
Therefore I counsel you clergy, carpenters of Holy Church,
Act as the Bible tells you, lest you too are excluded.
   I find that on Good Friday a felon was saved,
Who had lived all his life by lying and theft;
But because he confessed on the cross, and Christ
    absolved him,
He was sooner saved than St John the Baptist,
Or Adam, or Isaiah, or any of the prophets
Who had lain with Lucifer for many long years.[53]
A robber was ransomed, rather than all these,   420
Without penance in Purgatory, to perpetual bliss.
   What woman did worse than Mary Magdalen?
What man did worse than David, who devised Uriah's death?
Or Paul the Apostle, who was pitiless
In condemning many Christians to be killed?
Yet now they all sit like sovereigns among the
    saints in Heaven,
These whose works were the wickedest in the world, when
    they lived;
  And those whose words were wise, who wrote
    many books
Of worth and wisdom, dwell now with damned souls.

I think that what Solomon says is true, and certain
   of us all: 430
     Sunt justi et sapientes, et opera eorum in manu Dei:
       et tamen nescit homo utrum amore, an odio dignus sit.
     (The righteous and the wise, and their works,
       are in the hand of God: no man knoweth either love
       or hatred by all that is before them.)[54]
Wise men, and of worthy life, and their works, are hidden
In the hands of Almighty God; only He knows the truth,
Whether a man will be applauded for his love and loyal
   works,
Or otherwise used for ill-will and the envy in his heart –
Being used according to his life; for by evil, men know good.
   How should we know what is white, if all things
     were black,
Or who good men are, if none were evil?
Let us live on, then, with bad men – few are good, I believe.
For *qant* OPORTET *vyent en place, yl ny ad que* PATI.
(When MUST is upon men, they may only ENDURE.)[55]
And may He Who can amend all, have mercy on us all.   440
God never spoke words more certain than when He said
     nemo bonus –
     There is none good but one, that is, God.[56]
   Christ Himself commended clerisy only little,
For He said to St Peter, and to such as He loved,
     Ante praesides et reges stabitis propter me … Nolite
      praecogitare quid loquamini:
That is, though you come before kings and the clerks
   of the law,
Be not abashed, for I shall be in your mouths,
And give you wisdom at will, and the skill to confute
All those who argue against you and Christianity.[57]
David makes mention that he spoke among kings,
And none could overcome him by cunning speech.[58]
But wisdom and keen wits never won mastery   450
In a time of misfortune, without more grace from God.
   The doughtiest of the Doctors, the deepest expounder of
     the Trinity,

Was ancient Augustine, the greatest of all four;[59]
And he said in a sermon that I once saw written,

> *Ecce ipsi idioti rapiunt coelum, ubi nos sapientes in*
> *inferno mergimur.*
>> (Lo, the ignorant conquer Heaven swiftly, while
>> we wise men are plunged into Hell.)

This means, for English men of mean rank or high,
That none are more readily ravished from right thinking
Than are subtle scholars who study many books;
And none sooner saved, nor of solider faith,
Than ploughmen and porters and poor common labourers.
Shoemakers and shepherds, and such unlettered wretches,   460
Can pierce with one Pater-noster the palace of Heaven;
And, when they depart, pass painlessly through Purgatory
Into the bliss of Paradise, for their pure faith,
Imperfect though their learning and lives were, here below.
   You must have come across scholars who have cursed
      the time
That ever their minds mastered more than *I believe in*
   God the Father;
And many a parson has prized his pater-noster above all else.
I have seen examples myself and so have many others,
That the lesser servants of lords seldom fall into arrears,
Unlike those who administer his estate, such as clerks
      and reeves.   470
In like manner, laymen and others with little learning
Seldom fall so far or so foully into sin
As the clerks of Holy Church, the keepers of Christ's treasure,
The souls of men to be saved, as God says in the Gospel:

> *Ite vos in vineam meam.'*
>> (Go ye also into my vineyard.)[60]

Then Scripture grew scornful, and scolded me,
And said she thought little of me, and let me know it
      in Latin:
      'Multi multa sciunt, et seipsos nesciunt.'
      (Many who know many things are unmindful of
         themselves.)[1]
At these words I wept with grief and rage,
Till at last in a drowsy dudgeon I dropped asleep.
And there came to me then the most marvellous dream:
I was floated far away by the goddess Fortune,
Into the Land of Longing. There she brought me alone
To a mirror called Middle Earth, and made me look into it,
Saying, 'Herein you may see all sorts of wonders,
And your deepest desires – and attain them, perhaps.'   10
   Now, Fortune's followers were two fair damsels;
The elder of these ladies was called Lust-of-the-Flesh,
And Lust-of-the-Eyes was the other one's name;
And pursuant of this pair came Pride-of-Perfect-Living[2] –
Who bade me think lightly of Learning, but attend to
      my looks.
   Lust-of-the-Flesh laid her long arms round my neck,
And said, 'You are young and strong, and have many years
To live till old-age, and to love many ladies.
You may see in this mirror a multitude of pleasures,
That all your life long will give you delight.'   20
And the second said the same, 'And I will serve your wishes
Till you are a landed lord, and never leave
Your close companionship – so long as Fortune consents.'
And Fortune herself said, 'He shall find me his friend:
Folk who follow my wishes never fail to find happiness.'
   But a man called Old-Age stood by, and his aspect
      was heavy.
'Man, if you fall in with me, by St Mary in Heaven
You will find that Fortune fails you in your greatest need,

And Lust-of-the-Flesh will be altogether lost;
And bitterly then will you curse, both by day and by night,   30
That ever you even saw Lady Lust-of-the-Eyes,
Or that Pride-of-Perfect-Living brought you into such peril.'
But Recklessness appeared, all in rage: 'Bah! Pay no regard!
Follow after Fortune – you are still far from old:
Why start to stoop until your scalp starts to show?
Man proposes, said a poet called Plato,[3]
And God disposes – so let God do as He wishes.
If He himself will bear witness that it's well to follow
    Fortune,[4]
Then neither Lust-of-the-Flesh nor Lust-of-the-Eyes
Can bring you to *great* grief – nor beguile you against
    your will.'   40
  'Right! So long, cock!' cried Childishness, and carried
    me away
Till Lust-of-the-Flesh laid her rule upon all my doings.
Old-Age, and Holiness after him, cried, 'Alas,
That Reason should be ruined for the sake of will's revels!'[5]
  But Lust-of-the-Eyes was my consoler soon after,
And she followed me forty years, and five more on top
    of them;
Nor did I find delight in Do-Well or Do-Better;
I had no wish, believe me, to know anything about them.
Lust-of-the-Eyes lay more often in my mind
Than Do-Well or Do-Better among all my deeds.   50
And Lust-of-the-Eyes became my comforter often:
  'Have no heavy conscience about how you got
    your wealth;
Confess to some friar, as freely as you please.
For while Fortune is your friend, the friars will love you,
And embrace you in their brotherhood, and for your sake beg
Their Prior Provincial to obtain you a pardon;[6]
And they'll pray for you in person – if you've pennies enough.'
    Sed poena pecuniaria non sufficit pro spiritualibus delictis
    (Penance of money does not pay for spiritual
    trespasses),[7]
Yet I followed this wench's way, her words were so sweet,

Till my youth was over, and old-age fast approaching.
Then, Fortune became my foe, for all her fair promises,   60
And Poverty pursued me, and pushed me under;
And the friars seemed to fear me, they were so fleet-footed,
For all our first covenant – and this, because I refused
To be buried in *their* boneyard, but at my parish church.
For I had heard tell once how Conscience held
That by Nature a man should be buried where he had
    been christened,
And his grave be made in the ground on which he grew.
But the friars thought me a fool for saying this,
And liked me even less for my little speech.
I complained to my confessor, who thought himself
    cunning.   70
'For certain, friar,' said I, 'you are like those suitors
Who seek to wed widows only to have use of their wealth.
I declare by the Cross, you have never cared before
Where my body was buried, if you had my money about you.
It's a marvel to me, and to many others,
That your convent so covets to confess and bury people,[8]
Rather than baptise babies that want to be saved.'
Baptism and burial are both very necessary,
But baptism has far more merit, it seems to me;
A baptised man may, as masters of theology tell us,   80
Come at last to Heaven's courts, if he is contrite:
    Sola contritio delet peccatum
    (Only contrition can wipe out sin),[9]
But an unbaptised baby cannot be saved thus:
    Nisi quis renatus fuerit ex aqua
    (Except a man be born of water and of the Spirit, he
      cannot enter into the kingdom of God).[10]
Look and see, you lettered men, whether I lie or not!
  Then Loyalty looked at me, and saw me louring.
'Why do you frown so fiercely?' he said, and looked fixedly
    at me.
'I doubt if I dare,' said I, 'make this dream public.'
'Yes, by Peter and Paul, with their Epistles as proof!
    Non oderis fratres in corde tuo, sed publice argue illos.'

(Thou shalt rebuke the brothers in public, not be their
    secret hater.)[11]
'But they will adduce the Scriptures against *me*, and quote:
    Nolite judicare.'
    Judge not, that ye be not judged.)[12]
'What manner of use are morals that no man will uphold,
To stand against falsehood and faking? For the apostle said,   90
    Peccantes coram omnibus argue.
    (Them that sin, rebuke before all.)[13]
And also in the Psalter we find David saying,
    Existimasti inique quod ero tui similis: arguam te.
    (Thou thoughtest that I was altogether such an one as
      thyself: but I will reprove thee.)[14]
Laymen are allowed to lay the truth bare
If they are so inclined: the law grants it to all
Except parsons and priests and the prelates of Holy Church;
For it is not fitting that such folk should tell tales,
Even if the tales are true, and touch upon sin.[15]
  But why should you worry, when all the world knows
    them already,
To arraign with full rhetoric the friars' wrongdoings?
But never again be first to find and condemn the fault,
Howsoever evil; say nothing first; and be sorry if it is
    not amended.   100
Nor must you publish any piece of private knowledge,
Whether to laud it from love, or belittle from envy:
    Parum lauda, vitupera parcius.'
    (Sparingly praise, more sparingly reprove.)[16]
  'He speaks sense!' So said Scripture; and she skipped aloft,
    and preached.
But the substance of her sermon, could laymen understand it,
Would be little loved by them, as I believe.
For this was the text on which she talked – and I took
    good heed.
'Many folk were called to a feast, and all the good food;
And when the whole press was present, the porter unbarred
    the gate
And privately pulled in a few, and sent the rest packing!'[17]

Because of this troublous text, my heart trembled;   110
I was worked up with worry, and disputed within myself
Whether I were chosen or unchosen. I thought of
    Holy Church,
That admitted me at the font as one of God's elect;
Now, Christ called us all to come to him if we would:
Saracens and schismatics, and also the Jews –
    Omnes sitientes, venite ad aquas.
    (Every one that thirsteth come ye to the waters.) [18]
And he bade them, despite their sins, to suck from him safely,
And drink healing for their hurts, whosoever could use it.
  'So all Christians may come,' said I, 'and claim to enter,
By the blood with which he bought us, and then by baptism:
    Qui crediderit, et baptizatus fuerit, salvus erit.
    (He that believeth and is baptised, shall be saved.) [19]
For even should a Christian wish to cast-off his
    christening,   120
A real such reneguing is against reason.
No serf may sign a contract, or sell his goods,
Without his lord's leave – no law allows that.
He may run himself into arrears, and stray from his field,
And recklessly roam about, a renegade wretch,
But Reason shall bring him to his reckoning, and rebuke
    him at last,
And Conscience present his account, and convict him of debt,
And put him in the prison of Purgatory, to burn;
Doomed there for his debts until Judgment Day –
Unless Contrition comes, and he calls before death,   130
With mouth or with mind, for mercy upon his misdeeds.'
  'What you say, is so!' said Scripture. 'No sin is so deep
That Mercy may not atone for it, and Meekness with her.
For both of them, as the books tell us, are above all
    God's deeds:
    Misericordia ejus super omnia opera ejus.'
    (His tender mercies are over all his works.) [20]
'Ah, bah to books!' cried one who had burst out of Hell:
Trajan [21] his name, and a true knight once, by a pope's
    testimony:

He had died and been damned to dwell in torment
As an unChristian creature. 'Scholars know for sure
That all the clerisy under Christ could not claw me
    from Hell,
But only love and loyal faith and my own just laws.   140
St Gregory knew this well, and he wanted my soul
To be saved, for he saw that my works had been worthy.
So when he had wept, and wished that I were given
Grace, his boon was granted – and without benefit of
    bead-telling;
And I was saved, as you see, without the singing of Masses;
Merely by love, by enlightenment, and by upright living,
I was brought out of bitter torment, when mere prayers
    would have been useless.'
  'See, all you lords,' said Loyalty, 'how good life saved a
    Roman emperor,
Though an unChristian creature, as the clergy find in
    their books.
Not by the prayers of a pope, but for pure righteousness,   150
Was that Saracen saved, as St Gregory bears witness.
You lords who guard the laws should remember this lesson:
Remember Trajan's righteousness, and deal righteously with
    the people.
  This matter is a mystery to many of you men of
    Holy Church;
But in the Lives of the Saints you may learn more lavishly
    than from me.
Thus loyal love and righteous living
Pulled a Roman pagan from the pains of Hell.
Blessed be righteousness that so broke Hell's gate
And saved that Saracen from Satan and his power –
Which no clerisy could do, nor craft in Law.   160
Love and loyalty are a surer learning;
By them the Bible is blessed with hope of bliss and joy:
God wrought it and wrote it with His own finger,
And took it to Moses on the Mount, for all men to learn.'
'Law without love,' said Trajan, 'is worth less than a bean.
Every science under the sun, including the Seven Arts,[22]

Unless learned for love of Our Lord, is only time lost.'
'They are not for the making of money, or for a
      Master's degree,
But only for love of Our Lord, and to love the people
      better.
For what St John has said, is truly so: 170
      Qui non diligit, manet in morte.
      (He that loveth not his brother abideth in death.)[23]
   Believe me, the man without love is in living death.
John bade all manner of men, whether friends or enemies,
To love one another, and give as if to themselves:
Where nothing is given, there is no love; God knows
      that is true,
And commands all His creatures to conform themselves
      to love –
And especially to love poor people, and also one's enemy.
There is much merit in loving the man that hates us;
And if we give pleasure to the poor, their prayers may
      help us.
For our happiness and souls' health, Jesus Christ came
      from Heaven;
And, apparelled like a poor man, ever pursues us;   180
And in such likeness looks at us with loving countenance,
To discover the kindness of our hearts, and by the cast
      of our eyes
Whether we love earthly lords more than the Lord of bliss.
   And He exhorts us, through His evangelist, that when
      we hold feasts
We should not call our kinsmen to them, nor any kind of
      rich folk –
      Cum facis prandium, noli vocare amicos tuos …
      (When thou makest a dinner or a supper, call not
        thy friends, nor thy brethren, neither thy kinsmen,
        nor thy rich neighbours)[24] –
But we should invite the unfortunate, the deformed,
      and the poor:
For your friends would return the feast, and fully repay you
Your feasting and fine gifts, as is all friends' custom.

But, "*I* shall pay for the poor," says Christ, "and requite the
     expense in full,
Of those who give meals or money to them, and love them
     for my sake."   190
For the best men may be poor, or beggars, while some
     may be wealthy.
We are all Christ's creatures, and enriched from His coffers,
Brothers of one blood, whether beggars or earls.
For from Christ's blood on Calvary, Christendom sprang,
And there we became blood-brothers, redeemed by one Body,
"As new-born babes",[25] and each of us nobly born,
Neither beggar nor bondsman among us, but those made
     by sin:
     Qui facit peccatum, servus est peccati.
     (Whosoever committeth sin is the servant of sin.)[26]
  In the Old Law, as Holy Writ lets us learn,
Man's name for all mankind was "Sons of men" –
All the issue of Adam and Eve until the God-Man died.   200
Then, after His resurrection, His name was Redeemer;
And we, rich or poor, became the brothers of Him that
     bought us.
Therefore let us love like fond brothers, and all men
     laugh together;
And, so far as each can afford, give freely where there is need,
And let all men help each other; for all must go hence.
     Alter alterius onera portate.
     (Bear ye one another's burdens.)[27]
Let us not use our belongings meanly, nor our skills either,
For no man knows how soon he will be left with neither.
So, do not disparage another – though he *does* know
     more Latin! –
Nor coarsely reprove your neighbour, for no-one lacks faults.
For whatever the clergy contend about christening
     and so forth,   210
Christ said to a courtesan at a communal banquet
That her faith had saved her, and absolved her from
     her sins.[28]
  True belief is a loyal helper, above logic and law;

To logic and law, in the Lives of the Saints,
Little applause is given, unless faith assists them.
Logic would need long to make-out a lesson from those lives,
And law is loth to love unless to get money.
Both logic and law – if he does not like lying,
I counsel every Christian, "Do not clasp them too tightly."
I find written certain phrases that are part of
    faith's teaching,   220
And have saved sinful men, as St John bears witness:
    In qua mensura mensi fueritis, remetietur vobis.
    (With what measure ye mete, it shall be measured
       to you again.) [29]
  And so let us learn love's law, as Our Lord taught,
And St Gregory said for the good of our souls:
    Melius est scrutare scelera nostra, quam naturas rerum.
    (It is better to research our evil deeds than the natures
       of things.)
Why I make much of love, is mostly for the sake of the poor,
For it was in their likeness that Our Lord often let Himself
    be known.
For example, when He went to Emmaus, in Easter week, [30]
Cleophas could not recognise Him as Christ,
Because of His poor apparel and His pilgrim's clothing –
Not till He blessed and broke the bread that they ate.
It was by His works that they knew He was Jesus;   230
By His clothing they could not tell, nor by what His
    tongue declared.
  All this is an example to us sinners here on Earth,
That we should be lowly and loving in our language,
Let our apparels not be proud, for we are all pilgrims;
And in the apparel of a poor man, or a pilgrim's likeness,
Many times has God been met among needy people,
Unrecognised by any man in the ranks of the rich.
  St John and other saints were seen in poor clothing;
Like poor pilgrims they appealed for men's alms.
Jesus was born of a Jew's daughter, of gentle birth
    though she was,   240
And poor, though a pure maiden, and a poor man's wife.

Martha made huge complaints against Mary Magdalene;
And to Our Saviour Himself, she said as follows:
> *"Domine, non est tibi curae quod soror mea reliquit me
>   solam ministrare?"*
> (Lord, dost thou not care that my sister hath left me
>   to serve alone?)[31]

And Our Lord quickly answered, and so pleased them both
(Both Martha and Mary, as St Matthew bears witness):[32]
> *"Maria optimam partem elegit quae non auferetur ab ea."*
> (Martha, Martha, thou art careful and troubled about
>   many things ... and Mary hath chosen that good
>   part which shall not be taken away from her.)

Yet Our Lord had put poverty first, and praised it more
    highly.
All the wise men that ever were, for aught I can see,
Praise poverty as the best life, if patience goes with it,
And many times both better and more blessed than riches.
Though it is sour at first savouring, a sweetness follows;   250
Just as a walnut within its shell has a bitter husk,
But within both the shell and that bitter bark
Is a kernel both comforting and conducive to health:
So it is with poverty and penance patiently endured.
For they make a man's mind turn to God, with a great wish
To weep well and pray well – from which acts Mercy springs,
Of which Christ is the kernel that comforts the soul.
The poor man sleeps more soundly and securely,
For he has less dread of death, or of robbery in the darkness,
Than the rich man has – it stands to reason!   260
> *Pauper ego ludo, dum tu dives meditaris.*
> (I who am poor make merry, while you who are rich
>   must ponder.)

For although Solomon said, as we see in the Bible,
> *Mendicitatem, et divitias ne dederis mihi*
> (Give me neither poverty nor riches; feed me with food
>   convenient for me),[33]

One wiser than Solomon was bore witness and taught
That perfect poverty was to possess nothing:
The life that God likes most, as Luke bears witness:

Si vis perfectus esse, vende quae habes, et da pauperibus.
(If thou wilt be perfect, go and sell that thou hast, and
  give to the poor.)[34]
This means that all men living beneath the moon,
Who would reach pure perfection, must forsake possessions –
Or sell them, as the Book says, and give the silver
To beggars that go beseeching goods for the love of God.
  For no man ever lacked a meal if he served
    Almighty God: 270
    Non vidi justum derelictum, nec semen ejus quaerens
      panem.
    (I have not seen the righteous forsaken, nor his seed
      begging bread.)[35]
Thus David says in the Psalter; such as have the will
To serve God in good measure, no hardship grieves them:
    Nihil impossibile volenti
    (Nothing is impossible to him who has the will),[36]
Nor will they ever lack livelihood, nor linen and wool:
    Inquirentes autem Dominum non minuenter omni bono
    (They that seek the Lord shall not want any
      good thing).[37]
So if priests were perfect they would take no pay
For masses or for matins, nor their meals from usurers,
Nor kirtle nor coat, though they should die of cold;
For if they did their duty they would say like David
    in the Psalter,
    Judica me, Deus, et discerne causam meam.
    (Judge me, O God, and plead my cause against an
      ungodly nation.)[38]
Trust in the Lord[39] says to priests who have no
    spending-silver
That if they toil truly, and trust in God Almighty,
They shall never lack livelihood, nor wool nor linen.   280
And the title by which they take orders attests their
    advancement,
So they need not take silver for the masses that they sing:
It is his part, who made them priests, to pay their wages –
Or the bishop's who ordained them – if they deserve any.

Never yet did the king knight a man who had not
    the wealth
Befitting his title, or else he found the wealth himself;
He is a careworn knight, and of a caitiff king's dubbing,
Who has no land or rich lineage or lauded prowess.
And I say the same is true of all such priests
As have neither learning nor lineage, but only a tonsure   290
And a priest's title, a trifle, to live-on in time of trouble:
I think they count more on their shaven crowns to get
Curacies or livings than on learning or known purity of life.
I wonder why and wherefore, then, the bishop
Will ordain such priests, or let them betray the laity.

    A charter is challengeable before a Chief Justice:
If the language is false Latin, the Law will impugn it –
Or if it is illuminated between the lines, or has parts
    left out:
The scrivener who thus bescrawls documents is thought
    scatty.
So is the priest scatty, by God, who misreads the Gospel,   300
Or makes a mistake in his Mass or Matins.
    Quicumque . . . offendat autem in uno, factus est
      omnium reus.
    (For whosoever shall keep the whole law, and yet offend
      in one point, he is guilty of all.)[40]
David also, in the Psalter, speaks to those who skip texts:
    Psallite Deo nostro, psallite: psallite Regi nostro, psallite.
      Quoniam Rex omnis terrae Deus: psallite sapienter.
    (Sing praises to God, sing praises; sing praises unto our
      King, sing praises. For God is the King of all the earth:
      sing ye praises with understanding.)[41]
That bishop is guilty in God's eyes, I give my word,
Who ordains knights in His Order that *without*
    understanding
Sing or read psalms or say the Mass of the Day.
Nor is either ever blameless, bishop or priest,
For each is indicted by the rule, *ignorantia*
Non excusat episcopos nec idiotic priests:
Ignorance excuses neither bishops nor priests for incapability.

This look at unlettered priests had led me away from
    the praise
Of poverty, which in patient men is more perfect than
    wealth.'   310
Much more, so I dreamed, did someone dispute with me.
Then I saw other things in my sleep; and first I saw Nature.[42]
By my own name he called me, and bade me be heedful
To gather wisdom from the wonders of this world.
To a mountain called Middle Earth (such was my dream)
He fetched me forth, to learn from examples
Of creatures of all kinds, to love my Creator.
I saw the Sun; and the sea and the sand beside it,
And where the birds and the beasts went about with
    their mates;
Wild crawlers in the woods, and wonderful birds   320
With feathers flecked in fifty colours.
Man and his mate, also, I might see,
In poverty and plenty, in peace and war,
And in mirth and misery at the same moment;
And how some loved Meed the Maiden and hated Mercy.
    I saw how rigidly Reason ruled the beasts
In eating and drinking and engendering their species.
For after their sexual season, they no longer consorted
As when they had ridden in rutting-time; but right
    afterwards,
Males would mingle with males alone, at morning   330
And at evening alike, and keep away from females.
And no cow, or cowlike thing, once she had conceived,
Would bellow after the bull, nor the boar for the sow;
Nor would horse or hound or any other he-beast
Try to mount his mate in her months of pregnancy.
    I beheld the birds in the bushes, building their nests,
Of which no man's wits would ever have built the simplest.
I wondered when and from whom the magpie had learned
To intertwine the twigs in which she lays and breeds:
No weaver, I well know, could make it work,   340
And we should marvel at a mason who could make a
    model of it.

   Yet I marvelled still more at how many other birds
Could so secretly hide and cover-up their clutch,
On moors and marshes, so that men should not find it –
And hid their eggs when they left them awhile,
For fear of other wild-fowl, or of prowling beasts.
And some birds trod their mates, and bred, in the trees,
And brought forth their brood so, above the ground;
And some birds bred through the beak, only by breathing,[43]
And some by cackling, I recorded, and the curious ways
        of the peacock.[44]   350
But much I marvelled what master so many had,
Who taught them to timber their houses so high in trees
That neither man nor beast could reach their nest.

   Then again, I stared at the sea, and then at the stars,
And saw more wonders than I have space to describe.
I saw the flowers of the forest, with their fine colours,
Among the green grass growing so many-hued,
And thought how strange that some smelt sweet,
        others bitter;
But to describe all their kinds and colours would take
        too long.

   Yet what most moved me and impressed my mind   360
Was that Reason ruled and regarded all these creatures –
All except Man and *his* mate: how many a time
Did Reason disregard *them*! And so I reproached
That same Reason himself; and said plainly to him,
'I wonder at you,' I said, 'with the name of being wise,
That you do not shield Man and his mate from their
        mishaps.'

   But Reason rebuked me, and said roundly,
        'Never you mind
What I allow or do not; it is none of your business.
You make things better if you can; but I must bide my time.[45]
Long-suffering is a sovereign virtue, with a swift
        vengeance.   370
Who has more of it than God? No human, for sure!
God could amend in one moment all that is amiss,
But he forbears for the sake of a few; and all of us profit by it.

The Scriptures themselves teach men to suffer so:

> *Subjecti igitur estote omni humanae creaturae propter Deum.*
> (Submit yourselves to every ordinance of Man for the
>   Lord's sake.)[46]

And Frenchmen and English freemen thus inform their
  children:

> *Bele vertue est soffrance, mal dire est petyt veniance,*
> *Bien dire et bien soffrir fait lui soffrant a bien venir.*
> (Fair virtues lie in patient suffering,
> No more than small revenge in slandering;
> Soft answers turn away both parties' wrath,
> And bring the patient man to virtue's path.)

I would counsel you, accordingly, to control your tongue,
And do not attack others till you have taken a look at
  yourself.

No man beneath the moon can make his own nature;   380
If a man *could* remould himself to please other men,
Every man alive (believe me) would be blameless.
Besides, you will find few who are fond of hearing
Their ugly faults rehearsed for them, to their very faces.

  A wise and worthy king wrote these words in the Bible:

> *De re quae te non molestat, noli certare.*
> (Strive not in a matter that concerneth thee not.)[47]

Be a man hideous or handsome, you have no right to judge
The face and form that God Himself framed;
For all that was done by him was done well, as the Scriptures
  witness:

> *Viditque Deus cuncta quae fecerat: et erant valde bona.*
> (And God saw every thing that he had made, and
>   behold, it was very good.)[48]

And He bade every creature, after its kind, to increase and
  multiply,[49]

All to give pleasure to Man, who must suffer misery   390
From the temptations of the Flesh and of the Fiend as well.
For Man being made of flesh may not easily escape
From sometimes following the instincts of the flesh.
Cato is in accord – *nemo sine crimine vivit.*'

> (No man may live without misdemeanour.)

My face coloured with crimson because of my shame,
And so I awoke; and great was my woe
That in my dream I had not managed to learn more.
I chid my lost chance, and began to tell myself,
'Now I know what Do-Well is, or by dear God I think so.'
And as I glanced up, I saw someone regarding me,   400
Who said, 'And what is it?' 'Why, surely, sir,' said I,
'To see much and suffer more must be Do-Well.'

   'If you had suffered in good sooth, although asleep,
You could have learned as much as Clerisy, and collected
      more from Reason;
For Reason would have rightly explained what Clerisy ruled.
But because of your thrusting-in, they abandoned you here:
      Philosophus esses, si tacuisses.
      (You might be a philosopher – if you held your
         tongue.)[50]
So long as Adam said nothing, he had Paradise at command;
But when he argued about apples, and interfered
In the wisdom and will of God, he was barred from bliss.
So it was with Reason and you: you, with rude words,   410
Were praising and dispraising things beyond your purview;
He had no temptation to teach you more.

   Now, perhaps, Pride and Presumption will impeach you,
So that Clerisy will no longer care for your company.
No challenging or chiding will chasten a man so soon
As Shame will, that shows him his faults, and shapes him
      towards better things.
For if some daft drunkard falls into a ditch,
Let him lie there, leave him till he feels like stirring;
For if Reason rebuked him at once, he would not regard it,
And for Clerisy's counsel would not give a cress-leaf: 420
To abuse or beat him at once would be sheer sin.
But when dire need and the fear of death get him upright,
And Shame scrapes the shite off his clothes, and he cleans
      his shins,
Then that daft drunkard knows what he has done wrong.'
   'You are speaking sense,' I said. 'I have often seen it.
Nothing can slap more smartly, or smell more sour,

Than Shame, wherever he shows himself – and so people
    shun him.
Was your motive for telling me this my rebuke of Reason?'
'Certainly that is so.' And he started to walk off.
But I rose fast to my feet, and followed after him,   430
Asking as a favour if I might know his name.

PASSUS 12

'I am Imagination, and I was never idle
Though I sit by myself in sickness and in health.
By my faith, I have followed you these forty-five winters,
And many times have moved you to remember your end,
And how many yester-years have gone, and how few remain
      to you;
Of your wildness and wantonness when you were young –
To amend it in your middle age, ere your strength failed
In your *old* age, when one can ill endure
Poverty or hard penance or long praying.
> *Si venerit in secunda vigilia, et si in tertia.*
>> (If he shall come in the second watch, or come in the
>> third watch, and find them watching, blessed are
>> those servants.)[1]
Amend yourself while you may – you have often been
      warned 10
By the power of the Plague, by poverty and anguish:
For with such bitter birch-rods God beats His dear children –
> *Quem diligo, castigo.*
>> (Whom I love, I chastise.)[2]
And David says in the Psalter, of such as love Jesus,
> *Virga tua et baculus tuus, ipsa me consolata sunt.*
>> (Thy rod and thy staff, they comfort me.)
Although you strike me with your staff, with your stick
      or your rod,
It makes me the better pleased, for it amends my soul.[3]
Yet you mess about making poems when you might be
      reciting psalms
Or praying for those who provide your bread; there are
      plenty of books
To tell men what Do-Well is, and Do-Better and Do-Best,
And many a preacher, or pair of friars, to explain them.'
I well saw the truth of his speech; and a little to excuse
      myself, 20

I said, 'Cato, great clerk though he was, used to comfort
   his son,
Or amuse him at times, by making poems, as I do:
    Interpone tuis interdum gaudia curis.
    (Mingle, now and again,
    Some pleasures with your pain.)
And I have heard of holy men who sometimes
Would play, in many places, to perfect themselves.
But if there were anyone who would tell me
What Do-Well and Do-Better and Do-Best really are,
I would write no more works, but wend to Holy Church
And say my rosary except when eating or sleeping.'
   'St Paul, in an Epistle, explains Do-Well: 30
    Fides, spes, caritas . . . major autem horum est caritas.[4]
   Faith, Hope, and Charity, all of these are good,
And often save men's souls – but none sooner than Charity.
For doubtless a man does well to do as Loyalty teaches;
That is, if a man is married, to make his wife his love,
And live henceforth as the Law bids, for the rest of
    their lives.
   If you are a religious, do not go running
Away to Rome or Rochemadour; keep to your Rule,[5]
And hold to your obedience, the highway to Heaven.
If you are unmarried and maiden, and can maintain that state,
Stay so, seek no far saints, for your soul's health.   40
   For how did Lucifer come to lose High Heaven,
Or Solomon his wisdom, or Samson his strength?[6]
Job the Jew paid dearly for his joys,
And Aristotle, and others like Hippocrates and Virgil;
Alexander the all-conquering had a dismal end.[7]
Wealth and Mother-Wit were encumbrances to them all.
Felicia the Fair fell into disgrace;
And Rosamund so wretchedly misruled her life
That the beauty of her body was squandered in beastliness.[8]
I have read of many such, both men and women   50
Who would speak wise words, but whose works were
    the opposite:
    Sunt homines nequam bene de virtute loquentes.

(There do exist bad men who are praisers of virtue.)[9]
Just in this way, wealthy men will amass and be frugal,
For the men whom they hate most to administer it all in
    the end;
And, because they perceive and permit so many poor people,
Without loving them as Our Lord bade, they lose their
    souls too.
    Date, et dabitur vobis.
    (Give, and it shall be given unto you.)
So wealth and sharp wits will undo many people.[10]
Woe to him who wields them unless he uses them well:
    Scientes et non facientes variis flagellis vapulabunt.
    (They who know what is right, and do not perform it,
        are whipped with sundry scourges.)[11]
Sapience, the Bible says, makes a man's soul swell,
    Sapientia inflat
    (And wealth in the same way, unless it is rooted in
        worth),[12]
But the herb of Grace grows to relieve such griefs,   60
Yet Grace grows in no garden save among the humble:
Patience and Poverty are the plots in which it grows,
Among men of loyal life and holy living,
And only by gift of the Holy Ghost, as the Gospel tells us:
    Spiritus ubi vult spirat.
    (The wind bloweth where it listeth.)[13]
But informedness and intellect come from observation
    and teaching,
As the Book bears witness for bodies that can read:
    Quod scimus loquimur, et quod vidimus testamur.
    (We speak that we do know, and testify that we
        have seen.)[14]
From *that we do know* comes informedness, and
    acquaintance with Divinity;
And from *that we have seen*, and other things, arises intellect.
But Grace is a gift of God, and springs from great love;   70
Informedness does not know how it comes, nor intellect
    its ways:
    Nescis unde veniat; aut quo vadat.

> (Thou canst not tell whence it cometh and whither
>   it goeth.)[15]

Yet learning is laudable, and intellect no less;
And clerisy in particular, since its root is love of Christ.
Moses gives evidence that God wrote to give people
    knowledge;
In the Old Law, as *Leviticus* tells us of the laws of the Jews,
Any woman caught in adultery, whether rich or poor,
Should be stricken with stones till she was stunned
    to death.[16]
But one woman, as we may read, was guilty of that act,
And Christ in His courtesy used clerisy to save her;[17]
From the characters that Christ wrote, the Jews
    grew conscious   80
That they were guiltier in God's eyes, and greatly
    more sinful,
Than the woman before them was; and shame drove
    them away.
Literacy and learning were that woman's deliverers.
And Holy Church is aware that Christ's writing
    acquitted her;
It makes clerisy a comfort to creatures that repent,
But to men under malediction, great misery at their end.
    For bread could not become Christ's body, but for clerisy,
Which body is both blessing to the righteous
And death and damnation to those who die unabsolved.
As Christ's writing both comforted the woman and
    proved culpable   90
The Jews who had judged her there, though Jesus
    would save her –
    Nolite judicare, ut non judicemini
    (Judge not, that ye be not judged)[18] –
Just so, my brothers, God's Body – unless received
    by the blameless –
Means damnation on Doomsday, as Christ's writing
    damned those Jews.[19]
Therefore I counsel you: for Christ's sake love clerisy;
Mother-Wit is akin to it, and both are close cousins

To Our Lord Himself, believe me. And so I say, *love them*;
For we may use them as mirrors, to amend our faults,
And as leaders for learned and laymen alike.
    So never look askance at logic, nor its laws and customs,
Nor contradict clerisy. That is my counsel for ever.   100
No man may see if his eyes are missing,
And scholarship would be blind if there were no books.
Men made those books, but God was their master,
And the Holy Spirit their instructor, to say what they
        should write.
And just as sight serves a man to see his own high-street,
So literacy leads the unlearned to reason.
A blind man in a battle may bear weapons to fight with,
But has no hope of hitting an enemy with his axe:
No more has a man with Mother-Wit but untaught,
To come (for all his natural cleverness) to Christianity
        and salvation.   110
Christendom is Christ's treasure-chest, and scholars keep
        its keys;
They unlock it when they like, and dispense to laymen
God's mercy for misdeeds – if those men ask for it
Humbly, with good hearts, and as a gift of grace.
    Under the old Law, Levites looked after the Ark of the
        Covenant;
None but Levites were allowed to lay hands on that coffer,
Except priests and their sons, or patriarchs or prophets.[20]
Saul, for an unpriestly sacrifice, ended in sorrow,
And his sons were also punished for that sin;[21]
And many more un-Levitical men   120
Who went before the Ark in reverence and worship
And laid hands on it to lift it, lost their lives for the act.[22]
I counsel, then, all creatures *Do not despise clerisy*,
Nor think lightly of the learned, whatever their lapses:
Respect the worth of their words, for they witness truth.
Do not meddle much with them, in case you make
        them angry,
Lest strife should stir us up to strike one another;
        Nolite tangere christos meos.

(Touch not mine anointed.)[23]

For clerisy, under Christ in Heaven, keeps us safe;
And every knight that there is, was made knight by
    clerisy.

Mother-Wit comes from all kinds of experiences,   130
Of birds and beasts and of tests both true and false.
Our ancestors in olden days used to record
The strange things they saw, and teach them to their sons;
And they held it a high science, to have knowledge
    of such things.
But no soul was ever saved by all that science,
Nor brought by books into eternal bliss;
Their science was only a series of sundry observations.
So patriarchs and prophets disapproved of their science,
And said their so-called words of wisdom were but folly –
And compared with Christian philosophy, a contemptible
    thing.   140
    Sapientia enim hujus mundi stultitia est apud Deum.
    (For the wisdom of this world is foolishness
        with God.)[24]
For they knew that the high Holy Ghost would split
    Heaven asunder,
And Love leap out upon our low Earth,
And a clean virgin catch it, and clerks find it:
    Pastores loquebantur ad invicem.
    (The shepherds said one to another, Let us now go
        even unto Bethlehem.)[25]
Not rich men, be it noted, nor men of mere cleverness,
Nor unlettered lords, but the most learned men alive:
    Ecce Magi ab Oriente.
    (Behold, there came wise men from the East.)[26]
So if any friar was found there, I'll give you five shillings!
Nor was that boy born in a beggarly cottage,
But in the abode of the richest burgess in Bethlehem:[27]
    *Quia non erat eis locus in diversorio; et pauper non
        habet diversorium.*
    (Because there was no room for them in the inn;
        and a poor man has no inn.)[28]

To peasants and poets there appeared an angel
That bade them go to Bethlehem and honour God's birth,   150
And sang a song of solace – *Gloria in excelsis Deo!*[29]
While the rich men lay routing in their beds of rest,
There shone before the shepherds a vision of Heaven.

Wise Men were aware of this, and came with their gifts,
And paid humble homage to Him Who was almighty.

I have told you all this because I took good heed
Of how you contradicted Clerisy with crabbed words,
And said the unlettered were likelier to be saved than
    the learned,
The educated and intellectual among us Christians.
You spoke the truth about some; but see in what way: 160

Take two strong men, and throw them into the Thames,
Both naked as needles, and nothing to choose between
    them
Save that one is skilful at swimming and diving,
The other inexperienced in the sport, and unable to swim.
Which of those two in the Thames, do you think, has
    more to fear?
He who has never dived, and knows nothing of swimming,
Or the swimmer who is safe, and proceeds as he wishes
While his fellow floats along where the flood carries him,
In great dread of drowning, since he never dived or swam?'
'He who is unable to swim, I should imagine.'   170
'Obvious, is it not? And it stands to reason
That learned men are more able to climb out
Of sin, and be saved, even though they sin often,
Than the unlearned are – if the learned so wish.
If the lettered man is intelligent, he knows what sin is,
And how contrition even without confession may comfort
    the soul;
As you may see in the Psalter – in more psalms than one –
Contrition is commended for the carrying-off of sin:

    Beati, quorum remissae sunt iniquitates: et quorum tecta
        sunt peccata.
    (Blessed is he whose transgression is forgiven, whose
        sin is covered.)[30]

This comforts all who can read, and keeps off despair,
In which flood the Fiend most fiercely tests a man.   180
But the unlettered lies powerless and waits for Lent,
Having no contrition before confession (and then he can
    say very little),
And then believing and leaning on all his confessor has
    him learn.
And *he* will be a parson or a parish priest, and perhaps
Unable to instruct lay-folk, as Luke bears witness:
    Caecus autem si caeco ducatum praestet, ambo in
      foveam cadunt.
    (If the blind lead the blind, both shall fall into
      the ditch.)[31]
  The man who must wade with such leaders was marked
    out for woe!
Well may boys bless those who set them to their books,
So that, living with literature, they may save life and soul!
Dominus pars hereditatis meae is a cheerful text
(The Lord is the portion of my inheritance)
That has robbed Tyburn Tree of scores of tough thieves.   190
They hoist unlettered thieves high, but see how the lettered
    are saved![32]
That thief who obtained God's grace on Good Friday,
    as you say,
Did so by confessing his faith to Christ on the Cross, and
    acknowledging guilt,
And by asking grace from God – Who is ready to grant it
To them that biddably beseech it and are bent on amendment.
But though that thief reached Heaven, he has less high
    joy there
Than St John and other saints, who served God better:
Just as if some man gives me a meal, and seats me in the midst
    of the hall-floor,
And I have more than enough to eat, but not so much honour
As those that sit at the side-tables, with the seigneurs
    of that hall,   200
But sit like a beggar, with no table, by myself on the ground:
So it fared with that felon who was saved on Good Friday;

He sits neither with St John nor with Simon, nor with Jude,
Nor with the Virgins, nor with the Martyrs and Confessors
    and Widows,
But is served sitting on the floor by himself.
For he that has once been a thief is forever at risk
From the Law, that has the last word whether he lives or dies:
    De peccato propitiato, noli esse sine metu.
    (Concerning propitiation, be not without fear to add sin
      unto sin.)[33]
Should a saint and such a thief be served together?
It is neither right nor reason to reward them alike.
Just as the true knight Trajan was no tenant of *deep* hell,   210
So that Our Lord had him easily out, so I think of the
    thief in heaven –
That he is in the lowest level, if our beliefs are true,
And lolls there lubberly by the law of Holy Church;
    Quia tu reddes unicuique juxta opera sua.
    (Thou renderest to every man according to his works.)[34]
  And why one thief on the cross would confess himself
    Christian,
Rather than the other thief: were you to ask that,
All the clergy of Christendom could not clear up the mystery.
    Quare placuit, quia voluit.
    (Whatsoever the Lord pleased, that did he …)[35]
And so I say to you that seek for "why",
And that reasoned with Reason, and almost rebuked him,
About the flowers of the forest, and their fine colours,
And where those colours come from, so clear and bright;   220
And that asked about birds and beasts and their
    breeding-habits
(Why some breed low down, some aloft), and looked
    for an answer;
And are astonished at stones and at stars (are you not?),
And at how all birds and beasts have such able brains:
  Neither Clerisy nor Mother-Wit, but only Nature,
Can ever know all causes; no other creature.
He is the magpie's patron, and puts into its mind
That it is best to build and breed where the thorn is thickest.

It is he who found the pea-fowl their fashion of mating,
He who taught Adam to know his private parts,   230
And showed him and Eve how to hide them in leaves.
Unlettered men often ask of their learned masters
Why Adam did not first hide his mouth, which ate the apple,
Rather than his body, down low: thus laymen ask the learned,
But only Nature knows why, and no scholar at all.

  Now, from birds and beasts, by men in olden times,
Examples and parables were produced, as the poets tell:
For instance, the most beautiful birds are the foulest
      breeders,
And the feeblest fliers of all that fly or swim –
Namely, the peacock and peahen, who stand for the
      proud and rich;   240
For the peacock, when pursued, cannot rise up high,
And because of its trailing tail it is soon overtaken.
Its flesh is foul to eat, and its feet are ugly,
And its voice is revolting, and vile to hear.

  The rich man resembles it, if he hoards his riches
Unshared until he dies, like a trailing tail of sorrow;
For as the peacock's pen-feathers impede its flight,
So does possession of pence and pounds impede
All who hold on to them until Death's hand pulls
      their quills.
And though the rich man may repent then, and rue
      the day   250
That he ever gathered such great wealth, and gave so
      little of it;
And though he may cry to Christ, and no doubt in keen
      longing,
His appeal, in Our Lord's ears, will be like a magpie's chatter;
And when his corpse comes to the clay for burial,
I think it will spread its vile odour through all the
      surrounding earth,
And envenom with its evil all others that lie there.
The peacock's feet, as I find in the fables, mean
Executors and false friends, who do not fulfil his will
As it was written, though they bore witness that they would.

The poet[36] explains that the peacock is admired for his
        feathers,   260
And the rich man revered only by reason of his wealth.
    Though the lark is a far lighter bird, its voice is far lovelier,
And it is far and away more swift of wing than the peacock –
And its flesh manifoldly fatter and sweeter;
So the lark is likened to men of the lower classes;
The great scholar Aristotle tells of such interpretations,
And his *Logic* draws lessons from the littlest of birds.[37]
And whether he is saved or not, is known to no scholar;
Nor of Socrates nor of Solomon are there scriptures
        to tell that.
But God is so good that I hope, since he gave them
        wisdom   270
With which to teach us folk (and lead us towards salvation
All the better for their books), and we are bound to beseech
God in His grace to give their souls rest;
For men now learned would be unlearned had they lacked
        those men's books.'
    'All these clergy,' quoth I, 'who believe in Christ,
Say in their sermons that neither Saracens nor Jews,
Nor any other creature in Christ's likeness, will be saved
        without christening.'
    'Not so,' said Imagination, and frowned somewhat,
Saying, '*Justus vix salvabitur in die judicii*
        (The righteous scarcely shall be saved on Doomsday).[38]
Ergo salvabitur – "Therefore he *shall* be saved."' Then he
        stopped speaking Latin.
'Trajan was a true knight, although never baptised,   280
And he is saved, so the books say, and his soul is in Heaven.
For there is baptism by water and baptism by shedding
        of blood,
And baptism by fire: this is firm belief –
        Advenit ignis divinus, non comburens, sed illuminans.
        (The divine fire comes not to burn but to illuminate.)[39]
A true man, who has never trespassed nor transgressed his
        own law,
But lives as that law teaches, and believes there is no better

(And if there were, he would adopt it), and who dies in
    this outlook:
Surely no God of truth could reject a truth of this kind?
And whether that be so or be not so, such belief is mighty
    in truth,
And a hope hangs therefrom that such faith may have its
    reward.
      For *Deus dicitur quasi dans vitam aeternam suis, hoc est,*
         fidelibus
      (It is said that God gives eternal life to His own, that is,
        to the faithful),
      Et alibi
      (And we find elsewhere),[40]
      Si ambulavero in medio umbrae mortis
      (Yea, though I walk through the valley of the shadow
        of death, I will fear no evil).
And the gloss upon that text grants a great reward
    to truth.'   290
He added, 'Wisdom and reason were once thought
    treasure enough
To keep a commonwealth safe; they considered these
    properties best,
And the cause of much comfort and courage.' And at once
    he vanished.

With this I awoke, well-nigh out of my wits;
And, as a fellow free to do so, forth I went roaming
In the manner of a mendicant, for many years.
Many a time I thought much about my dream.
First, how Fortune had failed me in my greatest need,
And how Old Age had menaced me should we ever meet;
And how the Friars follow after rich folk,
And put little price upon poor people;
And how no corpse could lie in their graveyard, nor be
    buried in their crypt,
Unless when alive he had left them money or helped settle
    their debts;   10
And how covetousness has overcome the priests, and
    all clergy;
And how the unlettered are led (unless Our Lord helps them)
By such incompetent clergy to incurable agonies;
And how Imagination had told me in my dream
About Nature and His knowledge, and His kindness
    to animals,
And how loving He is to all animals of land or water;
He leaves nothing alive forsaken, whether small or big;
Even the creeping creatures were created by Nature.
I thought then how Imagination had said, 'The righteous
    scarcely shall be saved,'
And of when he had said so, and how suddenly he vanished. 20
Once I lay thinking for a long time, and at last slept;
And, as Christ willed, Conscience appeared, to give
    me comfort,
And invited me to come to his castle and dine there
    with Clerisy.
And because Conscience mentioned Clerisy, I came the
    more readily.
I met there a Master of Divinity – not then knowing more
    about him –

Who made low and loving obeisance to Lady Scripture.
Conscience was well acquainted with this cleric,
So they washed and wiped their hands, and went in
    to dinner.
  Now, Patience was outside that palace, in pilgrim's clothes,
Begging his food like a hermit, as holy charity.   30
Conscience called him in, and said courteously,
'Welcome, good man! Go and wash, and we shall sit
    down soon.'
  The Master, as most important, was made seated first;
Then Clerisy and Conscience; and Patience came last.
Patience and I were both put away from that party,
And seated by ourselves at a side-table.
Conscience called for the food, and Scripture came in
And served them swiftly with many sorts of dish –
Such as Augustine, and Ambrose, and all four Evangelists:
    Edentes et bibentes quae apud illos sunt.
    (Eating and drinking such things as they give.)[1]
But neither the Master nor his manservant ate such
    honest meat,   40
Only the richest stews, ratatouilles, and ragoûts:
From ill-gotten gains, they were used to good living.
Yet their sauce was too sour, and their seasoning ill-ground
In a mortar called Post Mortem, which holds much future
    pain for them
Unless they sing Masses for souls, and weep salt tears:[2]
    Vos qui peccata hominum comeditis, nisi pro eis lacrimas
    et orationes effunderitis, ea quae in deliciis comeditis,
    in tormentis evomitis.
    (You who feast upon the sins of men, unless for their
      sake you pour out tears and prayers, those things that
      now you eat among pleasures you shall vomit up
      among torments.)[3]
  Then Conscience very courteously requested Scripture
To bring some bread for both Patience and me.
She set a sour loaf before us, and said, '*Do penance*,'
And drew us a draught of a drink called *Long-endure*.
I said, 'Yes! As long as I live, and my body lasts out!'   50

Said Patience, 'This is proper service! No prince fares better!'
    Then she brought us a mess of other meat, of
        'Have-mercy-upon-me-O-God'.[4]
    Then she brought us 'Blessed-is-he',[5] made by
        'Blessed-is-the-man'[6]
And 'Whose-sin-is-covered',[7] in a dish
Of covert confession, 'I-said-I-will-confess-my-
        transgressions-to-the-Lord'.[8]
    'Bring Patience his special pittance,' said Conscience
        privately.
And Patience's pittance was 'For-this-shall-every-one-that-
        is-godly-pray-unto-thee-in-a-time-when-thou-mayst-
        be-found'.[9]
And Conscience encouraged us, and recounted cheerful
        things:
        '*Cor contritum et humiliatum, Deus, non despicies.*'
        (A broken and a contrite heart, O God, thou wilt
          not despise.)[10]
And Patience was proud of such proper service,
And he was mirthful over his meal; but I mourned
        throughout   60
Because that Divine on the high dais drank wine so fast –
        Vae qui potentes estis ad bibendum vinum
        (Woe unto them that are mighty to drink wine) –[11]
And devoured so many different dishes, ragoûts and puddings,
Tripes, wild-boar's brawn, eggs fried in butter ...
Then I said to myself – but so that Patience could hear it –
'It is not four days since this fellow, in front of the Dean of
        St Paul's,
Preached about the privations of Paul the Apostle
From fasting and cold and from flogging with scourges:
        Ter virgis caesus sum ... a Judaeis quinquies quadragenas,
        una minus, accepi.
        (Thrice was I beaten with rods ... Of the Jews five
          times I received forty stripes save one.)[12]
    But there is one phrase that they forget when such friars
        preach so,
One that Paul in his Epistle told to all people,

> *Periculis in falsis fratribus:*
> In perils among false brethren.[13]

The Scriptures bid us beware – but I will not write it here　70
In English, in case it is too often repeated,
And grieves good men; but grammarians shall read it:

> *Unusquisque a fratre se custodiat; quia, ut dicitur,*
> *periculum est in falsis fratribus.*

> (Let each of you be on guard against a friar; for it is
> said that there is danger in false friars.)[14]

I know of no fellow who, as a friar, spoke before folk
　in English
And took *that* for his text, and taught it without sophistry!
They preach that penance is a profit to the soul,
And what agonies Christ endured on behalf of Man;
　But this glutton of God, with his gross face,
Has no pity on the poor, and practises evil.
He does not practise what he preaches,' I said to Patience;
And I wished with all my heart and will　80
That the dishes and plates placed before that preacher
Were molten lead in his middle, and Mahound among them!
'I shall approach,' I said, 'this piss-pot with his puffed-out
　belly,
To explain what that penance *is*, that he preached-of earlier.'
But Patience had seen my intention, and signalled me to
　silence:
'You will see soon enough, when he can stuff no more,
He'll do *his* penance in his paunch, and burp when he speaks;
And his guts will gurgle, and he'll go gapy-faced;
For he's drunk so deeply that he'll soon start discoursing,
And prove by the *Gluttons' Apocalypse* and the passion of
　St Aurea,[15]　90
That bacon and brawn and hash and blanquette of chicken
Are neither fish nor flesh, but penitential food.
Then indeed he will talk about his "trinities", and make his
　companion testify
What is found in a frail after a friar has fed;
And unless his first words are lies, nevermore believe me!
That will be the time to take and question this "master"

Whether Do-Well and Do-Better and Do-Best mean
    "penance".
  So I sat still, as Patience said. And soon this Master,
As rubicund as a rose, rubbed his cheeks,
Coughed, and began to converse; and Conscience listened,   100
And told him of the trinity we sought. He looked towards us.
  'What is Do-Well, sir doctor?' said I. 'Is it doing penance?'
'Do-Well?' said this Divine, and took his cup, and drank:
'It is to do all you can to avoid harming others.'
'Then, by this day, sir doctor, you are not Do-Well's man;
You *have* harmed us two, by eating-up the hashes
And the puddings, and plenty more, of which *we* had
    no piece!
If the sick fare so in your infirmary, I find it amazing
If quarrelling is not their *caritas*, and the very choirboys
    complain!
I would permute my penance with yours though I *am*
    pursuing Do-Well.'   110
  But Conscience, with a courteous countenance,
Appeared to ask Patience to pray my silence,
And himself said, 'Sir Master, if you do not mind,
What *are* Do-Well and Do-Better? You Divines know
    such things.'
'Do-Well is to do what the clergy say is your duty,
And Do-Better is he that teaches, and toils to teach others,
And Do-Best is to do oneself all that one teaches and
    preaches.
    Qui autem fecerit et docuerit . . . hic magnus vocabitur in
      regno coelorum.'
    (Whosoever shall do and teach . . . shall be called great
      in the kingdom of heaven.)[16]
'Now, Clerisy,' said Conscience, 'give us *your* account of
    Do-Well.'
'I have seven sons,' said Clerisy, 'who serve in a castle
Where the Lord of Life lives and teaches them of
    Do-Well.   120
But till I see those seven reconciled with myself,
I am unwilling to explain it to any man.

For a certain Piers Ploughman has impugned us all,
And set all sciences at a crumb's worth, save only love.
And he takes no texts to maintain his opinion
Except *Love thy Lord* and *Lord, who shall abide in thy
     tabernacle?*[17]
He says that Do-Well and Do-Better are both infinite;
Which infinites, with faith's help, will find Do-Best;
And Do-Best will save Man's soul. Thus says Piers
     Ploughman.'
'I know nothing of that,' said Conscience, 'but I know
     Piers well;   130
I am certain that *he* will say nothing against Scripture,
So let this question pass until Piers comes to explain it
     in practice.
Patience has been in many places, and perhaps knows
What no clerk could tell us, for Christ bears witness:
     Patientes vincunt: "The patient conquer."'
'Since you wish it, I will,' said Patience, 'if no one objects.
Disce,' said he, '*Doce*, and *Dilige inimicos*;
Disce is Do-Well, *Doce* is Do-Better, and *Dilige* is Do-Best.
To learn is Do-Well; To teach is Do-Better; and Do-Best
     is To love your enemies.
This I learned from a lady called Caritas, whom I loved.
"In word and in deed," she said, "and with all your
     heart's will,   140
So long as you live you must faithfully love your soul;
Thus you will learn to love, for the love of Our Lord
     in Heaven,
Your enemy as much as yourself in every way.
Cast coals upon his head, with your kindly speech;
With both words and deeds, try to win his love,
Surround him so with love that he *must* smile on you –
And if such beating does not break him, may he go blind!
     But it would be foolish to treat your friend in such
         a fashion;
For a friend who is truly fond of you covets little of yours.
Instinctive affection asks to own nothing but speech,   150
With half-a-line limned in Latin, *ex vi transitionis*."

(From the power of passing over.)
Bound fast within these words, I bear Do-Well about
    with me,
As a sign of that Saturday which started the Calendar,
And the wisdom of the Wednesday in the week that followed;
And the middle of the moon gives might to both.
While I have it, I am welcome wherever I go.[18]
Undo it, then, let this Doctor decide if it holds Do-Well;
For by Him who made me, no lack of money,
No misfortune or calamity, no evil of men's tongues,
No cold or care, or the company of thieves,   160
Neither heat nor hail, nor any fiend from Hell,
Nor fire nor flood, nor fear of an enemy,
May at any time trouble you, if you take *that* with you:
    Timor non est in caritate.
    (There is no fear in love.)[19]
And also, as I hope to be saved, for only your asking
There's no emperor, empress, earl or king or baron,
Pope or patriarch, but by power of pure reason
You may master them, and all men, through the might of
    this riddle –
Not by witchcraft, but by wisdom. And if you yourself wish
You may make the King and the Queen, and the whole
    commonwealth too,
Give you all that they can give, as their best guardian;   170
And as you decide, so shall they do, for the rest of their days:
    Patientes vincunt.'
    (The patient conquer.)
  'This is only a diddle,' said the Doctor, 'a minstrel's deceit.
All the wisdom in the world, all the might of great war-lords,
Cannot patch-up a peace between the Pope and his enemies,
Or contrive a truce between two Christian Kings,
That shall please both the peoples.' Then he pushed away
    the table,
And took Clerisy and Conscience into conclave, as it were,
Saying Patience should push-off – 'since pilgrims are
    fine liars'.
  But Conscience cried aloud, and yet courteously,

'Farewell, my friends!', and spoke fair to Clerisy,   180
'If God gives me grace; I will go along with this man,
A pilgrim beside Patience, till experience teaches me more.'
    'What?' said Clerisy to Conscience, 'Are you covetous now
Of gold, or New Year's gifts? Do you want to guess riddles?
I could bring you a Bible, say a book of the Old Law,
And instruct you, if you wished, in the tiniest detail –
Which Patience the Pilgrim could never do properly.'
    'No, by Christ,' said Conscience to Clerisy, 'though may
        God reward you.
For all that Patience promises, I feel little pride;
But the earnest intent of the man, and of these other
        people,   190
Has so moved my spirit that I mourn for my sins.
A man's meaning to do good may never be wholly bought,
For an honest intention is more precious than any treasure.
Was not Mary Magdalen given more for a box of ointment[20]
Than Zacchaeus, though he said *Dimidium bonorum
        meorum, Domine, do pauperibus*?
        (Lord, the half of my goods I give to the poor.)[21]
And the poor widow more for her pair of mites
Than all of the others who offered-up into the Treasury?'[22]
So Conscience courteously took congé, first of the Friar;
After which he said softly in Clerisy's ear,
'By Our Lord, as I hope to live, I should sooner like   200
To own perfect patience than half of your pack of books!'
    But Clerisy would take no congé of Conscience.
He said very soberly, 'You will see the time
When you are wearied-out with walking, and want
        my advice.'
'That may well turn out true,' said Conscience, 'but
        I take God to witness,
Were Patience our sharing-partner, and personal friend
        of us both,
We three could put right every woe in the world;
We could make peace between all kings and countries,
And turn to the true faith, to one single creed,
The Syrians and the Saracens and the Jews themselves.'   210

'This is certainly so,' said Clerisy, 'and I see what you mean;
But I shall dwell where I do, and perform my duty
Of confirming the faith of infants and such partly-taught folk,
Till Patience has put you to the test, and made you perfect.'[23]
 So Conscience went forth with Patience, and they lived
  as pilgrims,
And Patience, like all pilgrims, had victuals in his pack –
Sobriety, simple speech, and steadfast faith –
To comfort him and Conscience when they should come
To the hungry countries of Unkindness and Covetousness.
 As they went their way, and spoke of Do-Well,   220
They met with a man who seemed to me a minstrel.
Patience approached him first, and prayed him tell
To Conscience his calling, and the country he was seeking.
 'I am a minstrel, and my name is *Activa Vita*;[24]
I abhor an idle man, for Active Life is my name.
If you want to know, I'm a waferer, and work for many lords;
But they furnish me with few robes or furred gowns.
Could I lie to make people laugh, I should latch on
To mantles and money among the lords' minstrels;[25]
But I play neither tabor nor trumpet, and cannot
  tell romances,   230
Or harp or fiddle or fart in tune at feasts,
Or tell jokes, or juggle, or pipe a jig,
Nor tumble, neither, nor dance, nor sing to the gittern.
So I get no good gifts from those great lords,
For all the bread I bake, except a blessing on Sunday
When the priest tells the people to say their Pater-noster
For Piers the Ploughman and all who help him prosper –
Of whom I, Active Life, am one, since I hate idleness;
For all true toilers and tillers of the soil,
From Michaelmas to Michaelmas, I make wafer-cakes. 240
Beggars and cadgers beseech my bread,
And fakers and friars and other very bald folk.
I provide bread for the Pope, and fodder for his palfrey,
And (God's my guarantee) he never gave me
Either prebend or parsonage, did the Pope;
Only a pardon and a piece of lead with a pair of heads on it![26]

If I'd a clerk, who could write for me, I'd convey a petition
That he send me, under his seal, a salve against the Plague,
And his blessing, and some Bulls to get rid of boils:

> *In nomine meo daemonia ejicient ... super aegros manus*
> *imponent, et bene habebunt.*
>
> (In my name shall they cast out devils ... they shall lay
> hands on the sick, and they shall recover.)[27]

Then I'd make pastry for the people *prestissimo*,   250
And be busy and obedient to find bread and drink
For the Pope and all his people if I found that his pardon
Could cure a man, as I consider it should.
For since the Pope has the powers that St Peter himself had,
It seems certain to me he has that little pot full of salve:

> *Petrus autem dixit: Argentum et aurum non est mihi:*
> *quod autem habeo, hoc tibi do: In nomine Jesu Christi*
> *Nazareni, surge, et ambula.*
>
> (Then Peter said, Silver and gold have I none; but such
> as I have give I thee: In the name of Jesus Christ
> of Nazareth rise up and walk.)[28]

But if he may not work miracles, then man's unworthiness
To receive God's grace is the cause, not the Pope's guilt.
No blessing can benefit us till we amend our behaviour,
Nor any man's Mass make peace among Christian people
Till pride is entirely uprooted – when people lack bread!   260
Before I make bread out of meal, I must sweat hard for it;
And before the crowd has corn enough, I see many cold
    mornings;
So before my wafers are baked, I have bothers enough.
All London, I believe, loves my wafers,
And grumbles at not getting them. Not long ago
They were a downcast crowd when no cart came to town
With baked bread from Stratford.[29] How the beggars wept!
And the workmen were scared for a while – they will long
    remember it.
This happened in our drought-days, the dry April
Of one thousand three hundred twice thirty and ten: 270
My wafers were not many when Chichester was mayor.'[30]
I took careful note, by Christ, and so did Conscience,

Of Haukyn the Active Man, and of his dress.
His coat is of Christendom, in Holy Church's cut,
But is marked in many places with all kinds of mess:
Here a patch of pride, and a patch here of bragging;
Scorn here, scoffing there, here uncouth behaviour –
In deportment as in apparel, a proud man in public,
To seem other than he is, or has, in heart or appearance,
Wishing all men to believe that he is what he is not.   280
Therefore he boasts and brags, with many brazen oaths,
Ignoring all reproof from anyone living.
He seems a law unto himself, in all men's sight –
None like him, a nonpareil, none so pope-holy,
As if habited like a hermit, but of his own Order,
A Religious with no Rule or obedience to Reason,
Disparaging the learnèd and the unlettered alike,
Laying claim to a loyal life, but in his heart a liar.
    His inward or outward mind, his imagination and scheming,
Are all for his body's benefit, and his bad reputation.   290
He interferes everywhere in what are not his affairs,
Meaning men to think *his* mind better than their own –
For his craft and cunning, the wisest of clerks,
And the strongest horse-bestrider, and the sturdiest-thewed,
And the loveliest to look at, and most loyal to his word,
None so holy as he, nor with purer habits,
Nor with finer features, nor so well-formed and strong;
The subtlest singer, the most skilful with his hands,
And the most lavish lender, even if he loses by it.
But if he does give to the needy, he blazons it abroad;   300
And though poorly provided in both purse and coffer,
He is lordly as a lion in both looks and speech;
Boldest of beggars, and a beggarly boaster,
In farmstead or tavern to tell tall stories,
Describing, and swearing true, such things as he never saw,
Declaring and bragging about deeds he never did –
And of anything he truly did, he will take testimony and oath:
'Look, now, if you don't believe me, if you think I'm a liar,
Ask So-and-So or Such-and-Such, and *they'll* tell you
What I suffered, what I saw, all the stuff I once had,   310

How clever I was, the things I could do, what kin I
    come of . . .'
All that he wished men to know of his words or doings
Was to impress other people, and praise himself.

    Si adhuc hominibus placerem, Christi servus non essem.
        Et alibi: Nemo potest duobus dominis servire.
    (If I yet pleased men, I should not be the servant
      of Christ.
        And elsewhere: No man can serve two masters.)[31]

  'By Christ, Haukyn,' said Conscience, 'your best coat
Shows many marks and spots – you must wash it.'

  'Yes, if anybody bothers to look at the back or the front,
Inside it or outside, or either left or right,
He will find many furrows and many foul spots.'

  He turned quickly about, and I was able to see
That his coat was filthier by far than at first it had seemed.   320
It was all spattered with anger and with wicked ill-will,
With envy and with evil speech that instigates fights,
With lying, malicious laughter, and loose angry speech
That would repeat whatever ill he knew of anyone,
To backbite people and to wish them bad luck.
Whatever he heard about Will, he would tell it to Walt,
And what he learned from Walt would go back to Will,
So that friends were turned into foes by his false tongue:
'By the might of the mouth, if not by male strength,
I am often avenged – for otherwise, inwardly,   330
I should gnaw away at myself like a shepherd's shear.'
Evil, accursed men! *Cujus maledictione os plenum est . . .*

    Et alibi: Filii hominum, dentes eorum . . .
    (His mouth is full of cursing and deceit and fraud . . .
      And elsewhere: The sons of men whose teeth are spears
      and arrows, and their tongue a sharp sword.)[32]

  'I love no man alive for very long,
And I tell such tales that no one trusts me.
If a man overmasters me I am seized with such melancholy
That I catch internal cramp or a cardiac pain,
Or an anguishing ague, or it may be a fever,
That is with me a twelvemonth, till I come to despise

All Christian modes of medicine, andd my trust goes
    to witches:
I claim that no doctor can cure, nor Christ Himself,
Like the shoemaker of Southwark or Dame Emma of
    Shoreditch!³³ 340
I grumble that God's word never yet got me cured;
My best chances and chief cures came from magic charms.'
    Considered yet more carefully, his coat was smeared
With a liking for lechery, and a lustful roving eye;
For to every miss he met, he made a sign
Suggesting that they should sin – and would sometimes
    taste her
About the mouth, and begin to grope her down below,
Till both of them were well aroused. Then to work
    they went,
On fast-days, Fridays, or forbidden nights,
In Lent or out of Lent – all times were alike; 350
That sort of work, with them, was never out of season.
Till, both tired out, they would tell funny stories,
And laugh and joke about lecherous lovers,
And (even in old age) talk of harlotry and of whoredom.
    Then Patience perceived that parts of Haukyn's coat
Were eroded by avarice and unnatural grasping;
Goods, rather than God, had got *this* fellow's love,
And he planned perpetually how to profit
From false measures, false weights, and false witness.
He loaned for lust of the pledge; and he loathed fair
    dealing, 360
Always awaiting some way to deceive.
He mixed up his merchandise to make a good display –
'But the worst was underneath – I've cunning ways, eh?
If someone had a servant, or perhaps an animal,
More valuable than mine, I would plan many tricks
For securing that same; I set all my wits to work
And even – for want of a better way – would steal it,
Or privately strip his purse, or pick his locks.
By night and by day I was always busy
Getting guilefully together such goods as I have. 370

Should I go to plough, I would shave my ground so short
That I would filch a foot or a furrow at least,
And so narrow my next-door neighbour's land.
And if I reaped, would reach over (or tell my reapers to)
And seize by the sickle what I had never sown.
Should a borrower be wishful to buy more time,
He must give me private presents, or a fixed down-payment,
So that whether he wished or not, I would make more profit.
To my own kith and kin I was close with my money.
Those who made offers for my merchandise, I abused   380
Unless they proposed to pay me a penny or two
More than the stuff was worth; and still I would swear
That it cost me more than they offered, and I added
        many oaths.
    On holidays, at Holy Church, when I heard Mass,
God knows I never tried to pray in earnest
For mercy on my misdeeds; I felt more sorrow,
Believe me, for bad bargains than for bodily sins,
Even had I done deadly ones; I dreaded them less
Than when I lent money and thought it lost, or it was long
        in repaying.
So even if I *could* show kindness, to help a fellow-
        Christian,   390
My heart was hung-up on the hardest avarice.
If I sent my servants overseas to Bruges,
Or my apprentices to Prussia, to seek my profit
By making exchanges or sales of merchandise or money,
Nothing could make me happy in the meantime:
Neither Mass nor Matins, nor amusement of any sort,
Nor any penance performed, nor Pater-noster said,
But my mind was on my goods, and in mortal fear,
Rather than on God's grace and His great mercies.'
        Ubi enim est thesaurus tuus, ibi est et cor tuum.
        (For where your treasure is, there will your heart
            be also.)[34]
    This glutton's garments were also soiled with
        great oaths,   400
And filthily beslobbered by foul and false speech –

Such as needless and idle use of the name of God,
By which he had sworn a swarm of times, till sweat came
    through his coat.
He had devoured more food and drink than nature could
    endure:
'Yes, and gone sick many a time because of my surfeiting.
Then I *was* put in dread of dying in deadly sin.'
Then he would drop into despair, and doubt his salvation –
A form of Sloth so stark, no skill can cure it,
And no mercy amend such a man who dies thus.
   What may the branches of sloth be, that bring men
    to despair?   410
When a man does not mourn his misdeeds, or feel sorry;
When he performs badly the penance his priest lays on him,
Does no deeds of charity, feels no dread of sin,
Lives contrary to religion, and holds to no law.
For him, all days are holidays or high feast-days;
And all he is willing to hear are the harlotries of buffoons.
When people converse about Christ, and cleanness of soul,
He grows angry indeed, and demands only jollity.
Penance and the poor, and the pangs of saints,
He hates to hear about – and all who discuss them.   420
These are the branches (beware them!) that bring men
    to despair.
   You lords and ladies, you lieutenants of Holy Church,
Who feed wise fools and flatterers and liars,
And love to listen to them when they make you laugh,
    Vae vobis qui ridetis nunc: quia lugebitis et flebitis.
      (Woe unto you that laugh now! for ye shall mourn
        and weep.)[35]
You give them food and fees, and refuse poor people:
On the day of your death, I deeply fear,
These three kinds of creature will cause you great sorrow:
    Consentientes et agentes pari poena punientur.
      (Assenters to evil shall bear the same penalties as
        those who commit it.)[36]
Patriarchs and prophets, and preachers of God's word,
By means of their sermons, save men's souls from Hell;

Just so, flatterers and fools are the Fiend's disciples,   430
Whose tales entice men to ribald talk and sin.
Priests learned in Holy Writ should let their lords know
What David said of such men, as the Psalter shows:

> *Non habitabit in medio domus meae qui facit superbiam;*
>   *qui loquitur iniqua, non direxit in conspectu oculorum*
>   *meorum.*

> (He shall not dwell in the midst of my house, that
>   acts proudly; he who speaks iniquities shall not tarry
>   in my sight.)[37]

No harlequin should have audience in the halls or chambers
Where wise men may be (God's word is my witness),
Nor any self-admiring man be allowed among lords.
    Clergy and cavaliers welcome the king's minstrels,
And for love of their liege-lord listen to them at banquets.
Much more, then, should the rich, it seems to me,
Call beggars to be their guests, who are *God's* minstrels.   440
Christ Himself says, as St John bears witness,

> *Qui vos spernit, me spernit.*

> (He that despiseth you, despiseth me.)[38]

So I recommend to you rich men, when you hold revels,
That you solace your souls with such minstrels as *these*:
A poor man, instead of a so-called wit, seated at your
      High Table;
A learned, to give you lessons of Our Lord's Passion,
That saved your souls from their enemy Satan,
And to fiddle for you, without flattery, the Ballad
      of Good Friday!
A blind man, or a bedridden woman, in place of your buffoon,
Who shall cry to Our Lord for largesse, and laud you to *Him*.
Such minstrels as these three might make you laugh
      wholesomely,   450
And, when you die the death, give you comforts indeed
Who listened to them when living, and loved to hear them.
These would solace your soul, which you would see grow
Into strong hope, for having so acted towards saints of worth.
But flatterers and fools, with filthy words,
Lead those that love them to Lucifer's feast,

And a lament called *Lasciviousness*, sung to Lucifer's fiddle.
   Thus had Haukyn the Active Man made his coat filthy,
Till Conscience courteously called him to account
For why he had not washed it, or wiped a brush over it.   460

'I have only one whole suit,' said Haukyn, 'and am hardly
    to blame
If it is soiled and seldom clean, for I sleep in it at night;
Also, at home I have a wife, and have servants and children,
Who many times muck it up, my protests notwithstanding!
    Uxorem duxi et ideo non possum venire.
    (I have married a wife, and therefore cannot come.)[1]
It has been lathered in Lent, and out of Lent, too,
With the soap of sickness, that sinks very deep in,
And with loss of belongings, that made me loth to offend
Either God or any good man, had I grace to avoid it.
The priest also heard me confess, and gave me for my sins
The penitence of patience and providing for the poor –   10
And of keeping my coat clean if I wished to stay Christian.
Yet I never could, by Christ, keep it clean for an hour;
For I soiled it with lewd looks or with worthless talk;
Or with wickedness of word or of deed or the will
    of my heart,
I have filthily befouled it, from morn till eve.'
  'I will acquaint you,' said Conscience, 'with the making
    of an act of contrition
That will scrape your coat free from all sorts of smut.
Take *Cordis contritio*, contrition of the heart:[2]
Do-Well shall wash it and wring it through a wise confessor.
Take *Oris confessio*, oral confession:
Do-Better shall boil it and beat it as bright as scarlet,
And engrain it with good-will, and with God's grace
    to amend you;   20
Then send you to sacramental penance – Do-Best –
    to sew-up its rents.
  Satisfactio Do-Best: Do-Best is sacramental penance.
No mist will ever mar it again, nor moth nibble it,
Nor fiends nor false men befoul it so long as you live;
No herald nor harper shall have a finer garment

Than Haukyn the Active Man may, if he follows
    my teaching.
No minstrel shall be made more of; among rich or poor,
Than the wife of Haukyn the waferer, with his *activa vita*.'
'I shall present you with your paste, even when no
    plough stirs,' said Patience.
'And with flour to feed folk with, for the good of
    their souls,
Even when no grain grows in the fields, nor grapes on
    the vines.   30
All that live and look for a living, I will supply,
And none shall have less than enough of what he needs.
Men should not be too busy about their livelihood:
    Ne soliciti sitis . . . patientes vincunt . . .'
      (Take no thought for your life, what ye shall eat . . .
        the patient conquer . . .)[3]
  Then Haukyn laughed a little, and lightly swore:
'By our Lord, to rely on you, I believe, would bring small
    comfort!'
'Not so!' said Patience, *with* patience; and he took from
    his pack
Some victuals of great value to every kind of creature.
'Lo! Here is livelihood enough, if our beliefs are true!
God lent no creature life without means of livelihood –
Whereof; or wherefore, or whereby, to live.   40
Consider the wild worm, under the wet earth,
Fish that live in the floods, and the cricket in the fire;
The curlew, by consuming air, has the cleanest flesh
    of all birds;
And cattle live on grass and grain and green roots.
The meaning is that all men might in like manner
Live by loyal faith and love – as Christ bore witness:
    Quodcumque petieritis Patrem in nomine meo, hoc faciam.
    (Whatsoever ye shall ask the Father in my name, that
      will I do.)[4]
And elsewhere
    Non in solo pane vivit homo, sed in omni verbo quod
      procedit de ore Dei.'

(Man shall not live by bread alone, but by every word
    that proceedeth out of the mouth of God.)[5]
Now I looked at this provender that Patience so praised,
And perceived that it was a piece of *Pater-noster* – 'Thy
    will be done.'
'Take it, Haukyn,' said Patience, 'and have some when you
    are hungry,
Or when you are clumsy with cold, or clemmed with
    drought.   50
Manacles shall not make you grieve, nor magnates' anger,
Nor prison nor pain, for – *the patient conquer.*
Be sober in your behaviour with both eye and tongue,
In eating and in handling, and in all your five senses,
And you will not care about corn, or cloth of wool or linen,
Nor for drink nor for death, but die as God wills,
By hunger or heat or however He chooses.
For if you live by His lore, the shorter your life, the better:
    Si quis amat Christum, mundum non diligit istum.[6]
    (He who loves the King of Kings
    Takes no delight in earthly things.)
It was by His breath that beasts grew, and wandered
    abroad: 60
    Dixit et facta sunt.
    (He commanded, and they were created.)[7]
And therefore through His breath must beasts and men live,
As Holy Scripture substantiates when men say grace:
    Aperis tu manum tuam, et imples omne animal benedictione.
    (Thou openest thy hand, and satisfiest the desire of every
      living thing.)[8]
  We find that for forty winters folk lived without husbandry,
And a flood sprang up out of the flint, for the folk and beasts
    to drink;[9]
And in Elijah's time Heaven's floodgates were closed,
And no rain ran down (so we read in the books);[10]
Yet the Tribes lived so, many winters, without either bread
    or tillage.
There were seven men that slept, says the book, for seven
    hundred winters,

Living without food or liquid, yet waking at last.[11]
And if all men lived in moderation, famine would cease   70
Among Christian creatures, if Christ's words are true.
Dearth causes unkindness among Christian people,
And overplenty brings pride among poor and rich;
But moderation has such merit, no man can overprice it.
For the sins and the sorrows that the Sodomites suffered
Rose from bread in abundance and unabated sloth:

> *Otiositas et abundantia panis peccatum turpissimum*
>   *nutrivit.*
>
> (Fullness of bread and abundance of idleness bred up
>   that vilest of sins.)[12]

Because they were immoderate in their eating and drinking,
And did that deadly sin that the Devil rejoiced at,
For their vile vices, vengeance fell on them;
And both of their cities sank into Hell.[13]   80
    Let us temper our tastes, then, and take faith for
        our shield;
For through faith comes contrition, as Conscience
        knows well,
Which drives off deadly sin and reduces it to venial.
And though a man were mute, contrition might save him
And bring his soul to bliss, if Faith bore witness
That while he lived he believed in the lore of Holy Church.
So contrition, faith, and conscience, are correctly Do-Well –
The surgeons for deadly sin when spoken shrift fails.
    But oral confession is more excellent for the inwardly
        contrite,
For that slays any sin, howsoever deadly.   90
By confession to a cleric, all sins are killed,
But contrition can do no more than cut them down
        to venial.
Thus David in the Psalter says, "Blessed whose sin is
        covered."[14]
But satisfaction seeks out sin's root, and both slays and
        expels it,
And annihilates deadly sin as if it had never existed;
The sin leaves no scar or soreness, but seems a healed wound.'

'Where does Charity live?' said Haukyn. 'For I never
    looked yet, in my life,
On any man who had met him, for all my wide wandering.'
   'With perfect truth, and poverty of spirit, and a patient
    tongue;
There dwells Charity, the chief of God's chamberlains!'   100
'So, is patient poverty,' said Haukyn, 'more pleasing to
    Our Lord
Than riches rightfully gained, and reasonably spent?'
   'Come, now, but *quis est ille?* Quick – *laudabimus eum!*'
(First find me such a man, then we'll praise the fellow!)
'You may teach men how to use riches till the end of
    the world;
But I never ran across a rich man who, when he reckoned
That the day of his death was near, was not sorely in dread,
Or who, in that last reckoning, was not in arrears rather
    than credit.
The poor man dares to plead, and to prove by pure reason,
His right to Our Lord's lenience; he claims by Law,
From that just Judge, the joys he never had.   110
He says, "Look at the birds and beasts, debarred from
    Heaven's bliss,
And the wild worms in the woods: You anguish them in
    winter,
And make them, with famine, almost meek and mild;
But then you send them summer, their sovereign joy,
The Heaven's-bliss of the beasts both tame and wild.
So beggars, like the beasts, wait to be comforted,
They who have lived all their lives in languishing want."
Unless God sent them sometime *some* kind of pleasure –
Either here on Earth or elsewhere, nature would not
    bear it;
What man was ever made with no means towards joy?   120
   The angels who are now in Hell, had joy at one time;
Dives lived among dainties and *la dolce vita*[15] –
As really, we know by reason, do *all* rich men;
And their ladies also live lives of pleasure.
   To Man's Mother-wit, God's will may seem strange,

That He gives many men their thank-money before they
    have earned it –
For thus it is that He treats the rich; and I think it worth pity
That they have their reward, and their Heaven as it were,
    here on Earth,
In luxury of life, without labouring bodily,
But are disavowed when they die – as David says in the
    Psalter: 130
    Dormierunt somnium suum, et nihil invenerunt.
    (They have slept their sleep, and all the men of wealth
        have found nothing in their hands.)[16]
And in another psalm too!
    Velut somnium surgente, Domine, in civitate tua,
        imaginem ipsorum ad nihilum redige.
    (As a dream when one awaketh, so shalt thou make
        their image to vanish out of the city.)[17]
Alas that riches should wrench and rob men's souls
From the love of Our Lord, at their late end!
Servants who take their salaries in advance are always needy;
He seldom dies out of debt, who has not earned his dinner
By first doing his full day's work and duty.
   When a workman has finished his work, one may
    see exactly
What that work is worth, and what he has earned:
Take no fee beforehand, for fear your work is refused.
So I say to all you rich folk, you do wrong to expect   140
Your Heaven here below and in the hereafter too,
Like a servant with prepaid salary, who claims it a
    second time,
As if he had nothing, but must have his hire now.
It must not be, you rich men, unless Matthew lies in
    God's face:
    De deliciis ad delicias, difficile est transire.
    (From delights to delights is a difficult passage.)[18]
   Yet if you rich are not ruthless, but reward the poor well,
And live as God's law teaches, acting justly towards all,
Christ in His courtesy will comfort you at your ending,
And reward with double riches those of ruthful heart.

As a servant with prepaid salary who has served well
May, before he is relieved, receive extra rewards –   150
Say, a coat on top of his contract – so Christ will give Heaven
To both prosperous and poor who show pity in their lives;
All who do their duty well shall have double pay for
      their toil –
Forgiveness here for their sins, and hereafter Heaven's bliss.
   But the holy saints say in their books that it is seldom seen
That God rewards a rich man with double repose.
For the rich make high merriment with their meals
      and clothes,
As in May there is high merriment among wild beasts;
And their high spirits stay as long as Summer does.
But beggars have no bread to their supper even about
      Midsummer;   160
And Winter is even worse, for they walk wet-footed,
Always thirsty and hungry, and abused so foully,
And so despised by the prosperous, it is piteous to hear.
Lord, send them their Summer, and some kind of pleasure –
Heaven when they go hence – who have known such
      want here!
For You might have made all men equal in means,
And quick-witted and wise, had Your wish been so.
Then pity the prosperous who give Your prisoners nothing;
For all the goods You gave them, ingratitude comes
      from many;
But, God, in Your goodness, give them grace to reform.   170
No dearth is dire to them, nor drought, nor flood,
Nor heat nor hail, so long as they have their health;
And of all they might want or wish, in this world they
      lack nothing.
   But the poor people, Lord, Your prisoners in the pit
      of misfortune:
Comfort those creatures, who are so careworn
By dearth and drought all their days here below –
Woeful in winter, for want of clothing;
Seldom, even in Summer, supping well:
Comfort the careworn, Christ, in Your Kingdom;

For how You comfort all creatures, the clergy bear witness: 180
    Si revertamini et quiescatis, salvi eritis.
    (In returning and rest shall ye be saved.)[19]
Thus, courteously incarnate, Jesus Christ said
To robbers and reavers, to rich and to poor.
You taught them, Lord, to take baptism in the name of
    the Trinity,
And grow clean, through that christening, from all kinds
    of sin;
And if it befell through our folly we should later fall into sin,
Confessing and acknowledging it, and craving Your mercy,
Would redeem us as often as any man might wish.
But if Apollyon counter-pleaded, and punished our conscience,
You would rapidly take our Reprieve for that wretch to see:
    Pateat . . . per Passionem Domini . . .
    (Be it known that by the Passion of Our Lord . . .)[20]
And so drive off the Devil and demonstrate our ransom.   190
But poverty must be the parchment of which this Patent
    is made,
And pure patience too, and perfect faith.
From pomp and pride, this parchment falls away,
And indeed from all except the poor in spirit:
All else is idle, that ever we wrote on it –
Pater-nosters and penances, and pilgrimages to Rome;
Unless our expense and spending spring from right motives,
All our labour is lost. See how men have their names cut
On friary windows, when the foundation of the act is false.[21]
All Christians should hold wealth in common, none
    covetous for himself.   200
  There are seven sins that continually assail us,
And the Fiend follows them all, and makes efforts
    to help them –
And it is with riches that that Wretch most readily traps men.
For where riches reign, reverence is found,
Which is pleasing to the pride of both rich and poor.
The rich man is reverenced by reason of his riches,
And the poor man is pushed back – though perhaps he
    has more

Of wit and wisdom in him – which are far and away better
Than riches or royalty, and reach Heaven oftener.
For the rich owe great reckonings, and walk really slowly   210
The highway to Heaven, for their riches hinder them:

> *Dives difficile intrabit in regnum coelorum.*
> (A rich man shall hardly enter into the Kingdom
>   of Heaven.)[22]

There, the poor press ahead of the rich, with packs
    on their backs:

> *Opera enim illorum sequuntur illos*
> (And their works do follow them),[23]

And blatantly and boldly, as beggars do, they ask
Perpetual bliss for their poverty and patience.

> *Beati pauperes spiritu: quoniam ipsorum est regnum
>   coelorum.*
> (Blessed are the poor in spirit: for theirs is the
>   kingdom of Heaven.)[24]

   But Pride reigns in riches rather than in poverty,
And his mansion is in the master more often than in
    the man;
For Pride has no power over patient poverty,
Nor may any of the Seven Sins stay long with it,
Nor have power over poverty if patience attend it:
The poor man is always prompt in pleasing the rich man,   220
And obedient to his bidding, for the sake of his bits of bread.
But obedience and boastfulness do constant battle,
And each hates the other in all human life.
   If Wrath wrestles with the poor man, Wrath comes
    off worse;
If they take a quarrel to Court, the poor man pleads quietly,
For loud and abusive language would lose his case.
So his looks are lowly, and he lets his speech be likeable,
Who must ask other men for meal or for money.
   If Gluttony grapples with poor men, he gains the less,
For their earnings do not run to buying rich food,   230
And gluttony for even good ale makes them go to
    a cold bed,
With head all uncovered, and awkwardly twisted;

And, when they shift or stretch, only straw for sheeting.
So, for their gluttony and great sloth, they do grievous
      penance,
And cry *welladay* when they wake and weep for cold,
And sometimes for their sins; so they are never merry
Without some admixture of mourning, and misfortune
      as well.
If Cupidity tries to trip the poor man, he can hardly
      take hold,
And neither can ever take the other by the neck!
It is common knowledge that Cupidity has keen desires   240
And has hands and arms of huge extent,
While Poverty is a poor shrimp who must peer up
      to his navel;
And a boring bout it is, between long and short!
   If Avarice would injure the poor, he has little advantage;
For Poverty has only pockets to put his wealth in,
Whereas Avarice keeps his in cupboards and in coffers
      bound with iron –
And which is more easily rifled? There is less row
From a beggar's bag than from a coffer bound in iron!
   Lechery does not like the poor, for they give little silver,
Cannot dine on delicate food, nor drink wine often.   250
Broken reeds in brothels! – which would all break down
If they depended on poor men, and be un-pantiled!
   If Sloth pursues the poor man, and he serves God ill,
Then Adversity will teach him to think again,
That God is his highest helper, and no human being,
And his lackey (as Our Lord Himself said)[25] in the livery
      of Mankind.
And whether He helps him or not, He bears the sign of
      poverty,
And in such garb Our Saviour saved all Mankind.
Therefore poor men who are patient may expect and ask,
After their earthly ending, the bliss of Heaven's kingdom.   260
   Much more hardily may he ask who might, here
      on Earth,
Have enjoyed lands and lordship and the lusts of the flesh,

But for love of God left it all and lived like a beggar.
He is like a maiden who leaves her mother for a man's love;
Leaves her father and all her friends, and follows her mate:
Such a maiden is much to be loved by the man who
    weds her,
More than a maiden who was married through brokage,
By assent of several parties, and money to seal the bargain –
An agreement made for avarice, not by affection shared.
The first girl is like all folk who forsake their possessions   270
Purposing to be patient and make Poverty their mate
(That sib to God Himself; and to His saints.)'
   'God hear my oath!' said Haukyn. 'This is high praise
    of poverty!
But what does patient poverty imply, exactly?'
    'Paupertas,' said Patience, *'est odibile bonum; remotio
     curarum, possessio sine calumnia, donum Dei,
     sanitatis mater; absque solicitudine semita, sapientiae
     temperatrix, negotium sine damno; incerta fortuna;
     absque solicitudine felicitas.'*[26]
   'I cannot construe that,' said Haukyn. 'You must counsel
    me in English.'
   'In English,' said Patience, 'it is hard to explain in full;
Yet I will say something about it, within your understanding:
    Poverty is a hateable good, the removing of cares,
     possession without cheating, a gift of God, the
     mother of good health; a narrow footpath without
     anxiety; the governess of wisdom, business without
     loss; doubtful fate; happiness without worry.
Poverty is the prime object of Pride's hatred,
And anything abhorrent to Pride can only be good!   280
Conscience knows well that contrition brings comfort
    to men;
Though in itself a sorrow, it brings solace to the soul;
Just so, poverty is properly penance done with joy,
And produces in the body pure and spiritual health.
   Therefore *paupertas est odibile bonum*,
As contrition is a comfort and a cure for souls.
Poverty seldom sits upon a sworn jury,

Nor are poor men enjoined as justices, to judge others,
Nor as mayors to lead other men, nor as ministers of
    the Crown;
Seldom is a poor man appointed to punish others:
    remotio curarum.
Therefore poverty and poor men put in practice the
    commandment,   290
    Nolite judicare quemquam
    (Judge not, that ye be not judged).
And thirdly – rarely does a poor man grow rich, save by
    rightful heirship;
He does not win money with false weights or warrantless
    measures,
Nor borrow from folk near-by too much to pay back easily:
    possessio sine calumnia.
Fourthly, it is a fortune by which the soul flourishes
In sobriety, far from all sin; and still there is more:
It makes the flesh forgo a great many foolish things,
With a corresponding comfort that this is Christ's own gift:
    donum Dei.
Fifthly, it is mother of health, and a friend in all ordeals,
Leechcraft for all the land, a lover of cleanness: *sanitatis mater.*
Sixth, it is the Path of Peace – yes, even through
    Alton Pass[27]   300
Poverty might progress without peril from robbers.
For where poverty passes, peace follows after;
And your heart is the hardier, the less you have upon you.
Therefore Seneca says *paupertas est absque solicitudine
    semita,*[28]
And makes a man hardy of heart among a host of thieves:
    Cantabit pauper coram latrone viator.
    (The poor traveller will sing in the presence of the
        highwayman.)
Seventh, it is wisdom's well, and few words come from it;
For lords praise it little, nor listen to its opinion;
It turns its tongue towards Truth, and desires no treasure:
    Sapientia temperatrix.
Eighth, it is an honest labourer, unwilling to take more

Than well-deserved wages, in winter or in summer,   310
And in commerce cares nothing for loss, but for increase
    of charity:
     Negotium sine damno.
Ninth, it is sweet to the soul, far sweeter than sugar;
For poverty's proper bread is perfect patience,
And sobriety is a sweet drink, and sickness's best doctor.
This I learned from a lettered man, for love of Our Lord –
St Augustine said to be poor is a blessed life, without bother
For body or for soul: *absque solicitudine felicitas.*
Now may God, Who gives all good things, grant rest
    to the soul
Of the man who first wrote to teach us what poverty
    might mean!'
  'Alas!' said Haukyn the Active Man, 'that after my
    baptism   320
I did not die and get buried, for Do-Well's sake!
How hateful it is, to live and have to sin!
Yet sin pursues us for ever.' And he grew sorrowful,
And wept from watery eyes, and bewailed the times
That ever he did a deed that displeased dear God;
He sobbed and sighed often, and well-nigh swooned,
For having ever owned land or lordship, no matter how little,
Or more mastery over other men than over himself.
'God's my witness, I'm unworthy to wear *any* clothes,
Neither shirt nor shoes, except only, for shame's sake,   330
One rag to cover my carcass!' He cried aloud for mercy,
And wept and wailed. And with all this, I awoke.

PASSUS 15

Yet after my waking, it was still a long while
Before I had full knowledge and feeling of Do-Well.
My wits waxed and waned until I was crazy;
Few men approved my life, and many abused it,
Alleging that I was a losel, and loth to be humble
Towards lords and ladies or any of that lot –
Such as parsons in furred apparel, with pendants of silver.
To Sergeants-at-Law and such I never once said,
'God bless you, my lords!' nor did low obeisance.
And so, folk thought me a fool; and I raved in that folly   10
Till Reason took pity on me, and rocked me to sleep.
    Then I saw, as if by sorcery, a most subtle creature:
He had neither tongue nor teeth, but he told me where
      I was going,
And whence I came, and my character. I conjured him, at last,
If he were a creature of Christ, for Christ's love to tell me.
    'I *am* a creature of Christ, widely known as a Christian,
Even in Christ's Court itself, and as one of His kinsmen.
Neither Peter the Porter nor St Paul with his falchion[1]
Will defend its door against me, knock I never so late.
At midnight or midday my voice is known,   20
And every member of His Court makes me right welcome.'
    'What are you called in that Court, among Christ's people?'
'When I quicken Man's carcass, I am called *Anima*: Life.
When I am a wisher, a user of will, I am *Animus*: Soul.
Because I know and comprehend, I am called *Mens*: Mind.
When I make moan to God, my name is *Memoria*:
      Recollection.[2]
When I lay down decrees, and do as Truth teaches,
Then *Ratio* is my right name – or, in English, Reason.
When I perceive what men say, my first name is Sense –
Which means wisdom and understanding, the well-spring
      of all skills.   30
When I claim or do not claim, buy or withdraw my custom,

Then I am called Conscience – God's clerk and notary.
When I love Our Lord truly, and all other men,
My name is Loyal-Love, or in Latin *Amor*.
When I flee from the flesh, and forsake the carcass,
I am inexpressible spirit, and *Spiritus* is my name.
Augustine and Isidore, the one as much as the other,
First found me these names; and it is for you to choose:
Call me what name you wish, now that you know them all.

> *Anima pro diversis actionibus diversa nomina sortitur:*
> *dum vivificat corpus, anima est; dum vult, animus est;*
> *dum scit, mens est; dum recolit, memoria est. Dum*
> *judicat, ratio est; dum sentit, sensus est; dum amat,*
> *amor est; dum negat vel consentit, conscientia est:*
> *dum spirat, spiritus est.'*

> (According to its different functions, the soul receives
> different names: in animating the body, its name is
> Life; in exercising will, its name is Soul; in having
> knowledge, it is Mind; in recollecting, it is Memory.
> In judging, it is Reason; in feeling, it is Sense; in
> loving, it is Love; in denying or consenting, it is
> Conscience; in being the breath of life, it is Spirit.)[3]

'You must be a bishop,' I said, by way of a joke.   40
'For bishops, once being ordained, go by all sorts of names,
Such as *presul* and *pontifex* and *metropolitanus*,
> *Episcopus* and *pastor*, and piles of others.'[4]

'That is true,' he returned. 'Now I see your intention!
You need to know the reason for the many names they have –
And for mine too, I fancy, from the way you speak!'

'Yes, sir,' I said, 'so long as no one minds.
All science under the sun, and all subtle arts,
Were it possible, I would know and hold naturally within
my heart!'

'That proves you imperfect,' he said, 'and one of Pride's
knights;   50
Such longings and lusts made Lucifer fall from Heaven:
> *Ascendam super altitudinem nubium, similis ero Altissimo.*
> (I will ascend above the heights of the clouds; I will be
> like the Most High.)[5]

It would be unnatural, and against all kinds of reason,
That any being should know all things, except Christ alone.
Solomon speaks against men such as you, and despises
    their minds.
    He says, *Sicut qui mel multum comedit, non est ei bonum:*
        sic qui scrutator est majestatis, opprimetur a gloria.
    (It is not good to eat much honey; so for men to search
        their own glory, is not glory.)[6]
Remade into English, this means, for men with their senses,
That the man who eats too much honey does a mischief to
    his belly,
And the more a man hears of profitable matters,
Unless he acts upon them, he is doubly harmed.
"Blessed is he," says St Bernard, "who reads the Scriptures
And turns their words to deeds, to his utmost ability."[7]   60
The hunger to have and apprehend great knowledge
Pushed our first parents out of Paradise:
    Scientiae appetitus hominem immortalitatis gloria spoliavit.
    (The lust for knowledge despoiled Man of the glory of
        immortality.)[8]
As honey is hard to digest, and harmful to the stomach,
So they who seek by reason to understand the roots
Of God and His great might, must forgo His grace.
For in such longing lie pride and lust of the flesh,
Against Christ's counsel, and all clerical teaching:
    Non plus sapere quam oportet sapere.
    (To know no more than is proper to know.)[9]
You friars, and experts in the Faith, the lay-folks' preachers,
You are mooting inscrutable matters when you mention
    the Trinity;
So that lay-folk lose their belief, all too often.   70
Better did the bulk of you Doctors abandon such teaching,
To teach men the Ten Commandments, and touch on the
    Seven Deadly Sins,
And the branches that burgeon from them, and bring men
    to Hell;
And of how folk will dissipate on follies all five senses:
Friars, like other church-folk, go to foolish expense

On their convents, their clothing, and conceit in their
    learning –
More in pomp than in pure charity. The people know
    that's true;
I'm not lying, look you! You become lords' toadies,
Paying reverence to the rich with regard to their money:
    Confundantur omnes qui adorant sculptilia.
    (Confounded be all they that serve graven images.) [10]
And elsewhere:
    Ut quid diligitis vanitatem, et quaeritis mendacium?
    (How long will ye love vanity, and seek after lying?) [11]
Go to the gloss on that text, all you great scholars;   80
If I lie to you, in my illiteracy, lead me out to be burned! [12]
For it seems to me you will forgo alms from no one,
Whether usurers or whores or grasping hucksters either;
You bow low to the lords who may load you with gold
(Against your Rule, and religion – I refer this to Jesus,
Who said to His disciples, *Ne sitis personarum acceptores*: [13]
    Thou shalt not respect persons, neither take a gift.)
  I could write a long book about all this business;
But I shall recount (of those with cure of Christian souls),
For truth's sake, what the Fathers tell: take heed who wishes!
  As holiness and high worth spring from Holy Church   90
Through religiously-living men who teach the Law of God:
Just so, out of Holy Church all evils arise
When an imperfect priesthood are the preachers and teachers.
We see a symbol of this on summer trees,
When some boughs bear leaves, but others are naked;
When boughs are thus bare, there must be badness at the roots.
Now, the parsons and priests and preachers of Holy Church
Are the roots of right belief; if they rule folk well;
And where those roots are rotten, reason requires
There shall be no flowers or fruits, nor fair green leaves.   100
So if you lettered men could leave your lust for rich clothing,
And be kind and courteous, as clerks should, in the use of
    Christ's bounty,
And be truthful of tongue, and keep your tails chaste,
Loathing to hear lewd talk, and loth to accept

Tithes from dishonest earnings by tillage or trade:
Then laymen would be loth to neglect your teaching,
And they would reform wrongdoers, if *you* were exemplars
Instead of preaching and not practising – which is pure
　　hypocrisy.
Hypocrisy in Latin[14] is likened to a dunghill
Concealed under snow, and with snakes inside it;　　　　　　110
Or to a whitewashed wall, with filth underneath.
Many priests and preachers and prelates are like that:
You are whitewashed with fine words, and with clothing too;
But most unwinning are the words and the works that
　　you hide.
　St John Chrysostom[15] speaks of clergy and priests:
　　　Sicut de templo omne bonum progreditur, sic de templo
　　　　omne malum procedit.
　　　Si sacerdotium integrum fuerit, tota floret ecclesia; si autem
　　　　corruptum fuerit, omnium fides marcida est.
　　　Si sacerdotium fuerit in peccatis, totus populus convertitur
　　　　ad peccandum.
　　　Sicut cum videris arborem pallidam et marcidam, intelligis
　　　　quod vitium habet in radice,
　　　Ita cum videris populum indisciplinatum et irreligiosum,
　　　　sine dubio sacerdotium ejus non est sanum.
　　(Just as all good proceeds from the Temple, so also from
　　　the Temple proceeds all that is evil.
　　If the priesthood be uncorrupted, the whole Church
　　　will flourish; but if it be corrupt, all men's faith is
　　　enfeebled.
　　If the priesthood be in the midst of sins, the whole
　　　people is directed towards sin.
　　Just as when you see a tree to be yellow and withered,
　　　you understand that there is rottenness at its root,
　　So when you see an undisciplined and irreligious
　　　populace, without doubt its priesthood is unsound.)
　If an ignorant man could correctly construe that Latin,
And identify the author, I should think it a wonder;
But how if many priests were to bear, not baselards and
　　brooches,[16]

But a rosary in their hand and a book under their arm?
Sir John and Sir Geoffrey[17] wear silver girdles,   120
And a short-sword or a stiletto with studs of silver-gilt.
But the breviary should be their instrument for reciting
    the Office,
Which they're unwilling to say unless someone slips
    them silver!
Alas, you unlettered men, you lavish too much on priests!
Wise God would not allow it, were not all of it gained
Wickedly and with falsehood – and goes to wicked men
(Namely, imperfect priests, and preachers who are venal,
And executors and sub-deans, and summoners and
    sweethearts),
So that what was gained by guile, is degradingly spent:
Pimps and prostitutes get the profit of such goods;   130
And God's folk, in default of them, are enfeebled and perish.
  Some curates and clerics of the Church, close-fisted all
    their lives,
Let all the gold they leave go straight to good-for-nothings;
Or one such dies intestate, and then the Bishop enters,
And he and his men make merry with the money,
Saying, "He was a niggard, and he never had a halfpenny
For friend or foreigner – may the Fiend have his soul!
He kept a wretched household all his life long;
All that he saved and scrimped, we'll spend on pleasure!"
  Be he learned or illiterate, that man loth to spend,   140
That's the way his goods go, when he gives up the ghost.
But for good men, God knows, there is great mourning;
Men bemoan good meal-givers, and bear them in mind
With prayers and penances, in perfect charity.'
  'What is Charity?' I asked. And he said: 'A childlike thing:
    Nisi efficiamini sicut parvuli, non intrabitis in regnum
      coelorum.
    (Except ye be converted, and become as little children,
      ye shall not enter into the kingdom of Heaven.)[18]
Yet it is not infantile or foolish, but free and liberal
    good will.'
  'Where can one find such a friend, with so free a heart?

I have lived in this land, and my name is Long Will,
But I never found free-handed Charity before or behind me!
Men are often merciful to mendicants and poor people,   150
Or will lend if they believe their loan will be honestly repaid;
But Charity such as Paul praised as best, such as pleased
    our Saviour –
    Non inflatur, non est ambitiosa, non quaerit quae sua sunt.
    (It is not puffed up, doth not behave itself unseemly,
      seeketh not her own.)[19]
I never saw such a man, so help me God,
As would not ask for his own, and also covet
Things that he did not need, and nab them if he could!
The clergy tells us that Christ can be found everywhere,
Though I certainly never saw Him, except mirrored in *me*:
    Per speculum in aenigmate; tunc enim facie ad faciem.
    (Through a glass darkly; but then face to face.)[20]
And by what I am told of Charity, I take it as truth
That he's not found where men fight, or haggle for bargains.'
  'Charity does not challenge or chaffer or claim;   160
He is as proud of a penny as if of a pound of gold,
As glad of a gown of grey homespun
As of a tunic from Tartary, or of choicest scarlet.[21]
He is glad with all who are glad, and is good to the wicked,
And believes and loves all whom Our Lord created.
He curses no creature, he does not continue in anger,
He does not like lying, or laughing men to scorn.
All that men say, he accepts, and receives with pleasure,
And mildly endures all manner of misfortunes;
He covets no earthly commodity, but bliss in the Kingdom
    of Heaven.'   170
  'He has no riches or rents, nor any rich friends?'
  'Of rents or of riches he makes no reckoning,
For no friend that finds him in need ever fails him.
Fiat-voluntas-tua, "Thy will be done", always finds him;
And he sups sparely on the soup of *Spera-in-Deo* –
    Trust-in-the-Lord.
He can portray the Pater-noster well, and paint it with
    Hail-Marys.[22]

At whiles it is his wont to walk on pilgrimage
To where the poor lie in prison awaiting pardon;
He brings them no bread, but a much sweeter food,
And loves them as Our Lord bids, and looks to their
    welfare.   180
   When he is weary of this work, he will sometimes
Labour for a mile's length in a laundry;[23]
For eagerly he addresses himself to youth's errors,
And to pride and its appurtenances, and presses them together
And batters them upon his breast till they are beaten clean.
Then he lays into them a long rime, labouring with groans
    of contrition,[24]
And with warm water from his eyes he afterwards washes
    them.
Yet he sings as he does so, and sometimes says, weeping,
    "*Cor contritum et humiliatum, Deus, non despicies.*"
    (A broken and a contrite heart, O God, thou wilt not
      despise.)[25]
  'By Christ!' quoth I, 'I wish I knew him – no creature
    more so!'
'Without help from Piers the Ploughman, you will never
    see him in person.'   190
  'Cannot the clergy find him, the keepers of Holy
    Church?'
  'The clergy can know man only by works or words,
But Piers the Ploughman can penetrate more deeply
Into men's motives, and the reason why so many suffer:
    Cum vidisset Jesus cogitationes eorum, dixit: Ut quid
      cogitatis mala in cordibus vestris?
    (And Jesus, knowing their thoughts, said, Wherefore
      think ye evil in your hearts?)[26]
For there are many proud-hearted men who are mild in
    their speech
And biddable in their bearing towards burgesses and lords,
Yet who, meeting poor people, have pepper in their noses,
And who lour like lions if someone belittles their doings.
There are beggars and bums one might take for beadsmen,
Looking meek as lambs, and of holy life-habit;   200

But it is more to get their meals in the easiest manner
Than for penance or self-perfection, that *these* assume poverty.

 Neither clerisy nor outward colour can reveal Charity to you,
Nor words, nor deeds, but only the knowledge of men's hearts;
And those are known to no clerk or other creature on Earth,
Except Piers the Ploughman alone: Peter, that is: Christ![27]

 The Lollards do not know Charity, nor do land-loping
  "hermits",[28]
Nor ancresses with alms-chests: all these are fakers.
Fie upon fakers and all who show them favour!
Charity is God's champion, though as gentle as a child; 210
He is the merriest of mouth when he sits at meals;
The love that lies in his heart makes him lively of speech
And as companionable and comforting as Christ Himself:
 Nolite fieri, sicut hypocritae, tristes.
 (Be not, as the hypocrites, of a sad countenance.)[29]
For I have seen him sometimes in silks, sometimes in
  homespun,
In both grey wool and grey furs with golden trappings,
But all alike giving gladly to any who were needy.

 Edmund and Edward were each of them kings,[30]
But esteemed as saints since Charity dwelt with them.

 I have also seen him reading and singing in Church;
Riding, or running along in ragged clothes; 220
But I never beheld him cadging like a beggar.
He is readiest to walk in rich robes,
Cleanly clothed in cyprus or in Tartary-cloth,
Capped, and with crimped hair round a shaven crown.[31]
In a friar's frock he was at one time found,
But those days are far-off, in the time of St Francis;
He has been seldom seen since then in that Order.

 He regards rich men highly, and accepts robes from them
If they live their lives honestly and without wile:
 Beatus est dives.
 (Blessed is the rich that is found without blemish, and
  hath not gone after gold.)[32]
He comes often to the King's court, when the counsellors
  are honest; 230

But if Covetousness joins the Council, he will not
     come to it.
He seldom consorts with the King's court-jesters,
For they brawl and backbite and bear false witness.
     In the Consistory, before the Commissary, he comes rarely,
For their law-suits are long-drawn-out, unless you use bribery;
And there they make and unmake marriages, for money;
What Christ and Conscience had closely conjoined,
Those Doctors of Law undo dishonestly.
     Among archbishops and bishops and prelates of
          Holy Church,
He was at one time wont to remain,   240
And share-out Christ's patrimony piecemeal to poor people.
But Avarice keeps the keys now, and saves everything for
     his kinsmen,
His executors, and his servants – and some for the Bishops'
     children.
     Now, I blame nobody; but – make us better, O Lord,
And give us grace, good God, to follow Charity!
For whoever may meet him, finds him hating such manners
As condemning and cursing and commending and boasting,
Fault-finding, flattering, frowning sternly,
Claiming and coveting and crying for more:
          In pace in idipsum dormiam, et requiescam.
          (I will lay me down in peace, and sleep.)[33]
All his living and livelihood is love under Christ's Passion;   250
He does not beg or beseech, nor borrows to repay;
He does mischief to no man, nor makes trouble with
     his mouth.
     Among Christian men, such mildness should prevail;
In all kinds of anguish, they should have this at heart,
That whatsoever they have suffered, God suffered more
     for us:
He showed by example what we should do – take no
     vengeance
On foes that treat us falsely: that is Our Father's will.
It is obvious to all, that if God had not willed it,
Judas and the Jews could never have put Jesus on the Cross,

Nor have martyred Peter and Paul, nor have imprisoned
     them.   260
Christ suffered as an example that we should suffer too,
And said to such as will suffer that *the patient conquer.*
There are texts enough,' said Reason, 'and true examples
     to study,
In *Legenda Sanctorum*, the Lives of the Holy Saints,
Of the penances and poverty and pains that they endured,
In hunger and heat and in all kinds of hurt.
Saints Antony and Aegidius, and other Holy Fathers,[34]
Dwelt in the wilderness among wild beasts;
And monks and mendicants, men living alone
In caverns and cubby-holes, conversed rarely.   270
Neither Antony nor Aegidius, nor any hermit then,
Had leopards or lions to bring them food to live on,
But, we read in books, the birds of the air.
(Except that Aegidius summoned to his cell a hind,
And managed to live on the milk of that mild creature;
Yet he did not have her daily to reduce his hunger,
But only from time to time, as the book teaches and tells us.)
    Antony, every day at about noontime,
Had a bird that brought him bread, by which he lived;
And God, if that saint had a guest, gave enough for both.   280
    Paul, the primary hermit,[35] had so pleached himself in
As to be out of sight behind moss and leaves;
But the birds for many winters brought him food,
     none-the-less;
And finally he founded the Augustinian Friars' Order.
Paul the Apostle, after preaching, wove baskets,[36]
Earning with his hands what his hunger demanded.
Peter fished for his food, like his friend Andrew.[37]
They sold some, and they seethed some; and so they
     both lived.
Mary Magdalen lived on morning-dew and roots,[38]
But more upon remorse and on memories of Our Lord.   290
In a week I could not recount all the cases
Of those who for love of Our Lord lived thus for long years.
Neither leopard nor lion that prowled those lands,

Nor bear nor boar, nor other wild beast,
But fell at their feet and fondled them with their tails.
And could the creatures have spoken, by Christ I believe
They would have fed those folk before the birds did.
For all such courtesy as beasts can, they showed often to
      those recluses,
In licking them, and in lowliness, in the lands where
      they walked.
But God sent the fowls of the air with food, and not
      fierce beasts,   300
In emblem that meek men should be fed by mild creatures.
By this rule, righteous men should feed the religious,
And loyal believers bring food to men of holy life.
Then lords and ladies would loathe injustice,
Or taking too much money from their tenants,
When they found the very friars refusing their alms
And bidding them take it back whence it was borrowed.
For we are all God's fowls, and are forced to wait
Till other birds bring us that by which we live.
If you had broth and bread enough, and small beer
      to drink,   310
And a single dish of some sort to set beside them,
You Religious would eat right well – and so your own
      Rule says.
      Nunquam rugiet onager cum habuerit herbam? aut mugiet
        bos cum ante praesepe plenum steterit?
      (Doth the wild ass bray when he hath grass? or loweth
        the ox over his fodder? ... The nature of the brute
        beasts condemns you, for among them ordinary food
        suffices; your sin proceeds from luxury.)[39]
   If laymen knew Latin enough, they would look where
      their gifts went,
And consider for five or six days before
They signed their estates away to monks or canons.
Alas! You lords and ladies are ill-advised
To take from your heirs all that your ancestors left you,
And render it, in return for prayers, to the rich
Who are already endowed and enfeoffed to pray for others.

Who today performs this prophecy, among living
    people –   320
    Dispersit; dedit pauperibus
    (He hath dispersed, he hath given to the poor)?[40]
If any people perform it, they are these "poor" friars!
For what they beg, all about, they spend on their buildings,
And some upon themselves and such as labour for them:
So they take from them that have, and give to those that
    have not!
    But you rich clergy and cavaliers and commoners
Are acting as I would be if I had a forest
Full of pleasant trees, but plotted and planned
How I might plant more in among the rest.
Just so you rich men give robes to clothe the rich,
And help those who help you, and give to those
    that have –   330
As if one filled a firkin with fresh river-water,
And went off with that water to widen the Thames!
You are really the same, you rich men, who give robes
    and food
And help to people who have as much as you have yourselves.
And the rich Religious should rather feed beggars
Than the rich burghers are bound to, as the Book teaches:
    Quia sacrilegium est res pauperum non pauperibus dare.
    Item, peccatoribus dare, est daemonibus immolare. Item,
    Monache, si indiges et accipis, potius das quam accipis.
    Si autem non eges, et accipis, rapis. Porro, non indiget
    monachus, si habeat quod naturae sufficit.
    (For it is sacrilege not to give to the poor what belongs
        to the poor. Also: *Giving presents to defaulters/Is laying*
        gifts on devils' altars. Also: O monk, if thou art needy,
        and takest gifts, thou givest more than thou takest.
        But if thou art not needy, to take gifts is to steal.
    Moreover: A monk is not poor if he has what suffices
        nature.)[41]
Therefore I counsel all Christians to conform with Charity;
For charity, unchallengeably, discharges sin from the soul,
And many a prisoner from Purgatory, by means of prayer.

But there are faults in the folk who should guard the Faith; 340
Whereby lay folk are feebler, and less firm, in theirs.
As snide contains base alloy, yet looks like sterling,
And is marked as if from the Mint, but of frangible metal:
So we find many folk nowadays, fair of speech,
In tonsure and christening the King of Heaven's currency,
But the metal (man's soul) misalloyed with sin.
Both lettered and illiterate are now thus misalloyed,
So that no man now loves his neighbour or Our Lord.
Through wars and wickedness and immoderate weather
The weatherwise seaman and well-read scholar 350
Have lost their faith in the skies and philosophers' lore.
    Astrologers every day find their art fails them,
Who once could warn us of things that were to come.
Shipmen and shepherds, in charge of ships and sheep,
Could read in the clouds what weather was coming,
And were able to warn us of whirlwinds and storms.
The tillers who tended the soil could tell their masters,
From the seed they had sown, how much it was best to sell
Or to lend or to live-on: the land was so trustworthy.
But now the folk of both flood and field fail, 360
The shipmen and the shepherds and the tillers shilly-shally
Between one course and another, having no certain
    knowledge.
Astrologers also are at their wits' end,
For what they computed from the spheres comes out the
    contrary.
Grammar, the ground of all teaching, now baffles girls
    and boys;
Not one of our new learners today takes pains enough
To write correct verses or compose a competent letter;
Not one in a hundred can construe the Classics,
Nor read one letter of any language but Latin and English.
Look at any level of learning, you'll find Flim-flam
    in charge, 370
And his colleague Toady as an apt assistant:
I marvel at such matters among us all.
Doctors who study decretals, Masters of Divinity,

Men who should have mastered all manner of knowledge,
And be able to answer all arguments in quodlibets:
(I scarcely dare say it, for shame) if such men were examined,
They would fail in philosophy and physic both.[42]
Therefore I fear that officials of Holy Church
May also make omissions, in their Offices and Hours.
If they do make omissions (and I hope not), our faith will
    supply them;   380
For, as clergy at the feast of Corpus Christi counsel and sing,
Simple faith is sufficient to save the ignorant.[43]

    Therefore Saracens may be saved, and Scribes and Jews;
Alas, then, that our teachers teach otherwise than they live,
And by their lax lives make laymen guiltier towards God.
For Saracens own something similar to our faith;
For they believe in, and love, one Almighty God,
As we, both learned and lay, believe in one God.
But a man called Mohammed brought the men of Syria
Into dire disbelief; and he did it thus:[44]   390
He was formerly of our faith, but, failing for the Papacy,
He strayed into Syria, where by subtle devices
He tamed a turtle-dove, and at all times fed her;
And the corn that she always ate, he laid in his ear.
Now, when he preached to the people in the places he visited,
He would let this culver come and seek corn from his ear,
For it was to this end that he had taught and trained her;
And he made the folk fall to their knees, for he swore in
    his sermons
That the culver had come down from God in Heaven
As a messenger to Mohammed, for men's instruction.   400
Thus, by his wily wits and a white dove,
Mohammed led men to misbelief, and women too;
And learned and unlearned, there, still live by his laws.

    Now, since our Saviour let the Saracens be so beguiled
By a once-Christian cleric, accursed of soul . . .
But for dread of death I dare not tell the truth,
How the clergy of England feed a culver, called Covetousness,
And act so in Mohammed's manner that no man follows
    honesty.

Anchorites and hermits and monks and friars
Are peers of the Apostles if they perfect their lives.   410
The Father of true faith would never wish that His ministers
Should take alms from tyrants that oppress true Christians,
But should do as Antony did, and Dominic and Francis,
And Benedict and Bernard, who had been their first teachers
Of how to live on little, in lowly houses, on loyal men's alms.[45]
Grace should grow like a green tree, through their
    good living;
And folk that have any form of sickness should find
    themselves
The better in body and soul for these men's beseeching God.
Their prayers and penances should pacify all
Who are at enmity, were these honest beadsmen: 420
    Petite, et dabitur vobis.
    (Ask, and it shall be given you.)[46]
Salt is a preservative, or so say housewives:
    Vos estis sal terrae.
    (Ye are the salt of the earth.)[47]
The heads of Holy Church, were they holy themselves,
Would be called by Christ "salt" for preserving
    Christian souls:
    Quod si sal evanuerit; in quo salietur?
    (But if the salt have lost his savour, wherewith shall
      it be salted?)[48]
For fresh meat or fish, with insufficient salt,
Is certainly insipid, whether seethed or baked.
So indeed is a man's soul, when set no good example
By those of Holy Church who should teach us the Highway,
And guide us, and go before us like good standard-bearers,
And by their own bravery embolden fallers-back.
   Eleven holy men converted all the world[49]   430
To the true faith; how much lighter a task it seems
If all manner of men (we have so many Masters
And priests and preachers, and a Pope as their head)
Became the salt that should save the souls of men!
   All England and Wales was at one time heathen,
Till Gregory appointed priests to come here and preach.

Augustine at Canterbury christened the King;[50]
And by miracles, as all men may read, converted that
    march-land
To Christ and Christendom and the honour of the Cross.
He baptised folk fast, and taught them the Faith   440
More through miracles than through much preaching,
As well through his works as through his holy words;
But he told them what baptism and faith were about.
    Cloth that comes straight from the loom cannot well
    be worn:
One must full it with one's feet, or in fulling-mills,
Wash it well in water, comb it with teasels;
Then, well tucked and tentered, it reaches the tailor's hands.
So a new-born baby, brought fresh from the womb,
Till christened in Christ's name, and confirmed by
    the Bishop,
Is a heathen still, and its soul is helpless to reach Heaven.   450
    "Heathen" means "of the heath" or untilled land,
Like the wild beasts that thrive in the wider wilderness,
Rude and unreasoning, and running without restraint.
    You will remember how in St Matthew a certain man
    planned a feast;
He fed his guests no deer-flesh or roast pheasants,
But on flesh of tame fowl that followed him when
    he whistled:
    Ecce, prandium meum paravi, tauri mei et altilia
      occisa sunt, et omnia parata.
    (Behold, I have prepared my dinner: my oxen and my
      fatlings are killed, and all things are ready.)[51]
Also on calves' flesh he fed those folk that he loved,
For the calf betokens cleanness and keeping of the laws:[52]
As the cow feeds the calf on her milk until it
    becomes an ox,
So love and loyalty sustain true believers;   460
And maidens and mild men desire mercy and truth;
Just as the cow's calf covets sweet milk
So must righteous men desire mercy and truth.
By the hand-fed fowls are meant those of God's folk

Who are loth to lose Him without learning by fables.
Just as capons in the courtyard come to men's whistle,
And follow the whistler for the sake of food,
So simple men without subtle reasoning
May love and believe by example of the learnèd,
And wise men's works and words are their thought
    and belief   470
And as fowls find their food by following a whistler,
So these hope to have Heaven by heeding the call of
    their pastors.
By the man who made the feast, Majesty is meant;
That is, God in His grace gives all men bliss:
Wonders and high winds are his warning whistles,
When He wishes to call us to come into His courtesy
And be fed and feasted for ever more.
    And who are those that excuse themselves? Parsons
    and priests,
The heads of Holy Church, who have all they want *here*,
And without trouble – taking their tithes from true
    men's toil.   480
They will be angry at my saying this, but as witnesses I call
Both Matthew and Mark, and the Psalm *Lord, remember*
    David.
    Ecce, audivimus eam in Ephratah.
    (Lo, we heard of it at Ephrata.)[53]
What Pope or prelate now performs what Christ bade?
    Euntes in mundum universum, praedicate Evangelium.
    (Go ye into all the world, and preach the Gospel to
      every creature.)[54]
Alas that men should remain, who believe in Mohammed,
While the Pope ordains so many prelates to preach
As Bishop of Nazareth, of Nineveh, of Naphtali or of
    Damascus![55]
Let them work as Christ wishes, if they want such titles,
And be true pastors, and preach the Passion of Jesus,
As He Himself said, and so live and die –
    Bonus pastor animam suam dat pro ovibus suis.
    (The good shepherd giveth his life for the sheep.)[56]

He said this for the salvation of Saracens and the like,   490
For unChristian as well as Christian he meant the words
    Ite vos in vineam meam.
    (Go ye also into the vineyard.)[57]
And since the Saracens and Scribes and Jews
Share a little of our belief, the lighter (surely) the task
Of whoever should try to convert them, and teach them
    the Trinity.
    Quaerite, et invenietis.
    (Seek and ye shall find.)[58]
  It arouses one's pity to read how the righteous lived,
Mortifying their flesh and forsaking their desires;
And, far from their kith and kin, they went poorly clad,
And barely bedded, conscience their only book,
And rejoicing in the Rood as their only riches:
    Mihi autem absit gloriari nisi in cruce Domini.
    (God forbid I should glory, save in the Cross of
      our Lord.)[59]
Then there was plenty and peace among poor and rich;   500
But now it rouses pity to read how the red gold-piece
Is reverenced more than the Rood, and received with
    more worship
Than Christ's Cross which overcame death and deadly sin.
  And now there is war and woe; and the reason why
Is covetousness for that cross on the gold crown-piece;
Both the rich and the religious honour the rood
That is graven on groats and on gold nobles.
For coveting that cross, the clergy of Holy Church
Shall be tumbled as the Templars[60] were – the time is
    coming fast.
Have you not heard, you wise men, how these men
    honoured   510
Treasure more than truth? I dare not tell all the facts,
But Reason and Rightful Judgment condemned that
    Religious Order.
Just so, you clergy, they shall quickly condemn your
    covetousness,
And doom the "Church's Dowry",[61] and dispose your pride:

Deposuit potentes de sede, et exaltavit humiles.
>   (He hath put down the mighty from their seats,
>   and exalted them of low degree.)[62]
>   If knighthood and native intelligence and the nation's
>   conscience
> Are loyal allies, then believe well, you Bishops,
> You shall soon lose for ever your lordships over lands,
> And live like Levites, as Our Lord teaches,
>   *Per decimas et primitias.*
>   (By your tithes and heave offerings.)[63]
>   When Constantine, of his courtesy, gave Holy Kirk
>   endowments
> Of lands and labourers and lordships and rents,   520
> An angel was heard to cry, in the air above Rome,
> "The Church's dowry has today drunk poison,
> And all who hold Peter's power are poisoned by it."[64]
> Would there might be a medicine to amend those prelates
> Who should pray for peace, but whose possessions
>   prevent them!
> Take their lands from them, you lords, let them live
>   upon tithes.
> If possessions are a poison, causing imperfect lives,
> Better unburden them, on behalf of Holy Church,
> And purge them of that poison before fresh perils befall us.
>   If the priesthood were perfect, all the people would
>   reform,   530
> Who conflict with Christ's law, and hold Christendom
>   in contempt.
> For the paynims all pray to, and perfectly believe in,
> The great and holy God, and His grace is their prayer,
> Though they make their appeals to Mohammed, as their
>   intermediary.
> Thus those folk have true faith, but a false intermediary;
> And this is a pity for the pious, who are part of God's
>   Kingdom,
> And perilous to the Pope and the prelates that he makes –
> Those who bear the names of Bishop of Bethlehem or
>   Babylon.[65]

When the High King of Heaven sent His Son to Earth,
He performed many miracles for Mankind's conversion,   540
As examples by which men should see that by sober reason
No man might be saved, but only by mercy and grace,
And by penance and pain, and by perfect belief.
He became man, born of a maiden, our great Metropolitan
     Bishop;[66]
He baptised, and bishoped, with the blood of His heart,
All who would willingly believe Him within their conscience.
Many a saint since then has suffered death
To affirm the Faith, in countries far and wide:
They have died in India, Alexandria, Armenia, and Spain,
Dying dreadful deaths for their Faith's sake.   550
For the saving of Faith, St Thomas accepted martyrdom;
Because he loved Christ, he died among Christian traitors,[67]
To keep the rights of God's Kingdom, and of all
     Christian realms.
Holy Church is highly honoured by his dying;
He is a pattern to all prelates, a polished mirror,
And especially to such as have "Sees" in Syria,
But career about in *this* country, consecrating altars,
And creep-in among local curates to hear confessions –
     against God's Law:
     Si intraveris in segetem amici tui, franges spicas, et manu
          conteres: falce autem non metes.
     (When thou comest into the standing corn of thy
          neighbour ... thou shalt not move a sickle.)[68]
In Rome there were many men martyred for love of Christ,
Before Christianity came there, or the Cross was
     honoured.   560
     Every Bishop who bears a crozier is bound by that
     symbol
To proceed through his province, that his people may
     see him,
And to tell them and teach them true belief in the Trinity,
And feed them with spiritual food, and find for the poor:
Isaiah speaks of *your* sort, and so does Hosea;
They say none should be a bishop but he who gives

Both spiritual food and bodily, where those boons are needed:

> *In domo mea non est panis, neque vestimentum: nolite*
> *constituere me principem populi.*
>
> (In my house is neither bread nor clothing: make me not
> a ruler of the people.)[69]

And Hosea says, for such as are sick or feeble,

> *Inferte omnem decimam in horreum, et sit cibus in domo mea.*
>
> (Bring ye all the tithes into the storehouse, that there
> may be meat in my house.)[70]

Let us Christian creatures, who believe in Christ's Cross,
Hold firm in our faith – God forbid otherwise! –   570
And have clergy to keep us in it, *and* those who come
        after us.
    The Jews live under a true Law, that the Lord God
        Himself laid down
In stone, that it should be steadfast, and stand forever:

> *Dilige Deum et proximum.*[71]

"Love God and love your neighbour" is Jewish Law to
        perfection,
And God gave it to Moses to teach men till Messiah
        should come.
Jews still live by that Law, and believe it the best.
Yet they could see that Christ, Christendom's founder,
Was a pure prophet, and that many people were saved
        by Him
From all sorts of sickness. They saw this often,
And other miracles and marvels: meals were given by Him, 580
From two loaves and five fishes, to five thousand people.[72]
By those meals, men should have seen that Messiah's look
        was on Him.
Likewise, He raised-up Lazarus, who had lain in the tomb
Dead, under a stone, and stank: in a strong voice He
        called him,

> *Lazare, veni foras.*
>
> (Lazarus, come forth.)[73]

And the dead man stood and strode where the Jews could
        see him.
Yet they said and swore it was by sorcery Christ did it;

And they set-about to destroy Him – and destroyed
    themselves,
For by His patience their power was brought to precisely
    nothing.
    Patientes vincunt.
    (The patient conquer.)
Daniel had predicted their undoing. He said,
    Cum Sanctus Sanctorum veniat, cessabit unctio vestra.
    (When the Holy of Holy comes, your anointment
      shall cease.)[74]
Yet those wicked ones still believe He was a pseudo-
    prophet,   590
And His teaching untrue; they contemn it all,
And believe their Redeemer to be unborn still,
Whether Moses again, or Messiah. Thus their Masters
    prophesy.
  But the Pharisees and Saracens and Scribes and Greeks
Are folk of one faith in that they worship God the Father;
And since, then, the Saracens and the Jews also
Recognise the first clause of our Creed:
    Credo in Deum Patrem Omnipotentem.
    (I believe in God the Father Almighty.)
The prelates of unChristian provinces should strive if possible
To make them learn, little by little,
    Et in Jesum Christum filium
    (And in Jesus Christ His only Son),
Until they could spell out *et in spiritum sanctum*   600
    (and in the Holy Ghost),
And read and remember "in the remission of sins",
Until "the resurrection of the body, and life everlasting.
    Amen." '

'A happy fate befall you,' I said, 'for your fine sermon;
On account of Haukyn the Active Man, I shall always
    love you.
And yet I am still anxious about the meaning of Charity.'
    'Truly to tell,' said Reason, 'it is a *tree*, of great virtue.
Mercy is the name of its root, the stem of it is Pity;
Its leaves are the loyal words of the law of Holy Church;
Its blossoms are biddable speech and benignant looks.
The perfect tree is called Patience or Poverty of Spirit;
And, through God and the work of good men, it grows fruit
    called Charity.'
    'To see this tree, I would travel two thousand miles;   10
And to eat my fill of that fruit, forsake all other food.
Lord! Can I learn of *no one* the land where it grows?'
    'It grows in a garden that God Himself planted,
For the root of that stem is in the midst of Man's body,
And his heart is the humus that nourishes it.
Free-Will is the lessee of that land
From Piers the Ploughman, to hoe it and pull out weeds.'
'Piers Ploughman!' I cried; and for pure joy
At hearing his name again, into a swoon I fell,
And lay a long while in a lonely dream; till at last it seemed   20
That Piers the Ploughman was showing me all that place,
And bidding me take note of the tree from top to bottom.
Three props were supporting it, as I soon perceived.
    'Piers,' I said, 'I pray you, what are these props for?'
'Why, in case of windy weather,' said he, 'to keep it
    from falling:
        Cum ceciderit justus, non collidetur: quia Dominus
            supponit manum suam.
    (Though [a good man] fall, he shall not be utterly cast
        down, for the Lord upholdeth him with his hand.)[1]
For in budding-time the blooms would wither, but for
    those props:

The world is an ill wind for them who wish Truth,
For Covetousness comes on that wind, and creeps among
    the leaves
And for all its fair appearance gnaws away near the fruit.
So I push him down with the first prop – the power of
    God the Father.   30
And the Flesh is a fierce wind; and in flowering time,
With lewdness and lust, it blows so loud
That it foments flirting looks and foul speech,
And the wicked works of the worms of sin
That bite-down the blossoms to the bare leaves.
So I set-to with the second staff – the wisdom of God
    the Father.
Namely, the Passion and power of the Prince Jesus.
And by prayer and by penance, and with that Passion
    in mind,
I save the tree till I see it ripen, and to some extent fruited.
But then the foul Fiend plots to destroy my fruit,   40
With all the wiles that he knows: he will shake the root of
    the tree,
Or hurl up at the harvest some hateful neighbours,
Or breach-of-the-peace backbiters, brawlers and quarrellers;
Or he lays a ladder up against it, with rungs of lies,
And sometimes filches my flowers before my very eyes.
But my lieutenant, who looks after the tree by my leave –
Free-Will – can for a while resist the Fiend:
    Qui autem dixerit contra Spiritum sanctum, non remittetur
    (Whosoever speaketh against the Holy Ghost, it shall
      not be forgiven him),
    Hoc est idem: qui peccat per liberum arbitrium non repugnat
    (And in like manner, [he speaks against the Holy
      Ghost] that sins of his free will, and resists not).[2]
But when the Fiend and the Flesh, in fellowship with
    the World,
Threaten furtively behind me to filch my fruit away,
Then Free-Will goes to work with the third prop,   50
And brings down the Devil by dint of pure grace
And help of the Holy Ghost; and so we have won.'

'Happy fate befall you, Piers,' I said, 'for so well
    describing
The power of those props, and their particular virtues.
But I still have thriving thoughts about those three posts:
Of what wood are they, and where did they grow?
For all are of the same length, and none larger than others:
All have the same degree of girth and of greenness.
And it seems to me they must have grown from one root.'[3]
    'Certainly what you have said may well be so.   60
I will tell you in a nutshell what this tree implies.
The ground in which it grows is called Goodness;
And as for the tree itself – I have told you it betokens
    the Trinity.'
And he shot me such a sharp look, I felt I should not
Enquire any more about that; but I gently asked him
To let me know more of the fruit that lay luscious on
    the boughs.
'On the lowest boughs, here within reach when I wish,
Is Marriage – a most juicy fruit, I may say.
Closer to the crown is a grafting of Cailloux pears, called
    Continence;
And topmost, the tree's purest fruit, and most natural,   70
Maidenhead, equal of the angels, and earliest to ripen,
Sweet without swelling-up, and never souring.'[4]
    Then I prayed Piers to pluck me an apple, if he would,
So that I could ascertain what sort of taste they had.
He cast something up at the tree's crown, and the tree
    began crying;
He wagged the branch called widowhood, and again it wept;
But when he meddled with Marriage, it made such a din,
And wailed so woefully when he shook it, that I pitied it.
For whenever fruits fell down, there was the Fiend,
Eager to gather them up, both big and small –   80
Adam, and Abraham, and Isaiah the Prophet,
Samson, and Samuel, and St John the Baptist –
And bore them off bodily, with nobody to stop him,
And made a hoard of holy men in the Marches of Hell,[5]
Where dread and darkness are, and the Devil is master.

Then Piers, in pure anger, picked up the prop
Called Son, by the Father's will and by grace of the
       Holy Spirit,
And hit out heedlessly at the Devil's hind-quarters,
To recapture from that wretch the fruits of his robbery.
    Then the Holy Ghost began speaking through
       Gabriel's mouth   90
To a maiden called Mary, of great meekness;
He said that one Jesus, a Judge's son, must sojurn in
       her bower
Till in *plenitudo temporis*, the fullness of time,[6]
Piers Ploughman's fruit had flowered and fully ripened.
Then Jesus should joust for that fruit, and judgment of arms
Should fix who should take the fruit, the Fiend or himself.
    The maiden meekly assented to this message,
And humbly said to him that she was God's handmaid,
Without sin, and willing to do as he wished.
       Ecce ancilla Domini; fiat mihi secundum verbum tuum.
       (Behold the handmaid of the Lord; be it unto me
          according to Thy word.)[7]
Then God was in her womb for forty weeks,   100
Till He was born from her flesh, a child fit to fight
And defeat the Fiend even before time was ripe.
But Piers the Ploughman[8] understood the plenary time,
And taught Him the art of healing, so as to save His life
Were He wounded by the enemy, and to work His own cure.
Piers made Him assay His skill upon sick people,
Till He was a perfect practitioner in any kind of peril.
And He sought-out the sick, and the sinful too,
And he cured the sick and the sinful, the crooked or blind,
And converted common whores to a clean life;   110
       Non est opus medicus valentibus, sed male habentibus.
       (They that be whole need not a physician, but they
          that are sick.)[9]
The dumb, and those with dysentery, and doomed lepers:
He often healed such people, and thought little of His
       powers –
Save when He lifted up Lazarus, who had lain in the grave

Four days dead, and arose living, and walked.
Then when He put forth His power, He was dispirited,
And wept water from His eyes, and was seen by many.[10]
Some that saw that sight said at the time
That He was Life's Healer, and Lord of High Heaven.
The Jews judged differently, and alleged by their laws
That He worked miracles by witchcraft, with the
     Devil's help: 120
     Daemonium habet, et insanit.
     (He hath a devil, and is mad.)[11]
  'Then you are serfs,' said Jesus, 'and your sons also,
And Satan is your saviour, as yourselves have borne witness.
I have saved you yourselves, and your offspring also,
Your bodies, and your beasts, and have cured blind men,
And fed you with two fishes and five loaves,
And left basketsful of broken meat to be borne-off by
     whoever wished.'
Then He abused the Jews boldly, and threatened to beat them,
And laid into them with a lash, and threw low the tables
Of those who traded in the Temple and trafficked in
     money;[12]
And He said to all that stood there, so that everyone heard, 130
'I shall overturn this Temple and destroy it utterly,
And in three days re-erect it anew,
In every respect of the same size, or bigger,
As ever it was, and as wide; so I would have you
Call this a place of prayer and of perfection:[13]
     Domus mea domus orationis vocabitur.'
     (My house shall be called the house of prayer.)[14]
Envy and ill-will imbued the Jews;
They cast-about and contrived to kill Him if they could;
And day by day they bided their time,
Till one Friday, a little before the Feast of the Passover.
He had made His Maundy[15] after the meal on Thursday 140
When, sitting at supper, He said these words:
'I am betrayed by one of you, who shall bitterly rue the day
That he sold his Saviour for silver, or at all.'[16]
  Judas questioned this judgment, but Jesus told him

The man was indeed himself, saying, 'Thou hast said.'
Then that wicked man went out, and met with the Jews,
And told them a token by which to recognise Jesus
(A token which to this day is too much used) –
A kiss from a friendly countenance, with unkindness
    at heart;
Which is how it was with Judas when he betrayed Jesus.   150
'Hail, Rabbi,' said that wretch, and went right up to Him,
And kissed Him, to have Him caught and killed by the Jews.
    Then Jesus said to Judas, and the Jews also,
'I find falsity in your fair speech,
Guile in your glad face, and gall in your laughter.
You shall be made a mirror, to deceive many men;
But your wickedness, and the worst fate, will fall upon *you*:[17]
    Necesse est enim ut veniant scandala: verumtamen vae
        homini illi, per quem scandalum venit.
    (It must needs be that offences come; but woe to that
        man by whom the offence cometh.)[18]
But though I am treacherously taken, by intent of you all,[19]
Leave my apostles in peace, peacefully to depart.'
    Thus was He taken after twilight on that Thursday,   160
By Judas and the Jews. Jesus was His name,
Who on the Friday following, for the sake of mankind,
Jousted in Jerusalem, a joy to us all.
On the Cross on Calvary, Christ gave battle
Against Death and the Devil, and destroyed the power
    of Hell;
Dying, He undid Death, and made day out of night.[20]
    With this I awoke, and wiped my eyes,
And peered and stared all around for Piers the Ploughman;
Eastward and Westward I eagerly searched for him
And set out as if insane, to search around the countryside   170
For Piers the Ploughman. I sought in many places,
Till on a Mid-Lent Sunday I met with a man
As hoary as a hawthorn; his name was Abraham.
At once I asked him where he had come from,
And where he lived, and whither he was bound.
    The old fellow said, 'I am Faith, I tell you no falsehood,

And a herald-of-arms in the house of Abraham.
I am seeking someone I have seen only once,
A bold knight-bachelor, whom I knew by his blazon.'
'What *is* the boy's blazon, God bless you?' I asked.   180
'Three persons in one body, all equal in height,
In majesty, and in might, and in all other measures.
What one does, all do, and each of his own accord.
The first has might and majesty, and made all things;
Pater is his proper name, this person being the Father.
Filius, the Son of that Sire, is the second, called Truth;
Warden of his sire's wisdom, he is without beginning.
The third has for name Holy Ghost, Himself a person,
The light of all that has life by land or water,
The comforter of all creatures, from whom comes all bliss.   190
A lord who lays claim to lordship needs three things:
Power, a path by which to prove that power,
And his servant's also, and what both suffer.[21]
Thus God Who could have no beginning unless it seemed
      good to Him,
Sent forth His Son as a servant for a while,
To be busy here until the birth of children –
That is, the children of Charity, with Holy Church
      for mother.
Patriarchs and prophets and apostles were those children,
Also Christ and Christendom and the Christian
      Holy Church.
   The meaning of this is that men must believe in
      one God,   200
Who, wherever He fashioned or favoured, took the form
      of three Persons.
Mankind itself is a sign that this is so in truth;
Wedlock and widowhood, with virginity named first,
In token of the Trinity, had their root in one man.
Adam, father of us all, had Eve spring from him;
And the issue that they had, sprang from them both,
And each is the other's joy, in three separate persons,
On Earth as in Heaven, yet with only one nature.
Thus mankind, and manhood, with marriage their source,

Betoken the Trinity, and true belief.   210
   Marriage is mighty, and multiplies the Earth,
And truly betokens, if I dare talk so,
The Father of Heaven, Who first framed all things.
The Son (if I dare say so) is a symbol of widowhood –
     Deus meus, Deus meus, ut quid dereliquisti me?
     (My God! My God! why hast thou forsaken me?)[22]
The Creator had become the creature, to know both kinds
     of being;
And as widows would not exist if wedlock did not,
No more could God become man except by means
     of a mother.
And if widowhood without wedlock is a contradiction,
So a sterile marriage is scarcely to be praised:
     Maledictus homo qui non reliquit semen in Israel.
     (Cursed is the man who has not left seed in Israel.)[23]
So mankind's perfection proceeds from three persons
     in unity,   220
Man and his mate and their legitimate offspring
(Though Jesus Christ in Heaven was engendered by one
     gender only.)[24]
The Father puts forth the Son, and free-will springs
     from both,
As also the Holy Ghost does, yet all are but one God:
     Spiritus procedens a Patre et Filio.
     (The Holy Ghost proceeding from Father and Son.)
Thus I saw Him one summer, as I sat in my porch.[25]
I rose up and did Him reverence, and greeted Him
     right fairly;
Yet it seemed that I saw and received three men.
I washed and wiped their feet, and afterwards they ate
Calves' flesh and cakebread; and they could read my mind.
Sure tokens passed between us, and I am free to tell them.   230
   First, He tested me to see if I loved better
Him or Isaac my heir, whom He ordered me to kill.[26]
Thus He grew aware of my will; and he will praise me for it,
And my son too; I am certain of that, in my soul.
For His sake I circumcised my son Ishmael;

And I myself too, and all the males of my household,
Bled for love of that Lord, and hope of His blessing.[27]
My faith and fealty are firm in this belief;
For He Himself has promised me, and all my issue,
Land and lordship and eternal life.[28]   240
Yet to me and to my issue he granted still more:
Mercy upon our misdeeds, as many times as we ask it:

> *Sicut locutus est ad patres nostros, Abraham, et semini*
>   *ejus in saecula.*
> (As he spoke to our fathers, to Abraham, and to his
>   seed for ever.)[29]

Then He sent me a message to say I should make sacrifice,
And worship Him with both bread and wine.[30]
He called me a foundation-stone of His faith, for the saving
    of His people,
And to defend from the Fiend all those who followed me.
Thus I have been His herald, both on Earth and in Hell,
Where I comforted many of the careworn that await His
    coming.[31]
And this is why I seek Him; for I recently heard say
That somebody baptised him, John Baptist by name –   250
Who to patriarchs and prophets and other people in that
    darkness
Has said that he saw here the Salvation of us all:

> *Ecce agnus Dei, ecce qui tollit peccatum mundi.'*
> (Behold the Lamb of God, which taketh away the sin
>   of the world.)[32]

   I wondered at his words, and at the width of his garments;
For in his bosom he bore something that he continually
    blessed.
I looked at the overlap, and saw that a leper lay there
Among patriarchs and prophets in great pleasure.
'Why are you waiting? What do you want?' he asked.
'I should like to learn what you have in your lap.'
So he let me see, saying, 'Lo!' 'Lord have mercy!' said I.
'That is a present of great price! What Prince is it for?'   260
'It is a precious present; but the Devil has appropriated it –
And me into the bargain; no pledge can buy us back,

Nor anybody go bail to bring us out of his power,
Nor any mainprise procure our release from his pound,
Till He of whom I tell (and Christ is His name)
Shall some day deliver us from the Devil's power
By offering a better pledge for us than we could be worth:
That is, life for life. Else, these will lie for ever
Lounging in my lap until such a lord comes for us.'
    'Alas,' I said, 'that sin should hinder so long   270
The might of God's mercy, that has power to amend us all!'
And I wept at his words. Then at once I saw someone else,
Rapidly running in our direction.
I enquired of him what he was called, and whence he came,
And where he was going; and he willingly told me.

He said, 'I am Spes, or Hope; and I seek a knight
Who gave me a commandment upon Mount Sinai
With which to rule all realms. Here *is* that writ.'
'Is it sealed?' I said. 'Can one see the script?'
And Hope said, 'No; I seek Him in whose charge the seal is,
That shows Christendom, and Christ hanging on the Cross.[1]
And when my writ is so sealed, I know for a certainty
That the lordship of Lucifer shall last no longer.'
'Let us see this letter,' I said, 'and learn that law.'
So he pulled out his patent – a piece of hard rock   10
Whereon there were written only eight words, and a comment:
> '*Diliges Dominum Deum, et proximum tuum sicut teipsum.*'
> (Thou shalt love the Lord thy God, and thy neighbour
>   as thyself.)[2]
This truly was all the text, for I took a good look;
But the gloss was gorgeously written in gold ink:
> '*In his duobus mandatis universa lex pendet, et prophetae.*'
> (On these two commandments hang all the Law and
>   the Prophets.)[3]
'Are these,' I asked, 'your Lord's only laws?' 'Believe me,
     they are.
And whoever lives by those laws, I will attest
That the Devil shall not daunt him nor Death affright his soul.
For though I say it myself, I have saved with this charm
Many score thousands of men, and of women too.'
   'He is telling the truth,' said the herald, 'as I myself
      can testify.
Look: here in my lap are some who believed in those laws: 20
Joshua, and Judith, and Judas Maccabaeus;
Oh, and sixty thousand besides, whom you do not see here.'
'Your words are wonderful. But which of you is truer?
Belief in whom is likelier for the life of the soul?
Abraham says that he saw the Holy Trinity,
Three separate Persons, distinct from each other

And all only one God. This is Abraham's teaching,
And has saved those who believed, and were sorry for
    their sins:
He cannot count them all, but he carries some in his lap.
Then I do not see the need for starting a new law,   30
Since the first is sufficient for salvation and Heaven.

   Yet here comes Hope, who claims to have found that law;
And he tells us nothing of the Trinity that gave him
    the statute
"Believe in, and love, one Lord God Almighty,
And love, as you love yourself, all other people."

   The man who walks with one staff is better off,
It seems to us all, than one who walks with two.
Precisely so, by the Rood, it stands to reason
That unlettered men will more easily learn one lesson
(The simplest a terrible task!) than be taught two.   40
It is not easy for any man to believe Abraham;
And how much worse − woe's me − to love wicked
    neighbours!
One more easily believes in three loveable Persons
Than one loves, or lets be, the louts as well as the likeable.
Gang your gate, Hope, for God's sake,' said I.
'Those who learn *your* law will not long observe it!'

   As we thus went our way, reasoning with one another,
We saw a Samaritan sitting on a mule,[4]
And rapidly riding in our direction.
He was coming from a country that men call Jericho,   50
And was jogging off quickly to a jousting in Jerusalem.[5]
Abraham the Herald, and Hope and he, all met together
Where a man was lying wounded, left there by highwaymen.
He could neither stagger nor stand, nor stir hand or foot,
Nor help himself anyhow, for he seemed half dead,
Naked as a needle, and no one to help him.

   Faith had first sight of him, and fled on the other side,
And would not come near him by nine fathoms' length.

   Then Hope came hiking by, he who had boasted
How with Moses' commandments he had saved
    many men;   60

But as soon as he saw that victim, he dodged aside –
With as much dread, by God, as a duck from a falcon.
    Yet as soon as the Samaritan had seen that man,
He got down off Dapple, and led it by the bridle
To where the man was. He examined his wounds,
And perceived by his pulse that he was in peril of death
And, unless he was rapidly roused, might never rise again.
So he bustled to his bottles, and opened them both,
And washed the man's wounds with oil and wine,
Anointed and bound-up his head, and laid him in his lap,   70
And brought him on the mule to a manor men call
        Christ's Law,
Some six miles, or seven, from the New Market.
He entered him at an inn, and said to the inn-keeper:
'Take this man in, and tend him till I return from the jousting.
Here is some silver to buy salve for his wounds.'[6]
And he gave him twopence extra towards the man's board,
Saying, 'If he spends more, I will see you repaid later;
I will not delay now.' So, astride on his Dapple,
He rode off in a rush on the direct road to Jerusalem.
    Faith, who wanted to meet him, followed him fast;   80
And Hope made haste, in case *he* had a chance
To overtake him and talk to him before they reached
        the town.
When I saw this, I did not stay, but started running
In pursuit of that Samaritan who had shown so much pity,
And offered myself as his servant. He said, 'I thank you;
But I offer you, rather, friendship and fellowship in need.'
    I thanked him too, and then began to tell him
How Faith and his friend Hope had fled away
When they found that poor fellow who had fallen
        among thieves.
'You may excuse them,' said he, 'for their help would not
        have been useful;   90
No medicine on Earth may bring that man back to health –
Neither Faith nor Hope – his wounds have festered so,
Except the blood of a boy born of a maiden.
If he is bathed, or baptised as it were, in that blood,

Then plastered with penance, and with the Passion
    of that child,
He will stand, and step forward; but he will never be stalwart
Till he has eaten all the child, and drunk its blood.
Not one man in the world has passed through that wilderness,
Whether walking or riding, without being robbed and rifled,
Except Faith and his friend Hope and myself as third –   100
And now *yourself*, since you follow suit with us.

    For outlaws lurk in the woods and below the banks,
Where they may see every man, and mark exactly
Who is behind, who before, and who is on horseback
(For a man on a horse has more courage than he who walks).
So when their chief saw me, a Samaritan, pursue Faith
    and Hope,
On my mount whose name is Flesh (which I got from
    Mankind),
That whoreson lost heart, and hid himself in Hell.
But I assure you, before three days are over
The felon shall be fettered fast in chains,   110
And never again grieve travellers who go that way.
    Ero mors tua, O mors!
    (Oh death, I will be thy death!)
    Then Faith shall be forester here, and walk this frith,
Escorting common folk who do not know the country
To the way that I went, which leads to Jerusalem.
And Hope shall serve the hosteller, where the traveller
    lies healing.
All who are feeble and faint, whom Faith cannot teach,
Hope shall lead on with love, as his own law bids;
He shall be their host and their healer through the faith of
    Holy Church,
Till I have salves for all sick men; then I shall be seen again:
I shall come again to this country, and comfort all the sick   120
Who crave or covet or cry out for a cure.
For that boy has been born in Bethlehem, whose blood
    shall save
All who live by Faith and follow his friend Hope's teaching.'
    'Ah, sweet sir, but what *shall* I believe?' said I.

'As Faith and his friend both informed me?
Three separate Persons living perpetually,
All three only one God – thus Abraham taught me.
And, afterwards, Hope instructed me to love
One God with all my might, and all other men afterwards;
To love them like myself, but Our Lord above all.'   130
'Set fast your faith and firm belief
Upon Abraham, that Herald-of-Arms.
And as Hope ordered, so I also say,
Love your fellow-Christians just as you love yourself.
And if Conscience or Common-sense should combat
        that teaching,
Or heretics heckle you – show them your hand.
For God is like a hand: hear me, and learn how.
    First is the Father, like a fist with fingers folded –
Until it was His liking to unloose them
And protrude them from the palm whenever He pleased.   140
For the palm is properly the hand, and protrudes the fingers
To make or administer as much as is in its power.
So it truly betokens – and so you may tell them –
The Holy Ghost in Heaven: *He* is the palm.
The fingers are free either to fold or to act,
And so symbolise the Son, who was sent to Earth
And touched and entered (at the Palm's teaching)
St Mary the Maiden, and became a man.
        Qui conceptus est de spiritu sancto – etc.
        (Who was conceived by the Holy Ghost – etc.)[7]
So the Father is a fist with Fingers that can touch
All that the Palm perceives as proper to handle.   150
        Quia omnia traham ad me ipsum.
        (I will draw all things unto me.)[8]
Thus all three of them are but one, as the hand is,
And yet are separate selves in a single Being.
Because the palm puts forth fingers and fist as well,
So, in the same way, as we can see is reasonable,
He Who is Holy Ghost puts forth both Father and Son.
    And, as the hand can hold things hard and fast
With four fingers, thumb, palm, and so forth,

So the Father and Son and the Holy Spirit
Hold all the wide world between the three of them:
The windy welkin, the earth and the water,   160
Heaven and Hell, and all that they hold.
Thus it is (and no man need believe any different)
That three Persons are present in our Heavenly Lord
Separate in themselves, yet sundered never –
Any more than my hand can move without my fingers.
My fist is a full hand when folded together;
Thus the Father is fully God, as former and creator:
    Tu fabricator omnium . . .
    (Thou the Maker of all things . . .)
And all the might He commands is as a Maker.
   The fingers form a full hand, for drawing or painting
Or carving or contriving, for their craft is such: 170
Just so, the Son is the *skill* of the Father,
Yet fully God as the Father is, neither feebler nor stronger.
The palm, that is properly the hand, has power of its own,
Apart from the clenched fist or the fingers' craft;
For the palm has power to project all the joints,
And unfold the clenched fist, for it is the palm's place
To receive or reject what the fingers reach for
When it feels the fist's or the fingers' wishes.
   So the Holy Ghost is God, neither greater nor less
Than Sire or Son, and of the same power.   180
And they are all one God, as my hands and fingers,
My fist, whether folded or unfolded, and my palm,
All form only one hand, however I turn it.
If a man is hurt in the middle of his hand,
It is obvious that he is unable to grasp anything;
For the fingers that should fold, and so form the fist,
Have lost their power, because of pain in the palm,
To clutch or clasp or take a close hold.
   If the middle of my hand were maimed or pierced,
I could retain really nothing of what I reached for.   190
Yet even if my thumb and fingers were all cut-about,
But the middle of my hand without maltreatment,
I might help myself in many kinds of ways –

Though my fingers might ache, I could move and
    adjust them.
  It seems to me that I see a symbol here:
Whoever sins against the Holy Spirit shall never be saved,
Neither here nor hereafter, as I have heard tell.
> *Qui autem blasphemaverit in Spiritum Sanctum non*
>   *habebit remissionem in aeternum*
> (He that shall blaspheme against the Holy Ghost hath
>   never forgiveness),[9]
For he who trespasses thus has pierced God's palm.
For God the Father is like a fist, the Son like a finger,
And the Holy Ghost in Heaven is as it were the
    hand's palm.   200
So to sin against the Holy Spirit, so to speak injures
God in the part He grasps with; and His grace is killed.[10]
  The Trinity is likened also to a torch or a taper,
Which has wax and wick as it were intertwined,
And a flame that comes flaring out from both;
Just as wax and wick and the warmth of fire combine
To form a flame and so light a fire,
So do Father and Son and Holy Spirit
Foster belief and love among folk,
And cleanse all kinds of Christians from their sins.   210
And as you will sometimes see a torch that suddenly
Has the blaze of it blown out, though the wick still burns
Without light or flame to ignite the tinder:
So the Holy Ghost is God and Grace without mercy,
To all who unnaturally wish to destroy
Loyal love or the life that Our Lord created.
  And as glowing embers are of less relief to workmen
Who must stay awake and work on winter nights
Than a link or a candle that has caught fire, and blazes:
No more do Sire and Son and Holy Spirit   220
Grant any grace or forgiveness of sins
Till the Holy Ghost begins to glow and blaze.
The Holy Ghost will glow as gloomily as an ember
Till true love lies by Him, and blows the flame;
Then He flames like a fire upon Father and Son,

And melts their might into mercy. You may see in winter
How icicles hanging from eaves, when the sun shines out,
Will melt in a minute into mist and water:
So, by grace of the Holy Ghost, the great might of
    the Trinity
Is melted into mercy – but for the merciful only.   230
And as wax, with nothing else, on a warm ember
Will blaze up and burn because they have met,
And bring solace to those who were sitting in darkness,
    and see it,
So will the Father forgive folk of humble heart,
Who remorsefully repent and make restitution,
And by making amends inasmuch as they may.
If his assets do not suffice, though he dies in such a mind,
Then Mercy, because of his meekness, will make up the rest.
And as wick and fire will make a warm flame,
And make men cheerful, who were sitting in murk,   240
So Christ of His courtesy (if men cry for His mercy)
Both forgives and forgets, and prays for us too,
To our Father in Heaven, to have forgiveness.
    But you may hack fire from a flint for four hundred
        winters,
And unless you have tow or tinder or kindling to
        catch the sparks,
All your labour and your long toil are lost;
No fire can make flame if it lacks a fellow-substance.
Thus the Holy Ghost is God and Grace without mercy
To all that act against nature – as Christ Himself says:
    Amen dico vobis, nescio vos.
    (Verily I say unto you, I know you not.)[11]
    Be unkind to your fellow-Christian, and you can pray,   250
Deal-out alms, and do penance, day and night for ever,
And purchase all the pardons in Pamplona and Rome,
And no end of indulgences: be ungrateful to your fellows,
And the Holy Ghost will not hear you, nor help you,
    because of it.
For unkindness quenches Him, so that He cannot shine,
Nor burn or blaze clearly, since unkindness blows Him out.

Paul the Apostle proves whether I lie:
> *Si linguis hominum loquar . . . etc.*
> (Though I speak with the tongues of men . . . etc.) [12]
So beware, you wise men of worldly affairs,
You who are rich and can reason, rule your souls well.
I counsel you, be not unkind to your fellow-Christians;   260
For upon my soul, many of you rich men, as men have
    told me,
May burn, but do not blaze: you are blind beacons.
> *Non omnis qui dicit mihi, Domine . . . etc.*
> (Not everyone that saith unto me, Lord, Lord, shall
>   enter into the Kingdom of Heaven.) [13]
Dives[14] died in damnation for his unkindness
In withholding meat and money from men who needed them.
I recommend all rich men to remember him,
And give their goods back to that God Whose grace
    provided them.
For those who misuse His people, I hope no better
Than that they dwell where Dives is, all the days of eternity.
Thus unkindness is God's contrary, and kills, as it were,
The Grace of the Holy Ghost, that is God's own nature.   270
What Nature does, unkindness undoes as do those cursèd
    thieves,
Unkind Christians, who for covetousness and envy,
And whether by mouth or by hand, will slay men for their
    moveables.
What the Holy Ghost has in keeping, those whoresons
    destroy;
That is, life and love, and the light in Man's body.
For all good men, in like manner, may be likened to torches
Or tapers, that are offered in reverence to the Trinity;
And whoever murders a good man, so it seems to my
    conscience,
Puts out the light that Our Lord loves most dearly.
  There are many more ways in which men offend the
    Holy Ghost,   280
But that is the worst way open to anyone,
Of sinning against the Holy Spirit; to destroy, of set purpose,

For covetousness of any kind, what Christ bought dearly.
How can a man ask for mercy, or mercy help him,
Who wickedly and willingly would extinguish mercy?
Innocence stands nearest to God, and it cries day and night,
"Vengeance, vengeance! May it never be forgiven,
The sin that ruined us, spilt our blood, and as it were
uncreated us!
Usquequo, Domine, non vindicas sanguinem nostrum?"
(How long, O Lord, doest thou not judge and avenge
our blood?) [15]
Thus, "Vengeance, vengeance!" even Charity may cry;
And since Holy Church and Charity charge this
so strongly,   290
I cannot believe that Our Lord will love those lacking
charity,
Nor pity them despite their mournful prayers.'
    'But suppose *I* had sinned so and, being about to die,
Were sorry that I had so offended the Holy Spirit;
That I made my confession, and cried to God the Creator
for grace
And meekly begged Him for mercy: might I not be saved?'
    'Yes,' said the Samaritan, 'it is possible that you might
repent so perfectly
That, through your repentance, the rigour of justice
might relax.
But it is seldom seen, after straightforward testimony,
That a criminal once condemned by a King's Justice   300
Is rescued by his repentance, once reasonably found guilty.
For when a plaintiff is the prosecutor, the imputation
is so grave
That the King himself cannot pardon unless both parties
come to terms,
And each is equally content, as Holy Writ says:
    Numquam dimittitur peccatum, donec restituatur ablatum.
    (A sin is never remitted until what has been taken
is restored.) [16]
Thus those folk fare who, in falsehood all their lives,
Live evilly, and do not leave off until life forsakes them;

Then dread of despair drives away grace,
And mercy may not enter their minds after that;
Hopelessness kills the good hope that should have
  helped them:
Not because God has no power, or is unable   310
To amend all that is amiss, for His mercy is greater
Than all our ill deeds, as is written in the Scriptures:
  Miserationes ejus super omnia opera ejus.
  (His tender mercies are over all his works.)[17]
But before He turns justice to mercy, men must make
  some restitution;
And sorrow will suffice if a man lacks all else.
  There are three things, as the Holy Scripture tells,[18]
That force a man to flee from his own house:
One is a scolding wife who will not be reproved,
And who forces her husband to take flight, for fear of
  her tongue.
The next is an ill-roofed house that leaks rain upon his bed,
So that he searches elsewhere for a dry place to sleep.   320
The third is when smoke and smoulder smother his eyes –
And that is worse than his wife, or sleeping wet.
For smoke and smoulder will smother his sight
Till he is bleary-eyed and half-blind, and hoarse in the throat,
And coughs and curses, "May Christ send them sorrow,
Who didn't bring in better wood, or blow till it burned well!"
  These three things that I tell-of, I interpret thus:
The wife is our wicked flesh, that will not be chastened,
For nature will not leave it, nor cease to war with the soul;
Yet if it falls, we find excuses in its frailty;   330
Fleshly sins are easily forgiven and forgotten
To a man who asks for mercy and means to do better.
  The rain that runs in where we should be resting,
Is the sicknesses and sorrows we so often suffer,
As St Paul the Apostle taught Christian people:
  Virtus in infirmitate perficietur.
  (My strength is made perfect in weakness.)[19]
And though men may make much ado of their infirmities,
And be impatient in such penances, pure reason shows

That they have cause to complain, being sick or sad.
And Our Lord will easily, at the end of their lives,
Have mercy on such men, who bemoaned their suffering.   340
    But the smoke and smoulder that smother men's eyes,
Those are covetousness and unkindness, and they put out
        God's mercy;
For unkindness is the contrary of any kind of reason,
And no one is so sick or sorrowful or so very wretched
That he cannot love if he elects to, and lend from his heart
Good will or good words, and wish for their sake
Mercy and forgiveness for all manner of men,
And love others as he loves himself and amend his life.
But I must delay no longer.' He laid spurs to his mount,
And went away like the wind. And with this, I awoke.   350

Wool next my skin, and wet-shod, I went on again,
As a reckless rover regardless of misfortune,
Wandering like a wastrel, all my life long,
Till at last I wearied of the world, and was yearning to sleep;
And at one Lent I relaxed, and slept a long time
So I stayed there, snoring hard, until Palm Sunday,
And dreamed long of Christ's Passion, and His penance that
    redeemed all people,
And of boys and girls singing *Gloria*, *Laus*, 'Praise
    and Glory',
And of how the old folk sang *Hosanna* to the organ.[1]
  Somebody like the Samaritan, yet somewhat like Piers
    Ploughman,   10
Came riding, bootless and barefoot, on an ass's back,
With neither spur nor spear. But he looked sprightly,
As is the nature of a knight newly coming to be dubbed
And get his golden spurs and gallant shoes.[2]
  Faith stood looking from a casement, and cried out,
    'O Son of David!'
Like a Herald-at-Arms announcing an adventurer come
    to joust,
And the aged Jews of Jerusalem sang for joy,
    Benedictus qui venit in nomine Domini!
    (Blessed is he that comes in the name of the Lord!)[3]
  I asked Faith the meaning of all this ado,
And who was coming to joust in Jerusalem. He said, 'Jesus,
To fetch back from the Fiend the fruit of Piers
    Ploughman.'[4]   20
'Is Piers in this place?' I asked; and his look pierced me:
'Jesus, out of gentilesse, will joust in Piers's blazon,
And in his helmet and hauberk, Human Nature by name,
So that Christ shall not be recognised here as the King
    of Heaven;
And Jesus shall joust in Piers Ploughman's jerkin,

For no blow He endures can dismay Him in His natural
      Divinity.'
'And who shall joust against Jesus? The Jews and Scribes?'
  'No; the foul Fiend, False Condemnation, and Death.
Death has threatened to undo and bring down
All things that live or lurk by land or water;   30
Life says that he lies, and has laid Himself as pledge
That for anything Death can do, within three days
He will go and fetch from the Fiend Piers Ploughman's fruit,
And lodge it where he likes, and chain-up Lucifer,
And batter down and destroy Death and Sorrow for ever.'
      Ero mors tua, O mors!
    (O death, I will be thy death.)[5]
Then Pilate came, with a swarm of people, and sat in the
      Judgment Seat
To see how doughtily Death would fight, and to umpire
      the dispute.
The Jews and the Judge himself sided against Jesus,
And all the Court cried-out shrilly, 'Crucify Him!'
Then a pillager appeared before Pilate, and said,   40
'This Jesus jeered at, and scorned, our Jewish temple;
He said he could destroy it in a day, and after three days
Erect it all anew – and there he stands, who said it! –
And would remake it the same in every measurement,
In length and latitude and loftiness and capacity.'
A constable cried, 'Crucify him! I'll warrant he's a warlock!'
Another cried, 'Off with him! Off with him!' And he took
      some sharp thorns
And twisted their spiny twigs into a chaplet
Which he savagely set on Christ's head, with mocking speech:
'Hail, Rabbi!' said that ribald, and poked reeds at Him,[6]   50
Then nailed Him naked, with three nails, to the Cross.
They pushed poison towards His lips, on the end of a pole,
And bade Him drink His death-draught, for His days
      were done.
'And if you have magic art, use it to help yourself.'
'If you are Christ, and a King's son, come down from
      the cross:

Then we shall believe that the Lord of Life loves you, and
    will not let you die!'
   Christ said, '*Consummatum est*,' and commenced to swoon,
As piteously pale as a dying prisoner;
Then the Lord of Life and Light laid His eyelids together.
The daylight withdrew in terror, the sun grew dark,   60
The Temple wall trembled and split, and the whole
    world shook.
Hearing that din, dead men left their deep graves,
And told why that tempest lasted such a long time.
Said one dead body, 'There is a bitter battle.
Life and Death, in this darkness, are trying to destroy
    each other,
Nor shall anyone know truly which of them has won,
Until Sunday, around sunrise.' And he sank back into the soil.
Some said Christ was God's son, so finely He died:
    '*Vere Filius Dei erat iste.*'
    (Truly this was the Son of God.)[7]
But some said He was a warlock, 'And we had better
    make certain
He is dead indeed, before taking him down.'   70
Two thieves also suffered death on that day,
On crosses beside Christ, as the Common Law then was.
A constable came and cracked the legs of both,
And afterwards the arms of either thief;
But nobody was so bold as to touch God's body:
Because He was a cavalier, and a King's son, Nature
    forbade for once
That any whoreson should have the courage to lay hands
    on Him.
   But [Nicodemus says] a knight soon came, with a
    sharp-ground spear;
Longinus was his name, and long since he had lost his sight.
He came to that place where Pilate and the other
    people were;   80
And demur as he might, they made him there and then
Take the spear into his hands and tilt against Jesus;
For none who was there, on horseback or foot, had courage

To attack or touch Him, or take Him down from the Cross.
But this blind knight-bachelor drove the blade through
	His heart
And the blood streamed down the spear and unsealed the
	knight's eyes.
Then the knight fell to his knees and asked forgiveness:
'Lord, it was not my will to wound you so sharply!'
He sighed then, and said, 'I sorely repent.
For the cruelty I have committed. I cast myself on your
	mercy. 90
Have pity on me, Just Jesus!' And with this, Longinus wept.
	Then Faith fiercely rebuked the false Jews,
Calling them caitiffs, accursed eternally
For their vile villainy – 'Vengeance light on you all!
To make a blind man strike a bound man was a beastly
	thought.
You cursèd cowards, it was never called chivalry
To abuse a dead body, by night or day.
But despite the great gash, Christ gains the prize;
For your champion of champions, chief knight of you all,
Yields himself recreant, resigned to the rule of Christ.   100
Once this darkness has departed, His death will be avenged;
And you, my lords, have lost, for Life shall be sovereign,
And the freedom of your franchise has fallen into slavery.
You and your children shall be churls, and achieve nothing,
Nor have lordship over lands, nor have land to till,
But be altogether barren, and live by usury –
A life that in all His laws Our Lord has cursed.
Now your good days are done, as Daniel prophesied:
When Christ came, crowning in that kingdom should cease!
	Cum veniat Sanctus Sanctorum, cessabit unctio vestra.'
	(When the Holy of Holies comes, your anointing
		shall cease.)[8]
	For fear of these phenomena, and the falsity of the Jews, 110
I withdrew through the darkness, and went down to
	the underworld.
And there in good sooth I saw (as we may read in the Psalms)[9]
A wench who came from the west (so went my dream).[10]

She came walking my way, and was looking towards Hell.
This maiden was called Mercy, and was of mild nature,
A gracious girl, and of goodly speech.
   Her sister, as it seemed, came softly walking
Exactly out of the East, and was looking westward:
She was indeed a comely creature, and was called Truth;
By reason of the power surrounding her, she was
     never afraid.   120
   When these two maidens, Mercy and Truth, had met,
Each asked the other about those great wonders –
The din, and the darkness, and the sudden daybreak –
And what were that gleam and that glory at the gates of Hell.[11]
Truth said, 'I am amazed indeed by all these matters,
And have come thus far to find out the meaning of the affair.'
Said Mercy, 'Do not marvel; it means great joy.
A maiden called Mary, unmeddled-with by man,
Or any kind of creature, has conceived by the Word
And Grace of the Holy Ghost, and grown big with child;   130
Without blame or blemish did she bring him into this world,
And that my tale is true, I take God to witness.
Since the boy was born, thirty winters have gone by;
And he endured death at almost noon today.
That is the cause of the eclipse that occludes the sun;
For its meaning is that Man shall be drawn from his murk,
While this gleam and this glory shall leave Lucifer blind.
Patriarchs and prophets have often preached
That man shall save man through the help of a maiden;
That that which was lost through a tree, a tree should
     restore,[12]   140
And that a death should raise up those whom Death
     brought down.'
   'What you are telling,' said Truth, 'is a tale of
     mumbo-jumbo.
Adam and Eve, and Abraham and others –
Patriarchs and prophets – that now lie in pain,
Will never be lifted aloft by that light over there,
Nor be heaved out of Hell. Hold your tongue, Mercy!
You are talking trash: I am Truth, and know what is *so*.

He who is once in Hell, comes out no more;
The prophet and patriarch Job disproves your sayings:

Qui descenderit ad inferos, non ascendet.'

(He that goeth down to the grave shall come up
no more.)[13]

Then Mercy answered mildly, in this manner: 150
'It is experience that makes me hope they shall be saved.
For poison casts out poison; as reason proves:
The vilest of all venoms is that of a scorpion;
No medicine may remedy the part that it stings,
Till the dead creature is laid on the wound, and undoes
the harm,
The first venom destroyed by the venom itself.
So shall this death undo, I dare wager my life,
All that Death first undid through the Devil's enticement;
And just as man was beguiled by guile,
So the Grace by which man was begun shall itself
beguile well: 160

Ars ut artem falleret.

(Art that shall deceive art.)[14]

Said Truth, 'Let us pause, for I seem to see
(Coming from the nip of the North, and not far away)
Righteousness running towards us: let our argument rest,
For she is our elder, and wiser than we.'
'For certain; and also I see, in the South,
Peace gaily approaching, robed in patience.
Love has longed for her so lastingly, I believe no less
Than that He sent her a message about what this light means,
That hovers over Hell: perhaps she will tell us.'

When Peace, robed in patience, had approached
the others,   170
Righteousness did her reverence for her rich dress,
And prayed Peace to tell her where she planned to go
In those gay garments, and whom she had hoped to greet.

'I will away,' she said, 'to welcome all those
Who have long been hidden from me by the hell-dark of sin:
Adam and Eve, and many more in Hell,
Moses among them, shall have mercy shown them.

And I shall dance at the sight – sister, dance too!
For since Jesus jousted well, joy's dawn begins.

> *Ad vesperum demorabitur fletus: et ad matutinum laetitia.*
> (Weeping may endure for a night, but joy cometh in
>   the morning.)[15]

Love, who is my belovéd, sent a letter to me,   180
Saying Mercy my sister and I should save Mankind;
That God has given and granted to Peace and Mercy
To be Mankind's mainpernors, now and for ever more.
See here the letters-patent!' said Peace. '*In pace in idipsum*;
And, that this Deed shall endure, *dormiam et requiescam.*'

> (I will both lay me down in peace, and sleep.)

Said Righteousness: 'Are you raving? Or roaring drunk?
Do you believe that that light can unlock Hell,
And save men's souls? Sister, never believe it!
God, in the beginning, gave this judgment Himself,
That Adam and Eve and all that came after them   190
Should die downright, and dwell in anguish afterwards,
If they touched a certain tree, and tasted its fruit.
After this, Adam, against that forbiddal,
Did feast on that fruit, and forsook, as it were,
The love of Our Lord, and His Law also,
And did as the Devil taught, and Eve desired,
Against all reason. I, Righteousness, record for certain
That their pains will be perpetual, and no prayer help them:
Let them chew as they chose; and let us not chide, sisters,
For what they bit off was a bane no balm will cure.'   200

'I shall prove,' said Peace, 'that their pains must
      have an end,
And woe turn to weal when the time is ripe;
For had they never known grief they could not know
      happiness –
No man knows what weal is, who has not met woe,
Nor what it is to hunger, who has never lacked food.
If there were no night, nobody, I believe,
Would understand entirely what is meant by day;
Nor any really rich man, living in rest and comfort,
Understand any distress, were natural death done away with.

So God, by Whom all began, of His great goodness   210
Became a man, born of a maiden, to save all men and women,
And allowed Himself to be sold, to learn the sorrow of death
That unravels all regret, and is the arrival of rest.
For until we meet meagreness, I may tell you,
None of us knows what "enough" may mean.
   Therefore God in His goodness gave the first man, Adam,
A condition of comfort and of complete bliss;
But soon He allowed him to sin, and experience sorrow,
So as to know within him the nature of happiness.
And then He set Himself at risk, and assumed
     Adam's nature,   220
So as to know his suffering, in three separate places –
In Heaven and on Earth and soon, he intends, in Hell,
To learn what utter woe is, Who knows utter joy.
So shall these folk fare; their folly and sin
Shall teach them torment first, then eternal bliss.
No person, where peace reigns, can appreciate war,
Nor utter contentment until *welladay* teaches him.'
   And now there appeared a person with two
     wide-open eyes;
Book was this bishop's name, a man of bold speech.
'By God's body,' said this Book, 'I will bear witness   230
That when this Boy was born, a star blazed forth,[16]
And all the wise men in the world were of one opinion –
That a boy had been born in Bethlehem city
Who should save men's souls and overcome sin.
And all the elements,' said Book, 'bear witness to it.
The airy sky first announced Him as God Who made all:
Those that were in Heaven took a starry comet
And lit it like a torch in tribute to His birth;
And the light followed the Lord to lowly Earth.
The water bore witness He was God, for He walked on it;   240
And the Apostle Peter perceived His approach
As He walked on the water, and knew Him well, and said,
     "*Jube me ad te venire super aquas.*"
     (Lord, bid me come unto thee on the water.)[17]
And lo! the sun has locked-up its light in itself,

At seeing Him suffer, Who made sun and sea.
The Earth, unhappy at seeing Him suffer,
Quakes like a living creature, and crushes the rocks.
Lo! Hell could not hold fast, but opened at His Passion,
And let out Simeon's sons,[18] at seeing Him hang on
    the Cross;
And Lucifer now must believe this, loth though he may be.
For Jesus the Giant has projected an engine   250
To break and beat-down all that may be against Him.
And let me, Book, be burned unless Jesus rises living,
With all the mights of Man, to make His Mother glad
And comfort all His kindred and carry them out of sorrow,
And leave all the joy of the Jews disjointed and shattered;
And unless they revere His Rood and His Resurrection,
And believe in a new Law, they are lost, body and soul.'
  'Stay a while,' said Truth, 'for I can both hear and see
A spirit that speaks to Hell, and bids them unbar the gates.'
From within the light, a loud voice cried to Lucifer: 260
    Attollite portas principes vestras, et elevamini, portae:
      aeternales; et introibit rex gloriae.'
    (Lift up your heads, O ye gates, even lift them up,
      ye everlasting doors; and the King of Glory shall
      come in.)[19]
'Princes of this place, unpin and unbar your portals!
Here comes, crowned, the King of Glory!'
Then Satan sighed, and said to them all,
'Such a light, without our leave, stole Lazarus away;
Discomfort and care are coming towards us.
If this King comes in, he will carry off mankind
And lead them where he likes, and have little trouble
    in binding me.
Patriarchs and prophets have proclaimed this for years,
That such a light and a lord should lead them all hence.'
  'Listen,' said Lucifer.[20] 'This lord is known to me –   270
The lord and the light as well – from long ago.
Neither Death nor devils' tricks can do him harm,
And he walks as he wishes. But he'd better beware of dangers:
If he robs me of my rights, he robs me by force.

By right and reason, all the rabble in Hell
Belong to me, body and soul, both the good and the wicked.
He himself said, the Sovereign of Heaven,
That if Adam ate the apple, all men should die
And dwell with us devils; thus did he threaten.
He who is Truth, he spoke those words.   280
And since I have had seisin these seven hundred winters,
I believe the Law will not allow him a jot.'
    'That is so,' said Satan. 'But I'm seriously worried
Because you gained them by guile – and broke into his garden
In the semblance of a serpent, and sat in the apple-tree,
And egged-on Eve, when alone, to eat,
And told her a tale full of treacherous words.
That is how you had them out, and brought here at last;
And to what is gained by guile, there is no good title.'
'God will not be beguiled,' said a goblin, 'nor befooled.[21]   290
We have no true title to them; it was treachery that
        damned them.'
    'That is so,' said Satan, 'and I fear Truth will steal them.
These thirty winters, I think, he has walked the world,
        preaching;
I have tested him with temptations, and one time asked him
If he were God or God's son – and I got a curt answer.[22]
And so he has traipsed around these thirty-two winters.
And when I saw things were so, in her sleep I went
And warned Pilate's wife what kind of man Jesus was.[23]
For though the Jews hated him, and have put him to death,
I would have had him live longer. I believed if he died   300
His soul would suffer no sin to be in its sight;
For his body, when flesh and bone, was busy all the time
To save men from sin, if they themselves were willing.
And now I see a soul come sailing towards us
Amid glory and great light: it is God, I well know.
My advice to us all,' said he, 'is to get out fast;
We'd be better off dead than be seen by *him*.
Your lying, Lucifer, has lost us all our prey.
It was your fault that we first fell from High Heaven –
Because we believed your lies, we all leapt out with you.   310

And now, because of your latest lie, we have lost Adam,
And all our lordship, I believe, over land and water:

> *Nunc princeps hujus mundi ejicietur foras.'*
>
> (Now shall the prince of this world be cast out.)[24]

   Again the Light bade them unlock; and Lucifer answered.
'What lord art thou?' asked Lucifer. '*Quis est iste?*

> (Who is this?)'

'*Rex gloriae,*' the Light said at once. 'The King of Glory,
The Lord of might and mastery and all manner of virtues.
Dukes of this dark place, undo these gates,
That Christ may come in, the Son of the King of Heaven.'[25]
At His breath, Hell broke open, for all Belial's bars,
And the gates went wide despite their warders.   320
   Patriarchs and prophets, 'the people who sat in darkness',
Sang the song of St John, 'Behold the Lamb of God'.[26]
Lucifer could not look at them, for the light had blinded him.
Then Our Lord lifted up into His light all those that
      loved Him,
And said to Satan: 'Lo! Here is my soul as ransom
For all souls of sinners, to save those who deserve it.
They are mine, and part of me; my claim to them is better.
Though Reason may rule, and I myself recognise,
That from eating of the apple all must die,
I did not order them held here in Hell for ever.   330
For the deed that they did was incited by deceit;
With guile you gained them, against all justice;
In my palace of Paradise, in the appearance of an adder,
You treacherously took from me the two that I loved.
   There like a lizard with a lady's face[27]
You wrongfully robbed me. The Old Law reads
That beguilers shall be beguiled, and that is good sense:

> *Oculum pro oculo, dentem pro dente.*
>
> (Eye for eye, tooth for tooth.)[28]

Therefore, soul shall buy soul and sin shall cure sin;
All that Mankind has misdone, I as man will amend.
Member for member was the Old Law's "amends",   340
And life for life also: by that Law I claim
Adam and all his issue, to be at my will for ever.

What Death has undone in them, *my* death shall restore,
And shall quicken and requite all that is quenched.
Good law demands that grace shall undo guile:
Never believe, then, Lucifer, that I unlawfully seize them;
By reason and by right I ransom my vassals:

> *Non veni solvere legem, sed adimplere.*
> (I am not come to destroy the law, but to fulfil.)[29]

Falsely and feloniously, in my own fields,
Against all equity, you stole my own. Now in law
I recover them by ransom, and by no recourse else,   350
So that what you gained by guile is regained by grace.
You, Lucifer, in the likeness of a loathsome adder,
Got by guile that which God loved;
And I, Who am Heaven's Lord, in human likeness,
Have repaid your guile with grace – let guile combat guile!
And as a tree caused the death of Adam and all his seed,
So a tree shall make Adam and all his seed alive again;
Thus guile is beguiled, and its own guile traps it:

> *Incidit in foveam quam fecit.*
> (And is fallen into the ditch which he made.)[30]

Now your guile begins to turn against you,
And my grace to grow greater and wider.   360
The bitter draught you brewed, now you must brook:
You who are Doctor of Death – drink your own potion!

  For I who am Lord of Life, *my* drink is love;
And for that drink, today, I died on Earth.
I fought so for Man's souls, I am still athirst;
No drink may refresh me, nor slake my thirst,
Till it is vintage time in the Valley of Jehoshaphat,
And I drink the ripe grape of the resurrection of the dead.[31]
Then I shall come as a King, with a crown of angels,
And hoist all human souls out of Hell.   370
Fiends and fiendlets shall stand before me
And be at my bidding and go about my business.
My human nature demands I be merciful to Mankind,
For we are blood-brothers, though not all of one baptism.
But none who are my brothers both in blood and in baptism
Shall be damned to the death that has no ending.

Tibi soli peccavi.
(Against thee only, have I sinned.)[32]
On Earth it is not the custom to hang a criminal
Twice, if the first time fails; not even a traitor;
And if the King of a country should come in time
To the place of execution or of other punishment,   380
The law says the man shall live if the King but looks
    at him.[33]
   I, who am King of Kings, shall come at such a time,
When all the wicked are doomed to death and damnation;
And if the law lets me look at them, it will lie with my mercy
Whether they die or do not, for their evildoing.
And if they have paid in part for their presumptuous sins,
I may rightfully use mercy, yet all my words remain true.
And though Holy Writ requires my revenge on evildoers –
    Nullum malum impunitum
    (No evil unpunished)[34] –
They shall be cleansed completely, and washed clean of
    iniquity
In my prison called Purgatory, till pardon behoves,   390
And my mercy shall be shown to many of my brethren;
For kinsmen may let kinsmen go cold or hungry,
But cannot without compassion see kinsmen bleed.'
    Et audivi arcana verba, quae non licet homini loqui:
    And I heard unspeakable words, which it is not lawful
      for a man to utter.[35]
'But my righteousness and my right shall rule all Hell,
And my mercy rule all mankind before me in Heaven,
How unkind a King I should be, not to help my own kin,
And especially in such straits as most sorely need help –
    Non intres in judicium cum servo tuo, Domine:
    Enter not into judgment with thy servant, O Lord.[36]
Thus it will be by law that I shall lead hence
Those that loved me and believed in my coming.
And, Lucifer, for the lies that led Eve astray,   400
You will bear a bitter sentence!' And He bound him in chains.
Ashtaroth[37] and the rest of his rout ran off to hide in corners,
For the boldest of the lot dared not look at Our Lord,

But left Him to do as he liked, and lead off whom he pleased.
   Then many hundreds of angels harped and sang the hymn
     Culpat caro, purgat caro;
     Regnat deus dei caro.
     (The flesh offends, the flesh atones;
     The flesh of God now reigns as God.)[38]
And Peace played on her pipe to this piece of poetry:
'*Clarior est solito post maxima nebula Phoebus,*
Post inimicitias clarior est et amor . . .'[39] said Peace,
'After sharp showers, does the sun show fairest;
No weather is warmer than after watery clouds;   410
No love is liever nor friendship loyaller
Than after warfare and woe, when Love and Peace are
     the captains.
Never was war in this world, nor wickedness so bitter,
That Love, if He liked, could not change it into laughter,
And Peace, by means of patience, prevent its perils.'
Then Truth called a truce: 'Your words are true, by Jesus!
Let us clasp each other in covenant, sealed with a kiss!'
'And let no person,' said Peace, 'perceive that we ever
     disputed;
For nothing is ever impossible to the Almighty.'
   'You are in the right,' said Righteousness, and reverently
     kissed her;   420
And Peace kissed *her*, saying, 'Now let peace be perpetual!
     Misericordia et veritas obviaverunt sibi, justitia et pax
      osculatae sunt.'
     (Mercy and truth are met together; righteousness and
      peace have kissed each other.)[40]
Then Truth blew a trumpet and sang *Te Deum laudamus*;
And Love played on the lute, loudly singing the Psalm
     Ecce quam bonum, et quam jucundum, habitare fratres
      in unum.
     (Behold, how good and how pleasant it is for brethren to
      dwell together in unity.)[41]
Then until day dawned, these damsels danced.
   But then the bells rang out for Easter, and rapidly woke me.
So I called to Kitty my wife and Colette my daughter,

'Arise, and do reverence to God's resurrection!
Creep to the Cross on your knees, and kiss it as a jewel!
For it bore God's blessèd body for our redemption;
And it frightens the Fiend, for such is its might   430
That no grisly ghost dares glide into its shadow!'

So I awoke, and wrote down what I had dreamed,
Put on my most expensive clothes, and proceeded to church,
To hear the whole Mass, and later have the Eucharist.
In the middle of Mass, when men went to make their
    offerings,
I suddenly fell asleep again, and soon after dreamed
That Piers the Ploughman appeared, as if painted with blood,
And carrying a cross, before the common people,
And like in all his lineaments to Our Lord Jesus.
I called upon Conscience to make the meaning clear.
'Is this Jesus the Jouster?' I asked, 'Whom the Jews killed?   10
Or is it Piers Ploughman? And who painted him red?'[1]
Quoth Conscience, and knelt, 'Those are Piers's coat-of-arms,
His colours and bearings; but he who is here bloodstained so,
Is Christ with His Cross, the Conqueror of the Christians.'
'Why do you call Him Christ, when the Jews called
    Him Jesus?
Patriarchs and prophets have prophesied in the past
That every kind of creature should incline and kneel
Whenever men named the holy name of Jesus.
Therefore no name can match the name of Jesus,
Nor is any so necessary to name by night or day.   20
For all dark devils dread to hear it,
And sinners are solaced and saved by that name.
Yet you call Him Christ: for what cause, I beg?
Is Christ a name of more power or more worth
Than Jesu or Jesus, from whom all our joy comes?'
    'Now, you know very well, and are not without reason,
That cavalier, king, and conqueror may be one person.
To be called a cavalier is fine, because men will kneel to him;
To be called a king is fine, for he can *make* knights;
But to be called a conqueror comes only by special charisma, 30
And from uncommon courage, and the courtesy of
    knighthood;

He makes lords of low folk in the lands that he conquers,
And foul thralls of freemen that refuse his laws.

The Jews had been like gentlefolk; but, Jesus once despised,
And His love and His law, are now like lowly villeins:
Through all the wide world, not one of them lives
Except under tribute and tax, like tillers and peasants.
But those that became Christian, as counselled by
    the Baptist,
Are like freemen and franklins, from the virtues of baptism,
And are gentlefolk with Jesus (for Jesus was baptised,   40
And on His Cross upon Calvary was crowned King of
    the Jews).

It is fitting for a King to defend and maintain,
In lands he has conquered, his laws and his liberties.
Jesus did so for the Jews; He justified and taught them
The laws of that life that lasts for ever;
He defended them from foul evils such as fevers and fluxes,
And from fiends that possessed them, and from false beliefs.
Then the Jews called Him Jesus, a gentle prophet,
And King of their Kingdom – though His crown
    was of thorns.

Then on the Cross He became a great conqueror,   50
Whom Death could not bring down or undo for ever;
For He arose and reigned, and ravaged Hell.
He was called the Conqueror then, of the quick and the dead,
For He gave bliss to Adam and Eve and many others
Who had long been lying in Hell as Lucifer's slaves.
And since, to His loyal liegemen, He has given great largesse –
Such as places in Paradise when they depart this world,
He may well be called Conqueror, because that is the
    meaning of "Christ".[2]

    And the cause that He comes thus to us, with the Cross
    of His Passion,
Is to teach us, when we are tempted, to use the Cross   60
And let it fight for us and defend us from falling into sin,
And to see by His suffering that whosoever wants happiness
Must first apply himself to penance, and to poverty also,
And be willing to endure in this world a wealth of woe.

But now to speak more of the name, and why Jesus was
    named so,
To be fair, it is a fact that He was first called Jesus,
When He was born in Bethlehem, as the Bible tells,
And came to redeem Mankind. Then Kings and angels
Reverenced Him royally with all Earth's riches.
Angels came down from the skies, and knelt and carolled   70
    Gloria in excelsis Deo
    (Glory to God in the highest).
  Afterwards Kings came and kneeled, carrying gifts
Of myrrh and much gold, and demanding no thanks,
Nor any kind of recompense, but acknowledging His
    kingship
Over sun and earth and sea. And so they went back
To their kingly kinsmen, conducted by angels.
And there the words of which you spoke were fulfilled:
    In nomine Jesu omne genu flectatur coelestium, terrestrium,
    et infernorum.
    (At the name of Jesus every knee should bow, of things
      in heaven, and things in earth, and things under
      the earth.)[3]
For all the angels of Heaven kneeled at His birth,
And the wisdom of the world was in those three kings;
Reason and Righteousness and Ruth were their offerings,[4]
Which is why the wise men of those days –   80
The Masters, and men of letters – called them Magi.
  The first King came with Reason, represented by incense.
The second king offered, in sooth, when he came,
Righteousness, Reason's colleague, in the form of red gold;
For gold is likened to Loyalty that lasts for ever,
And Reason to the rich gold of truth and righteousness.
The third King came, and likewise kneeling,
Presented Him with Pity in the appearance of myrrh;
For myrrh means mercy, and a tongue of mild speech.
Thus were three things of like worth offered at once   90
By rulers of three races, kneeling from respect for Jesus.
  But, for all these precious presents, Our Lord Prince Jesus
Was neither King nor conqueror till the coming of the time

That He moved towards manhood, and to much wisdom.
Now, it becomes a Conqueror to know cunning skills,
And have many wiles and much wisdom, if he wants
    to lead men;
Jesus did have these, in His days, had I time to describe them:
Sometimes He suffered, and sometimes He hid Himself;
Sometimes He fought fiercely, and fled at other times;
Sometimes He gave gifts, and granted health too,   100
And restored life or limb however He liked.
Jesus came among men in the manner of a conqueror,
Till all were His, for whom His blood was shed.

   When He was a young man, Jesus went to a Jewish feast
And there turned water into wine, as we are told in
    the Scriptures;[5]
It was then that God of His grace began to Do-Well.
For wine is an emblem of the Law, and a life of holiness,
And the Law then was lacking, for men did not love
    their enemies.
But Christ both counsels and commands us,
Lettered and unlettered alike, to love our enemies.   110
Therefore it was at this feast first, as I said before,
That God began of His grace and goodness to Do-Well.
As yet He was not called or accounted Christ, but Jesus,
As a fine young fellow, and full of wisdom, and Son of Mary.

   He worked this miracle in his mother Mary's presence
So that she, first and foremost, should firmly believe
That He was begotten by God's grace, and by none other;
And He worked it, not by some sleight, but only by His word,
Accordant to the Nature He came of. So He commenced
    to Do-Well.

   When He had grown to more manhood, away from
    His mother,   120
He made lame men leap, and gave light to the blind,
And fed with two fishes and five loaves
More than five thousand folk who were truly famished.
Thus He comforted the careworn, and acquired a greater
    name,
Wherever He went; and that was *Do-Better*.

For His deeds made the deaf to hear, and the dumb to speak;
And all whom He healed and helped asked for His grace.
So the common people of His country called Him,
Because of the deeds he did, "Jesus, Son of David".
For David, in his own day, did the doughtiest deeds,   130
So that maidens sang, "Saul has slain his thousands, and
    David his ten thousands."[6]
Therefore He came in that country to be called "Son
    of David",
And they named Him after Nazareth, and thought none
    worthier
To be King and Kaiser of the Kingdom of Judah
And the Jews' Chief Justice, than Jesus was.
    Caiaphas and his Jewish company became envious of this;
And to do Him to death, they conspired day and night.[7]
They killed Him on a cross at Calvary, one Friday,
Then buried His body, and bade certain men
To keep it from night-comers, with a company of
    armed men,   140
So that no friends should fetch it away. For prophets had
    told them
That the Blessèd Body should arise from burial
And go to Galilee and gladden the Apostles
And His mother Mary: so men had believed.
    The soldiers set to guard it themselves confessed
That angels and archangels, before the arising of the day,
Had come and knelt to the corpse, singing *Christus resurgens*
    (Christ being raised from the dead dieth no more).[8]
And that He rose alive before them all, and went forth
    with them.
The Jews begged the guards to be discreet, and besought them
To tell the common folk there had come a company
    of Apostles   150
That bewitched them while they watched, and stole away
    the corpse.
    But Mary Magdalen met Him by the roadside,
Going towards Galilee as both God and man,
Alive and alert; and loudly she cried

To all company she came into, *Christus resurgens!* [9]
Thus it came out that Christ had conquered, recovered,
    and lived:
    Sic oportebat Christum pati, et resurgere a mortuis tertia die.
    (Thus it behoved Christ to suffer, and to rise from the
        dead the third day.) [10]
For what a woman knows cannot well be concealed!
   Peter perceived all this, and pursued Mary Magdalen,
With James and John, to seek Jesus out;
Thaddaeus was with them, and Thomas of India, [11] and
    ten others.   160
Then, as all these wise ones were together,
Shut in a building, behind bolted doors,
Christ came in to them, through the closed gates and doors,
And said, "Peace be unto you!" to Peter and the Apostles.
He took Thomas by the hand, and told him to search
And feel with his fingers the flesh of His heart.
   And Thomas touched it, and his tongue exclaimed,
    "*Dominus meus, et Deus meus.*
    (My Lord and my God.)
You are my Lord, and I believe, O Lord God Jesus!
You suffered and died, and will be deemster of us all;
For now you are alive and alert, and will live for ever!"   170
   Then Jesus gently rejoined to him,
"Thomas, because you attest this now, and truly believe it,
You shall be blessèd both now and for ever.
And blessèd shall all be, in body and soul,
Whose sight is never set on me, as *you* see me now,
Yet loyally believe all this: I love them and bless them.
    Beati, qui non viderunt, et crediderunt."
    (Blessèd are they that have not seen, and yet have
        believed.)
   And when He had done this, He taught the disciples
    Do-Best,
And gave Piers the power to grant pardon
And mercy and forgiveness to all manner of men,
And authority to remit all sins of whatever kind,   180
So long as men acknowledged to his entire satisfaction

His pardoning-power and its proviso – *Pay back
what you owe.*[12]
So Piers has power, his pardon thus paid for,
To bind and unbind both here and elsewhere,
And set men free of all sins save only that of debt.
And soon after this, on high into Heaven
Christ went, and will dwell there, but at last will come
To reward all men who *pay back what they owe* –
That is, pay completely, as pure honesty dictates.
Any person who does not so pay, Christ means to punish: 190
On Doomsday He will be Deemster of both quick and dead,
And send the good up to God and to great joy,
And the wicked to dwell in woe without end.'
Thus Conscience discoursed to me of Christ and of
the Cross,
And bade me do it obeisance. But then in my dream
The Paraclete came to Piers and his companions;[13]
In the likeness of lightning He alit on them all,
And made them understand and interpret many tongues.
I wondered what it might be, and touched Conscience
with my arm,
Being afraid of that light – for now in the likeness of fire   200
The Spirit of the Paraclete had quite overspread them.
Quoth Conscience, and knelt, 'That is Christ's Messenger;
He comes from the great God, and His name is Grace.
Kneel, and if you can sing, let *Veni Creator Spiritus*,[14]
"Come, Holy Ghost", be your hymn to welcome and
worship Him.'
So I sang that song, and so did hundreds of others,
And cried, together with Conscience, 'God of Grace, help us!'
Then Grace began to go along with Piers the Ploughman,
And counselled both Piers and Conscience to summon
the common people;
'For I shall distribute today a division of Grace   210
To all sorts and species of creatures that have five senses:
Treasure to live by until the end of their life,
Weapons to fight with that will never fail.
For Antichrist and his apostles shall harm all the world

And overmaster you, Conscience, unless Christ comes
    to your aid.[15]
    And many false prophets, and flatterers and fakers,
Shall come with Cure of Souls over Kings and earls,
And Pride shall be made Pope, the Prince of Holy Church,
With Covetousness and Unkindness as his Cardinal
    Counsellors.
Therefore I, Grace, will give you treasure before I go,   220
And weapons to fight with when Antichrist attacks you.'
And He gave every man a grace by which to guide himself
Lest Idleness or Envy or Pride overcame him.
    Divisiones vero gratiarum sunt, idem autem Spiritus.
    (There are diversities of gifts, but the same Spirit.)[16]
    To some He gave wisdom, and a way with words,
And eloquence by which to live in such worldly callings
As priests and preachers and apprentices to the Law.
All these should live uprightly by the labours of their tongues,
And use intelligence to teach others as Grace taught *them*.
To some He taught subtlety and keenness of sight,
To earn their daily bread by buying and selling;   230
To some He taught labouring, an honest and excellent life;
Others He taught to delve, to ditch, or to thatch –
And earn their living by the lore they learned from Him.
Some He gave knowledge of numbers, in all kinds of
    computing;
He taught some to compose clever pictures, and mix colours;
Some to foresee and foretell what should befall –
Whether for weal or woe, to give warning beforehand,
As astrologers do by their art, and subtle philosophers.
    Some He taught how to ride, and recover the spoils of
    robbery,
Getting them back by the use of bodily ability,   240
Forcing them from those felons by lynch-law.
With some he left the wish to be in another world,
Here to live in poverty and penance, praying for all Christians.
He told all to live in unity, trades loving each other,
Forbidding all disputes or debates between them.
'Some crafts are cleaner than others, as you can well see;

But I could have put the cleanest worker to the filthiest
    occupation.
I gave you, by my grace, such gifts as you have:
Be like brothers, then, to each other, none calling
    another base;
  Let whoever masters most skills be mildest of manners;   250
Crown Conscience as your king; make Capability your
    steward;
And as Capability counsels you, clothe and feed yourselves.
I appoint Piers the Ploughman my agent and bailiff,
And my registrar for the receipt of *Return what you owe.*
My purveyor and ploughman, too, shall Piers be on Earth,
And he shall have an ox-team to till Truth's field.'
So Grace gave Piers a team of four great oxen.
The first was Luke, a large beast, but of gentle looks;
Then Mark, and Matthew for a third, both mighty beasts;
And to them he added John, the gentlest of all,   260
The prize beast of Piers's plough-team, surpassing the others.
  And Grace in his goodness gave Piers four stots[17]
To harrow all the land that his oxen had ploughed.
One was called Augustine, and Ambrose another,
And Gregory (a great scholar), and good Jerome;
These four followed Piers's team, for teaching the faith,
And harrowed in half no-time all Holy Scripture,
With two harrows that they had, an old and a new,
    Id est, vetus Testamentum et novum.
   (That is, the Old Testament and the New.)
  And Grace gave Piers grains of corn, called the
    Cardinal Virtues,[18]
To sow in men's souls; and he explained their names.   270
The Spirit of Prudence, the first seed was called;
And whosoever ate it would use his imagination,
And consider the outcome before committing himself
    to action;
Thus, learned men buy a ladle with a long handle
To collect floating fat, and keep their crocks in good order.
  The second seed was called the Spirit of Temperance.
Whoever ate of that seed acquired such a nature

That his stomach would never swell from excess food
    or drink,
And no scorning or scolding spoil his even balance,
No winning of wealth or of worldly riches   280
Make him waste idle words or use wicked speech:
No uncommon clothing would ever come on his back,
Nor the meat in his mouth have been spiced by
    master-cook John.
  The third seed that Piers sowed was the Spirit of Fortitude.
Whosoever ate of that seed would be always strong-hearted
To suffer all that God sent of sickness and misfortune;
No lying or libel, nor loss of worldly goods,
Could move him to mourning, nor make his soul un-merry;
He was dauntless and enduring under all indignities,
To pass them off in patience with *parce mihi, Domine*,   290
And cover himself with the counsel of Cato the Wise:
    Esto forti animo, cum sis damnatus inique.
    (Be strong in courage when unjustly condemned.)[19]
  The fourth seed that Piers sowed was the Spirit of Justice,
And he that ate of that seed would always be honest
Towards God, and fear only guile, giving way to no fear else;
For guile goes about so secretly, that sometimes good faith
And the Spirit of Justice itself cannot be seen.
The Spirit of Justice is unsparing to punish
Those that are guilty, or even to correct
The King himself if he falls into malfeasance or sin.   300
For he counts the King's wrath as nothing, when he sits
    in Court
As a Justice, to judge cases; just so, he never fears
A Duke, or Death itself, but does as Law demands;
He cares nothing for presents or prayers, or princes' letters;
He gives equity to all, to the full extent of his power.
  Piers sowed these four seeds, and set about harrowing them
With the Old Law and the New Law, so that Love might
    sprout up
Among the four virtues, and the vices be destroyed.
For it is common in the country that kexes and weeds
Grow among the fruits of the field, and foul *their* growth;   310

And that is what vices do to worthy virtues.
Said Piers, 'Harrow all who have mother-wit, with these
      Doctors' teachings,
And cultivate, by their counsel, the Cardinal Virtues.'
  Said Grace, 'Before your grain begins to grow ripe,
Piers, you should build yourself a barn to bestow your
      corn safely.'
  'By God, Grace,' said Piers, 'then you must give me
      the timber,
And act as architect yourself, ere you depart.'
  So Grace gave him the Cross and the Crown of Thorns
From which Christ had suffered on Calvary for the sake
      of mankind;
And from the water of His baptism, and the blood He
      bled on the Cross,   320
Grace made a kind of mortar; and Mercy was its name.
With these Grace began to make a good foundation.
Then he walled it and wattled it with Christ's pains
      and Passion,
And afterwards made a roof out of all Holy Scripture;
And he called that house Unity – or in English,
      Holy Church.
  And when these deeds were done, Grace devised
A cart, called Christendom, to carry Piers's sheaves;
And he gave him caples for his cart, named Contrition
      and Confession,
And made Priesthood his hay-warden while he himself went
Over the width of the world, with Piers, to cultivate Truth. 330
  Piers having gone to plough, Pride saw his chance,
And gathered a great host in order to march against
Conscience, all Christians, and the Cardinal Virtues –
Which he meant to beat-down and bruise, and bite their
      roots apart.
So he sent forth Surquedry,[20] his Sergeant-at-Arms,
And his spy Love-Spoiler Speak-evil-behind-men's-backs.
These two came to Conscience and the Christian people,
And Surquedry told them their tidings. 'You are to lose
The seeds that Piers sowed, that is to say, the Four Virtues;

Piers's barn shall be broken down, and all who may be
    in Unity 340
Shall be scattered. And, Conscience, your two caples
Confession and Contrition and your cart of the Faith
Shall be coloured so cunningly, so concealed under sophistry,
That you cannot contrive to tell by Contrition,
Nor by Confession, who is Christian or unChristian,
Nor any merchant-man who handles money,
Whether what he earns is won fairly, or unfairly by way
    of usury.
    In such camouflage and cunning does Pride come armed,
Together with Lord Lechery who lives for bodily lust,
To lay waste the whole world, in a little while, 350
By using their wits, with luxury and wicked ways.'
    Quoth Conscience then to all Christians, 'My counsel
    is to go
As quickly as we can into Unity, and keep inside,
And pray for peace in the barn of Piers the Ploughman.
For I am certain that we two have not strength between us
To go forth against Pride, unless Grace is with us.'
    Then Commonsense came to advise Conscience,
And cried out his command to all Christian people –
That they should dig a deep dyke around Unity,
So that Holy Church might stand in Unity like a stela. 360
    So Conscience commanded all Christians to delve
An immense moat, such as might make a fortress
To help Holy Church and her guardians.
Then every kind of Christian except common whores
Repented, and repudiated sin: all but those, and rogues,
False men such as flatterers, and filchers and usurers,
False-witnesses, and jurymen who were often forsworn
And wittingly and wilfully sided with injustice,
Forswearing for silver what they knew to be so.
    No Christian creature that knew Commonsense, 370
Except such ill-doers as those I have spoken of,
But lent a helping hand to enlarge the Moat of Holiness:
Some by telling beads, and some by pilgrimages,
Others by private penance or by gifts of their few pence.

Then the water came welling up, as wicked deeds
Started it streaming saltily from men's eyes.
The pure lives of laymen and of clergy alike
Soon had Holy Church standing amidst the Moat
    of Holiness.
  Said Conscience, 'I care not though Pride *should*
    come now,
And the lord of lust shall be hindered all this Lent, I hope.   380
Come, then, all you Christians; now we can dine,
All who have laboured loyally throughout this Lent.
Here is blest bread, that conceals God's body:
Grace, by God's word, gave Piers the right
And might to make it, and men then to eat it
To aid their souls towards health, once in a month,
Or as often as they need, if they have paid
For Piers Ploughman's pardon, with *Repay what you owe.*'
  Then the common folk cried, 'What? You require us
    to pay back
All that we owe anyone, before we go to Mass?'   390
'I counsel and require,' said Conscience, 'and so do the
    Cardinal Virtues,
That all men forgive each other; and the Pater-noster asks it:
    Et dimitte nobis debita nostra, sicut et nos dimittimus
      debitoribus nostris.
    (And forgive us our debts as we also forgive
      our debtors.)
Only after this may you be absolved, and make true
    Communion.'
  'Ah, bah!' said a brewer, 'I won't be ruled,
By Jesus, for all your jabber, by any "Spirit of Justice",
Nor by Conscience himself, by Christ, while I can sell
Both dregs and draff, and draw from the same hole
Both thick ale and thin; for that's my nature,
And I don't haggle around after holiness: hold your tongue,
    Conscience,
You talk a lot to no purpose about "Spirit of Justice".'   400
  'You paltry poltroon!' said Conscience. 'You profane
    wretch!

You are unblest, brewer, unless God be your rescuer;
Unless you live by love of the Spirit of Justice
(The chief seed that Piers sowed), you will never be saved.
Unless Conscience and the Cardinal Virtues feed the
    common folk,
(Indeed believe it!) they are lost, both life and soul.'
  'Then many a man,' said an unlearnèd vicar,[21] 'must be lost!
I have Cure of Souls in Holy Kirk, and there never in my
    time came to me
Anyone able to tell me about cardinal virtues,
Or who cared a cock's feather – or a hen's either –
    for Conscience.   410
The only cardinals *I've* come across came from the Pope;
And we clergy, *when* they come, have to pay for their keep –
And all their fine furs and their palfreys' fodder, and the
    pillagers that follow them!
Every day I can hear the common folk cry out against them,
That the country is accursed into which cardinals come,
And that where they linger longest, lechery reigns.
Therefore I would wish, as God is my witness,
That no cardinals came among the common people,
But that they held fast in holiness to their habitation
At Avignon, among the Jews[22] –   420
    Cum sancto sanctus eris!
    (With the holy thou shalt be holy!)[23] –
Or in Rome, where their own Rule says they should guard
    the Relics.
And you, Conscience, should stay at King's Court for ever;
So should that Grace you grind on about, as guide to
    the clergy;
And Piers with his new plough and his old one also
Should be Emperor of all Middle Earth, to make all
    men Christian.
  That's an imperfect Pope who should help all people
Yet sends men to slay those whom he should be saving.[24]
I wish well to Piers Ploughman, who imitates God in
    his works,
    Qui pluit super justos et injustos:

Who sendeth rain on the just and the unjust alike,[25]
And sends the sun to sweeten a sinner's tilth   430
With as bright a blaze as for the best man or woman.
Just so, Piers the Ploughman takes pains, and tills
No worse for the wastrels or the brothel-wenches
Than for himself and his servants – though those *are*
          served first.
And he toils and tills just as hard for a traitor,
And at all times, as for a true and trusty man.
And worshipped be He Who made all, both heinous
          and good,
And lets sinners go on living, so that at last they may repent.
And may God improve the Pope, who pillages Holy Church,
And claims, above the King, to be keeper of all Christians: 440
Yet accounts it nothing when Christians are killed
          and robbed,
And even furnishes forces to fight and spill Christian blood,
Against both Old Law and New, as St Luke bears witness:
          Non occides ... Mihi vindicta:
          Thou shalt not kill ... Vengeance belongeth to me,
             I will recompense, saith the Lord.[26]
It seems that so long as he himself has his will,
He doesn't care a curse for the rest of Creation.
And may Christ in His courtesy save the Cardinals too,
And turn their quick wits towards wisdom, and the welfare
          of souls!
As for the common folk, they feel very little
The counsels of Conscience or of the Cardinal Virtues,
Unless they catch sight of something that will serve
          their ends.   450
Dishonesty or deceit do not trouble them at all;
For the Spirit of Prudence among the people is *guile*,
And all those lovely Virtues appear as vices.
Everyone schemes some deceit by which to hide sin,
And passes it off as pure art, and honest practice.'
   A lord who heard this, laughed, and said, 'By this light,
I think it right and reasonable to take from my Reeve
All that my auditor, or it may be my steward,

Records in his accounts, and my clerks write out.
With the Spirit of Wisdom they search the Reeve's rolls,   460
And with the Spirit of Fortitude I scrape in the cash!'
   Then a king came there, and said, 'By my crown,
I was crowned king to rule the common people,
And defend Holy Kirk and her clergy against criminals.
And whatever livelihood I lack, the Law lets me take it
Where I can most quickly come by it; for I am the head
   of the Law;
You are only the limbs, and I am above you all.
Now, since I am head of you all, I am also your healer –
The chief helper of Holy Church, and headman of the
   Commons.
What I take from those two, I take at the teaching   470
Of the Spirit of Justice; for I am Judge over you all.
So I may have Communion freely, for I borrow from no man.
Nor cadge from the Commons except as required by my rank.'
   'Upon condition,' said Conscience, 'that you can duly
   defend
And rule your realm well, by reason and by truth,
Then your Law allows you to claim what you need –
   within reason.
     Omnia tua sunt ad defendendum, sed non ad depredandum.'
     (All things are yours for defending, but not for
     despoiling.)
The vicar, being far from home, took friendly leave.
Thereupon I awoke, and wrote down what I had dreamed.

Well, having thus awakened, on my way I went,
My expression mournful, and misery in my heart;
Nor did I know where to eat, nor where to find food.
When it was nearly noon, I met with Need,
Who accosted me with abuse, and called me an impostor.
'Could you not have excused yourself as the King and
    others did,
That only out of necessity did you take food and clothing,
As taught and told by the Spirit of Temperance,
And never took any more than directed by Need –
Need who knows no law, nor acknowledges any debt?   10
For he makes free of three things for his life's preservation.
The first is food, if man refuses him it and he has no money
And no one will go bail for him, and he has nothing
    worth pawning.
    If he is caught in such a case, and acquires food by theft,
He certainly commits no sin by getting it so.
And he may acquire clothing so, if he cannot bargain better:
Need will soon stand his surety in such a case.
And if his lips long for water, the Law of Nature
Will make him drink from any ditch rather than die of thirst.
So Need, in real necessity, may annex things to himself   20
Without consulting Conscience or the Cardinal Virtues,
So long as he submits to the Spirit of Temperance.
    For no virtue is so sovereign as the Spirit of Temperance,
Neither the Spirit of Justice nor the Spirit of Fortitude;
For the Spirit of Fortitude fails very often
By being immoderate, as may be often seen:
It may have men beaten too badly, or not beaten enough,
Or give men greater grief than good measure suggests.
And the Spirit of Justice must judge, willy nilly,
According to the King's Council, or the Commons' wish.   30
And the Spirit of Prudence will in many points fail
When it wants to foresee the future, for that rests with wisdom;

Opinions are not always wise, nor informed guesses, either:
Man proposes, God disposes – and governs all good virtues.
And Need is near God in this: that he humbles men in
    a moment,
And makes them as meek as lambs when they miss necessities.
Wise men have forsaken wealth, wishing rather to be needy;
They went to live in wildernesses, and would not grow rich;
God left His great joy and spiritual good,
Assuming human nature, and becoming needy –   40
So needy, as the Scriptures say in sundry places,
That He Himself said in His sorrow on the Cross,
'Both foxes and fowls of the air may creep or fly to shelter,
And the fishes have fins that take them fleetly to rest;
But Need has so seized me here, that I must needs stay
And suffer most bitter sorrows, that will soon turn to joy."[1]
So do not be bashful about begging and being needy,[2]
When He Who made all the world was needy from choice –
Never a man more needy, nor who died poorer.'
When Need had so reproved me, I soon fell asleep,   50
And had a most marvellous dream: that in Man's shape
Antichrist came, and tore up by the roots
The tender crop of Truth, turned it upside down
And made falsehood spring up and spread and serve
    men's needs.
In every quarter he came to, he cut away Truth,
And made Guile grow in its place, as if it were good.
The friars followed this fiend, for he gave them vestments,
And the religious orders reverenced him, and rang all
    their bells,
And whole convents came out to welcome that tyrant
And all his hangers-on, too – except the fools,[3]   60
Which fools preferred to die first, rather than live
Any longer, since Loyalty was so insulted,
And the false fiend Antichrist ruled over all folk.
For these fools were mild and holy men, fearing no misuse,
Defying all falseness, and the folk who practised it;
And should any king comfort or consort awhile with
    such men,

Antichrist's crowd would curse him, and their counsel,
    whether cleric or layman.
  So Antichrist soon saw hundreds follow his banner.
Pride bore it boldly all about,
Beside the Lord who lived for bodily lust,   70
And who came to fight Conscience, that safe-keeper
    and guide
Of the Christian Company and the Cardinal Virtues.
  Said Conscience, 'I counsel all you fools to come with me
Into Unity, Holy Church's stronghold, and hide there,
And cry unto Nature to come and keep us fools safe
From the limbs of this fiend, for love of Piers Ploughman.
Let us call to the common people that they come into Unity,
To abide there and battle against Belial's children.'
  Nature heard the cry of Conscience, and came out of
    the planets[4]
And sent forth his fore-runners, fevers and fluxes,   80
Coughs and carditises, cramps and toothaches,
Rheums and retinitises, and running sores,
Boils and blains and burning agues,
Frenzies, and other foul evils. These fore-runners of Nature
Pierced and preyed-upon great presses of people
Till a legion, more or less, had soon lost their lives.
Then were heard cries of *Woe's me!* and *Help! Here comes Nature*
With dreadful kinds of death, to undo us all!
And the Lord that lived for lust cried aloud
To Comfort, his knight, to come and carry his banner.   90
  'To arms, to arms!' cried that Lord, 'Every man for
    himself!'
The two sides met each other before the trumpets could sound
Or Heralds-at-Arms call out the titles and names of the lords.
Hoary Old Age came, and he was in the spearhead,
Bearing the banner before Death, as by right he could.
Nature followed near him, with a flock of fierce diseases,
Such as poxes and pestilences, that undid many people.
Thus Nature's contagions killed whole companies –
Death came driving after him, and dashed into dust
Kings and cavaliers and kaisers and popes;   100

Learnèd or unlettered, he let no man stand
That once he had hit, for he never stirred again.
Many a lovely lady, and many knights' lemans,
Dropped senseless, and died, from the bitterness of
      Death's blows.
   Now Conscience, in pure kindness, requested Nature
To pause and be patient, and see if such people
Would secretly leave Pride's party, and become perfect
      Christians.
So Nature held his hand, in hope that folk would reform.
But then Fortune began to flatter those few left alive,
Promising them long lives. And she sent out Lust   110
Among all sorts of men, married or single,
And he gathered a great host to fight against Conscience.[5]
   This Lust laid about him with cheerful looks,
And with secret speeches and subtle words,
And armed himself with idleness and with arrogance.
He bore a bow in his hand, and many bloodstained arrows
That were feathered with fine promises and not a few
      false betrothals.
With his unchaste chatter he often troubled
Conscience and his companies the teachers of Holy Kirk.
   Then Covetousness came, and cast about for means   120
Of overcoming Conscience, and the Cardinal Virtues.
He armed himself in avarice, and lived as if ravenous.
His weapons were wiles for winning and hoarding:
With feigning and falsehood he fooled all the people.
Simony had sent him to assail Conscience,
And these two preached to the people, and chose prelates
      for themselves
Who would take Antichrist's side, to save their temporalities.
He came to the King's Court as a cruel baron,
And in that Court kneeled to Conscience before the
      whole company –
And made Good Faith flee the place, but Falsehood
      remain;   130
He boldly overbore with many bright gold-pieces
Much of the worth and wisdom of Westminster Hall.

He would jog up to a Justice and joust at his ear,
Unseating Honesty with, 'Take this to amend your
    judgment';
Then would afterwards be off in haste to the Archbishop's
    Court,
There turning Civil Law towards Simony, with a bribe
    for the officer.
For a mantle of miniver he would make a true marriage
Disband before Death came, and frame a divorce.
    Quoth Conscience, 'Alas! I wish Christ, of His grace,
Had made Covetousness a Christian, he fights so keenly   140
And is so bold and stubborn while there's money by him.'
    But Life only laughed, and had scallops cut in his clothes,
And armed himself hastily in whorish words,
Thinking sanctity absurd, and courtesy wasteful;
He thought Loyalty a labourer, and Liar a freeman;
Conscience and Good Counsel he counted as fools.
Thus, with a little luck, Life was revived,
And pranced away with Pride, praising no virtue,
Nor caring how Nature can slay, and will come at last
To kill all earthly creatures except only Conscience.   150
No; Life leapt away and found himself a light-of-love.
Said he, 'Health and I, and high-heartedness,
Will save you from dread of Death or of Old Age;
You shall forsake all sorrow, and think nothing of sin.'
    Life and his leman, Fortune, liked this very well;
Till at last they begat in their glory a lazy lout
Called Sloth, who was to cause much calamity.
He matured amazingly fast, and was soon a man;
Then he wedded a brothel-wench whose name was Despair.
Her sire had been an Assize-juror who was always
    foresworn,   160
A certain Tom Two-Tongues, attainted at every inquest.
Sloth was a wary warrior, and made himself a sling
That cast the dread of Despair a dozen miles round.
    Conscience, in consternation, called upon Old Age,
And bade him make efforts to fight, and frighten
    Despair away.

Old Age hefted the sword of Good Hope, and made
    ready in haste;
He drove Despair into outlawry, and did battle with Life.
Life fled away in fear, and sought help from Physic,
And begged for salvation from some of his elixir,
And gave him hard-earned gold that gladdened his heart;   170
And for this gold, Physic gave him a cap of glass.[6]
Life had faith that Physic's art could foil Old Age,
And drive away Death with doses and drugs;
But Old Age attacked Life again, and at last chanced to hit
A physician in a furred hood, who fell into a palsy;
And that doctor died not three days later.
    Said Life, 'Now I see that neither Physic nor Surgery
Is even a ha'porth of help against Old Age.'
But in hope of healing he took good heart,
And rode to the house of Revel, a rich and merry mansion: 180
'The Company of Comfort', men sometimes call it.
    Soon after, Old Age attacked *me*, and walked over my head,
And battered me bald in front and bare on the crown;
He rode so rough-shod on my head, I shall bear the marks
    for ever.
'Sir Ill-bred Old Age,' I said, 'may bad manners attend you!
How long have you had right-of-way over men's heads?
Could you not have had the courtesy,' quoth I, 'to ask leave?'
He answered, 'Ah, so? Be quiet, you oaf!' And attacked me
    with ageing.
He hit me under the ear, and now I'm hard of hearing;
He beat me about the mouth, and battered my teeth out;   190
He fettered me so firmly with gout, I can't stir from home.
And for all the woe I was in, my wife too was sorry,
And wished with all her heart that I were in Heaven;
For the limb she loved me for, and delighted to feel –
At night in especial, when we were naked –
By no means could I manage to make it to her liking:
Old Age, and she, had entirely undone it.
    Then, as I sat there in sorrow, I saw Nature pass by,
And Death drew near me. I shook with dread,
And cried out to Nature to cure my cares: 200

'See how Hoary Old Age has handled me!
Avenge me, if it be your will, for I long to get away!'
    'If you want revenge, you must go into Unity,
And stay there, without stirring out, until I send for you;
And be careful to learn some craft, before you do come out.'
'Counsel me, Nature,' quoth I. '*What* craft shall I learn?'
    'Learn to love, and leave all else aside.'⁷
'But how shall I gain goods, and get food and clothing?'
'If you love loyally, you shall never lack
A meal or a worldly garment while your life lasts.'   210
    So on Nature's advice I set out to wander
Through the lands of Contrition and Confession, till I
        came to Unity.
Conscience was its Constable, the saviour of Christians,
But I saw it was besieged by seven great giants,
Who in Antichrist's company harassed it hard.
Sloth with his sling made a fierce assault;
And proud priests, more than a thousand, accompanied him
In bum-freezers and pointed boots, and with bloody great
        knives:⁸
These came against Conscience, in company with
        Covetousness.
    'By Mary!' said a banned priest from the Irish border,   220
'So long as I get silver, I set Conscience at no more
Than I do to drink a draught of good ale!'
And so said sixty more from the same country,
And sent showers of shot at him, and many sheaves of oaths,
Broad-barbed arrows like 'By God's heart and nails!',
And they almost had Holiness and Unity helpless.
    Conscience cried, 'Help, Clerisy, or I shall fall
Before these perverted priests and prelates of Holy Church!'
The Friars heard his cry, and came to his help;
But they knew their business badly, and Conscience
        abandoned them.   230
    Then Need came near, with news of a warning for
        Conscience,
That they had come out of covetousness, in hope of a curacy:
'Because they are poor, perhaps, and have no patrimony,

They flatter rich folk for the sake of good living.
But since they *chose* the chill of wretched poverty,
Let them chew the mouthful they chose – and charge them
    with no parish!
He is likelier to lie, who must beg for his living,
Than he who labours for his living and lets beggars share it.
Since friars forsook the felicities of this world,
Let them live as beggars – or eat angels'-food only!'   240
    When he heard this counsel, Conscience commenced
    laughing,
And courteously comforted the friars, having called them in,
Saying, 'Sirs, you are certainly all welcome
To Unity and to Holy Church. But one thing I beg of you:
That you remain in Unity, and keep yourselves from envy
Of lettered folk or lay, and live according to your Rule.
Then I will be your bailsman; you shall have bread
    and clothing
Enough, and your other necessities; you shall not lack
If only you leave your logic and learn how to love.
For love they gave up lordship and lands and learning,   250
Friars Francis and Dominic – for the love of holy living.
    If you long for livings, take a lesson from Nature:
God made in their proper measure all manner of things,
And set them at certain decisive numbers,
And gave new things names, and numbered the stars:
    Qui numerat multitudinem stellarum: et omnibus eis
      nomina vocat.
    (He telleth the number of the stars; he calleth them
      all by their names.)[9]
    Kings and cavaliers, likewise, keepers and defenders,
Have officers under them, all in fixed numbers;
And for costing a campaign, one must record men's numbers,
Or no purse-bearer will pay them, however hard people fight –
Others who might be on the battlefield would be thought
    bandits,   260
Pillagers and armour-plunderers, in all places accursed.
    What is more, monks and members of all Religious Orders
Are required by their Rule to restrict their numbers:

Of learned and unlearned alike the Law demands
A certain quota for each class – except only friars.
I may tell you, then, by Christ, Mother Wit informs me
That it would be wicked to give you wages, for you are
    growing innumerable!
The Heavenly Host is numbered, but not that of Hell;[10]
And so I especially wish you were all well registered,
And numbered under a notary's seal, neither more nor less!' 270
Envy heard this, and had friars haste off to school
To learn logic and law – and contemplation, too –
And preach to men about Plato, and prove it by Seneca,
That everything on Earth ought to be common property.[11]
    Yet he lies, I believe, who preaches this to unlettered men,
For God made a law for Man, and Moses taught it:

> *Non concupisces domum proximi tui ... nec omnia quae*
>   *illius sunt.*

> (Thou shalt not covet thy neighbour's house ... nor
>   anything that is thy neighbour's.)

But how ill is this observed in the parishes of England!
For parsons and parish priests, who should be the people's
    confessors,
Are called 'curates' because they must know and heal
All their parishioners, and impose penances on them,   280
And make them ashamed in their shrifts; but that shame
    makes men go
Fleeing off to the friars, as defaulters do to Westminster
(Bearing borrowed money there, then begging the lenders
Frantically for forgiveness, or a few more years' grace;
But while they are at Westminster, they will go to work hard
To make themselves merry on other men's goods).[12]
    So it fares with many folk who confess to the friars –
Like assizers and executors, who will award the friars
A few pence to pray for a dead man, then proceed to
    make merry
With the remains of the riches that the other had
    drudged for,   290
Thus leaving the dead man in debt until the Day of Doom.
On this score, Envy abhorred Conscience,

And founded a school for teaching the friars philosophy.
   Meanwhile, Covetousness and Unkindness were attacking
      Conscience;
But he held firm in Unity and Holy Church.
He appointed Peace his Portress, to bar the gates
Against all idle tale-tellers and hesitants.
Hypocrisy and she had a hard struggle,
For Hypocrisy made a heavy assault on her gates,
And wickedly wounded many wise teachers   300
Who accorded with Conscience and the Cardinal Virtues.
Conscience called for a Doctor skilled in hearing confessions:
'Go, give your salve to those who are sick, and wounded
      by sin.'
Doctor Shrift prepared painful salves, and made the sick
      do penance,
Every man of them for the misdeeds they had committed,
Till Piers's pardon had been paid for by *Repay what you owe.*
   Some found this treatment distasteful, and sent letters
      to discover
If any surgeon there besieged used less stringent cures.
Sir Like-to-Live-in-Lechery lay there and groaned,
For fasting on a Friday made him feel like death: 310
'There *is* a surgeon in this seat who deals more softly,
And knows far more of physic, and plasters a fellow
      more gently.
He is called Friar Flatterer, Physician and Surgeon.'
Contrition said to Conscience, 'Have this man come to Unity,
For here we may have many men whom Hypocrisy has hurt.'
Quoth Conscience, 'There is no need. I know of no better
      healers
Than the parson, the parish priest, the bishop, or the
      Grand Penitentiary –[13]
Except Piers Ploughman, who has power over them all,
And may deal men indulgences unless they are in
      debt to him.
Still, since you so wish, I am willing to sanction   320
That Friar Flatterer be fetched, and physic your patients.'
   The friar had heard of this, and went in haste

To My Lord Bishop, for a licence giving him leave to *cure*
Just like a *curate*. So he came with his certificates,
As boldly as you like, to the Bishop; and he soon had his brief
To hear confessions in whatever quarter he came to.[14]
So he came to where Conscience was, and knocked to come in.
    Peace, the Portress of Unity, opened the gate,
And hurriedly asked him what he might want.
The friar said, 'In faith, both for profit and for health,   330
I would like to converse with Contrition. That is why
      I have come.'
Said Peace, 'He is sick, and so are many others.
Hypocrisy hurt them so badly, they will hardly recover.'
'I am a surgeon, and understand salves;
Conscience knows me well, and can vouch for my skill, too.'
Peace then said, 'I pray you, before you proceed,
What is your name? Please tell it, and not conceal it.'
    'Certainly!' said his friend, 'It is Sir Slip-into-Houses.'[15]
'Ah, so! Then gang your gate, by God, for all your physic;
Unless you have learned something better, I shall not
    let you in!   340
I knew such a one as you, not eight winters ago,
Who came, in such a cope, to a Court where I dwelt.
He was doctor to My Lord and to My Lady too;
And at last this licenced beggar, when My Lord was away,
Gave our women-folk such *salves*[16] that some grew with child!'
    But Courtesy commanded Peace to cast the gates open:
'Let in the friar and his friend; give them full hospitality;
He may know this or that, and there is no telling
But that Life may learn from him to leave Covetousness,
To be in dread of Death, and withdraw from Pride,   350
And come to accord with Conscience, and all kiss
      each other.'
And so, because of Courtesy, the friar came in
To where Conscience was, who greeted him warmly.
Quoth Conscience, 'You are welcome! Can you heal the sick?
My cousin Contrition is confined here wounded:
Comfort him if you can, and take care of his sores.
The parson's plasters and powders are too mordant;

And he leaves them on too long, being loth to change them –
From one Lent to the next Lent he will let them burn.'
The licentiate said, 'That is too long. I shall amend it.'   360
　　So he goes and fingers Contrition, and gives him a plaster
Called Private-Payment, and says, 'I shall pray for you,
And for all those whom you love, all my life long.'
And to Peace, 'You, my lady, shall have Matins and Masses,
And the fellowship of our fraternity – for a little silver.'[17]
So he creeps around collecting cash, and cajoling whom
　　　　he confesses,
Till Contrition has quite forgotten to cry out, or weep,
Or be wakeful for his wicked acts, as he had once done.
In the comfort of a mild confessor, he was contrite no more,
Though that is the most sovereign salve for all sins.   370
　　Sloth saw this, and so did Pride,
And they came back with cruel intent to the attack on
　　　　Conscience.
Conscience cried out again for Clerisy to help him,
And called on Contrition to keep the gates.
But Peace said, 'He's asleep and dreaming, and so are
　　　　many others.
That friar has bewitched these folk with his physic,
And salved them so mildly that they fear no sin.'
　　Said Conscience then, 'By Christ, I will become a pilgrim,
And walk as wide as the whole world stretches,
To find Piers the Ploughman, who may overthrow Pride   380
And find fitter work for the friars who flatter for their keep
And run counter to me, Conscience. I call Nature to
　　　　avenge me
And send me happy fortune and health, till I have found
　　　　Piers Ploughman!'[18]
And while he was crying out for grace, I awoke.

> *Explicit hic dialogus Petri Plowman.*
> (Here ends the discourse concerning
> Piers Ploughman.)

APPENDIX

The 'Autobiographical Episode'

C, 5, 1–104

Thus I woke up, God knows, when I lived in Cornhill,
Kit and I in a cottage, clothed as a loller,[1]
And not highly thought of, trust me, it's true,
By lollers of London and ignorant hermits,
Because I wrote about them as Reason taught me.
For as I came by Conscience I met with Reason
In a hot harvest when I had my health
And limbs to labour with and loved to live well
And to do nothing but drink and sleep.
I was sound in mind and body and someone questioned me; 10
Roaming in remembrance, thus Reason rebuked me.
'Can you serve,' he said, 'or sing in a church,
Put the hay into haycocks or pitch it into carts,
Mow or stack or make bindings for the sheaves,
Reap or oversee the reaping and rise early,
Or have a horn and guard the hay and sleep out at night
And keep my corn in my croft from cadgers and thieves?
Or make shoes or cloth, or tend the sheep and cattle,
Hedge or harrow or drive the hogs and geese,
Or any other craft the community needs,   20
To improve the life of those who provide for you?'
'Surely,' I said, 'so God help me,
I am too weak to work with the sickle or the scythe,
And too tall,[2] trust me, to bend over low.
If I worked as a workman I wouldn't last long.'
'Then have you lands to live on,' said Reason, 'or a rich family
To find you your food? For you seem an idler,
A spendthrift who has to spend or a timewaster.
Or do you beg for your living at people's doors
Or con them at churches on Fridays and feast-days?   30

That is the life of lollers and it's praised little
Where Righteousness rewards men right as they deserve.

>*Reddet unicuique iuxta opera sua*
>(He will repay every man in accordance with what he
>   has done.)[3]

Or perhaps you are maimed in body or member,
Or injured in some accident which might be an excuse?'
'When I was young,' I said, 'many years since,
My father and my family sent me to school
Until I knew certainly what Scripture meant
And what is best for the body, as the Bible says,
And safest for the soul, so long as I continue.[4]
And I never found, in faith, since my family died   40
Any life that pleased me but in these long clothes.[5]
And if I ought to live and earn my living by labour,
I should live by the labour that I learned best.[6]

>*In eadem vocacione in qua vocati estis*
>([Remain] in the same state to which you are called.)

And so I live in London and in the land round it;
The tools that I toil with and take my wages with
Are *Pater-Noster* and my primer[7] and *Placebo* and *Dirige*
And my psalter sometimes and my seven psalms.
These I say for the souls of such people as help me,
And those who provide my food promise, I believe,
That I'll be welcome when I come, once a month or so,   50
Now to him, now to her; in this way I beg,
Without bag or bottle but only my belly.[8]
And also, moreover, it seems wrong to me, Sir Reason,
To constrain clerks to do the work of common men,
For by the law of Leviticus[9] that our Lord ordained,
Tonsured clerks, by common understanding,
Should neither sweat at manual work nor swear oaths
    at inquests
Nor fight in the front line nor injure the foe.[10]

>*Non reddas malum pro malo*
>(Do not return evil for evil.)

For those who are tonsured are the heirs of heaven,
And in choir and in church the ministers of Christ.[11]   60

Dominus pars hereditatis meae. Et alibi: Clemencia
    non constringit
(The Lord is the portion of my inheritance. Mercy is
    not constrained.)
It is fitting for clerks to serve Christ
And for untonsured lads to labour on the land.
For no clerk should be crowned with the tonsure unless he
    has come
From franklins and free men and folk who are married.
Bondsmen and bastards and beggars' children,
These belong to labour and lords' kin to service
Of God and good men, which goes with their rank,
Some to sing masses or sit and write,
Read and receive what Reason ought to spend.
But since bondsmen's children have been made bishops   70
And their children's bastards have become archdeacons
And cobblers and their sons knights on payment of silver,
And lords' sons their labourers, pawning their lands
To ride against our enemies for the right of this realm
For the comfort of the commons and the king's worship,
Since monks and nuns, who should feed the mendicants,
Have made their kin knights and purchased knight-fees,[12]
And popes and patrons have spurned poor nobles
And taken the sons of Simon[13] to keep the sanctuary,
Life-holiness and Love have been long distant,   80
And will be till it's over or changed some other way.
    So please don't rebuke me, Reason, I pray,
For in my conscience I know what work Christ wants of me.
The prayers of a perfect man and his wise penance
Are the dearest labour that pleases our Lord.
Truly "Man does not live",' I said, ' "by bread alone"[14].
The prayer "*Pater-Noster*" provides proof of that:
"Thy will be done" will look after us in all things.'
'By Christ,' said Conscience, 'I can't see that this lies.[15]
But begging in cities doesn't seem perfect   90
Unless one's in an order, obedient to prior or abbot.'[16]
'That is true,' I said, 'and so I acknowledge
That I have wasted time and I have misspent time.

And yet, I hope, like a man who has ventured his money
And always lost and lost, and at last struck lucky
And made such a bargain he was better off for ever,
And at last wrote off his losses as light,
His winnings were so great through the words of grace.[17]
> *Simile est regnum celorum thesauro abscondito in agro.*
> *Mulier qui invenit dragmam . . . etc.*

> (The kingdom of heaven is like a treasure hidden in
> a field. The woman that found a silver coin . . .)

So I hope to have of him who is almighty
A gobbet of his grace and begin a time   100
That all times of my time to profit shall turn.'
  'I counsel you,' said Reason, 'to get on with beginning
The life that is laudable and lawful for your soul.'
'Yes, and continue in it,' said Conscience, and I went
  to church.*

*This translation of the 'Autobiographical Episode' is by Priscilla Martin.

NOTES

The poet sees, in a dream, the whole maze of activity that constitutes 'Middle Earth' – a plain lying between Heaven and Hell (lines 13–16). Corruption is everywhere, nowhere more flagrantly than in the Church: all men's standards – including, we detect, his own – are materialistic rather than spiritual. Already, however, we meet honest ploughmen, since one of them is not only the 'hero' of the poem but is also to be an instrument of human salvation.

1 The citation is inexact, but there are similar passages in several epistles, notably Ephesians 5:4.
2 The shrine of St James the Greater, at Compostela.
3 The site of a popular shrine dedicated to the Virgin.
4 A pardoner was originally a man (usually lay or in minor orders) licensed to give papal indulgences that remitted temporal penalties for sins. Gradually, pardoners began selling what they claimed were plenary remissions of the consequences of sins (past, present or to come), besides arrogating to themselves other privileges and powers. Cf. Chaucer's Pardoner in *The Canterbury Tales*.
5 The Black Death, at its worst during 1348–50, killed off so many people that many parishes could not support a priest.
6 Consistory Courts were episcopal courts of great power in cases involving the clergy. Langland often uses them as emblems of Judgment Day.
7 Matthew 16:19.
8 'Cardinal' does in fact derive from the Latin *cardo*, 'a hinge'. The four Cardinal Virtues are Fortitude, Temperance, Prudence and Justice (see Passus 19, lines 269ff). Langland glances satirically at the other meaning of *Cardinal*.
9 There follows an allegorical account of England's political structure and situation in the 1370s. The king was still a child, so that the country was in theory ruled by a Council of Peers. In fact, however, much of the power lay with

John of Gaunt, Duke of Lancaster, and his overbearing followers. In the fable of lines 146–207 (after a sketch of the duties of king, nobles, clergy and commons), the Cat represents John of Gaunt, with Richard II as the Kitten. The Rats are probably the upper-class members of Parliament, the Mice rich City merchants. The whole fable represents a plea for maintaining the present situation for fear of creating a worse.

10 Usually a lapsed cleric turned wandering poet.

11 Ecclesiastes 10:16.

12 'God preserve you, Dame Emma.' Some lost song – possibly about the sorceress of Passus 13, line 340?

PASSUS I

Passus 1 constitutes a moralising commentary on what Langland has described in the Prologue. We are given, as it were, the spiritual aspects of, and background to, what has so far been observed temporally and materialistically. By association, rather than by argument, Lady Holy Church draws us towards the basic theme of the poem: the identity of Truth and Love, and their personification in Christ as the incarnation of God. Langland is quick to ask the question upon which the whole epic hangs – 'How shall I save my soul?' He receives, but does not yet recognise, the same answer as crowns his entire long quest.

1 For the edifying story of Lot, see Genesis 19. The quotation is from verse 32.

2 For the conspiracy of World, Flesh and Devil against mankind, see also Passus 16, lines 24–52.

3 Matthew 22:17–22.

4 Langland's phrase (here as in the Prologue) is *kynde witte*, which might also be rendered as 'natural – or innate – intelligence', implying an inborn sense of right and wrong.

5 The elder-tree is apocryphal, but the belief was widespread, perhaps because of the tradition that the Cross was made of elderwood (though a Celtic tradition has it made from the wood of a descendant of Adam's tree). For the hanging itself, see Matthew 27:3–5. See also Bennett.

6 The *locus classicus* is 1 John 4:16.

7 St Luke (apparently Langland's favourite evangelist) does not say so. Langland may still be thinking of the context cited above.

8 This anachronism, common medieval currency, may be variously interpreted; but it probably refers to 2 Samuel 23:8ff.

9 The seven lower orders of faithful angels are Thrones, Dominions, Virtues, Powers, Principalities, Archangels, Angels. The rebellious angels, that became fiends, fairies and other supernatural beings, form a tenth order.

10 A misquotation, occurring elsewhere in the poem, from Isaiah 14:13–14.

11 Cf. Deuteronomy 10:12.

12 Cf. Isaiah 53:2.

13 John 1:14.

14 Matthew 7:2. The Latin, below, is the Vulgate of this passage.

15 James 2:26.

PASSUS 2

Having been instructed in the recognition of Truth, the Dreamer must now learn how to recognise Falsehood (personified in the Devil). Holy Church shows him (on the ill-omened left side, which in this case is the North – the Devil's quarter) several examples of personified evil. Gradually, these begin to act out their allotted parts.

1 Langland uses *Fauvel* to mean – primarily – Flattery. The name may ultimately derive from the Latin *fabella*, 'fable, invention, lie', but Langland will probably have borrowed it from the earlier fourteenth-century *Roman de Fauvel*, by Gervais du Bus. In this poem, the name is made cognate with *fauve* and *faux*, 'tawny' (a colour of deceit), and 'false'. The name is also an acronym – which must be slightly adjusted, in English – of Flattery, Avarice, Uncleanness of heart, Variety (fickleness), Envy and Lachete (baseness of soul).

2 Properly speaking, 'meed' means simply 'reward' – including fair payment for honest work. Langland uses personified Meed to represent *corrupt* payments of all kinds. Her clothing may be intended to suggest the Scarlet Woman, the Whore of Babylon (though she is introduced as a maiden – since she cannot properly be said ever to have belonged to any man). She is in any case the enemy and antithesis of Holy Church.

3 The first phrase is proverbial, the second from Matthew 7:17.

4 Psalm 15:1ff – one of Langland's favourite texts.

5 The suggestion of incest is quite possibly intentional. Cf. line 25.

6 Assize-jurors were originally witnesses, upon oath, but had begun to move towards the present-day function of jurors; they were in either case susceptible to bribery. Summoners were officers of the Church whose duty was to bring sinners before ecclesiastical courts. Their corruption and venality were notorious: cf. Chaucer's Summoner in *The Canterbury Tales*. Pre-emptors were 'purveyors', royal officials who oppressed market-folk by buying-up their goods (at arbitrary low prices), during a royal progress. Provisioners, 'vitaillers', were those who did this with foodstuffs. 'Brokers' here means marriage-brokers – professional go-betweens. The Court of the Arches was the London law-court of the Archbishop of Canterbury. Its (clerical) lawyers charged high fees.

7 What follows is a gorgeous parody of the 'deeds of gift' that often accompanied marriage-settlements.

8 'Pauline' may be a reference to the Crutched Friars ('crutched' = 'crossed' – *cruciati*, from the crosses on their clothes and staffs), a theoretically mendicant order that busied itself in lawsuits. But it is difficult to see a pardoner in such an Order or function; and the reference may be to the preaching that was common at Paul's Cross (pardoners, of course, having no right to preach: see Prologue, line 68; cf. also Passus 10, note 9). All such, together with beadles and reeves and millers, were proverbial for greed and dishonesty.

9 In the passage that follows, Langland (through the mouth of Theology) makes play with the double meaning of 'meed' noted above. Theology's at first surprising defence is of honest payment for services rendered; not of bribery and corruption. Hence his contradictory account of her ancestry.

10 Luke 10:7.

11 What I have called 'pope's-priests' were 'prouisoures' – clerics arbitrarily given benefices, over the heads of other eligible priests, by the pope or by his delegates. Such appointments were open to accusations of simony. Note that in the whole of this splendidly satirical passage, *all* the officials (clerical or not) who ride or are ridden to the King's Court at Westminster, are implicitly accused of corrupt venality. It may also be a fresh satirical touch that it is *Fauvel* who orders the mounts: in Gervais du Bus he is himself a tawny stallion.

12 The Commissary was an episcopal officer to whom bishops delegated special legal powers outside the Consistory Court itself.

PASSUS 3

Meed is brought for trial before the King at Westminster. She is treated at first as an innocent victim of unscrupulous people; but very soon the venal frequenters of the Court are 'making up' to her. In this Passus, the attack upon Meed by Conscience is a counterbalance to her defence in Passus 2 by Theology. It constitutes the Dreamer's first ideally spiritual – as distinct from piously practical – advance.

1 It was a fairly common practice, for people who could afford it, thus to decorate and restore a Friary or its church – and have one's name and portrait recorded there in stained glass. To be one of the Friars' Lay Sisters was to become, with no further effort unless a little more money, a participant in their spiritual privileges. Langland several times mentions the practice, with disapproval.

2 Cf. Matthew 6:1–4. The Vulgate quotation and Authorised Version paraphrase after line 72 are from the same source.

3 Pillories were at this time used to punish various kinds of dishonest trading, especially those involving food. The 'penal stools' were ducking-stools, an equivalent punishment for female offenders.

4 Not Solomon, but Job 15:34. I have not given the Authorised Version, since Langland himself at once paraphrases the passage.

5 There is no known historical connection between bribery and the dethronement and murder of Edward II – the king presumably referred to.

6 Again, no literal connection can be made with the poisoning of a pope; but see Passus 15, lines 521–2, and the notes on that couplet.

7 A reference to the secret and illicit use of the Privy Seal for the obtaining of benefices.

8 Love-days were sessions of the Manorial Courts, for the settling of minor local disputes.

9 Meed is referring to the disastrous French Campaign by Edward III, 1359–60, which resulted in his signing away most of his French possessions – for money – and in which the troops were indeed demoralised by great storms. It is hard to see how *Conscience* can be blamed for any of the misfortunes and misdeeds alleged by her; and while meed as *soldiers' pay* is certainly a great heartener of troops, it was meed as *pusillanimous greed* that caused Edward to sign the Treaty of Brétigny. Perhaps Langland intends Meed's arguments to be confused and false? Later in her defence, however, she copies Theology in assuming the righteous interpretation of her name; and for a while, this convinces the king.

10 Psalm 15 again, as are the texts after lines 236 and 240.

11 A reference to Luke 6:38, and to the bottomless greed of the corrupt.

12 Psalm 26:10.

13 Matthew 6:5.

14 The story is in 1 Samuel 15, *et seq.*

15 Ibid.

16 Isaiah 2:4.

17 Ibid.

18 This is a parody, but a half-serious one, of fake astrological predictions. There is no point in attempting a Nostradamian interpretation for every detail; the purport is plain enough – eventual salvation for all the peoples of the world.

19 Proverbs 22:1.

20 Langland paraphrases the Vulgate of Proverbs 22:9. The Authorised Version differs. The joke, expounded by Conscience, is that Meed's mock-bashful claim to be unlearned is howlingly confirmed: the last phrase of (Vulgate) 22:9 is by no means to Meed's purpose, and is quoted by Conscience after line 345. It is not found in the Authorised Version.

21 Thessalonians 5:21.

22 See note 20.

PASSUS 4

Meed's trial, or rather examination, is suspended while Conscience rides away to bring Reason back to Court. Meanwhile, there has begun a case that is to end in the overthrow of Meed and most of her adherents. The king pledges himself to reform the State, and to use Conscience, Reason and Obedience to that end – and also for the reformation of society *per se*. Note that all moral advances are still those of *practical* good behaviour, and imply no real spiritual change.

1 'Cato' refers to neither of the great Romans, but to a collection of moral proverbs called *Catonis Disticha* – 'Cato's Couplets'. They are the work of one Dionysius Cato, *fl.* fourth century AD. They formed part of every grammar-school curriculum, and were a favourite source of quotations for Langland. The point is that basic education (Cato) is the servant of Reason (see Bennett). 'Tom True-tongue (etc.)' represents decent and sensible conversation. The horse represents watchful patience, and its girths are

good advice. Its bridle must be heavy so as to encourage humility.

2 These two represent *worldly* wisdom and native cunning (Bennett).

3 Romans 3:16–17.

4 Ibid., verse 18.

5 'Wrong' is no longer the Devil, as in Passus 1, but a purveyor (see Passus 2, note 6). 'Peace' is here an oppressed farmer.

6 This was another abuse – under-payment by a tally that could in theory, but not always in practice, be off-set against taxes.

7 Because when criminals were convicted in Royal Courts, all their property escheated (was forfeited) to the Crown – unless, as Wisdom hints, the criminal could buy himself off. Later, Wisdom suggests to the king another such transaction: that Wrong be released by Mainprise (or suretyship); that is to say, upon bail which he would promptly skip. Meed shall be his mainpernor, or surety, after which no more need be said about his crimes.

8 Emblem of a proudly-dressed woman. Cf. Passus 5, lines 26 and 63.

9 Religious who forsake their cloisters either for pure pleasure, or to go on needless pilgrimages, such as (lines 126–7) to the shrine of St James at Compostela.

10 Perhaps meant literally; but most likely a reference to fees taken by officials or the Papal Court in exchange for judgments or benefices.

11 See Passus 2, note 11.

12 The riddle derives from a precept of Pope Innocent III's: that that man is a just judge '*qui nullum malum praeterit impunitum, nullum bonum irremuneratum*' – who lets no evil go unpunished, no good unrewarded.

PASSUS 5

This Passus marks the beginning of the true quest, Reason's sermon moving everyone to repentance; the poet puns on his name, Will, to show that human resolve is beginning to reform.

The goal is now spiritual as well as practical. The Seven Deadly Sins, personified, confess and repent and are shriven. Christ's aid must be enlisted before Truth can be found and redemption achieved; and meanwhile, who can guide the world along the right path? Not the false palmer (lines 523ff. – the corrupt Church), but the true pilgrim – Piers. At this stage, he personifies natural and instinctive goodness (as described by Holy Church in Passus 1). Further, as a ploughman, he represents honest and productive toil, which Langland repeatedly maintains to be the root and bedrock of sincere practical Christianity. Piers Ploughman's description of the Way to Truth is an allegory of spiritual progress, and leads to an allegorical description of the human soul itself.

1 The Plague was by now very seldom quite absent; but there were serious outbreaks on at least four occasions between 1369 and 1375. There was a great storm on Saturday, 15 January 1361 (1362 by modern reckoning).

2 See Passus 4, note 8.

3 To beat his wife so as to save her from the ducking stool that was the fate of scolds.

4 Half-a-mark was 6s.8d., or nearly 34p in modern currency. A mark was a good month's wages for an artisan.

5 Proverbs 13:24.

6 Matthew 25:12.

7 The Holy Ghost.

8 Here, the personified Sin of Pride.

9 Since Envy was a sin commonly attributed to friars (Bennett).

10 Sugar was considered medicinal. I have used 'twisted canes of candy' to translate Langland's *diapenidion*, a medical form of barley-sugar (Bennett).

11 It is noteworthy that Wrath is not presented as himself an angry man (as, in fact, Envy *is*), but as a cause of anger and contention in others.

12 Limiters were friars licensed to beg only in specific areas. 'Lectors' *may* here mean 'lecturers'; but a Lector is one of the lowest Minor Orders of the Church.

13 This must be meant allegorically, for of course he had no right within the convent walls (for, in fact, despite line 136, as a gardener he would have been a layman; and even friars needed a special dispensation).

14 It was Gregory IX (Pope 1227–41), not St Gregory I or St Gregory VII, who forbade abbesses to hear confessions.

15 Probably a reference to 1 Peter 4:7.

16 The purpose of this portrait is to demonstrate that every trade and profession uses dishonest tricks to increase profits; hence the diverse occupations pursued by Covetousness and his wife. For no clearly known reason, Langland in line 189 calls him 'Sir Harvey'.

17 So that it would stretch.

18 Pudding-ale was thick and inferior, but she sold it mixed with smaller quantities of good ale (Bennett).

19 In other words, at nearly three times the normal price for good ale.

20 Strictly 'regrater' – one who buys cheaply and gains a local monopoly, then sells dearly.

21 The priory of St Andrew, near Bromholm in Norfolk, had a cross reputed to have been made from the True Cross. It was not far from the shrine at Walsingham, a favourite resort for pilgrims (Goodridge & Bennett).

22 Punning on *French* in its meaning of 'cant' or 'jargon'. Norfolk was supposed to be a particularly dishonest county.

23 Even more than the Jews, whom at this period they outnumbered in England, the Lombards were hated as extortionate money-lenders.

24 The 'cross' was the 'heads' side of a coin (the reverse being *pile*). The pun is of course on Christ's Cross.

25 I do not know the origin of this couplet.

26 From St Augustine's *Epistles* (Bennett).

27 Psalm 51:6. The 'gloss' will be the *Glossa Ordinaria* (see Bennett).

28 Psalm 18:25–6; but the Authorised Version does not translate *sanctus*, 'holy'.

29 Psalm 145:9.

30 Nowhere literally in the Scriptures. 'Scintilla' really means *spark*.

31 These bits-and-pieces are too trivial to interfere with his fast – or so she would persuade him.

32 This curious game was a kind of barter in which appointed judges estimated the difference in value to be paid by one or other owner of two articles offered for exchange. Here, the difference in value between Hicks's hood and Clement's cloak is only a mug of ale which was no doubt the primary purpose of the game.

33 Robin Hood was a real person, alive and in trouble with the law in the early thirteenth century. His exploits, of course, are fictitious. It is doubtful which Randolph of Chester Langland had in mind; but it is interesting to learn that ballads about both people were already current. Cf. Bennett & Goodridge.

34 Duty should have called him to *early* Mass, and at his parish church. Even at the Friary Mass he arrives only when it is virtually over.

35 The opening phrases of Psalms 1 and 128.

36 Langland calls this person *Vigilate*, 'Be watchful', in reference either to Mark 13:35–7, or to Matthew 26:41. *Leveilleur* = 'the waker'.

37 Romans 13:7. The theme of *restitution* is central to the two closing Passus, but is in a sense basic to Langland's view of Christianity.

38 This is the name given, in the apocryphal Gospel of Nicodemus, to the penitent thief, though his name also appears as Dimas and even Titus. (The impenitent one was Gestas or Gesmas.) For the canonical account of the incident, see Luke 23:3–43, as also for 'remember me' in line 474.

39 *Latro* is Latin (and masculine) for 'robber'. It is the word used in the Vulgate for Christ's fellow-sufferers on Cavalry.

40 Genesis 1:26.

41 1 John 4:16. The Latin before line 499 is from Ephesians 4:8.

42 Isaiah 9:2.

43 Mark 16:9, etc.

44 Luke 5:32.

45 John 1:14.

46 Psalm 71:20 – though the Authorised Version differs.

47 Psalm 32:1.

48 Psalm 36:6–7.

49 A representation of the kerchief reputedly lent by Veronica to Christ, to wipe His face – which left its likeness on the cloth.

50 That of St Thomas à Becket, in Canterbury. As perhaps the most popular in England, it was notable for its rich endowments.

51 Exodus 20:12. Others of the Ten Commandments are paraphrased in the lines that follow. Cf. also Deuteronomy 5:7–21.

52 The human soul.

53 A theme often found in medieval literature. Cf. the ninth-century hymn *Ave maris stella* – 'Hail, Star of the Sea' – stanza 1, line 4: in this the Virgin is called *felix coeli porta*, 'blissful gate of Heaven'.

54 Cf. Hosea 13:3.

55 That is, your soul may linger in Purgatory.

56 Seven Virtues (though not the conventional list) to balance the Seven Deadly Sins.

57 Bishops' bulls were letters authorising the sale of indulgences.

PASSUS 6

As we have seen, Langland believed honest labour to be an essential part of practical Christianity. Those people who agree to follow Piers, in search of Truth, must work in his field until the harvest is complete. Piers's 'half acre' of course represents all Middle Earth; and, while both work and harvest are *literally* meant, they are also emblematic of spiritual cultivation. Human nature being what it is, the whole project quickly comes to a standstill.

1 Luke 14:10.

2 But not for the profitless, dishonest and immoral callings

that he lists: they are *ipso facto* damned, short of repentance and amendment. Cf. the Prologue, lines 35–45.

3 Psalm 69:28.

4 Ibid.

5 Cf. Deuteronomy 24:10–13. Again the theme of restitution.

6 An eighth-century image of Christ, crucified but regally dressed, in Lucca Cathedral.

7 Perhaps an uncloistered monk, or a goliard.

8 Bretons, like Gascons at a later period, had a reputation for boasting.

9 Bayard was a common, and hence generic, name for a horse. The food is presumably bran-mash, since *baken*, like modern German *backen*, did not have the limited meaning of modern English 'bake', though I have used that word for convenience.

10 Galatians 6:2.

11 Hebrews 10:30 and Romans 12:19.

12 Luke 16:9.

13 Genesis 3:19.

14 Proverbs 20:4.

15 The image of a man, or of a man's face, was the emblem of this evangelist.

16 See Matthew 25:14ff.

17 Ibid., verse 29.

18 Psalm 128:2.

19 I do not know what particular kind of fur *Calabrian* fur was, except that it was grey (Bennett); but physicians were a byword for (ill-gotten) wealth.

20 From *Cato's Couplets*. See Passus 4, note 1, and Bennett.

21 The ineffective Statutes of Labourers attempted to halt the increased demands of workmen (prompted by the scarcity of labour, and the widespread emancipation of villeins, after the Black Death). But Hunger's Law, says Langland, is always observed.

22 As with the 'prophecy' in Passus 3 (see note 18 on that Passus), there is little point in labouring for detailed explanations of this passage. But a few points may be noted. 'Waken with the waters' does suggest the floods of

line 326; Saturn is (astrologically) malignant, and associated with winter, famine and certain diseases. The sun standing awry suggests an eclipse (there was one in 1377); and the monks' heads remind us of the lack of charity in the Church. The maiden having mastery refers to Meed and her continuing reign with even greater power. Further suggestions are made by Bennett and Goodridge.

PASSUS 7

Piers's project having broken down, all thoughts of a literal pilgrimage, even within the terms of allegory, have been abandoned (except, in later Passus, for Langland individually; and even that is emblematic). The precept now is to be: *Cultivate your own fields; save your soul at home, by honest labour, humble devoutness and practical charity.* This will prove more effective than all the indulgences and false pardons that you may purchase: there is a *true* pardon, summed-up in the words 'Do well'.

This Passus ends the first part of the epic, but with hints of what is to come – namely, Langland's quest (within himself) for the meaning of 'Do-Well', personified, and his companions Do-Better and Do-Best. The later significance of Piers is also foreshadowed: already he is offering himself as a mediator for the salvation of others.

1 Such a plenary (and hereditary) pardon is beyond the power of any Church official, even the highest: only God can remit the guilt itself; as well as the punishment for it.

2 Goodridge says that this means the two divisions of the Ten Commandments – those relating to God, and those relating to our neighbours. Bennett says it means Canon Law and Civil Law. Most probably it refers to the Old and the New Testaments, as elsewhere in the poem.

3 A misquotation from Psalm 15:5.

4 Not in the Bible.

5 Psalm 15:5. Substituted for Langland's 15:1.

6 'Very small'.

7 Matthew 7:12.

8 Cato here is the Cato who wrote the *Disticha* or Couplets. See notes above. The 'Clerk of the Stories' was the twelfth-century Peter Comestor, who wrote an *Historia Scholastica* which was a (legendarily) expanded version of the Bible (Skeat).

9 Not Gregory, but Jerome in his commentary on Ecclesiastes (Bennett).

10 Luke 19:23.

11 From St Jerome's Epistles (Bennett).

12 Psalm 37:25.

13 Cf. the Athanasian Creed, and its basis in Matthew 25:46. Piers is infuriated (line 116) because this is *not* a full pardon for all his helpers, but merely a restatement of what he and they have already been taught: it is valid as a pardon *only conditionally* – upon good behaviour. Piers thereupon resolves to live like a hermit, offering his own piety on behalf of mankind.

14 Psalm 23:4. This verse has sometimes been interpreted as a resolve to live faithfully and piously, without fear, even when surrounded by malicious unbelievers (Goodridge). If that is its import here, it may mean that Piers rejects the Priest's casual dismissal of the pardon – which, though not what Piers expected (see previous note), is nevertheless a guarantee of salvation *upon terms*.

15 Psalm 42:3.

16 A paraphrase of Matthew 6:31.

17 Psalm 14:1.

18 I have corrected Langland's misquotation of the Vulgate (Proverbs 22:10).

19 Langland is here muddling Daniel 2 with Daniel 5. The dream cited by him in fact concerned Belshazzar.

20 Genesis 37:9–10, 41:39–41, and succeeding chapters.

21 Biennial and triennial masses were those endowed, for such periods, on behalf of a dead person. For Bishops' Bulls, see Passus 5, note 57.

22 Matthew 16:19.

23 By the Four Orders, Langland means the Augustinians, Carmelites, Dominicans and Franciscans. Friars could give

lay people (sometimes whole families) 'letters of fraternity', thus creating them 'confraters' or associate-members of the Order. Cf. Passus 3, note 1. This gave them the privilege of being prayed for during life and after death; but it cost money. The Provincial was the monastic head of a given district, and had the power to distribute letters of indulgences. Such indulgences (see note 1) were in fact limited; but pardoners, and others, let it be thought that one could thus buy one's way into Heaven.

PASSUS 8

This Passus describes the Dreamer's hesitant beginning in his quest for Do-Well, Do-Better and Do-Best. Passus 7 was the start of a transition from *temporal* to *spiritual* concerns (hints of which had been given in earlier Passus). But, misled by his encounters with the two Friars, and with Thought, the poet still continues for several Passus (*a*) to believe that Do-Well, Do-Better and Do-Best are *separate* modes of life (only towards the end does he see that, like the Trinity itself, they are triune); (*b*) to look for them in the worldly and practical kind of Life that he has explored in the Prologue and the first seven Passus, rather than looking for them in spiritual development. He must learn that they are not constituted by *actions*, merely, but by an attitude of mind that must necessarily *bring about* good actions.

Langland sees quite easily through the Friars' facile and superficial complacency. But Thought is harder to reject, since he represents the limit of the Dreamer's present ability. Only Reason, says Thought, can teach Langland how to *apply* his moral principles.

1   Franciscan Masters of Divinity.
2   Latin: 'On the contrary!' This was the formal signal of a rebuttal in the debates or 'quodlibets' of the Theological Schools.
3   Proverbs 24:16.
4   An echo of Luke 16:9. Cf. Passus 6, line 230.
5   2 Corinthians 11:19. Langland misunderstands, or perhaps for dramatic reasons allows Thought to misunderstand, St

Paul's *statement* – and takes it to be an injunction. See also Passus 20, note 3, and Goodridge.

6 The word in Langland is *Witte*, which throughout the poem has many shades of meaning. In this context, the name could also be rendered as Intelligence or Native Good Sense.

PASSUS 9

Reason's answer to Will's question begins as an allegory of the human body – for it is in the healthy interaction of the natural human faculties (bodily and mental) that Reason claims Do-Well is to be found. Most of the evil in the world, he says, arises from the misuse of one or more of these faculties: Do-Well is rational obedience to God's laws; and whatever is contrary to Nature and Good Sense, is criminal. Do-Well is therefore basically spiritual in origin, though physical in its effects.

1 In Langland, *Kynde* – another word with several shades of meaning. It can mean 'Nature', 'human nature', 'all that is naturally ordained', 'all that is innate'. Therefore, 'unkynde' can mean *unnatural* as well as *cruel* (Langland would have found the difference very slight, in any case). In this context, of course, Kynde (or Nature) means *God*.

2 The doctrine of Empedocles, that all things were composed of various admixtures of four 'elements'. My translation modifies Langland's text: he omits Fire, since for him *eyre* meant the fire of the upmost atmosphere, whereas the air that we breathe he called *wynde*.

3 The human soul.

4 Satan. See John 12:31.

5 That is, Do-Well guards the frontiers of body and soul from the invasion of evil.

6 For metrical convenience (and anyway not without justification!) I have thus translated Langland's *Inwitte*, which might also be rendered as Good Sense, and elsewhere also carries the modern meaning of conscience.

7 Psalm 148:5.

8 All three Persons of the Trinity acted simultaneously in

creating Man. 'Let *us* make ...' (Genesis 1:26) implies this. Langland's text is very confused, but not in fact contradictory, since the Word may be used either as an intermediary or as part of a simultaneous act. See Goodridge.

9 The word used here by Langland is the same *Inwit* (so spelt in this context) as in line 18; but it does not refer to the *person*.

10 Philippians 3:19.

11 1 John 4:16.

12 Matthew 25.12 and Psalm 81.12, respectively.

13 St Jerome, St Gregory, St Augustine and St Ambrose. Cf. Passus 19, lines 262–8.

14 There is nothing directly relevant in Luke. Goodridge suggests Acts 6:1–4 or James 1:27.

15 Both quotations are from Peter Cantor's *Compendium* (Goodridge).

16 Proverbs 9:10.

17 James 2:10.

18 Psalm 34:10.

19 At the marriage at Cana. John 2:1–10.

20 It was believed that Cain was conceived during a time when his parents should by duty have abstained from intercourse (in penance for their sin). Though, in any case, Jewish law too proscribed certain times. Cf. Leviticus 12: 2–5 and 15:16–28, etc. This meant that he was born cursed with wickedness, and all his descendants would be cursed and wicked too.

21 Psalm 7:14.

22 This tradition is not in canonical scripture; but it was believed that Genesis 6:1–4 referred to the intermarriage of Cainites with Sethites.

23 Genesis 6:6–7.

24 Genesis 6:14–20.

25 Ezekiel 18:20.

26 Matthew 7:16.

27 John 14:6 – 'I am the way and the truth.'

28 An ancient Essex ceremony, still observed, was that if a couple could swear that they had never quarrelled, nor

regretted their marriage (and could maintain their word under severe cross-examination), they would be awarded with a flitch – a whole side, salted and cured – of bacon.

29 Goodridge says that the Latin is by John of Bridlington.
30 On days of fasting or other penitence.
31 1 Corinthians 7:2.

PASSUS 10

Reason's speech displeases his wife, Dame Study. She believes Langland to be a sensual hypocrite merely toying with amateur theology, rather than genuinely seeking Do-Well. She attacks all quibbling arguments and fine distinctions unless they are undertaken by serious, expert and devout scholars. When Langland protests his own earnestness, she relents and sends him off to her kinsfolk Clerisy (or Learning) and his wife Scripture (which means not merely the Old and New Testaments, but all sacred or devout writings). Together, this couple imply *all* knowledge proper for a Christian to possess. It should be noted that Langland has gained virtually nothing from Reason and Study, but still clings to his intellectual preconceptions. Even from Clerisy and Scripture he gains little more save to be driven into the opposite camp and to regard faith alone (without intellect or learning) as Do-Well.

1 Matthew 7:6.
2 'Gem' derives from the Latin *gemma*, a bud – and reflects the belief that such stones grew organically.
3 The 'love-days' previously noted (Passus 3, note 8).
4 Cf. Job 21:7ff. and Jeremiah 12:1.
5 Psalm 73:12.
6 Psalm 11:3 in the Vulgate; but both the Prayer Book and the Authorised Version differ from the Latin.
7 Cf. Passus 2, line 111.
8 Psalm 132:6. Langland has completely misunderstood the text. As the biblical 'gloss' points out, and the New English Bible makes plain, David is talking about a new home for the Ark of the Covenant. Langland believes the text to imply that God Himself is found among the fields and

woods, and their inhabitants, rather than among rich townsfolk.

9 Not in the Cathedral, but outside, at St Paul's Cross.

10 Isaiah 58:7.

11 The Apocrypha rather than the Bible properly so called. Tobit 4:8.

12 Ezekiel 18:20.

13 Galatians 6:5.

14 The English is Authorised Version, Romans 12:3. The words of the Vulgate mean 'not to have more wisdom than it is proper to have'.

15 Langland's word is *clergye* – 'clerkship', not necessarily implying ordination, but only the state of being literate and well read.

16 Medieval education comprised two main groups of studies. The Trivium consisted of grammar, logic and rhetoric; the Quadrivium, of arithmetic, geometry, astronomy and music.

17 This is again Cato of the *Disticha*. But cf. Passus 18, note 14.

18 Galatians 6:10.

19 Romans 12:19. See also, as previously noted, Hebrews 10:30.

20 Do-Well, in short, is adherence to Christian faith. Although Will comes to embrace this as the literal and exclusive nature of Do-Well, he is not much advanced by it – nor by Clerisy's denunciation of corruption in the Church (which he himself has already denounced).

21 John 14:9–10.

22 A dictum of St Gregory's (Goodridge).

23 I cannot trace the quotation verbatim; but the motto is familiar enough.

24 Again untraceable by me.

25 Matthew 7:3.

26 Ibid., verse 5.

27 Not Mark, but Luke 6:39.

28 The story is in 1 Samuel 4.

29 Psalm 50:21.

30 Isaiah 56:10.

31 Cf. the Prologue to *The Canterbury Tales*, lines 177–82. The

origin of the saying appears *not* to be Gregory, but Gratian's *Decretum*. Still, the 'fish out of water' simile is widespread.

32 Matthew 21:12; Mark 11:15; Luke 19:45.

33 Psalm 1:1.

34 Psalm 20:7–8.

35 An allusion to the pretended Donation of Constantine (d. 337), by which the Emperor allegedly endowed Pope Sylvester and his successors in perpetuity with wealth and temporal power. Cf. Passus 15, lines 519–23. It was Gregory who sent Augustine to Britain, where he founded monasticism; hence 'Gregory's godchildren'. See also Passus 15, note 50.

36 An old and rich abbey, taken as typical.

37 Isaiah 14:4–5.

38 Here an emblem of Antichrist, who shall eventually be defeated by the King of Heaven and His loyal followers – not, as Will here supposes, by secular power.

39 1 Timothy 6:9–11.

40 Ecclesiasticus 10:9.

41 From Cato's *Disticha*.

42 James 2:5–6. Also Luke 16:19ff. – the parable of Dives and Lazarus.

43 Cf. note on Passus 8, line 20.

44 There is nothing explicitly to this purpose in either Peter or Paul. Perhaps Langland was thinking of Mark 16:16.

45 Colossians 3:1.

46 Exodus 20:13 – the sixth Commandment. See also Deuteronomy 5:17.

47 Romans 12:19, with the Authorised Version and (lines 370–1) with Langland's gloss. See also Hebrews 10:30.

48 Cf. Revelation 20:12–15.

49 John 3:13 – i.e., a man's fate is known only to God.

50 Even in Minor Orders, Langland must have known that the Church *could* not pronounce finally on such a matter.

51 Matthew 23:2.

52 Psalm 36:6.

53 See Luke 23:39ff. The Harrowing of Hell – the release from damnation of certain patriarchs, prophets and others – is

not specifically recounted in the canonical Gospels, but in that of Nicodemus (which was, in the Middle Ages, accorded virtually canonical respect).

54 Ecclesiastes 9:1.
55 Latin and early Middle French. Origin unknown to me.
56 The Latin, 'nobody good', is too terse for a certain attribution. Psalm 14:1? Matthew 19:17? The latter is likelier.
57 Langland's paraphrase of Mark 13:9–11.
58 Langland's paraphrase of Psalm 119:46.
59 Cf. Passus 9, line 72, and note 13 on that Passus.
60 Matthew 20:4.

PASSUS II

Langland has in effect rejected secular power, learning and reason, and even good works, as fallible if not fallacious means to Do-Well. For this, he is rebuked by Scripture. Now thoroughly discouraged, he abandons his quest for many years – which he spends in idle and lascivious pleasure. He is pulled up sharply, however: first by fear, then by Loyalty (which in this context means general uprightness and honest living, and adherence to the basic tenets of the Church). Now he is made to see that all that he has rejected *may* be valid, but only if inspired and infused by love – by *caritas*, or Christian charity and loving-kindness. Also, he must stop *questioning* everything for a reason. This he cannot yet do, until brought by Imagination into a broader view both of the world and of the inner self (the process only begins in this Passus, and belongs chiefly to the next).

1 From St Bernard.
2 See 1 John 2:16. The phrase 'pride of perfect living' does not occur there in the Authorised Version, nor in the Vulgate. The New English Bible renders the phrase as 'all the glamour of [the world's] life'.
3 Not Plato, but a familiar adage perhaps derived from Proverbs 16:9.
4 Perhaps based upon Matthew 6:34.
5 Complex puns are involved here. 'Reason' – *witte* – is both the Dreamer's, and generically human, good sense, and the

character called by me *Intelligence* (and by Langland Witte) in Passus 8 and 9. 'Will', as on certain other occasions – as in Passus 5, line 62 – puns upon the Dreamer's name and on childishly human obstinacy and self-seeking.

6 See Passus 3, lines 35ff., and elsewhere, for the notoriously easy penances given by well-fed friars. Cf. Passus 7, lines 191–3, for Provincials' letters, pardons and acceptance into Fraternities. See *passim* for friars' venality!

7 Untraced by me in this form, but related to the basic theme of *restitution*. But cf. Passus 5, note 26.

8 But of course Langland knows that their motive was the high burial-fee they would charge.

9 Untraced by me; but, again, related to the theme of penitence and restitution. See note 7.

10 John 3:5.

11 There is nothing quite like this in either of Peter's Epistles or any of Paul's. The general principle may, however, be found in several texts; and as the words stand, they are a misquotation of Leviticus 19:17. Langland is punning (I believe he is pretending to do so naïvely) upon the Latin *frater*, which translates both as *brother* and as *friar*.

12 Matthew 7:1.

13 I follow Goodridge here in replacing Langland's repetitive *Non oderis fratrem* – 'Thou shalt not hate thy brother' – with 1 Timothy 5:20, which is more to the poet's point.

14 Psalm 50:21.

15 They must observe the seal of the Confessional.

16 Untraced by me.

17 The reference is to Matthew 22:1–14.

18 Isaiah 55:1.

19 Mark 16:16. The second, unquoted, part of the verse is also meant to be in readers' minds: 'but he that believeth not shall be damned'.

20 Psalm 145:9.

21 The account given by Langland, and by Trajan himself, closely follows a widespread medieval legend. The point is that St Gregory's prayers for Trajan's salvation would not *in themselves* have sufficed to redeem an unbaptised

misbeliever; but Trajan's own instinctive excellence of character, *plus* the prayers, *did* suffice. Some versions have it, however, that he first had to be restored to life, and baptised.

22 See Passus 10, note 16.
23 1 John 3:14.
24 Luke 14:12–13.
25 Cf. 1 Peter 2:2.
26 John 8:34.
27 Galatians 6:2.
28 The story is in Luke 7:37–50.
29 Matthew 7:2.
30 See Luke 24:13–31.
31 Luke 10:38–42.
32 Obviously, therefore, not Matthew. This quotation is from the same source as the last.
33 Proverbs 30:8.
34 Again, not Luke; it is Matthew 19:21.
35 Psalm 37:25.
36 Based upon Matthew 17:20.
37 Psalm 34:10.
38 Psalm 43:1.
39 Langland misquotes the Vulgate, giving *Deo*, 'God', instead of *Domino*, 'Lord'. It is Psalm 37:3.
40 James 2:10.
41 Psalm 47:6–7.
42 Here, as sometimes elsewhere, to be taken as God the Creator.
43 A superstition traceable, like so many, to Aristotle.
44 It was believed that the lecherous peacock sought out the eggs of his hen so as to break them – thus inducing her to fresh copulation; see Skeat.
45 Adjured by St Paul (1 Corinthians 4:5), Reason must suspend judgment and so must Langland.
46 1 Peter 2:13.
47 Ecclesiasticus 11:9.
48 Genesis 1:31.
49 Genesis 1:22–6.

50 Boethius, Book One, Prosa 7. Cf. Chaucer's version: 'This
    feynede philosophre took pacience a litel while; and when
    he hadde resceyved wordes of outrage, he, as in stryvynge
    ayen and rejoysynge of hymself; seide at the laste ryght
    thus: "undirstondistow nat that I am a philosophre?" The
    tother man answerede ayen ful bytyngly and seyde: "I
    hadde wel undirstonden it yif thou haddest holde thi tonge
    stille."'

PASSUS 12

Imagination is to set Will's muddled and extremist thoughts in
order; he sorts out, for the poet, the tangled strands of various
theories, relates them to each other, and leads the dreamer
towards *acceptances* – towards something like Keats's 'Negative
Capability', the ability to remain in uncertainty.

1 Luke 12:38.
2 A misquotation of Revelation 3:19. Cf. also Proverbs 3:12.
3 Psalm 23:4. Langland misunderstands the *protective* pur-
   pose of the shepherd's crook and staff, which he takes to
   be instruments of (loving) punishment.
4 1 Corinthians 13:13. I have not quoted the Authorised
   Version, since Langland himself immediately paraphrases
   the text.
5 Rochemadour was a shrine of the Virgin, near Cahors.
6 These are all examples of straying from one's proper
   concern and duty.
7 Aristotle, as a heathen, could in any case be *presumed* to
   be damned. Hippocrates murdered his nephew, the even
   greater physician Galen. Virgil (not the poet, but the
   medieval necromancer) was carried off by Satan. Alexander
   died young, murdered by poison.
8 Felicia was the hero Guy of Warwick's wife, who plagued
   her husband until he deserted her. Rosamund, for centuries
   a fabulous beauty, was Henry II's mistress until poisoned
   by his wife.
9 I have not traced this.

10 Luke 6:38.

11 A misquotation of Luke 12:47. I have translated Langland's Latin, and ignored the Authorised Version.

12 1 Corinthians 8:1.

13 John 3:8.

14 John 3:11.

15 John 3:8 again.

16 Leviticus 20:10 is the passage Langland has in mind, but it does not specify death by stoning. Cf. Deuteronomy 22:20–24.

17 John 8:3–11. That Christ wrote *something* on the ground, is canonical; that He wrote about the Jews' sins, is not.

18 Matthew 7:1.

19 One must not partake of Holy Communion if in a state of sin. Cf. 1 Corinthians 11:27–9.

20 Cf. Numbers 1:50–3.

21 1 Samuel 13:9–14.

22 2 Samuel 6:6–7 gives one example.

23 Psalm 105:15.

24 1 Corinthians 3:19.

25 Luke 2:15.

26 Matthew 2:1.

27 This belief is based on the word 'house' in Matthew 2:11 (Goodridge).

28 Luke 2:7, with a comment perhaps of Langland's own.

29 'Glory to God in the Highest!'

30 Psalm 32:1.

31 Matthew 15:14.

32 All who could read must be tried by ecclesiastical courts (if at all), not by secular; thus they escaped hanging. Tyburn, of course, was long one of the most famous gibbet-sites. The quotation from Psalm 16 suggests that this was used as a test of literacy; but the more famous 'neck-verse' (the implication is obvious!) was Psalm 51.

33 Ecclesiasticus 5:5.

34 Psalm 62:12.

35 Psalm 135:6.

36 It is not known to which poet Langland refers – he tends,

in any case, to use the word 'poet' loosely – as, for instance, of Plato.

37 Not in his *Logic*, but in his *Natural History*.

38 1 Peter 4:18.

39 I have not been able to identify this and the next Latin quotation.

40 Psalm 23:4.

PASSUS 13

In this Passus, the Dreamer's quest moves even farther from *literal* towards *spiritual* concepts of 'doing'. The pilgrim called Patience reaffirms that *to love* is to 'Do Best'; and in token of this, the name of Piers Ploughman is heard again: he is now the embodiment of the *caritas* that may save mankind, and of the unpretentious life of the devout poor. In addition to this, the Dreamer himself learns patience and humility. To emphasise the importance of this achievement (and, indeed, of the Passus itself), Langland reintroduces the Seven Deadly Sins by way of Haukyn, the man of Active Life. Haukyn symbolises all worldly, superficial, venal thought and activity – and therefore all the sins that arise from these. He does this very neatly by way of his own inveighing against both laymen and clergy. Gradually, Conscience and Patience begin the cleansing of his coat – the reformation of his sins; his penitence, and his redemption.

1 Luke 10:7.

2 That is to say, after death such sinful friars as this Master (cf. Passus 8, lines 8ff.) will suffer in Purgatory or even in Hell unless they repent and do penance.

3 I do not know the origin of this quotation.

4–9 All these emblematic dishes are phrases from penitential psalms. See Passus 12, note 32 for 4, which is Psalm 51:1, the 'neck-verse'. The remainder are all from Psalm 32.

10 Psalm 51:17.

11 Isaiah 5:22.

12 See 2 Corinthians 11:24–8.

13 Ibid. As earlier, Langland plays on the double meaning of *frater* – either 'brother' or 'friar'.

14 I cannot identify the quotation; but see previous note.

15 *The Apocalypse of Gluttons* was written by Walter Mapes (*c.* 1140–1209), who eventually became Archdeacon of Oxford. He contributed to some versions of the Arthurian Legend, as well as composing this and other satirical works (this one contains specific descriptions of clerical gluttony). By contrast, St Aurea was an eleventh-century Spanish anchoress of (literally) legendary abstemiousness (Goodridge).

16 Matthew 5:19.

17 The first quotation is universal; the second is from Psalm 15:1.

18 This is a riddling way of saying that he carries with him, as a talisman, an image of the *Agnus Dei*, 'the Lamb of God which taketh away the sin of the world' (John 1:29). The days mentioned are those of Easter Week – the Saturday being Passover Day. It was on this day that the pope ritually blessed the *Agnus Dei* images; and it 'starts the calendar' because it was the first day after the redemption of mankind on Good Friday. The 'middle of the moon' will be Easter Day. On Easter Wednesday, church services concentrated upon the neophytes who had been baptised on the preceding Saturday: that in itself was a kind of 'passing over'. Cf. Goodridge.

19 1 John 4:18.

20 See Mark 14:3–9. Though unnamed in that context, the woman is traditionally assumed to have been Mary Magdalen.

21 Luke 19:2–8.

22 Luke 21:1–4.

23 A glancing reference to James 1:3–4.

24 This is Haukyn. In line 221 he looks like a minstrel because of his disreputable clothing (see below). He *calls* himself one because he envies their pay and their abilities (which he affects to despise); but his dissolute life also makes him resemble those minstrels decried in the Prologue, lines 35–9. In fact (line 226) he is a 'waferer': besides being an ordinary baker, he also bakes both sweet wafer-bread and

what will become Holy Wafers. I am not sure what allegor-
ical subtlety lies behind these facts, except the (as it were)
two-faced nature of his business; but 'bread' in line 243
means – astonishingly for this period! – *money*. Haukyn is
named Active Life *not*, as he claims, because he is a busy
and honest trader (and a helper of Piers Ploughman: cf.
lines 236–40), but because he interferes in all men's business
– for his own aggrandisement (lines 283–313).

25 These are of course *household* minstrels, not itinerants.

26 The heads of St Peter and St Paul on the seal of a papal
indulgence.

27 Mark 16:17–8.

28 Acts 3:6. It is perhaps needless to remark that all this argu-
ment (including, I think, the recantation in lines 256–8) is
Langland's irony rather than Haukyn's naïvety.

29 Stratford-at-Bow (the odd French of which was spoken by
Chaucer's Prioress). It was a busy bread-making centre just
outside London (Skeat).

30 Which is very good history. The reference is to John de
Chichestre.

31 The first quotation is a slight misrendering of part of
Galatians 1:10. The second is Matthew 6:24.

32 The first quotation is slightly misremembered from Psalm
10:7; the second is from Psalm 57:4.

33 Unidentified people, and perhaps imaginary.

34 Matthew 6:21.

35 Luke 6.25.

36 According to Skeat, not a quotation but a general maxim.

37 Psalm 101:7; but both Prayer Book and Authorised Version
differ considerably from the Vulgate (and each other).
I have given a slightly paraphrased version of the Vulgate.

38 Not John, but Luke 10:16.

PASSUS 14

The active and sinful life of the world, as allegorised in Haukyn,
begins to give way. In its place come the spiritual values – and
techniques – taught by Patience. These are: patience itself,

humility, contrition, happy poverty and, above all, *faith and love* (*caritas*).

1 Luke 14:20.
2 The three phrases between lines 17 and 23 constitute the three aspects or acts of Contrition. Sacramental Penance is indeed often referred to as Satisfaction – see line 94.
3 The first part is from Matthew 6:25–6; the second is Langland's (and Patience's) recurrent motto.
4 A slightly garbled version of John 14:13.
5 Matthew 4:4.
6 I do not know the origin of this Leonine hexameter.
7 Psalm 148:5.
8 Psalm 145:16.
9 Exodus 17:6. For the forty years in the wilderness (line 63), see Deuteronomy 1:1–3.
10 1 Kings 17 and 18.
11 These were the legendary Seven Sleepers of Ephesus. The legend varies from one source to another, but all agree that seven young Christians fell asleep and were walled up in a cave. The length of their sleep and their eventual fate also vary from one account to another, but the period usually given is two hundred years.
12 A very confused memory of Ezekiel 16:49–50.
13 Sodom and Gomorrah, the Cities of the Plain. See Genesis 18:20 to 19:25.
14 Psalm 32:1.
15 Luke 16:19ff. Neither Vulgate nor Authorised Version has the *name* Dives; it is a Latin adjective, meaning 'rich', mis-interpreted as a personal name. *La dolce vita* – 'the pleasant life' – is perhaps more familiar to modern ears than Lang-land's medieval French equivalent, *douce vye*.
16 Psalm 76:5 – but Vulgate, Prayer Book and Authorised Version all differ widely in their wording. I have made my own translation.
17 Psalm 73:20. Again, the three sources mentioned differ widely. I have used the Prayer Book version.

18 Source dubious, though the spirit is that of Matthew 19:23–4.

19 I have corrected the Latin, which Langland badly misquotes from Isaiah 30:15.

20 Langland is (reverently) parodying the formal introduction to a legal certificate, patent or declaration – that mankind is redeemed by the death of Christ.

21 See above, Passus 3, note 1 – and elsewhere.

22 Langland's Latin reads *Ita impossibile diviti, etc.* – 'Thus it is impossible for a rich man, etc.' – which occurs nowhere in the Bible but is obviously a sketch of Matthew 19:23–4. So I have substituted that, as above.

23 Revelation 14:13.

24 Langland's Latin corresponds exactly neither to Luke 6:20 nor to Matthew 5:3, but is much nearer the latter, which I have substituted.

25 Strictly speaking, it was St Paul who said it, in Philippians 2:7.

26 According to Skeat, this derives from Vincent de Beauvais's *Speculum Historiale* (a paraphrase, says Goodridge). Vincent was a thirteenth-century Dominican, whose major work was this outline of world history – with many legends included.

27 A notorious haunt of robbers, between Surrey and Hampshire (Skeat).

28 Not Seneca, but another quotation from the main Latin passage above; and the Latin after line 305 is from Juvenal's Tenth Satire (Goodridge).

PASSUS 15

Almost stealthily, as it were, the true concept of Do-Well has been arrived at; and this long Passus is a kind of prologue to Do-Better. Though the Dreamer is rebuked for insatiably wanting to *know*, he is taught that knowledge and learning are perfectly good in themselves *provided* that they operate together with charity (which again, as nearly always in this poem, means *caritas* – though 'charity' in the more usual sense is of course one practical expression of loving-kindness, and is often implied by

Langland). And charity can truly operate only through Piers Ploughman – who is now explicitly identified as Christ (line 206).

The perspective of the poem, and of the Dreamer, broadens to take in – for the Church and for all mankind – a vision of this loving-kindness working hand-in-hand with learning, wisdom, contented poverty and the virtues already learnt. The personal and purely temporal are being more and more transcended: we are now concerned with the possibility of universal salvation, by means of Charity; and the Dreamer is almost ready for the vision (in the next Passus) of Piers tending the Tree of Charity.

1 Peter is 'porter', of course, by virtue of his holding the keys of Heaven (Matthew 16:19). St Paul's falchion is an emblem of his martyrdom.

2 An example of Langland's shaky Latin. His source (Isidore only, not Augustine as he claims: see Goodridge) has *recolit*, 'remembers', which makes sense of *Memoria*. Langland confuses the verb *recolo* with some other that means 'to complain' – perhaps *recuso*, 'to object, to take exception'. Strictly speaking, moreover, even *recolo* (used figuratively as here) means less 'recollect' than 'turn over in one's mind'.

3 This is of course the passage in Isidore (*Etymologiarum Liber*) cited earlier by Langland.

4 *Presul* (Classical Latin *praesul*) originally meant a public dancer; did it acquire its clerical meaning from the story of David's dance before the Ark of the Covenant (2 Samuel 6:14)? *Pontifex*, originally 'bridge-builder', came to mean 'high-priest', hence 'pontiff', 'archbishop' and even 'pope'. A metropolitan bishop (*metropolitanus*) is also an archbishop, the bishop of a metropolis. *Episcopus* is the general term for a plain diocesan bishop. *Pastor*, 'shepherd', can mean any cleric with Cure of Souls, but specifically an ecclesiastical Visitor, or inspector, who would usually be of episcopal rank.

5 Isaiah 14:14.

6 Proverbs 25:27.

7 In St Bernard's *Epistles* (Goodridge).

8 Unidentified by me, but of course referring to Genesis 3:1–19.

9 The Latin is Romans 12:3. But see Passus 10, note 14.

10 Psalm 97:7.

11 Psalm 4:2; but I have substituted 'lying' for the Authorised Version's archaic 'leasing'.

12 In other words, 'Go to St Augustine's commentary, and check whether I am a heretic.'

13 The Latin is a misquotation from either James 2:1 or Deuteronomy 16:19. I have opted for the latter. Cf. also Leviticus 19:15.

14 I do not know where; but the likeness to a 'whited sepulchre' (not as in Langland) is in Matthew 23:27; and there is a 'whited wall' in Acts 23:3.

15 Not in fact from his works, but from an anonymous set of homilies (Goodridge).

16 A baselard was a kind of dagger, or sometimes a short sword. Priests were in fact forbidden to wear either weapons or frivolous adornments (see also below, lines 120–1, and elsewhere in the poem).

17 'Sir' was formerly a title of priests as well as of knights.

18 Matthew 18:3.

19 1 Corinthians 13:4–5 (slightly compressed).

20 The quotation is from 1 Corinthians 13:12. 'Mirrored in me' implies *both* Christ's assumption of human form, *and* that Will can understand Christ as perfect Man, but not as Charity incarnate.

21 A tunic from Tartary would probably be of silk, and a costly rarity. At this time, 'scarlet' was not necessarily red, but a particular kind of fine cloth, of any colour.

22 Obscure. Perhaps it means simply that he is devoted to prayer, of which he 'makes a fine art'.

23 The laundry is of course a symbol for contrition and penance (it is often forgotten that 'contrite' derives ultimately from the Latin *tero*, 'to rub, as in cleaning', and *contero*, 'to wear away by rubbing or battering' – still methods of laundry in Ireland and Egypt). The quaint location 'a mile's length', as a measure of *time*, may refer to

the time it takes an average man to walk a mile; but this does not seem a very long period of contrition.

24 The original line ends in Latin – *laboravi in gemitu meo*, 'I am weary with my groaning', from Psalm 6:6.

25 Psalm 51:17.

26 Matthew 9:4. This quotation, as applied to Piers, prepares us for the *identity* stated in line 206.

27 Langland gives the last four words in Latin: *petrus, id est, Christus*. This is done deliberately, to recall 1 Corinthians 10:4 – '*petra autem erat Christus*' – 'and that rock was Christ' (which itself echoes the well-known pun in Matthew 16:18: '*tu es Petrus, et super hanc petram aedificabo ecclesiam meam*' – 'thou art Peter, and upon this rock I will build my church').

28 The Lollards ('idlers', or possibly 'canters') were followers of Wycliffe. While they decried the same Church abuses as those attacked by Langland, unlike him they also disbelieved in transubstantiation and clerical celibacy. They were peripatetic preachers. For 'landloping hermits', see Prologue, lines 53–7 and elsewhere.

29 Matthew 6:16.

30 Edmund, King of the East Angles, was allegedly martyred by the Danes in 869. Edward may be either Edward the Confessor (1004–66), who is more likely, or Edward the Martyr (962–78) – unjustly so called.

31 Cyprus was a thin silken fabric, usually black, resembling crape, often confused with the tree *cypress*. For Tartary cloth, see note 21 on this Passus. The point, from lines 219–24, is that charity may be found with high-ranking priests or monks, but never with mendicant friars.

32 Ecclesiasticus 31:8.

33 Psalm 4:8.

34 This is the earliest St Antony, the lavishly-tempted hermit, who died at about the middle of the fourth century. He spent much of his life in the Egyptian desert. St Aegidius, or Giles, was French; he is known almost only from a tenth-century (and self-evidently spurious) 'Life' – which embodies the tale cited by Langland.

35 St Paul of Thebes, traditionally the Christian proto-hermit

(although he died only a few years before Antony, he was a centenarian even senior to that saint). St Jerome wrote a chimerical 'Life' of him: one would have expected few pleachable leaves, and less moss, in the Theban desert.

36 No; he made tents (Acts 18:3).

37 Cf. Matthew 4:18. But Andrew was in fact Peter's *brother*.

38 A widespread and quite uncanonical legend.

39 Job 6:5, followed by a gloss.

40 Psalm 112:9.

41 Partly from Peter Cantor, partly from Jerome (Goodridge).

42 See above for the Medieval Seven Arts (Passus 10, note 16). The Masters and Doctors had theoretically qualified in the higher studies of philosophy and medicine.

43 This refers to the hymn by St Thomas Aquinas, *Pange, lingua, gloriosi corporis mysterium* ('Declare, oh tongue, the Mystery of the glorious Body'). Stanza Four reads, in part:

> *Fitque sanguis Christi merum;*
> *et, si sensus deficit,*
> *ad firmandum cor sincerum*
> *sola fides sufficit.*

It is tempting to render this as English verse; but it means: 'And the pure wine becomes the Blood of Christ; and, if the understanding fails [to grasp this], faith alone suffices to support the untainted heart.'

44 What follows, about Mohammed, is common medieval legendary material.

45 For Antony, see above, note 34. St Dominic (1170–1221) was the founder of the Order of Friars Preachers, and a model of frugal living. *Francis* here means St Francis of Assisi (1181–1226), founder of the Friars Minor (Minorites), who were originally itinerant and penniless. The Benedict intended here (480–547) founded the monastery of Monte Cassino. Bernard of Clairvaux (1090–1153) founded the Cistercian Order.

46 Matthew 7:7.

47 Matthew 5:13.

48 Ibid.

49 Of course, the Apostles except Judas; but Langland must have been aware that a good deal of this work was delegated.

50 St Gregory the Great (540–604) despatched Augustine and forty other monks to convert Britain (596). St Augustine of Canterbury (d. 605) soon converted Ethelbert, and became Canterbury's first archbishop.

51 See Matthew 22:2–14. For Langland, the wild game signified the heathen; the tame fowls, oxen; and 'fatlings' (calves, piglets, etc., specially fattened for the table) are young neophytes that need particular attention.

52 As in Leviticus 11, and elsewhere.

53 Psalm 132; but see Passus 10, note 8.

54 Mark 16:15.

55 Honorary, not to say imaginary, bishoprics in the Holy Land necessarily treated as sinecures, despite Langland's missionary zeal.

56 John 10:11.

57 Matthew 20:4.

58 Matthew 7:7.

59 Galatians 6:14.

60 The military Order of Knights of the Temple was founded in 1118. Though they had begun as an order practising poverty, their wealth and influence increased rapidly: they were soon objects of jealousy and therefore of calumny. It is certain that some corruption had crept into the Order, but equally certain that none of the panoramic atrocities alleged against them was true. Nevertheless, after and amid many and great barbarities, the Church suppressed the Order in 1312.

61 Her 'rightful possessions', beginning with the 'Donation of Constantine'. See lines 519–23, and Passus 10, note 35.

62 Luke 1:52.

63 Deuteronomy 12:6. A 'heave-offering' was usually a lamb's (or sheep's, or other animal's) shoulder, held up as a sacrifice.

64 A widespread, now forgotten, legend. Cf. Passus 3, note 6.

65 See above, note 55, and below, lines 557–8.

66 See above, note 4.

67 This is fabled to have happened at Mailapur (or Mylapore) in India, after Thomas had baptised the ruler and many of his subjects.

68 Deuteronomy 23:25.

69 Isaiah 3:7. In this and the last quotation, I have corrected Langland's Latin.

70 Not Hosea, but Malachi 3:10.

71 Cf. Leviticus 19:18, as well as the better-known Matthew 19:19.

72 Matthew 14:15–21.

73 John 11:43.

74 Distantly based upon Daniel 9:24–7.

PASSUS 16

We now re-encounter Piers, in his new role – that of Christ Himself (though somewhat ambiguously) – as Keeper of the Tree of Charity. This Tree represents many things, all of them under constant threat from the Devil. It is the growth of goodness and holiness in this world from the Jewish patriarchs onwards; it is the growth of the Church with all the saints (and other holy folk) borne by it as fruit; it is the growth of goodness – Do-Well, Do-Better and Do-Best – in the soul of Man (which is imperfect, however, until crowned with the 'theological' virtues of Faith, Hope and Charity). Personifications of these we shall soon encounter, after this vision of how Charity grows in the world. All three of the main emblematic *themes* of the Tree combine in the life of Christ, of which Langland now has a vision. Just before Passiontide, he meets Faith (in the person of Abraham), and is confirmed in his belief in the Trinity.

1 Psalm 37:24, slightly altered by Langland. I have correspondingly altered the Authorised Version.

2 The first part of the Latin comes from Matthew 12:32. The second part is apparently Langland's gloss: that voluntary sin is tantamount to sin against the Holy Ghost, Whose help could always have been sought against temptation (Goodridge).

3 Skeat mentions a legend that the tree from which the Cross

was made grew in three stems (as emblem, presumably, of the Trinity). There is also, however, a Celtic legend (see the Cornish *Ordinalia*, and Passus 1, note 5) that Adam's tree gave rise to three others: one from which Noah's keel was built, one which formed the roof-tree of Solomon's temple and one from which the Cross was made. The three staves, of course, are themselves symbols of the Trinity.

4 The three *physical* states correspond, in ascending order of excellence, to three *social* states (matrimony, chaste widowhood, virginity), and to the three *spiritual* states of Do-Well, Do-Better and Do-Best. Later (lines 200ff.), the Trinity itself is symbolically tied into the analogy. See also Goodridge.

5 That is to say, not in *deep* Hell, but in Limbo.

6 Cf. Galatians 4:4. Cf. also the *Pange, lingua* hymn by Venantius Fortunatus (*c.* 530–610), line 10 of which reads: *Quando venit ergo sacri plenitudo temporis* ... ('When, therefore, the fullness came of [that holy] time ...).

7 See Luke 1:28–38.

8 Piers, in this passage, is not strictly speaking Christ Himself, but His Divine destiny.

9 Matthew 9:12.

10 John 11:33–8.

11 John 10:20.

12 John 2:13–16.

13 John 2:19–21, though the end of the speech belongs to the next note.

14 Matthew 21:13.

15 'Maundy', which gives its name to Maundy Thursday (the day before Good Friday), was the ceremony of washing the Disciples' feet (John 13:5–15), and is now a ritual washing of the feet of the poor. The word comes from *mandatum*, 'a command', because of the injunction at the end of the above passage and in verse 34 of the same chapter.

16 Langland's version of John 13:21 and of Matthew 26:21–5 (whence also line 145).

17 Langland's expansion of Matthew 26:48–50.

18 Does not belong in this context at all: it is Matthew 18:7.

19 John 18:8–9.
20 See 1 Corinthians 15, *passim*, and Hebrews 2, *passim*.
21 The Parable of the Hand, elaborated by Charity in Passus 17, lines 136 and 202, to explain the Trinity, is a kind of expansion of this obscure passage. Though the Trinity is triune, Son and Holy Spirit are *in some sense* dependent upon the Father. In this context, 'what both suffer' implies such interdependence – though Langland's human analogy is inexact. The passage that follows (cf. note 4, above) symbolically, in various ways, relates human life to the Trinity. Further, it continues the symbolism of the Tree of Charity: all human life, says Faith, depends upon *trinities* of things.
22 Matthew 27:46 – though Christ was in fact quoting Psalm 22:1.
23 Not biblical, but it echoes God's command to Noah and his family in Genesis 9:1.
24 Jesus, as a man on earth, must have a mother; as the Son of God in Heaven, He needs a Father only.
25 See Genesis 18:1–8. The incident is written as the entertainment of three angels; Langland – I do not know with what authority – treats it as *really* having been a visit of the Trinity, in person and speaking to Abraham *directly* rather than through the mouths of messengers (which is what I take 'And the Lord appeared ... and the Lord said ...' to mean).
26 Genesis 22:1–12. Langland's chronology goes awry here: see next note.
27 These events are recounted earlier, in Genesis 17:23–4.
28 Genesis 12:2–3, referred to in Romans 4:13.
29 Luke 1:55.
30 Genesis 14:18–20. This is held to foreshadow the Last Supper and the Mass – hence, also, Christian priesthood. Thus Abraham, 'Faith', is linked both to the New Law of Christ and to Piers.
31 Abraham's function as herald and protector of the righteous is justified by the previous note. See also Luke 16:22–3, Romans 4:9–14 and, of course, lines 254–69 of this Passus.
32 John 1:29.

PASSUS 17

Faith has been established; we await Hope and Charity. Hope
appears in the person of Moses: though the recorder of the Old
Law, he nevertheless foreshadows the New Law of *caritas*. In
Langland's opening line of this Passus, Hope calls himself 'a
spye' – a scout or explorer – in search of Christ the Combatant.
The Dreamer's last intellectual (and moral and emotional)
difficulties begin to crumble with the appearance and doctrine
of Charity – here personified in the Good Samaritan, himself
treated as an emblem of Piers/Christ. Charity, of course,
preaches the doctrine of that Love which proceeds from God
and should imbue all mankind. And he practises it, while Faith
and Hope remain inactive (lines 52–78).

1 The Old Law shall be consummated, and the New Law
  (springing from it) be validated, by Christ upon the Cross.
2 The 'piece of hard rock' refers back to the Two Tables
  brought down by Moses from Mount Sinai (Exodus 31:18).
  But it is also symbolic of the *permanence* of the Law
  inscribed on it (which is adumbrated by Leviticus 19:18 and
  Matthew 19:19; but see next note).
3 Matthew 22:37–40.
4 For the parable of the Good Samaritan, see Luke 10:30–7.
5 This 'jousting' is Christ's Passion, represented as a tourna-
  ment in which He overcomes the Devil, Hell and Death.
6 This whole episode (lines 52–123) is emblematic of Christ's
  Ministry, of that of the *righteous* Church, of the Passion
  and Resurrection and of the Second Coming. Lines 93–7
  refer to Baptism and the Eucharist (as well as to confession
  and penance). Lines 98ff. mean that hitherto the path to
  Heaven has been so beset by the Powers of Hell that only
  the faithful (or those that in righteousness *seek* the true
  faith) could pass it. But the Incarnation of Christ, and His
  imminent Passion, have made it safe for all who follow in
  His footsteps. The Latin after line 111 (more than once
  quoted by Langland) is from Hosea 13:14. 'Jerusalem' in
  line 114 implies the New Jerusalem – Heaven.
7 From the Catechism.

8 The Vulgate *omnia* means 'all things', which I have retained. The Authorised Version reads 'all men' (John 12:32).

9 Mark 3:29.

10 Cf. 1 Thessalonians 5:19 – which is also relevant to the succeeding passage likening the Trinity to a taper, ignited (for the individual) only by *caritas*.

11 Matthew 25:12.

12 1 Corinthians 13:1.

13 Matthew 7:21.

14 See Passus 14, note 15.

15 Revelation 6:10, misquoted and greatly shortened by Langland. I too have given a compressed version.

16 A rhyming adage, rather than strictly 'Holy Writ'. But cf. Passus 5, note 26.

17 Psalm 145:9.

18 The passage that follows is a conflation of, and gloss upon, four texts in Proverbs: 10:26; 19:13; 21:19 and 27:15 (Goodridge).

19 2 Corinthians 12:9.

PASSUS 18

This Passus gives us Will's vision of the Passion and the Harrowing of Hell. The Samaritan, Piers Ploughman and Jesus fuse into one personage, who will 'joust in Piers's blazon' (line 22 – i.e. in human flesh and nature) and overthrow the powers of Hell: cf. preceding Passus, note 5. The doctrine of atonement and redemption is expounded; Christ justifies His release of the Righteous from Hell; and the reconciliation of Mercy, Truth, Peace and Righteousness (=Justice) reflects the reconciliation of conflicts within Will himself. The redemption of all mankind is hinted at, and Christ's absolute victory on the Day of Judgment is foretold. The Dreamer wakes, finds it is (for himself, personally, an important piece of symbolism!) Easter Day; and he calls his family to worship. Though he has more *practical* lessons to learn, he has come *spiritually* almost as far as he ever will.

1 These are references to the service for Palm Sunday (the Sunday before Easter, and so-called from the strewing of palm-leaves before Christ at His entry into Jerusalem – John 12:13).

2 'Gallant shoes' in Langland is *galoches ycouped* – shoes with ornamentally slashed uppers. The golden spurs were emblems of new knighthood.

3 Matthew 21:9 – and also from the antiphon hinted at in line 8.

4 Cf. Passus 16, lines 40–52.

5 Hosea 13:14, and also from an antiphon for Holy Saturday.

6 Langland's account of the trial and crucifixion is a mixture of all four gospels (which are in some respects contradictory), with some additions of his own. No gospel, however, mentions *poison* (line 52); the vinegar and/or wine, variously admixed or not, is claimed by Robert Graves to have been a merciful anaesthetic. See *The Nazarene Gospel Restored*, p. 988. The soldier with the spear, in John 19:34, was expanded in the apocryphal Gospel of Nicodemus into the whole legend of Longinus (lines 78–91).

7 Matthew 27:54.

8 As elsewhere in the poem, a garbling of Daniel 9:24ff.

9 The whole encounter of Mercy, Truth, Peace and Righteousness is based upon Psalm 85:10–13.

10 The four maidens arrive from different quarters of the globe not merely because of their different natures, but in order to emphasise the universality of their coming reconciliation.

11 We must remember that Will is now *underground*, on the borders of Hell; the 'daybreak' and the glory are Christ's invasion of that kingdom.

12 Another quotation from Venantius Fortunatus's *Pange, lingua* hymn to the Holy Cross, lines 5–6. This hymn lies in the background of both the 17th and 18th Passus.

13 Badly misquoted from Job 7:9. The Vulgate *inferos* means, as Langland intends, 'the underworld'; but the Authorised Version reading, 'the grave', is also relevant, of course.

14 Again from Venantius Fortunatus's hymn, line 8 – slightly misquoted by Langland, and paraphrased by me.

15 Psalm 30:5. Lines 184–5 quote Psalm 4:8.

16 Matthew 2:2.

17 Matthew 14:28.

18 The Simeon of the *Nunc dimittis* (Luke 2:25–35) is said, in the Gospel of Nicodemus (which, as has already been shown, was treated in the Middle Ages as virtually canonical), to have had two dead sons who resurrected at the Crucifixion.

19 Psalm 24:9. It should be noted that most of Langland's quotations throughout this Passus are relevant to one or more church services between Palm Sunday and Easter Monday – or later.

20 In common with many medieval writers, Langland treats Lucifer and Satan as different personages; nor does he make it clear which (if either!) he thinks of as *the* Devil. Even up to the seventeenth century, and after, demonology remained confused, not to say illiterate, to the point of extravagance.

21 Apropos of the preceding note, Langland has *Gobelyn* as a proper name.

22 Matthew 4:3–7.

23 Matthew 27:19. Medieval literature (cf. the Cornish Passion sequence) attributed this dream to diabolical intervention with exactly the motive to which Satan here admits.

24 John 12:31.

25 This dialogue is based upon Psalm 24:7–10.

26 Line 321 from Isaiah 9:2, quoted in Matthew 4:16. Line 322 from John 1:36.

27 We must not expect modern precision in distinguishing the reptilian orders from writers to whom a dragon could be a 'worm'. Not only the Serpent in Eden, but other snakes, were often represented with forefeet, and sometimes with hindfeet as well. The 'lady's face' is also traditional, but much harder to explain. Originally it may not have been that of a woman at all, but the last relic of a fallen (but not yet utterly damned) angel – though the Serpent is described in line 352 as a loathsome adder. The Vulgate

word, *serpens*, means any creeping thing, and is common to both the masculine and feminine genders, though there treated as masculine.

28 Exodus 21:24, repeated in Deuteronomy 19:21 and quoted in Matthew 5:38.

29 Matthew 5:17.

30 Psalm 7:15. Note, in the preceding line, another reference to the *Pange, lingua* hymn.

31 A double reference, Joel 3:2 and 11–16, for the Valley of Jehoshaphat as the site of the Last Judgment. For the beautiful (in the original!) line 368 – 'That I drynke righte ripe must *resureccio mortuorum*' – see Matthew 26:29.

32 Psalm 51:4. (And therefore, the argument runs, pardon rests with me alone.)

33 None of this (lines 377–81) was ever actually Law; but examples have been known of popular insistence on royal prerogative being so used.

34 See Passus 4, note 12.

35 2 Corinthians 12:4. I follow Langland's slight misquotation.

36 Psalm 143:2. Again slightly misquoted by author and translator.

37 Cf. note 20. Ashtaroth = Astarte (among other versions) was in fact a moon-goddess – and one aspect or avatar of the White Goddess particularly celebrated by Robert Graves. Yet (like *Mahound* = Mohammed) the name often turns up as that of a male demon.

38 From an Ascension Day hymn.

39 Paraphrased by Langland in the lines that follow. Origin uncertain; but the idea of *'Amantium irae redintegratio amoris'* – or 'The falling out of faithful friends is the renewing of love' (Richard Edwards, 1523–66) – is of course immemorial.

40 See note 9.

41 Psalm 133:1.

PASSUS 19

Christ having risen, the foundation of Holy Church can begin; and this is the subject of Will's next vision. Piers Ploughman now changes from Christ Himself (at the opening of the Passus), to Christ's Vicar on Earth – St Peter and his papal successors – under the image of a faithful ploughman and sower of seeds in God's field. But already the corruption of the Church, and the coming of Antichrist, are casting their shadows before. In some ways we are moving back to earlier Passus, even to the maze of the Prologue itself (though the return of the Seven Deadly Sins, and the full war against them and Antichrist, belongs to Passus 20). It is already apparent, however, that Do-Best will see active engagement in that war. Piers vanishes; and the Church – and Will – are left in conscious imperfection, to defend themselves as best they may.

1 Cf. Isaiah 63:1–3. Apropos of that passage, it may be noted that *Edom* (like *Adam*) comes from a root meaning *red*. Cf. also the Cornish Ascension episode in the *Ordinale de Resurrexione Domini Nostri Ihesu Christi*. Christ, reaching Heaven, is greeted by a succession of angels with various forms of the question, 'Wherefore are thy garments red?' His answers are precisely those that apply in these lines of the Passus to Christ in Piers's armour (i.e. in human flesh). He has been scourged; He has worn a crown of thorns; He has been crucified; and so forth.

2 It is not, of course; 'Christ' means 'anointed'. Nevertheless, as established in the previous Passus, Christ Crucified, Christ the Harrower of Hell, must be regarded as both King and Conqueror.

3 Philippians 2:10.

4 This symbolic interpretation of gold, frankincense and myrrh is traditional, and relates to three essential qualities of kingship.

5 John 2:1–10. Wine is called an emblem of the Law (in line 107) because this, Christ's first miracle, was an emblem of the New Law of *caritas* – as, indeed, John implies in verse 11.

6 1 Samuel 18:7.

7 Cf. Matthew 26:3–5 or John 18:13–14.

8 Romans 6:9.

9   Mark 16:9–10 or John 20:14–18.

10   Luke 24:46. The reference there is to Daniel 9:24–7.

11   There is no canonical evidence that 'doubting' Thomas evangelised India; but see Passus 15, note 67. For the incidents and quotations given in lines 158–77, see John 20, especially verses 19–29 (which Langland has garbled).

12   This (derived from Matthew 18:28–35) is in a sense the theme of the entire epic, and especially of the two closing Passus: the dangers into which the Church, and the soul, fall, are due not merely to sin *in itself*, but to their neglect to *make restitution*, literally as well as spiritually, to Man and to God. Cf. Passus 5, line 232, and many other contexts.

13   Acts 2:3–4 and 17–18. Piers has now become St Peter.

14   The Pentecostal hymn ascribed to Hrabanus Maurus (d. 856).

15   Cf. 1 John 2:18–22.

16   1 Corinthians 12:4.

17   'Stots' are *young* oxen, fit only for lighter work. Those given to Piers are the four greatest Fathers of the Church, often cited by Langland, either separately or together.

18   Cf. Prologue, lines 100–10.

19   From one of the *Distichs* of Cato. Latin, line 290, 'Spare me, O Lord!'

20   'Surquedry' is often translated as 'arrogance', but is in fact closer to 'overweening' or 'presumption'.

21   This vicar is 'unlearnèd' (*lewed*) only in the sense that he is uncontaminated by 'the dirty devices of this world'. Unlike the still-complacent Conscience, he sees clearly what is *really* wrong with the Church – and the world.

22   Many cardinals preferred to station themselves at Avignon rather than at Rome, and their presence there contributed to the Great Schism of 1378–1417. Urban VI was elected Pope in Rome, Clement VII in Fondi. Clement and his Court later moved to Avignon, where they were largely supplied – and partly financed – by Jewish merchants, who received special privileges.

23   Psalm 18:25 – though the Authorised Version differs from

the sense of the Vulgate. I have given the Prayer Book version.

24 Urban VI declared a crusade against his rival, and the Roman supporters almost at once did battle with the French. In any case, Langland would have preferred the crusades in the Holy Land, to say nothing of those against such heretics as the Albigenses, to have been crusades not of destruction but of conversion: see Passus 15, lines 561 to end; and cf. lines 483–94 of the same Passus.

25 Matthew 5:45.

26 St Luke has nothing to do with either quotation. The first is Exodus 20:13 and Deuteronomy 5:17; the second Hebrews 10:30 (and elsewhere).

PASSUS 20

At last all the agents of Antichrist march forth against the Church. Conscience calls upon Nature (here, God) for help, and great afflictions are sent to turn men back to righteousness. Though many sins are resisted, many return; and the Church and its flock are at last undone by folly, hypocrisy, greed and the complacency that Conscience has shown earlier. The end of the epic is inconclusive: Conscience, and Will himself, have still to search the world anew for Piers Ploughman and redemption.

1 Langland's expansion (and attribution out of context) of Matthew 8:20.

2 As Goodridge remarks, Will's chief remaining fault is the *opposite* of those that he has previously shown: he has replaced arrogance and despair with excessive meekness and trust. (Not *all* action is evil!)

3 A reference to 1 Corinthians 1:19–27 and 2 Corinthians 11:19. With what authority, I do not know, but Robert Graves suggests (in *King Jesus*) that there may have been punning, among the early converts, upon *Christian* and *Chrestian* – the latter deriving from *chrestos*, which can mean 'foolishly simple' as well as 'worthy, wholesome, useful'.

4 'Out of the planets' because in traditional astrology their

positions affect (under God's preordinances) all human good and bad fortune.

5 It is true that the plagues, particularly the catastrophic 'Black Death', caused a relaxation of morality in some people (and a greater strictness in others). But copious venery was by many believed to be a prophylactic. See Nohl's book on the Black Death (or, indeed, others).

6 That is to say, a useless medicine or formula – or talisman – against disease and old age.

7 Will's last lesson, learned in old age, is virtually the same as his first, insufficiently understood by him from Holy Church's teaching in Passus 1.

8 Their short (secular) coats, their weapons and their ornamental footwear were forbidden to priests. Cf. Passus 15, lines 118–21. 'Bloody great knives' appears to me a fair modern version of Langland's *pisseres longe knyves*.

9 Psalm 147:4.

10 There is good Scriptural evidence (including the above reference) that Heaven, and the affairs of Heaven, are orderly, proportionable, symmetrical and precise; whereas (*pace* Dante!) Hell is equivalent to uncharted and unmeasured chaos. The point is that the friars are – hellishly – multiplying beyond control.

11 The citations of Plato and Seneca are – at any rate in this context and intention – either meaningless or satirical. They are in any case put down by the quotation that follows line 276 (Exodus 20:17 and Deuteronomy 5:21 – the Tenth Commandment). *Christian* community of goods is another matter; it is of the non-observance of this among the learned, and the danger and difficulty of trying to make the unlearned understand it, that Langland is complaining.

12 That is to say, friars are bribable for easy penances (*passim* throughout the poem), as Westminster judges are bribable for favourable decisions. In each case, the money belongs rightfully to someone else – the parish priest or the defrauded creditor.

13 A specially appointed (and usually very senior) cleric who

heard the confessions of magnates or of very grievous sinners.

14 Such licences and abuses have been condemned *passim* throughout the poem. The signalled (by me) pun in lines 323–4 is in Langland: the friar is wrongfully being granted a parish priest's (or higher cleric's) *cure of souls*.

15 As previously noted (cf. Passus 8, lines 8ff., and Passus 13, lines 40ff., though my translation somewhat obscures the latter), friars tended to travel in pairs. This particular friar's name derives from 2 Timothy 3:6.

16 A salve is a soothing balm – the word used here with both sexual implications and those of mild penances – see above. It is also the Latin greeting *Salve!* – 'Hail!' – as in the antiphon *Salve Regina*, addressed to the Virgin Mary. This is one of Langland's most complicated and bitterly ironical puns.

17 A further reference to the selling, by friars, of honorary fellowship in their Order; and the lines that follow repeat the accusations made frequently above (e.g. note 12, or Passus 3, note 1)

18 Lines 380–3. Pride is recognised as the *basis* for *all* sins – of course including the primal sin, that of Lucifer's rebellion. 'Nature', in this context, still means God – whose help must be sought until Piers Ploughman (once more a merging of Christ, the *righteous* Church and its priests, and the actively devout Common Man) may return to Earth.

THE 'AUTOBIOGRAPHICAL EPISODE'

1 The word 'loller' means wastrel or vagabond. During the fourteenth century a similar word 'lollard' was borrowed from the Dutch *lollaert*, a devout layman, and applied to the followers of Wycliff. These words were sometimes confused. Langland was not a Lollard but the piety, satire and indignation of the poem might have suggested a false connection to his contemporaries as they did to Robert Crowley, his sixteenth-century Protestant editor.

2 Will describes himself as 'to long', too tall. His nickname is Long Will.

3 Matthew 16:27.

4 'Continue' in the sense of persevere. Conscience repeats the word at line 104.

5 The clothes of a cleric.

6 1 Corinthians 7:20.

7 A book of basic religious instruction and prayer. *Placebo* and *Dirige*: antiphons in the Office for the Dead. Will's main service to others is prayer for the dead.

8 Will justifies his begging as due always to immediate necessity. He fills 'only [his] belly' and does not save anything in bag or bottle.

9 Leviticus 21.

10 1 Thessalonians 5:15.

11 Psalm 16:5, a text used in the ceremony of tonsuring.

12 'The amount of land for which the services of an armed knight were due to the sovereign' (*Oxford English Dictionary*).

13 The 'sons of Simon' are followers of Simon Magus (Acts 8:18) and practise simony, traffic in sacred things.

14 Matthew 4:4.

15 'Lyeth' could be one of two verbs. I take it to mean 'lies' but it is usually translated as 'applies'. If the former is right, the next word 'Ac' (90) has the adversative sense 'but'; if the latter, the connective sense 'and'.

16 As often, the unstructured and individualistic nature of Will's profession and piety is questioned. Conscience suggests that a life of contemplation and mendicancy is more obviously legitimate for those in religious orders.

17 Matthew 13:44, Luke 15:8–9.

SIR GAWAIN AND THE GREEN KNIGHT

I

When the siege and the assault had ceased at Troy, and the
fortress fell in flame to firebrands and ashes, the traitor who
the contrivance of treason there fashioned was tried for his
treachery, the most true upon earth – it was Æneas the noble
and his renowned kindred who then laid under them lands,
and lords became of well-nigh all the wealth in the Western
Isles. When royal Romulus to Rome his road had taken, in
great pomp and pride he peopled it first, and named it with
his own name that yet now it bears; Tirius went to Tuscany
and towns founded, Langaberde in Lombardy uplifted halls,
and far over the French flood Felix Brutus on many a broad
bank and brae Britain
> established full fair,
> where strange things, strife and sadness,
> at whiles in the land did fare,
> and each other grief and gladness
> oft fast have followed there.

2 And when fair Britain was founded by this famous lord,
bold men were bred there who in battle rejoiced,
and many a time that betid they troubles aroused.
In this domain more marvels have by men been seen
than in any other that I know of since that olden time;
but of all that here abode in Britain as kings
ever was Arthur most honoured, as I have heard men tell.
Wherefore a marvel among men I mean to recall,
a sight strange to see some men have held it,
one of the wildest adventures of the wonders of Arthur.
If you will listen to this lay but a little while now,
I will tell it at once as in town I have heard
> it told,
> as it is fixed and fettered
> in story brave and bold,
> thus linked and truly lettered,
> as was loved in this land of old.

3 This king lay at Camelot at Christmas-tide
   with many a lovely lord, lieges most noble,
   indeed of the Table Round all those tried brethren,
   amid merriment unmatched and mirth without care.
   There tourneyed many a time the trusty knights,
   and jousted full joyously these gentle lords;
   then to the court they came at carols to play.
   For there the feast was unfailing full fifteen days,
   with all meats and all mirth that men could devise,
   such gladness and gaiety as was glorious to hear,
   din of voices by day, and dancing by night;
   all happiness at the highest in halls and in bowers
   had the lords and the ladies, such as they loved most dearly.
   With all the bliss of this world they abode together,
   the knights most renowned after the name of Christ,
   and the ladies most lovely that ever life enjoyed,
   and he, king most courteous, who that court possessed.
   For all that folk so fair did in their first estate
        abide,
      Under heaven the first in fame,
      their king most high in pride;
      it would now be hard to name
      a troop in war so tried.

4 While New Year was yet young that yestereve had arrived,
   that day double dainties on the dais were served,
   when the king was there come with his courtiers to the hall,
   and the chanting of the choir in the chapel had ended.
   With loud clamour and cries both clerks and laymen
   Noel announced anew, and named it full often;
   then nobles ran anon with New Year gifts,
   Handsels, handsels they shouted, and handed them out,
   Competed for those presents in playful debate;
   ladies laughed loudly, though they lost the game,
   and he that won was not woeful, as may well be believed.
   All this merriment they made, till their meat was served;
   then they washed, and mannerly went to their seats,
   ever the highest for the worthiest, as was held to be best.

Queen Guinevere the gay was with grace in the midst
of the adorned dais set. Dearly was it arrayed:
finest sendal at her sides, a ceiling above her
of true tissue of Tolouse, and tapestries of Tharsia
that were embroidered and bound with the brightest gems
one might prove and appraise to purchase for coin
     any day.
  That loveliest lady there
  on them glanced with eyes of grey;
  that he found ever one more fair
  in sooth might no man say.

5 But Arthur would not eat until all were served;
his youth made him so merry with the moods of a boy,
he liked lighthearted life, so loved he the less
either long to be lying or long to be seated
so worked on him his young blood and wayward brain.
And another rule moreover was his reason besides
that in pride he had appointed: it pleased him not to eat
upon festival so fair, ere he first were apprised
of some strange story or stirring adventure,
or some moving marvel that he might believe in
of noble men, knighthood, or new adventures;
or a challenger should come a champion seeking
to join with him in jousting, in jeopardy to set
his life against life, each allowing the other
the favour of fortune, were she fairer to him.
This was the king's custom, wherever his court was holden,
at each famous feast among his fair company
     in hall
  So his face doth proud appear,
  and he stands up stout and tall,
  all young in the New Year;
  much mirth he makes with all.

6 Thus there stands up straight the stern king himself,
talking before the high table of trifles courtly.
There good Gawain was set at Guinevere's side,

with Agravain a la Dure Main on the other side seated,
both their lord's sister-sons, loyal-hearted knights.
Bishop Baldwin had the honour of the board's service,
and Iwain Urien's son ate beside him.
These dined on the dais and daintily fared,
and many a loyal lord below at the long tables.
Then forth came the first course with fanfare of trumpets,
on which many bright banners bravely were hanging;
noise of drums then anew and the noble pipes,
warbling wild and keen, wakened their music,
so that many hearts rose high hearing their playing.
Then forth was brought a feast, fare of the noblest,
multitude of fresh meats on so many dishes
that free places were few in front of the people
to set the silver things full of soups on cloth
    so white.
  Each lord of his liking there
  without lack took with delight:
  twelve plates to every pair,
  good beer and wine all bright.

7 Now of their service I will say nothing more,
for you are all well aware that no want would there be.
Another noise that was new drew near on a sudden,
so that their lord might have leave at last to take food.
For hardly had the music but a moment ended,
and the first course in the court as was custom been served,
when there passed through the portals a perilous horseman,
the mightiest on middle-earth in measure of height,
from his gorge to his girdle so great and so square,
and his loins and his limbs so long and so huge,
that half a troll upon earth I trow that he was,
but the largest man alive at least I declare him;
and yet the seemliest for his size that could sit on a horse,
for though in back and in breast his body was grim,
both his paunch and his waist were properly slight,
and all his features followed his fashion so gay
    in mode;

for at the hue men gaped aghast
in his face and form that showed;
as a fay-man fell he passed,
and green all over glowed.

8 All of green were they made, both garments and man:
a coat tight and close that clung to his sides;
a rich robe above it all arrayed within
with fur finely trimmed, shewing fair fringes
of handsome ermine gay, as his hood was also,
that was lifted from his locks and laid on his shoulders;
and trim hose tight-drawn of tincture alike
that clung to his calves; and clear spurs below
of bright gold on silk broideries banded most richly,
though unshod were his shanks, for shoeless he rode.
And verily all this vesture was of verdure clear,
both the bars on his belt, and bright stones besides
that were richly arranged in his array so fair,
set on himself and on his saddle upon silk fabrics:
it would be too hard to rehearse one half of the trifles
that were embroidered upon them, what with birds
        and with flies
in a gay glory of green, and ever gold in the midst.
The pendants of his poitrel, his proud crupper,
his molains, and all the metal to say more, were enamelled,
even the stirrups that he stood in were stained of the same;
and his saddlebows in suit, and their sumptuous skirts,
which ever glimmered and glinted all with green jewels;
even the horse that upheld him in hue was the same,
        I tell:
a green horse great and thick,
a stallion stiff to quell,
in broidered bridle quick:
he matched his master well.

9 Very gay was this great man guised all in green,
and the hair of his head with his horse's accorded:
fair flapping locks enfolding his shoulders,

a big beard like a bush over his breast hanging
that with the handsome hair from his head falling
was sharp shorn to an edge just short of his elbows,
so that half his arms under it were hid, as it were
in a king's capadoce that encloses his neck.
The mane of that mighty horse was of much the same sort,
well curled and all combed, with many curious knots
woven in with gold wire about the wondrous green,
ever a strand of the hair and a string of the gold;
the tail and the top-lock were twined all to match
and both bound with a band of a brilliant green:
with dear jewels bedight to the dock's ending,
and twisted then on top was a tight-knitted knot
on which many burnished bells of bright gold jingled.
Such a mount on middle-earth, or man to ride him,
was never beheld in that hall with eyes ere that time;
     for there
   his glance was as lightning bright,
   so did all that saw him swear;
   no man would have the might,
   they thought, his blows to bear.

10 And yet he had not a helm, nor a hauberk either,
not a pisane, not a plate that was proper to arms;
not a shield, not a shaft, for shock or for blow,
but in his one hand he held a holly-bundle,
that is greatest in greenery when groves are leafless,
and an axe in the other, ugly and monstrous,
a ruthless weapon aright for one in rhyme to describe:
the head was as large and as long as an ellwand,
a branch of green steel and of beaten gold;
the bit, burnished bright and broad at the edge,
as well shaped for shearing as sharp razors;
the stem was a stout staff, by which sternly he gripped it,
all bound with iron about to the base of the handle,
and engraven in green in graceful patterns,
lapped round with a lanyard that was lashed to the head
and down the length of the haft was looped many times;

and tassels of price were tied there in plenty
to bosses of the bright green, braided most richly.
Such was he that now hastened in, the hall entering,
pressing forward to the dais – no peril he feared.
To none gave he greeting, gazing above them,
and the first word that he winged: 'Now where is,' he said,
'the governor of this gathering? For gladly I would
on the same set my sight, and with himself now talk
    in town.'
  On the courtiers he cast his eye,
  and rolled it up and down;
  he stopped, and stared to espy
  who there had most renown.

11 Then they looked for a long while, on that lord gazing;
for every man marvelled what it could mean indeed
that horseman and horse such a hue should come by
as to grow green as the grass, and greener it seemed,
than green enamel on gold glowing far brighter.
All stared that stood there and stole up nearer,
watching him and wondering what in the world he would do.
For many marvels they had seen, but to match this nothing;
wherefore a phantom and fay-magic folk there thought it,
and so to answer little eager was any of those knights,
and astounded at his stern voice stone-still they sat there
in a swooning silence through that solemn chamber,
as if all had dropped into a dream, so died their voices
    away.
  Not only, I deem, for dread;
  but of some 'twas their courtly way
  to allow their lord and head
  to the guest his word to say.

12 Then Arthur before the high dais beheld this wonder,
and freely with fair words, for fearless was he ever,
saluted him, saying: 'Lord, to this lodging thou'rt welcome!
The head of this household Arthur my name is.
Alight, as thou lovest me, and linger, I pray thee;
and what may thy wish be in a while we shall learn.'

'Nay, so help me,' quoth the horseman, 'He that on high
     is throned,
to pass any time in this place was no part of my errand.
But since thy praises, prince, so proud are uplifted,
and thy castle and courtiers are accounted the best,
the stoutest in steel-gear that on steeds may ride,
most eager and honourable of the earth's people,
valiant to vie with in other virtuous sports,
and here is knighthood renowned, as is noised in my ears:
'tis that has fetched me hither, by my faith, at this time.
You may believe by this branch that I am bearing here
that I pass as one in peace, no peril seeking.
For had I set forth to fight in fashion of war,
I have a hauberk at home, and a helm also,
a shield, and a sharp spear shining brightly,
and other weapons to wield too, as well I believe;
but since I crave for no combat, my clothes are softer.
Yet if thou be so bold, as abroad is published,
thou wilt grant of thy goodness the game that I ask for
     by right.'
    Then Arthur answered there,
    and said: 'Sir, noble knight,
    if battle thou seek thus bare,
    thou'lt fail not here to fight.'

13 'Nay, I wish for no warfare, on my word I tell thee!
Here about on these benches are but beardless children.
Were I hasped in armour on a high charger,
there is no man here to match me – their might is so feeble.
And so I crave in this court only a Christmas pastime,
since it is Yule and New Year, and you are young here
     and merry.
If any so hardy in this house here holds that he is,
if so bold be his blood or his brain be so wild,
that he stoutly dare strike one stroke for another,
then I will give him as my gift this guisarm costly,
this axe – 'tis heavy enough – to handle as he pleases;
and I will abide the first brunt, here bare as I sit.

If any fellow be so fierce as my faith to test,
hither let him haste to me and lay hold of this weapon –
I hand it over for ever, he can have it as his own –
and I will stand a stroke from him, stock-still on this floor,
provided thou'lt lay down this law: that I may deliver
    him another.
    Claim I!
  And yet a respite I'll allow,
  till a year and a day go by.
  Come quick, and let's see now
  if any here dare reply!'

14 If he astounded them at first, yet stiller were then
  all the household in the hall, both high men and low.
  The man on his mount moved in his saddle,
  and rudely his red eyes he rolled then about,
  bent his bristling brows all brilliantly green,
  and swept round his beard to see who would rise.
  When none in converse would accost him, he coughed
      then loudly,
  stretched himself haughtily and straightway exclaimed:
  'What! Is this Arthur's house,' said he thereupon,
  'the rumour of which runs through realms unnumbered?
  Where now is your haughtiness, and your high conquests,
  your fierceness and fell mood, and your fine boasting?
  Now are the revels and the royalty of the Round Table
  overwhelmed by a word by one man spoken,
  for all blench now abashed ere a blow is offered!'
  With that he laughed so loud that their lord was angered,
  the blood shot for shame into his shining cheeks
    and face;
  as wroth as wind he grew,
  so all did in that place.
  Then near to the stout man drew
  the king of fearless race,

15 And said: 'Marry! Good man, 'tis madness thou askest,
  and since folly thou hast sought, thou deservest to find it.

I know no lord that is alarmed by thy loud words here.
Give me now thy guisarm, in God's name, sir,
and I will bring thee the blessing thou hast begged
    to receive.'
Quick then he came to him and caught it from his hand.
Then the lordly man loftily alighted on foot.
Now Arthur holds his axe, and the haft grasping
sternly he stirs it about, his stroke considering.
The stout man before him there stood his full height,
higher than any in that house by a head and yet more.
With stern face as he stood he stroked at his beard,
and with expression impassive he pulled down his coat,
no more disturbed or distressed at the strength of his blows
than if someone as he sat had served him a drink
    of wine.
    From beside the queen Gawain
    to the king did then incline:
    'I implore with prayer plain
    that this match should now be mine.'

16 'Would you, my worthy lord,' said Wawain to the king,
    'bid me abandon this bench and stand by you there,
    so that I without discourtesy might be excused from
        the table,
    and my liege lady were not loth to permit me,
    I would come to your counsel before your courtiers fair.
    For I find it unfitting, as in fact it is held,
    when a challenge in your chamber makes choice so exalted,
    though you yourself be desirous to accept it in person,
    while many bold men about you on bench are seated:
    on earth there are, I hold, none more honest of purpose,
    no figures fairer on field where fighting is waged.
    I am the weakest, I am aware, and in wit feeblest,
    and the least loss, if I live not, if one would learn the truth.
    Only because you are my uncle is honour given me:
    save your blood in my body I boast of no virtue;
    and since this affair is so foolish that it nowise befits you,
    and I have requested it first, accord it then to me!

If my claim is uncalled-for without cavil shall judge
    this court.'
  To consult the knights draw near,
  and this plan they all support;
  the king with crown to clear,
  and give Gawain the sport.

17 The king then commanded that he quickly should rise,
and he readily uprose and directly approached,
kneeling humbly before his highness, and laying hand on
    the weapon;
and he lovingly relinquished it, and lifting his hand
gave him God's blessing, and graciously enjoined him
that his hand and his heart should be hardy alike.
'Take care, cousin,' quoth the king, 'one cut to address,
and if thou learnest him his lesson, I believe very well
that thou wilt bear any blow that he gives back later.'
Gawain goes to the great man with guisarm in hand,
and he boldly abides there – he blenched not at all.
Then next said to Gawain the knight all in green:
'Let's tell again our agreement, ere we go any further.
I'd know first, sir knight, thy name; I entreat thee
to tell it me truly, that I may trust in thy word.'
'In good faith,' quoth the good knight, 'I Gawain am called
who bring thee this buffet, let be what may follow;
and at this time a twelvemonth in thy turn have another
with whatever weapon thou wilt, and in the world with
    none else but me.'
  The other man answered again:
  'I am passing pleased,' said he,
  'upon my life, Sir Gawain,
  that this stroke should be struck by thee.'

18 'Begad,' said the green knight, 'Sir Gawain, I am pleased
to find from thy fist the favour I asked for!
And thou hast promptly repeated and plainly hast stated
without abatement the bargain I begged of the king here;
save that thou must assure me, sir, on thy honour

that thou'lt seek me thyself, search where thou thinkest
I may be found near or far, and fetch thee such payment
as thou deliverest me today before these lordly people.'
'Where should I light on thee,' quoth Gawain, 'where look
     for thy place?
I have never learned where thou livest, by the Lord that
     made me,
and I know thee not, knight, thy name nor thy court.
But teach me the true way, and tell what men call thee,
and I will apply all my purpose the path to discover:
and that I swear thee for certain and solemnly promise.'
'That is enough in New Year, there is need of no more!'
said the great man in green to Gawain the courtly.
'If I tell thee the truth of it, when I have taken the knock,
and thou handily hast hit me, if in haste I announce then
my house and my home and mine own title,
then thou canst call and enquire and keep the agreement;
and if I waste not a word, thou'lt win better fortune,
for thou mayst linger in thy land and look no further –
    but stay!
  To thy grim tool now take heed, sir!
  Let us try thy knocks today!'
  'Gladly,' said he, 'indeed, sir!'
  and his axe he stroked in play.

19 The Green Knight on the ground now gets himself ready,
leaning a little with the head he lays bare the flesh,
and his locks long and lovely he lifts over his crown,
letting the naked neck as was needed appear.
His left foot on the floor before him placing,
Gawain gripped on his axe, gathered and raised it,
from aloft let it swiftly land where 'twas naked,
so that the sharp of his blade shivered the bones,
and sank clean through the clear fat and clove it asunder,
and the blade of the bright steel then bit into the ground.
The fair head to the floor fell from the shoulders,
and folk fended it with their feet as forth it went rolling;
the blood burst from the body, bright on the greenness,

and yet neither faltered nor fell the fierce man at all,
but stoutly he strode forth, still strong on his shanks,
and roughly he reached out among the rows that stood there,
caught up his comely head and quickly upraised it,
and then hastened to his horse, laid hold of the bridle,
stepped into stirrup-iron, and strode up aloft,
his head by the hair in his hand holding;
and he settled himself then in the saddle as firmly
as if unharmed by mishap, though in the hall he might
      wear no head.
   His trunk he twisted round,
   that gruesome body that bled,
   and many fear then found,
   as soon as his speech was sped.

20 For the head in his hand he held it up straight,
    towards the fairest at the table he twisted the face,
    and it lifted up its eyelids and looked at them broadly,
    and made such words with its mouth as may be recounted.
    'See thou get ready, Gawain, to go as thou vowedst,
    and as faithfully seek till thou find me, good sir,
    as thou hast promised in this place in the presence of
          these knights.
    To the Green Chapel go thou, and get thee, I charge thee,
    such a dint as thou hast dealt – indeed thou hast earned
    a nimble knock in return on New Year's morning!
    The Knight of the Green Chapel I am known to many,
    so if to find me thou endeavour, thou'lt fail not to do so.
    Therefore come! Or to be called a craven thou deservest.'
    With a rude roar and rush his reins he turned then,
    and hastened out through the hall-door with his head in
          his hand,
    and fire of the flint flew from the feet of his charger.
    To what country he came in that court no man knew,
    no more than they had learned from what land he had
          journeyed.
       Meanwhile,
    the king and Sir Gawain

at the Green Man laugh and smile;
yet to men had appeared, 'twas plain,
a marvel beyond denial.

21 Though Arthur the high king in his heart marvelled,
he let no sign of it be seen, but said then aloud
to the queen so comely with courteous words:
'Dear Lady, today be not downcast at all!
Such cunning play well becomes the Christmas tide,
interludes, and the like, and laughter and singing,
amid these noble dances of knights and of dames.
Nonetheless to my food I may fairly betake me,
for a marvel I have met, and I may not deny it.'
He glanced at Sir Gawain and with good point he said:
'Come, hang up thine axe, sir! It has hewn now enough.'
And over the table they hung it on the tapestry behind,
where all men might remark it, a marvel to see,
and by its true token might tell of that adventure.
Then to a table they turned, those two lords together,
the king and his good kinsman, and courtly men served them
with all dainties double, the dearest there might be,
with all manner of meats and with minstrelsy too.
With delight that day they led, till to the land came the
        night again.
    Sir Gawain, now take heed
    lest fear make thee refrain
    from daring the dangerous deed
    that thou in hand hast ta'en!

II

With this earnest of high deeds thus Arthur began the young
year, for brave vows he yearned to hear made. Though such
words were wanting when they went to table, now of fell work
to full grasp filled were their hands. Gawain was gay as he
began those games in the hall, but if the end be unhappy, hold
it no wonder! For though men be merry of mood when they

have mightily drunk, a year slips by swiftly, never the same
returning; the outset to the ending is equal but seldom.
And so this Yule passed over and the year after, and severally
the seasons ensued in their turn: after Christmas there came
the crabbed Lenten that with fish tries the flesh and with food
more meagre; but then the weather in the world makes war on
the winter, cold creeps into the earth, clouds are uplifted,
shining rain is shed in showers that all warm fall on the fair
turf, flowers there open, of grounds and of groves green is the
raiment, birds are busy a-building and bravely are singing for
sweetness of the soft summer that will soon be on

> the way;
> and blossoms burgeon and blow
> in hedgerows bright and gay;
> then glorious musics go
> through the woods in proud array.

23 After the season of summer with its soft breezes,
   when Zephyr goes sighing through seeds and herbs,
   right glad is the grass that grows in the open,
   when the damp dewdrops are dripping from the leaves
   to greet a gay glance of the glistening sun.
   But then Harvest hurries in, and hardens it quickly,
   warns it before winter to wax to ripeness.
   He drives with his drought the dust, till it rises
   from the face of the land and flies up aloft;
   wild wind in the welkin makes war on the sun,
   the leaves loosed from the linden alight on the ground,
   and all grey is the grass that green was before:
   all things ripen and rot that rose up at first,
   and so the year runs away in yesterdays many,
   and here winter wends again, as by the way of the world

> it ought,
> until the Michaelmas moon
> has winter's boding brought;
> Sir Gawain then full soon
> of his grievous journey thought.

24 And yet till All Hallows with Arthur he lingered,
    who furnished on that festival a feast for the knight
    with much royal revelry of the Round Table.
    The knights of renown and noble ladies
    all for the love of that lord had longing at heart,
    but nevertheless the more lightly of laughter they spoke:
    many were joyless who jested for his gentle sake.
    For after their meal mournfully he reminded his uncle
    that his departure was near, and plainly he said:
    'Now liege-lord of my life, for leave I beg you.
    You know the quest and the compact; I care not further
    to trouble you with tale of it, save a trifling point:
    I must set forth to my fate without fail in the morning,
    as God will me guide, the Green Man to seek.'
    Those most accounted in the castle came then together,
    Iwain and Erric and others not a few,
    Sir Doddinel le Savage, the Duke of Clarence,
    Lancelot, and Lionel, and Lucan the Good,
    Sir Bors and Sir Bedivere that were both men of might,
    and many others of mark with Mador de la Porte.
    All this company of the court the king now approached
    to comfort the knight with care in their hearts.
    Much mournful lament was made in the hall
    that one so worthy as Wawain should wend on that errand,
    To endure a deadly dint and deal no more
          with blade.
       The knight ever made good cheer,
       saying, 'Why should I be dismayed?
       Of doom the fair or drear
       by a man must be assayed.'

25 He remained there that day, and in the morning got ready,
    asked early for his arms, and they all were brought him.
    First a carpet of red silk was arrayed on the floor,
    and the gilded gear in plenty there glittered upon it.
    The stern man stepped thereon and the steel things handled,
    dressed in a doublet of damask of Tharsia,
    and over it a cunning capadoce that was closed at the throat

and with fair ermine was furred all within.
Then sabatons first they set on his feet,
his legs lapped in steel in his lordly greaves,
on which the polains they placed, polished and shining
and knit upon his knees with knots all of gold;
then the comely cuisses that cunningly clasped
the thick thews of his thighs they with thongs on him tied;
and next the byrnie, woven of bright steel rings
upon costly quilting, enclosed him about;
and armlets well burnished upon both of his arms,
with gay elbow-pieces and gloves of plate,
and all the goodly gear to guard him whatever
        betide;
    coat-armour richly made,
    gold spurs on heel in pride;
    girt with a trusty blade,
    silk belt about his side.

26 When he was hasped in his armour his harness was splendid:
the least latchet or loop was all lit with gold.
Thus harnessed as he was he heard now his Mass,
that was offered and honoured at the high altar;
and then he came to the king and his court-companions,
and with love he took leave of lords and of ladies;
and they kissed him and escorted him, and to Christ him
            commended.
And now Gringolet stood groomed, and girt with a saddle
gleaming right gaily with many gold fringes,
and all newly for the nonce nailed at all points;
adorned with bars was the bridle, with bright gold banded;
the apparelling proud of poitrel and of skirts,
and the crupper and caparison accorded with the saddlebows:
all was arrayed in red with rich gold studded,
so that it glittered and glinted as a gleam of the sun.
Then he in hand took the helm and in haste kissed it:
strongly was it stapled and stuffed within;
it sat high upon his head and was hasped at the back,
and a light kerchief was laid o'er the beaver,

all braided and bound with the brightest gems
upon broad silken broidery, with birds on the seams
like popinjays depainted, here preening and there,
turtles and true-loves, entwined as thickly
as if many sempstresses had the sewing full seven winters
    in hand.
  A circlet of greater price
  his crown about did band;
  The diamonds point-device
  there blazing bright did stand.

27 Then they brought him his blazon that was of brilliant gules
with the pentangle depicted in pure hue of gold.
By the baldric he caught it and about his neck cast it:
right well and worthily it went with the knight.
And why the pentangle is proper to that prince so noble
I intend now to tell you, though it may tarry my story.
It is a sign that Solomon once set on a time
to betoken Troth, as it is entitled to do;
for it is a figure that in it five points holdeth,
and each line overlaps and is linked with another,
and every way it is endless; and the English, I hear,
everywhere name it the Endless Knot.
So it suits well this knight and his unsullied arms;
for ever faithful in five points, and five times under each,
Gawain as good was acknowledged and as gold refinéd,
devoid of every vice and with virtues adorned.
    So there
  the pentangle painted new
  he on shield and coat did wear,
  as one of word most true
  and knight of bearing fair.

28 First faultless was he found in his five senses,
and next in his five fingers he failed at no time,
and firmly on the Five Wounds all his faith was set
that Christ received on the cross, as the Creed tells us;
and wherever the brave man into battle was come,

on this beyond all things was his earnest thought:
that ever from the Five Joys all his valour he gained
that to Heaven's courteous Queen once came from her Child.
For which cause the knight had in comely wise
on the inner side of his shield her image depainted,
that when he cast his eyes thither his courage never failed.
The fifth five that was used, as I find, by this knight
was free-giving and friendliness first before all,
and chastity and chivalry ever changeless and straight,
and piety surpassing all points: these perfect five
were hasped upon him harder than on any man else.
Now these five series, in sooth, were fastened on this knight,
and each was knit with another and had no ending,
but were fixed at five points that failed not at all,
coincided in no line nor sundered either,
not ending in any angle anywhere, as I discover,
wherever the process was put in play or passed to an end.
Therefore on his shining shield was shaped now this knot,
royally with red gules upon red gold set:
this is the pure pentangle as people of learning
     have taught.
   Now Gawain in brave array
   his lance at last hath caught.
   He gave them all good day,
   for evermore as he thought.

29 He spurned his steed with the spurs and sprang on his way
so fiercely that the flint-sparks flashed out behind him.
All who beheld him so honourable in their hearts were sighing,
and assenting in sooth one said to another,
grieving for that good man: 'Before God, 'tis a shame
that thou, lord, must be lost, who art in life so noble!
To meet his match among men, Marry, 'tis not easy!
To behave with more heed would have behoved one of sense,
and that dear lord duly a duke to have made,
illustrious leader of liegemen in this land as befits him;
and that would better have been than to be butchered
     to death,

beheaded by an elvish man for an arrogant vaunt.
Who can recall any king that such a course ever took
as knights quibbling at court at their Christmas games!'
Many warm tears outwelling there watered their eyes,
when that lord so beloved left the castle
    that day.
  No longer he abode,
  but swiftly went his way;
  bewildering ways he rode,
  as the book I heard doth say.

30 Now he rides thus arrayed through the realm of Logres,
  Sir Gawain in God's care, though no game now he found it.
Oft forlorn and alone he lodged of a night
where he found not afforded him such fare as pleased him.
He had no friend but his horse in the forests and hills,
no man on his march to commune with but God,
till anon he drew near unto Northern Wales.
All the isles of Anglesey he held on his left,
and over the fords he fared by the flats near the sea,
and then over by the Holy Head to high land again
in the wilderness of Wirral: there wandered but few
who with goodwill regarded either God or mortal.
And ever he asked as he went on of all whom he met
if they had heard any news of a knight that was green
in any ground thereabouts, or of the Green Chapel.
And all denied it, saying nay, and that never in their lives
a single man had they seen that of such a colour
    could be.
  The knight took pathways strange
  by many a lonesome lea,
  and oft his view did change
  that chapel ere he could see.

31 Many a cliff he climbed o'er in countries unknown,
  far fled from his friends without fellowship he rode.
At every wading or water on the way that he passed
he found a foe before him, save at few for a wonder;

and so foul were they and fell that fight he must needs.
So many a marvel in the mountains he met in those lands
that 'twould be tedious the tenth part to tell you thereof.
At whiles with worms he wars, and with wolves also,
at whiles with wood-trolls that wandered in the crags,
and with bulls and with bears and boars, too, at times;
and with ogres that hounded him from the heights of the fells.
Had he not been stalwart and staunch and steadfast in God,
he doubtless would have died and death had met often;
for though war wearied him much, the winter was worse,
when the cold clear water from the clouds spilling
froze ere it had fallen upon the faded earth.
Wellnigh slain by the sleet he slept ironclad
more nights than enow in the naked rocks,
where clattering from the crest the cold brook tumbled,
and hung high o'er his head in hard icicles.
Thus in peril and pain and in passes grievous
till Christmas-eve that country he crossed all alone
     in need.
    The knight did at that tide
    his plaint to Mary plead,
    her rider's road to guide
    and to some lodging lead.

32 By a mount in the morning merrily he was riding
into a forest that was deep and fearsomely wild,
with high hills at each hand, and hoar woods beneath
of huge aged oaks by the hundred together;
the hazel and the hawthorn were huddled and tangled
with rough ragged moss around them trailing,
with many birds bleakly on the bare twigs sitting
that piteously piped there for pain of the cold.
The good man on Gringolet goes now beneath them
through many marshes and mires, a man all alone,
troubled lest a truant at that time he should prove
from the service of the sweet Lord, who on that selfsame night
of a maid became man our mourning to conquer.
And therefore sighing he said: 'I beseech thee, O Lord,

and Mary, who is the mildest mother most dear,
for some harbour where with honour I might hear the Mass
and thy Matins tomorrow. This meekly I ask,
and thereto promptly I pray with Pater and Ave
    and Creed.'
  In prayer he now did ride,
  lamenting his misdeed;
  he blessed him oft and cried,
  'The Cross of Christ me speed!'

33 The sign on himself he had set but thrice,
  ere a mansion he marked within a moat in the forest,
  on a low mound above a lawn, laced under the branches
  of many a burly bole round about by the ditches:
  the castle most comely that ever a king possessed
  placed amid a pleasance with a park all about it,
  within a palisade of pointed pales set closely
  that took its turn round the trees for two miles or more.
  Gawain from the one side gazed on the stronghold
  as it shimmered and shone through the shining oaks,
  and then humbly he doffed his helm, and with honour
      he thanked
  Jesus and Saint Julian, who generous are both,
  who had courtesy accorded him and to his cry harkened.
  'Now bon hostel,' quoth the knight, 'I beg of you still!'
  Then he goaded Gringolet with his gilded heels,
  and he chose by good chance the chief pathway
  and brought his master bravely to the bridge's end
      at last.
    That brave bridge was up-hauled,
    the gates were bolted fast;
    the castle was strongly walled,
    it feared no wind or blast.

34 Then he stayed his steed that on the steep bank halted
  above the deep double ditch that was drawn round the place.
  The wall waded in the water wondrous deeply,
  and up again to a huge height in the air it mounted,

all of hard hewn stone to the high cornice,
fortified under the battlement in the best fashion
and topped with fair turrets set by turns about
that had many graceful loopholes with a good outlook:
that knight a better barbican had never seen built.
And inwards he beheld the hall uprising,
tall towers set in turns, and as tines clustering
the fair finials, joined featly, so fine and so long,
their capstones all carven with cunning and skill.
Many chalk-white chimneys he chanced to espy
upon the roofs of towers all radiant white;
so many a painted pinnacle was peppered about,
among the crenelles of the castle clustered so thickly
that all pared out of paper it appeared to have been.
The gallant knight on his great horse good enough thought it,
if he could come by any course that enclosure to enter,
to harbour in that hostel while the holy day lasted
    with delight.
  He called, and there came with speed
  a porter blithe and bright;
  on the wall he learned his need,
  and hailed the errant knight.

35 'Good sir,' quoth Gawain, 'will you go with my message
to the high lord of this house for harbour to pray?'
'Yes, by Peter!' quoth the porter, 'and I promise indeed
that you will, sir, be welcome while you wish to stay here.'
Then quickly the man went and came again soon,
servants bringing civilly to receive there the knight.
They drew down the great drawbridge, and duly came forth,
and on the cold earth on their knees in courtesy knelt
to welcome this wayfarer with such worship as they knew.
They delivered him the broad gates and laid them wide open,
and he readily bade them rise and rode o'er the bridge.
Several servants then seized the saddle as he alighted,
and many stout men his steed to a stable then led,
while knights and esquires anon descended
to guide there in gladness this guest to the hall.

When he raised up his helm many ran there in haste
to have it from his hand, his highness to serve;
his blade and his blazon both they took charge of.
Then he greeted graciously those good men all,
and many were proud to approach him, that prince to honour.
All hasped in his harness to hall they brought him,
where a fair blaze in the fireplace fiercely was burning.
Then the lord of that land leaving his chamber
came mannerly to meet the man on the floor.
He said: 'You are welcome at your wish to dwell here.
What is here, all is your own, to have in your rule
    and sway.'
   'Gramercy!' quoth Gawain,
   'May Christ you this repay!'
   As men that to meet were fain
   they both embraced that day.

36 Gawain gazed at the good man who had greeted him kindly,
and he thought bold and big was the baron of the castle,
very large and long, and his life at the prime:
broad and bright was his beard, and all beaver-hued,
stern, strong in his stance upon stalwart legs,
his face fell as fire, and frank in his speech;
and well it suited him, in sooth, as it seemed to the knight,
a lordship to lead untroubled over lieges trusty.
To a chamber the lord drew him, and charged men at once
to assign him an esquire to serve and obey him;
and there to wait on his word many worthy men were,
who brought him to a bright bower where the bedding
    was splendid:
there were curtains of costly silk with clear-golden hems,
and coverlets cunning-wrought with quilts most lovely
of bright ermine above, embroidered at the sides,
hangings running on ropes with red-gold rings,
carpets of costly damask that covered the walls
and the floor under foot fairly to match them.
There they despoiled him, speaking to him gaily,
his byrnie doing off and his bright armour.

Rich robes then readily men ran to bring him,
for him to change, and to clothe him, having chosen
      the best.
As soon as he had donned one and dressed was therein,
as it sat on him seemly with its sailing skirts,
then verily in his visage a vision of Spring
to each man there appeared, and in marvellous hues
bright and beautiful was all his body beneath.
That knight more noble was never made by Christ
    they thought.
    He came none knew from where,
    but it seemed to them he ought
    to be a prince beyond compare
    in the field where fell men fought.

37 A chair before the chimney where charcoal was burning
was made ready in his room, all arrayed and covered
with cushions upon quilted cloths that were cunningly made.
Then a comely cloak was cast about him
of bright silk brocade, embroidered most richly
and furred fairly within with fells of the choicest
and all edged with ermine, and its hood was to match;
and he sat in that seat seemly and noble
and warmed himself with a will, and then his woes were
      amended.
Soon up on good trestles a table was raised
and clad with a clean cloth clear white to look on;
there was surnape, salt-cellar, and silvern spoons.
He then washed as he would and went to his food,
and many worthy men with worship waited upon him;
soups they served of many sorts, seasoned most choicely,
in double helpings, as was due, and divers sorts of fish;
some baked in bread, some broiled on the coals,
some seethed, some in gravy savoured with spices,
and all with condiments so cunning that it caused him delight.
A fair feast he called it frankly and often,
graciously, when all the good men together there pressed him:
    'Now pray,

this penance deign to take;
'twill improve another day!'
The man much mirth did make,
for wine to his head made way.

38 Then inquiry and question were carefully put
touching personal points to that prince himself,
till he courteously declared that to the court he belonged
that high Arthur in honour held in his sway,
who was the right royal King of the Round Table,
and 'twas Gawain himself that as their guest now sat
and had come for that Christmas, as the case had turned out.
When the lord had learned whom luck had brought him,
loud laughed he thereat, so delighted he was,
and they made very merry, all the men in that castle,
and to appear in the presence were pressing and eager
of one who all profit and prowess and perfect manners
comprised in his person, and praise ever gained;
of all men on middle-earth he most was admired.
Softly each said then in secret to his friend:
'Now fairly shall we mark the fine points of manners,
and the perfect expressions of polished converse.
How speech is well spent will be expounded unasked,
since we have found here this fine father of breeding.
God has given us of His goodness His grace now indeed,
Who such a guest as Gawain has granted us to have!
When blissful men at board for His birth sing blithe
        at heart,
    what manners high may mean
    this knight will now impart.
    Who hears him will, I ween
    of love-speech learn some art.'

39 When his dinner was done and he duly had risen,
it now to the night-time very near had drawn.
The chaplains then took to the chapel their way
and rang the bells richly, as rightly they should,
for the solemn evensong of the high season.

The lord leads the way, and his lady with him;
into a goodly oratory gracefully she enters.
Gawain follows gladly, and goes there at once
and the lord seizes him by the sleeve and to a seat leads him,
kindly acknowledges him and calls him by his name,
saying that most welcome he was of all guests in the world.
And he grateful thanks gave him, and each greeted the other,
and they sat together soberly while the service lasted.
Then the lady longed to look at this knight;
and from her closet she came with many comely maidens.
She was fairer in face, in her flesh and her skin,
her proportions, her complexion, and her port than all others,
and more lovely than Guinevere to Gawain she looked.
He came through the chancel to pay court to her grace;
leading her by the left hand another lady was there
who was older than she, indeed ancient she seemed,
and held in high honour by all men about her.
But unlike in their looks those ladies appeared,
for if the younger was youthful, yellow was the elder;
with rose-hue the one face was richly mantled,
rough wrinkled cheeks rolled on the other;
on the kerchiefs of the one many clear pearls were,
her breast and bright throat were bare displayed,
fairer than white snow that falls on the hills;
the other was clad with a cloth that enclosed all her neck,
enveloped was her black chin with chalk-white veils,
her forehead folded in silk, and so fumbled all up,
so topped up and trinketed and with trifles bedecked
that naught was bare of that beldame but her brows all black,
her two eyes and her nose and her naked lips,
and those were hideous to behold and horribly bleared;
that a worthy dame she was may well, fore God,
    be said!
  short body and thick waist,
  with bulging buttocks spread;
  more delicious to the taste
  was the one she by her led.

40 When Gawain glimpsed that gay lady that so gracious
        looked,
   with leave sought of the lord towards the ladies he went;
   the elder he saluted, low to her bowing,
   about the lovelier he laid then lightly his arms
   and kissed her in courtly wise with courtesy speaking.
   His acquaintance they requested, and quickly he begged
   to be their servant in sooth, if so they desired.
   They took him between them, and talking they led him
   to a fireside in a fair room, and first of all called
   for spices, which men sped without sparing to bring them,
   and ever wine therewith well to their liking.
   The lord for their delight leaped up full often,
   many times merry games being minded to make;
   his hood he doffed, and on high he hung it on a spear,
   and offered it as an honour for any to win
   who the most fun could devise at that Christmas feast –
   'And I shall try, by my troth, to contend with the best
   ere I forfeit this hood, with the help of my friends!'
   Thus with laughter and jollity the lord made his jests
   to gladden Sir Gawain with games that night
        in hall,
      until the time was due
      that the lord for lights should call;
      Sir Gawain with leave withdrew
      and went to bed withal.

41 On the morn when every man remembers the time
   that our dear Lord for our doom to die was born,
   in every home wakes happiness on earth for His sake.
   So did it there on that day with the dearest delights:
   at each meal and at dinner marvellous dishes
   men set on the dais, the daintiest meats.
   The old ancient woman was highest at table,
   meetly to her side the master he took him;
   Gawain and the gay lady together were seated
   in the centre, where as was seemly the service began,
   and so on through the hall as honour directed.

When each good man in his degree without grudge had
        been served,
there was food, there was festival, there was fullness of joy;
and to tell all the tale of it I should tedious find,
though pains I might take every point to detail.
Yet I ween that Wawain and that woman so fair
in companionship took such pleasure together
in sweet society soft words speaking,
their courteous converse clean and clear of all evil,
that with their pleasant pastime no prince's sport
        compares.
    Drums beat, and trumps men wind,
    many pipers play their airs;
    each man his needs did mind,
    and they two minded theirs.

42 With much feasting they fared the first and the next day,
    and as heartily the third came hastening after:
    the gaiety of Saint John's day was glorious to hear;
    [with cheer of the choicest Childermas followed,]
    and that finished their revels, as folk there intended,
    for there were guests who must go in the grey morning.
    So a wondrous wake they held, and the wine they drank,
    and they danced and danced on, and dearly they carolled.
    At last when it was late their leave then they sought
    to wend on their ways, each worthy stranger.
    Good-day then said Gawain, but the good man stayed him,
    and led him to his own chamber to the chimney-corner,
    and there he delayed him, and lovingly thanked him,
    for the pride and pleasure his presence had brought,
    for so honouring his house at that high season
    and deigning his dwelling to adorn with his favour.
    'Believe me, sir, while I live my luck I shall bless
    that Gawain was my guest at God's own feast.'
    'Gramercy, sir,' said Gawain, 'but the goodness is yours,
    all the honour is your own – may the High King repay you!
    And I am under your orders what you ask to perform,
    as I am bound now to be, for better or worse,

by right.'
Him longer to retain
the lord then pressed the knight;
to him replied Gawain
that he by no means might.

43 Then with courteous question he enquired of Gawain
what dire need had driven him on that festal date
with such keenness from the king's court, to come forth alone
ere wholly the holidays from men's homes had departed.
'In sooth, sir,' he said, 'you say but the truth:
a high errand and a hasty from that house brought me;
for I am summoned myself to seek for a place,
though I wonder where in the world I must wander to find it.
I would not miss coming nigh it on New Year's morning
for all the land in Logres, so our Lord help me!
And so, sir, this question I enquire of you here:
can you tell me in truth if you tale ever heard
of the Green Chapel, on what ground it may stand,
and of the great knight that guards it, all green in his colour?
For the terms of a tryst were between us established
to meet that man at that mark, if I remained alive,
and the named New Year is now nearly upon me,
and I would look on that lord, if God will allow me,
more gladly, by God's son, than gain any treasure.
So indeed, if you please, depart now I must.
For my business I have now but barely three days,
and I would fainer fall dead than fail in my errand.'
Then laughing said the lord: 'Now linger you must;
for when 'tis time to that tryst I will teach you the road.
On what ground is the Green Chapel – let it grieve you
              no more!
In your bed you shall be, sir, till broad is the day,
without fret, and then fare on the first of the year,
and come to the mark at midmorn, there to make what
        play you know.
    Remain till New Year's day,
    then rise and riding go!

We'll set you on your way,
'tis but two miles or so.'

44 Then was Gawain delighted, and in gladness he laughed:
'Now I thank you a thousand times for this beyond all!
Now my quest is accomplished, as you crave it, I will
dwell a few days here, and else do what you order.'
The lord then seized him and set him in a seat beside him,
and let the ladies be sent for to delight them the more,
for their sweet pleasure there in peace by themselves.
For love of him that lord was as loud in his mirth
as one near out of his mind who scarce knew what he meant.
Then he called to the knight, crying out loudly:
'You have promised to do whatever deed I propose.
Will you hold this behest here, at this moment?'
'Yes, certainly, sir,' then said the true knight,
'while I remain in your mansion, your command I'll obey.'
'Well,' returned he, 'you have travelled and toiled from afar,
and then I've kept you awake: you're not well yet, not cured;
both sustenance and sleep 'tis certain you need.
Upstairs you shall stay, sir, and stop there in comfort
tomorrow till Mass-time, and to a meal then go
when you wish with my wife, who with you shall sit
and comfort you with her company, till to court I return.
        You stay,
    and I shall early rouse,
    and a-hunting wend my way.'
    Gawain gracefully bows:
    'Your wishes I will obey.'

45 'One thing more,' said the master, 'we'll make an agreement:
whatever I win in the wood at once shall be yours,
and whatever gain you may get you shall give in exchange.
Shall we swap thus, sweet man – come, say what you think! –
whether one's luck be light, or one's lot be better?'
'By God,' quoth good Gawain, 'I agree to it all,
and whatever play you propose seems pleasant to me.'
'Done! 'Tis a bargain! Who'll bring us the drink?'

So said the lord of that land. They laughed one and all;
they drank and they dallied, and they did as they pleased,
these lords and ladies, as long as they wished,
and then with customs of France and many courtly phrases
they stood in sweet debate and soft words bandied,
and lovingly they kissed, their leave taking.
With trusty attendants and torches gleaming
they were brought at the last to their beds so soft,
          one and all.
     Yet ere to bed they came,
     he the bargain did oft recall;
     he knew how to play a game
     the old governor of that hall.

III

Before the first daylight the folk uprose: the guests that were to
go for their grooms they called; and they hurried up in haste
horses to saddle, to stow all their stuff and strap up their bags.
The men of rank arrayed them, for riding got ready, to saddle
leaped swiftly, seized then their bridles, and went off on their
ways where their wish was to go. The liege-lord of the land was
not last of them all to be ready to ride with a rout of his men;
he ate a hurried mouthful after the hearing of Mass, and with
horn to the hunting-field he hastened at once. When daylight
was opened yet dimly on earth he and his huntsmen were up
on their high horses. Then the leaders of the hounds leashed
them in couples, unclosed the kennel-door and cried to them
'out!', and blew boldly on bugles three blasts full long. Beagles
bayed thereat, a brave noise making; and they whipped and
wheeled in those that wandered on a scent; a hundred hunting-
dogs, I have heard, of the best
          were they.
     To their stations keepers passed;
     the leashes were cast away,
     and many a rousing blast
     woke din in the woods that day.

47 At the first burst of the baying all beasts trembled;
   deer dashed through the dale by dread bewildered,
   and hastened to the heights, but they hotly were greeted,
   and turned back by the beaters, who boldly shouted.
   They let the harts go past with their high antlers,
   and the brave bucks also with their branching palms;
   for the lord of the castle had decreed in the close season
   that no man should molest the male of the deer.
   The hinds were held back with hey! and ware!,
   the does driven with great din to the deep valleys:
   there could be seen let slip a sleet of arrows;
   at each turn under the trees went a twanging shaft
   that into brown hides bit hard with barbéd head.
   Lo! they brayed, and they bled, and on the banks they died;
   and ever the hounds in haste hotly pursued them,
   and hunters with high horns hurried behind them
   with such a clamour and cry as if cliffs had been riven.
   If any beast broke away from bowmen there shooting,
   it was snatched down and slain at the receiving-station;
   when they had been harried from the height and hustled to
         the waters
   the men were so wise in their craft at the watches below,
   and their greyhounds were so great that they got them at once,
   and flung them down in a flash, as fast as men could see
     with sight.
     The lord then wild for joy
     did oft spur and oft alight,
     and thus in bliss employ
     that day till dark of night.

48 Thus in his game the lord goes under greenwood eaves,
   and Gawain the bold lies in goodly bed,
   lazing, till the walls are lit by the light of day,
   under costly coverlet with curtains about him.
   And as in slumber he strayed, he heard stealthily come
   a soft sound at his door as it secretly opened;
   and from under the clothes he craned then his head,
   a corner of the curtain he caught up a little,

and looked that way warily to learn what it was.
It was the lady herself, most lovely to see,
that cautiously closed the door quietly behind her,
and drew near to his bed. Then abashed was the knight,
and lay down swiftly to look as if he slept;
and she stepped silently and stole to his bed,
cast back the curtain, and crept then within,
and sat her down softly on the side of the bed,
and there lingered very long to look for his waking.
He lay there lurking a long while and wondered,
and mused in his mind how the matter would go,
to what point it might pass – to some surprise, he fancied.
Yet he said to himself: 'More seemly 'twould be
in due course with question to enquire what she wishes.'
Then rousing he rolled over, and round to her turning
he lifted his eyelids with a look as of wonder,
and signed him with the cross, thus safer to be kept
    aright.
    With chin and cheeks so sweet
    of blended red and white,
    with grace then him did greet
    small lips with laughter bright.

49 'Good morning, Sir Gawain!' said that gracious lady.
'You are a careless sleeper, if one can creep on you so!
Now quickly you are caught! If we come not to terms,
I shall bind you in your bed, you may be assured.'
With laughter the lady thus lightly jested.
'Good morning to your grace!' said Gawain gaily.
'You shall work on me your will, and well I am pleased;
for I submit immediately, and for mercy I cry,
and that is best, as I deem, for I am obliged to do so.'
Thus he jested in return with much gentle laughter:
'But if you would, lady gracious, then leave grant me,
and release your prisoner and pray him to rise,
I would abandon this bed and better array me;
the more pleasant would it prove then to parley with you.'
'Nay, for sooth, fair sir,' said the sweet lady,

'you shall not go from your bed! I will govern you better:
here fast shall I enfold you, on the far side also,
and then talk with my true knight that I have taken so.
For I wot well indeed that Sir Wawain you are,
to whom all men pay homage wherever you ride;
your honour, your courtesy, by the courteous is praised,
by lords, by ladies, by all living people.
And right here you now are, and we all by ourselves;
my husband and his huntsmen far hence have ridden,
other men are abed, and my maids also,
the door closed and caught with a clasp that is strong;
and since I have in this house one that all delight in,
my time to account I will turn, while for talk I chance
    have still.
    To my body will you welcome be
    of delight to take your fill;
    for need constraineth me
    to serve you, and I will.'

50 'Upon my word,' said Gawain, 'that is well, I guess;
though I am not now he of whom you are speaking –
to attain to such honour as here you tell of
I am a knight unworthy, as well indeed I know –
by God, I would be glad, if good to you seemed
whatever I could say, or in service could offer
to the pleasure of your excellence – it would be pure delight.'
'In good faith, Sir Gawain,' said the gracious lady,
'the prowess and the excellence that all others approve,
if I scorned or decried them, it were scant courtesy.
But there are ladies in number who liever would now
have thee in their hold, sir, as I have thee here,
pleasantly to play with in polished converse,
their solace to seek and their sorrows to soothe,
than great part of the goods or gold that they own.
But I thank Him who on high of Heaven is Lord
that I have here wholly in my hand what all desire,
    by grace.'
    She was an urgent wooer,

that lady fair of face;
the knight with speeches pure
replied in every case.

51　'Madam,' said he merrily, 'Mary reward you!
For I have enjoyed, in good faith, your generous favour,
and much honour have had else from others' kind deeds;
but as for the courtesy they accord me, since my claim is not
　　　equal,
the honour is your own, who are ever well-meaning.'
'Nay, Mary!' the lady demurred, 'as for me, I deny it.
For were I worth all the legion of women alive,
and all the wealth in the world at my will possessed,
if I should exchange at my choice and choose me a husband,
for the noble nature I know, Sir Knight, in thee here,
in beauty and bounty and bearing so gay –
of which earlier I have heard, and hold it now true –
then no lord alive would I elect before you.'
'In truth, lady,' he returned, 'you took one far better.
But I am proud of the praise you are pleased to give me,
and as your servant in earnest my sovereign I hold you,
and your knight I become, and may Christ reward you.'
Thus of many matters they spoke till midmorn was passed,
and ever the lady demeaned her as one that loved him much,
and he fenced with her featly, ever flawless in manner.
'Though I were lady most lovely,' thought the lady to herself,
'the less love would he bring here,' since he looked for
　　　his bane, that blow
　　that him so soon should grieve,
　　and needs it must be so.
　　Then the lady asked for leave
　　and at once he let her go.

52　Then she gave him 'good day', and with a glance she laughed,
and as she stood she astonished him with the strength of
　　　her words:
'Now He that prospers all speech for this disport repay you!
But that you should be Gawain, it gives me much thought.'

'Why so?' then eagerly the knight asked her,
afraid that he had failed in the form of his converse.
But 'God bless you! For this reason,' blithely she answered,
'that one so good as Gawain the gracious is held,
who all the compass of courtesy includes in his person,
so long with a lady could hardly have lingered
without craving a kiss, as a courteous knight,
by some tactful turn that their talk led to.'
Then said Wawain, 'Very well, as you wish be it done.
I will kiss at your command, as becometh a knight,
and more, lest he displease you, so plead it no longer.'
She came near thereupon and caught him in her arms,
and down daintily bending dearly she kissed him.
They courteously commended each other to Christ.
Without more ado through the door she withdrew
         and departed,
and he to rise up in haste made ready at once.
He calls to his chamberlain, and chooses his clothes,
and goes forth when garbed all gladly to Mass.
Then he went to a meal that meetly awaited him,
and made merry all day, till the moon arose
      o'er earth.
    Ne'er was knight so gaily engaged
    between two dames of worth,
    the youthful and the aged:
    together they made much mirth.

53 And ever the lord of the land in his delight was abroad,
   hunting by holt and heath after hinds that were barren.
   When the sun began to slope he had slain such a number
   of does and other deer one might doubt it were true.
   Then the fell folk at last came flocking all in,
   and quickly of the kill they a quarry assembled.
   Thither the master hastened with a host of his men,
   gathered together those greatest in fat
   and had them riven open rightly, as the rules require.
   At the assay they were searched by some that were there,
   and two fingers' breadth of fat they found in the leanest.

Next they slit the eslot, seized on the arber,
shaved it with a sharp knife and shore away the grease;
next ripped the four limbs and rent off the hide.
Then they broke open the belly, the bowels they removed
(flinging them nimbly afar) and the flesh of the knot;
they grasped then the gorge, disengaging with skill
the weasand from the windpipe, and did away with the guts.
Then they shore out the shoulders with their sharpened knives
(drawing the sinews through a small cut) the sides to
   keep whole;
next they burst open the breast, and broke it apart,
and again at the gorge one begins thereupon,
cuts all up quickly till he comes to the fork,
and fetches forth the fore-numbles; and following after
all the tissues along the ribs they tear away quickly.
Thus by the bones of the back they broke off with skill,
down even to the haunch, all that hung there together,
and hoisted it up all whole and hewed it off there:
and that they took for the numbles, as I trow is their
  name in kind.
 Along the fork of every thigh
 the flaps they fold behind;
 to hew it in two they hie,
 down the back all to unbind.

54 Both the head and the neck they hew off after,
and next swiftly they sunder the sides from the chine,
and the bone for the crow they cast in the boughs.
Then they thrust through both thick sides with a thong
   by the rib,
and then by the hocks of the legs they hang them both up:
all the folk earn the fees that fall to their lot.
Upon the fell of the fair beast they fed their hounds then
on the liver and the lights and the leather of the paunches
with bread bathed in blood blended amongst them.
Boldly they blew the prise, amid the barking of dogs,
and then bearing up their venison bent their way homeward,
striking up strongly many a stout horn-call.

When daylight was done they all duly were come
into the noble castle, where quietly the knight
    abode
  in bliss by bright fire set.
  Thither the lord now strode;
  when Gawain with him met,
  then free all pleasure flowed.

55 Then the master commanded his men to meet in that hall,
and both dames to come down with their damsels also;
before all the folk on that floor fair men he ordered
to fetch there forthwith his venison before him,
and all gracious in game to Gawain he called,
announced the number by tally of the nimble beasts,
and showed him the shining fat all shorn on the ribs.
'How does this play please you? Have I praise deserved?
Have I earned by mine art the heartiest thanks?'
'Yea verily,' the other averred, 'here is venison the fairest
that I've seen in seven years in the season of winter!'
'And I give it you all, Gawain,' said the good man at once,
'for as our covenant accorded you may claim it as your own.'
'That is true,' he returned, 'and I tell you the same:
what of worth within these walls I have won also
with as good will, I warrant, 'tis awarded to you.'
His fair neck he enfolded then fast in his arms,
and kissed him with all the kindness that his courtesy knew.
'There take you my gains, sir! I got nothing more.
I would give it up gladly even if greater it were.'
'That is a good one!' quoth the good man. 'Greatly I thank you.
'Tis such, maybe, that you had better briefly now tell me
where you won this same wealth by the wits you possess.'
'That was not the covenant,' quoth he. 'Do not question me more!
For you've drawn what is due to you, no doubt can you
    have 'tis true.'
  They laugh, and with voices fair
  their merriment pursue,
  and to supper soon repair
  with many dainties new.

56   Later by the chimney in chamber they were seated,
     abundant wine of the best was brought to them oft,
     and again as a game they agreed on the morrow
     to abide by the same bond as they had bargained before:
     chance what might chance, to exchange all their trade,
     whatever new thing they got, when they gathered at night.
     They concluded this compact before the courtiers all;
     the drink for the bargain was brought forth in jest;
     then their leave at the last they lovingly took,
     and away then at once each went to his bed.
     When the cock had crowed and cackled but thrice,
     the lord had leaped from his bed, and his lieges each one;
     so that their meal had been made, and the Mass was over,
     and folk bound for the forest, ere the first daybreak,
          to chase.
        Loud with hunters and horns
        o'er plains they passed apace,
        and loosed there among the thorns
        the running dogs to race.

57   Soon these cried for a quest in a covert by a marsh;
     the huntsman hailed the hound that first heeded the scent,
     stirring words he spoke to him with a strident voice.
     The hounds then that heard it hastened thither swiftly,
     and fell fast on the line, some forty at once.
     Then such a baying and babel of bloodhounds together
     arose that the rock-wall rang all about them.
     Hunters enheartened them with horn and with mouth,
     and then all in a rout rushed on together
     between a fen-pool in that forest and a frowning crag.
     In a tangle under a tall cliff at the tarn's edges,
     where the rough rock ruggedly in ruin was fallen,
     they fared to the find, followed by hunters
     who made a cast round the crag and the clutter of stones,
     till well they were aware that it waited within:
     the very beast that the baying bloodhounds had spoken.
     Then they beat on the bushes and bade him uprise,
     and forth he came to their peril against folk in his path.

'Twas a boar without rival that burst out upon them;
long the herd he had left, that lone beast aged,
for savage was he, of all swine the hugest,
grim indeed when he grunted. Then aghast were many;
for three at the first thrust he threw to the ground,
and sprang off with great speed, sparing the others;
and they hallooed on high, and ha! ha! shouted,
and held horn to mouth, blowing hard the rally.
Many were the wild mouthings of men and of dogs,
as they bounded after this boar, him with blare and with
    din to quell.
  Many times he turns to bay,
  and maims the pack pell-mell;
  he hurts many hounds, and they
  grievously yowl and yell.

58 Hunters then hurried up eager to shoot him,
aimed at him their arrows, often they hit him;
but poor at core proved the points that pitched on his shields,
and the barbs on his brows would bite not at all;
though the shaven shaft shivered in pieces,
back the head came hopping, wherever it hit him.
But when the hurts went home of their heavier strokes,
then with brain wild for battle he burst out upon them,
ruthless he rent them as he rushed forward,
and many quailed at his coming and quickly withdrew.
But the lord on a light horse went leaping after him;
as bold man on battle-field with his bugle he blew
the rally-call as he rode through the rough thickets,
pursuing this wild swine till the sunbeams slanted.
This day in such doings thus duly they passed,
while our brave knight beloved there lies in his bed
at home in good hap, in housings so costly
    and gay.
  The lady did not forget:
  she came to bid good day;
  early she on him set,
  his will to wear away.

59 She passed to the curtain and peeped at the knight.
   Sir Wawain graciously then welcomed her first,
   and she answered him alike, eagerly speaking,
   and sat her softly by his side; and suddenly she laughed,
   and with a look full of love delivered these words:
   'Sir, if you are Wawain, a wonder I think it
   that a man so well-meaning, ever mindful of good,
   yet cannot comprehend the customs of the gentle;
   and if one acquaints you therewith, you do not keep them
           in mind:
   thou hast forgot altogether what a day ago I taught
   by the plainest points I could put into words!'
   'What is that?' he said at once. 'I am not aware of it at all.
   But if you are telling the truth, I must take all the blame.'
   'And yet as to kisses,' she quoth, 'this counsel I gave you:
   wherever favour is found, defer not to claim them:
   that becomes all who care for courteous manners.'
   'Take back,' said the true knight, 'that teaching, my dear!
   For that I dared not do, for dread of refusal.
   Were I rebuffed, I should be to blame for so bold an offer.'
   'Ma fay!' said the fair lady, 'you may not be refused;
   you are stout enough to constrain one by strength, if you like,
   if any were so ill bred as to answer you nay.'
   'Indeed, by God,' quoth Gawain, 'you graciously speak;
   but force finds no favour among the folk where I dwell,
   and any gift not given gladly and freely.
   I am at your call and command to kiss when you please.
   You may receive as you desire, and cease as you think
           in place.'
       Then down the lady bent,
       and sweetly kissed his face.
       Much speech then there they spent
       of lovers' grief and grace.

60 'I would learn from you, lord,' the lady then said,
   'if you would not mind my asking, what is the meaning of this:
   that one so young as are you in years, and so gay,
   by renown so well known for knighthood and breeding,

while of all chivalry the choice, the chief thing to praise,
is the loyal practice of love: very lore of knighthood –
for, talking of the toils that these true knights suffer,
it is the title and contents and text of their works:
how lovers for their true love their lives have imperilled,
have endured for their dear one dolorous trials,
until avenged by their valour, their adversity passed,
they have brought bliss into her bower by their own
   brave virtues –
and you are the knight of most noble renown in our age,
and your fame and fair name afar is published,
and I have sat by your very self now for the second time,
yet your mouth has never made any remark I have heard
that ever belonged to love-making, lesser or greater.
Surely, you that are so accomplished and so courtly in
   your vows
should be prompt to expound to a young pupil
by signs and examples the science of lovers.
Why? Are you ignorant who all honour enjoy?
Or else you esteem me too stupid to understand your
   courtship?
  But nay!
  Here single I come and sit,
  a pupil for your play;
  come, teach me of your wit,
  while my lord is far away.'

61 'In good faith,' said Gawain, 'may God reward you!
Great delight I gain, and am glad beyond measure
that one so worthy as you should be willing to come here
and take pains with so poor a man: as for playing with
   your knight,
showing favour in any form, it fills me with joy.
But for me to take up the task on true love to lecture,
to comment on the text and tales of knighthood
to you, who I am certain possess far more skill
in that art by the half than a hundred of such
as I am, or shall ever be while on earth I remain,

it would be folly manifold, in faith, my lady!
All your will I would wish to work, as I am able,
being so beholden in honour, and, so help me the Lord,
desiring ever the servant of yourself to remain.'
Thus she tested and tried him, tempting him often,
so as to allure him to love-making, whatever lay in her heart.
But his defence was so fair that no fault could be seen,
nor any evil upon either side, nor aught but joy
      they wist.
   They laughed and long they played;
   at last she him then kissed,
   with grace adieu him bade,
   and went whereso she list.

62 Then rousing from his rest he rose to hear Mass,
and then their dinner was laid and daintily served.
The livelong day with the ladies in delight he spent,
but the lord o'er the lands leaped to and fro,
pursuing his fell swine that o'er the slopes hurtled
and bit asunder the backs of the best of his hounds,
wherever to bay he was brought, until bowmen
      dislodged him,
and made him, maugre his teeth, move again onward,
so fast the shafts flew when the folk were assembled.
And yet the stoutest of them still he made start there aside,
till at last he was so spent he could speed no further,
but in such haste as he might he made for a hollow
on a reef beside a rock where the river was flowing.
He put the bank at his back, began then to paw;
fearfully the froth of his mouth foamed from the corners;
he whetted his white tusks. Then weary were all
the brave men so bold as by him to stand
of plaguing him from afar, yet for peril they dared not
      come nigher.
   He had hurt so many before,
   that none had now desire
   to be torn with the tusks once more
   of a beast both mad and dire.

63 Till the knight himself came, his courser spurring,
and saw him brought there to bay, and all about him his men.
Nothing loth he alighted, and leaving his horse,
brandished a bright blade and boldly advanced,
striding stoutly through the ford to where stood the felon.
The wild beast was aware of him with his weapon in hand,
and high raised his hair; with such hate he snorted
that folk feared for the knight, lest his foe should worst him.
Out came the swine and set on him at once,
and the boar and the brave man were both in a mellay
in the wildest of the water. The worse had the beast,
for the man marked him well, and as they met he at once
struck steadily his point straight in the neck-slot,
and hit him up to the hilts, so that his heart was riven,
and with a snarl he succumbed, and was swept down the
    water straightway.
  A hundred hounds him caught,
  and fiercely bit their prey;
  the men to the bank him brought,
  and dogs him dead did lay.

64 There men blew for the prise in many a blaring horn,
and high and loud hallooed all the hunters that could;
bloodhounds bayed for the beast, as bade the masters,
who of that hard-run chase were the chief huntsmen.
Then one that was well learnéd in woodmen's lore
with pretty cunning began to carve up this boar.
First he hewed off his head and on high set it,
then he rent him roughly down the ridge of the back,
brought out the bowels, burned them on gledes,
and with them, blended with blood, the bloodhounds
    rewarded.
Next he broke up the boar-flesh in broad slabs of brawn,
and haled forth the hastlets in order all duly,
and yet all whole he fastened the halves together,
and strongly on a stout pole he strung them then up.
Now with this swine homeward swiftly they hastened,
and the boar's head was borne before the brave knight himself

who felled him in the ford by force of his hand
   so great.
    Until he saw Sir Gawain
    in the hall he could hardly wait.
    He called, and his pay to gain
    the other came there straight.

65 The lord with his loud voice and laughter merry
gaily he greeted him when Gawain he saw.
The fair ladies were fetched and the folk all assembled,
and he showed them the shorn slabs, and shaped his report
of the width and wondrous length, and the wickedness also
in war, of the wild swine, as in the woods he had fled.
With fair words his friend the feat then applauded,
and praised the great prowess he had proved in his deeds;
for such brawn on a beast, the brave knight declared,
or such sides on a swine he had never seen before.
They then handled the huge head, and highly he praised it,
showing horror at the hideous thing to honour the lord.
'Now, Gawain,' said the good man, 'this game is your own
by close covenant we concluded, as clearly you know.'
'That is true,' he returned, 'and as truly I assure you
all my winnings, I warrant, I shall award you in exchange.'
He clasped his neck, and courteously a kiss he then gave him
and swiftly with a second he served him on the spot.
'Now we are quits,' he quoth, 'and clear for this evening
of all covenants we accorded, since I came to this house,
   as is due.'
    The lord said: 'By Saint Gile,
    your match I never knew!
    You'll be wealthy in a while,
    such trade if you pursue.'

66 Then on top of the trestles the tables they laid,
cast the cloths thereon, and clear light then
wakened along the walls; waxen torches
men set there, and servants went swift about the hall.
Much gladness and gaiety began then to spring

round the fire on the hearth, and freely and oft
at supper and later: many songs of delight,
such as canticles of Christmas, and new carol-dances,
amid all the mannerly mirth that men can tell of;
and ever our noble knight was next to the lady.
Such glances she gave him of her gracious favour,
secretly stealing sweet looks that strong man to charm,
that he was passing perplexed, and ill-pleased at heart.
Yet he would fain not of his courtesy coldly refuse her,
but graciously engaged her, however against the grain
    the play.
    When mirth they had made in hall
    as long as they wished to stay,
    to a room did the lord them call
    and to the ingle they made their way.

67 There amid merry words and wine they had a mind once more
to harp on the same note on New Year's Eve.
But said Gawain: 'Grant me leave to go on the morrow!
For the appointment approaches that I pledged myself to.'
The lord was loth to allow it, and longer would keep him,
and said: 'As I am a true man I swear on my troth
the Green Chapel thou shalt gain, and go to your business
in the dawn of New Year, sir, ere daytime begins.
So still lie upstairs and stay at thine ease,
and I shall hunt in the holt here, and hold to my terms
with thee truly, when I return, to trade all our gains.
For I have tested thee twice, and trusty I find thee.
Now "third time pays for all", bethink thee tomorrow!
Make we merry while we may and be mindful of joy,
for the woe one may win whenever one wishes!'
This was graciously agreed, and Gawain would linger.
Then gaily drink is given them and they go to their beds
    with light.
    Sir Gawain lies and sleeps
    soft and sound all night;
    his host to his hunting keeps,
    and is early arrayed aright.

68 After Mass of a morsel he and his men partook.
　　Merry was the morning. For his mount then he called.
　　All the huntsmen that on horse behind him should follow
　　were ready mounted to ride arrayed at the gates.
　　Wondrous fair were the fields, for the frost clung there;
　　in red rose-hued o'er the wrack arises the sun,
　　sailing clear along the coasts of the cloudy heavens.
　　The hunters loosed hounds by a holt-border;
　　the rocks rang in the wood to the roar of their horns.
　　Some fell on the line to where the fox was lying,
　　crossing and re-crossing it in the cunning of their craft.
　　A hound then gives tongue, the huntsman names him,
　　round him press his companions in a pack all snuffling,
　　running forth in a rabble then right in his path.
　　The fox flits before them. They find him at once,
　　and when they see him by sight they pursue him hotly,
　　decrying him full clearly with a clamour of wrath.
　　He dodges and ever doubles through many a dense coppice,
　　and looping oft he lurks and listens under fences.
　　At last at a little ditch he leaps o'er a thorn-hedge,
　　sneaks out secretly by the side of a thicket,
　　weens he is out of the wood and away by his wiles from
　　　　　the hounds.
　　Thus he went unawares to a watch that was posted,
　　where fierce on him fell three foes at once
　　　　all grey.
　　　He swerves then swift again,
　　　and dauntless darts astray;
　　　in grief and in great pain
　　　to the wood he turns away.

69 Then to hark to the hounds it was heart's delight,
　　when all the pack came upon him, there pressing together.
　　Such a curse at the view they called down on him
　　that the clustering cliffs might have clattered in ruin.
　　Here he was hallooed when hunters came on him,
　　yonder was he assailed with snarling tongues;
　　there he was threatened and oft thief was he called,

with ever the trailers at his tail so that tarry he could not.
Oft was he run at, if he rushed outwards;
oft he swerved in again, so subtle was Reynard.
Yea! he led the lord and his hunt as laggards behind him
thus by mount and by hill till mid-afternoon.
Meanwhile the courteous knight in the castle in comfort
      slumbered
behind the comely curtains in the cold morning.
But the lady in love-making had no liking to sleep
nor to disappoint the purpose she had planned in her heart;
but rising up swiftly his room now she sought
in a gay mantle that to the ground was measured
and was fur-lined most fairly with fells well trimmed,
with no comely coif on her head, only the clear jewels
that were twined in her tressure by twenties in clusters;
her noble face and her neck all naked were laid,
her breast bare in front and at the back also.
She came through the chamber-door and closed it behind her,
wide set a window, and to wake him she called,
thus greeting him gaily with her gracious words
    of cheer:
  'Ah! man, how canst thou sleep,
  the morning is so clear!'
  He lay in darkness deep,
  but her call he then could hear.

70 In heavy darkness drowsing he dream-words muttered,
as a man whose mind was bemused with many mournful
      thoughts,
how destiny should his doom on that day bring him
when he at the Green Chapel the great man would meet,
and be obliged his blow to abide without debate at all.
But when so comely she came, he recalled then his wits,
swept aside his slumbers, and swiftly made answer.
The lady in lovely guise came laughing sweetly,
bent down o'er his dear face, and deftly kissed him.
He greeted her graciously with a glad welcome,
seeing her so glorious and gaily attired,

so faultless in her features and so fine in her hues
that at once joy up-welling went warm to his heart.
With smiles sweet and soft they turned swiftly to mirth,
and only brightness and bliss was broached there between
    them so gay.
   They spoke then speeches good,
   much pleasure was in that play;
   great peril between them stood,
   unless Mary for her knight should pray.

71 For she, queenly and peerless, pressed him so closely,
led him so near the line, that at last he must needs
either refuse her with offence or her favours there take.
He cared for his courtesy, lest a caitiff he proved,
yet more for his sad case, if he should sin commit
and to the owner of the house, to his host, be a traitor.
'God help me!' said he. 'Happen that shall not!'
Smiling sweetly aside from himself then he turned
all the fond words of favour that fell from her lips.
Said she to the knight then: 'Now shame you deserve,
if you love not one that lies alone here beside you,
who beyond all women in the world is wounded in heart,
unless you have a lemman, more beloved, whom you
    like better,
and have affianced faith to that fair one so fast and so true
that your release you desire not – and so I believe now;
and to tell me if that be so truly, I beg you.
For all sakes that men swear by conceal not the truth
    in guile.'
   The knight said: 'By Saint John,'
   and softly gave a smile,
   'Nay! lover have I none,
   and none will have meanwhile.'

72 'Those words,' said the woman, 'are the worst that could be.
But I am answered indeed, and 'tis hard to endure.
Kiss me now kindly, and I will quickly depart.
I may but mourn while I live as one that much is in love.'

Sighing she sank down, and sweetly she kissed him;
then soon she left his side, and said as she stood there:
'Now, my dear, at this parting do me this pleasure,
give me something as thy gift, thy glove it might be,
that I may remember thee, dear man, my mourning to lessen.'
'Now on my word,' then said he, 'I wish I had here
the loveliest thing for thy delight that in my land I possess;
for worthily have you earned wondrously often
more reward by rights than within my reach would now be,
save to allot you as love-token thing of little value.
Beneath your honour it is to have here and now
a glove for a guerdon as the gift of Sir Gawain:
and I am here on an errand in unknown lands,
and have no bearers with baggage and beautiful things
(unluckily, dear lady) for your delight at this time.
A man must do as he is placed; be not pained nor
        aggrieved,' said he.
    Said she so comely clad:
    'Nay, noble knight and free,
    though naught of yours I had,
    you should get a gift from me.'

73 A rich ring she offered him of red gold fashioned,
    with a stone like a star standing up clear
    that bore brilliant beams as bright as the sun:
    I warrant you it was worth wealth beyond measure.
    But the knight said nay to it, and announced then at once:
    'I will have no gifts, fore God, of your grace at this time.
    I have none to return you, and naught will I take.'
    She proffered it and pressed him, and he her pleading refused,
    and swore swiftly upon his word that accept it he would not.
    And she, sorry that he refused, said to him further:
    'If to my ring you say nay, since too rich it appears,
    and you would not so deeply be indebted to me,
    I shall give you my girdle, less gain will that be.'
    She unbound a belt swiftly that embracing her sides
    was clasped above her kirtle under her comely mantle.
    Fashioned it was of green silk, and with gold finished,

though only braided round about, embroidered by hand;
and this she would give to Gawain, and gladly besought him,
of no worth though it were, to be willing to take it.
And he said nay, he would not, he would never receive
either gold or jewellery, ere God the grace sent him
to accomplish the quest on which he had come thither.
'And therefore I pray you, please be not angry,
and cease to insist on it, for to your suit I will ever
    say no.
  I am deeply in debt to you
  for the favour that you show,
  to be your servant true
  for ever in weal or woe.'

74 'Do you refuse now this silk,' said the fair lady,
  'because in itself it is poor? And so it appears.
See how small 'tis in size, and smaller in value!
But one who knew of the nature that is knit therewithin
would appraise it probably at a price far higher.
For whoever goes girdled with this green riband,
while he keeps it well clasped closely about him,
there is none so hardy under heaven that to hew him were able;
for he could not be killed by any cunning of hand.'
The knight then took note, and thought now in his heart,
'twould be a prize in that peril that was appointed to him.
When he gained the Green Chapel to get there his sentence,
if by some sleight he were not slain, 'twould be a sovereign device.
Then he bore with her rebuke, and debated not her words;
and she pressed on him the belt, and proffered it in earnest;
and he agreed, and she gave it very gladly indeed,
and prayed him for her sake to part with it never,
but on his honour hide it from her husband; and he then agreed
that no one ever should know, nay, none in the world
    but they.
  With earnest heart and mood
  great thanks he oft did say.
  She then the knight so good
  a third time kissed that day.

75 Then she left him alone, her leave taking,
    for amusement from the man no more could she get.
    When she was gone Sir Gawain got him soon ready,
    arose and robed himself in raiment noble.
    He laid up the love-lace that the lady had given,
    hiding it heedfully where he after might find it.
    Then first of all he chose to fare to the chapel,
    privately approached a priest, and prayed that he there
    would uplift his life, that he might learn better
    how his soul should be saved, when he was sent from
            the world.
    There he cleanly confessed him and declared his misdeeds,
    both the more and the less, and for mercy he begged,
    to absolve him of them all he besought the good man;
    and he assoiled him and made him as safe and as clean
    as for Doom's Day indeed, were it due on the morrow.
    Thereafter more merry he made among the fair ladies,
    with carol-dances gentle and all kinds of rejoicing,
    than ever he did ere that day, till the darkness of night,
            in bliss.
        Each man there said: 'I vow
        a delight to all he is!
        Since hither he came till now,
        he was ne'er so gay as this.'

76 Now indoors let him dwell and have dearest delight,
    while the free lord yet fares afield in his sports!
    At last the fox he has felled that he followed so long;
    for, as he spurred through a spinney to espy there the villain,
    where the hounds he had heard that hard on him pressed,
    Reynard on his road came through a rough thicket,
    and all the rabble in a rush were right on his heels.
    The man is aware of the wild thing, and watchful awaits him,
    brings out his bright brand and at the beast hurls it;
    and he blenched at the blade, and would have backed if
            he could.
    A hound hastened up, and had him ere he could;
    and right before the horse's feet they fell on him all,

and worried there the wily one with a wild clamour.
The lord quickly alights and lifts him at once,
snatching him swiftly from their slavering mouths,
holds him high o'er his head, hallooing loudly;
and there bay at him fiercely many furious hounds.
Huntsmen hurried thither, with horns full many
ever sounding the assembly, till they saw the master.
When together had come his company noble,
all that ever bore bugle were blowing at once,
and all the others hallooed that had not a horn:
it was the merriest music that ever men harkened,
the resounding song there raised that for Reynard's
     soul awoke.
  To hounds they pay their fees,
  their heads they fondly stroke,
  and Reynard then they seize,
  and off they skin his cloak.

77 And then homeward they hastened, for at hand was now night,
making strong music on their mighty horns.
The lord alighted at last at his beloved abode,
found a fire in the hall, and fair by the hearth
Sir Gawain the good, and gay was he too,
among the ladies in delight his lot was most joyful.
He was clad in a blue cloak that came to the ground;
his surcoat well beseemed him with its soft lining,
and its hood of like hue that hung on his shoulder:
all fringed with white fur very finely were both.
He met indeed the master in the midst of the floor,
and in gaiety greeted him, and graciously said:
'In this case I will first our covenant fulfil
that to our good we agreed, when ungrudged went the drink.'
He clasps then the knight and kisses him thrice,
as long and deliciously as he could lay them upon him.
'By Christ!' the other quoth, 'you've come by a fortune
in winning such wares, were they worth what you paid.'
'Indeed, the price was not important,' promptly he answered,
'whereas plainly is paid now the profit I gained.'

'Marry!' said the other man, 'mine is not up to't;
for I have hunted all this day, and naught else have I got
but this foul fox-fell – the Fiend have the goods! –
and that is price very poor to pay for such treasures
as these you have thrust upon me, three such kisses
  so good.'
 ''Tis enough,' then said Gawain.
'I thank you, by the Rood,'
and how the fox was slain
he told him as they stood.

78 With mirth and minstrelsy and meats at their pleasure
as merry they made as any men could be;
amid the laughter of ladies and light words of jest
both Gawain and the good man could no gayer have proved,
unless they had doted indeed or else drunken had been.
Both the host and his household went on with their games,
till the hour had approached when part must they all;
to bed were now bound the brave folk at last.
Bowing low his leave of the lord there first
the good knight then took, and graciously thanked him:
'For such a wondrous welcome as within these walls I have had,
for your honour at this high feast the High King reward you!
In your service I set myself, your servant, if you will.
For I must needs make a move tomorrow, as you know,
if you give me some good man to go, as you promised,
and guide me to the Green Chapel, as God may permit me
to face on New Year's day such doom as befalls me.'
'On my word,' said his host, 'with hearty good will
to all that ever I promised I promptly shall hold.'
Then a servant he assigns him to set him on the road,
and by the downs to conduct him, that without doubt or delay
he might through wild and through wood ways most
  straight pursue.
 Said Gawain, 'My thanks receive,
such a favour you will do!'
The knight then took his leave
of those noble ladies two.

79 Sadly he kissed them and said his farewells,
and pressed oft upon them in plenty his thanks,
and they promptly the same again repaid him;
to God's keeping they gave him, grievously sighing.
Then from the people of the castle he with courtesy parted;
all the men that he met he remembered with thanks
for their care for his comfort and their kind service,
and the trouble each had taken in attendance upon him;
and every one was as woeful to wish him adieu
as had they lived all their lives with his lordship in honour.
Then with link-men and lights he was led to his chamber
and brought sweetly to bed, there to be at his rest.
That soundly he slept then assert will I not,
for he had many matters in the morning to mind, if he
        would, in thought.
    There let him lie in peace,
    near now is the tryst he sought.
    If a while you will hold your peace,
    I will tell the deeds they wrought!

IV

Now New Year draws near and the night passes, day comes
driving the dark, as ordained by God; but wild weathers of the
world awake in the land, clouds cast keenly the cold upon earth
with bitter breath from the North biting the naked. Snow
comes shivering sharp to shrivel the wild things, the whistling
wind whirls from the heights and drives every dale full of drifts
very deep. Long the knight listens as he lies in his bed; though
he lays down his eyelids, very little he sleeps: at the crow of
every cock he recalls well his tryst. Briskly he rose from his bed
ere the break of day, for there was light from a lamp that
illumined his chamber. He called to his chamberlain, who
quickly him answered, and he bade him bring his byrnie and
his beast saddle. The man got him up and his gear fetched
him, and garbed then Sir Gawain in great array; first he clad
him in his clothes to keep out the cold, and after that in his
harness that with heed had been tended, both his pauncer and

his plates polished all brightly, the rings rid of the rust on his
rich byrnie: all was neat as if new, and the knight him
    thanked with delight.
  He put on every piece
  all burnished well and bright;
  most gallant from here to Greece
  for his courser called the knight.

81 While the proudest of his apparel he put on himself:
  his coat-armour, with the cognisance of the clear symbol
  upon velvet environed with virtuous gems
  all bound and braided about it, with broidered seams
  and with fine furs lined wondrous fairly within,
  yet he overlooked not the lace that the lady had given him;
  that Gawain forgot not, of his own good thinking;
  when he had belted his brand upon his buxom haunches,
  he twined the love-token twice then about him,
  and swiftly he swathed it sweetly about his waist,
  that girdle of green silk, and gallant it looked
  upon the royal red cloth that was rich to behold.
  But he wore not for worth nor for wealth this girdle,
  not for pride in the pendants, though polished they were,
  not though the glittering gold there gleamed at the ends,
  but so that himself he might save when suffer he must,
  must abide bane without debating it with blade or with
    brand of war.
  When arrayed the knight so bold
  came out before the door,
  to all that high household
  great thanks he gave once more.

82 Now Gringolet was groomed, the great horse and high,
  who had been lodged to his liking and loyally tended:
  fain to gallop was that gallant horse for his good fettle.
  His master to him came and marked well his coat,
  and said: 'Now solemnly myself I swear on my troth
  there is a company in this castle that is careful of honour!
  Their lord that them leads, may his lot be joyful!

Their beloved lady in life may delight befall her!
If they out of charity thus cherish a guest,
upholding their house in honour, may He them reward
that upholds heaven on high, and all of you too!
And if life a little longer I might lead upon earth,
I would give you some guerdon gladly, were I able.'
Then he steps in the stirrup and strides on his horse;
his shield his man showed him, and on shoulder he slung it,
Gringolet he goaded with his gilded heels,
and he plunged forth on the pavement, and prancing no
    more stood there.
  Ready now was his squire to ride
  that his helm and lance would bear.
  'Christ keep this castle!' he cried
  and wished it fortune fair.

83 The bridge was brought down and the broad gates then
    unbarred and swung back upon both hinges.
    The brave man blessed himself, and the boards crossing,
    bade the porter up rise, who before the prince kneeling
    gave him 'Good day, Sir Gawain!', and 'God save you!'
    Then he went on his way with the one man only
    to guide him as he goes to that grievous place
    where he is due to endure the dolorous blow.
    They go by banks and by braes where branches are bare,
    they climb along cliffs where clingeth the cold;
    the heavens are lifted high, but under them evilly
    mist hangs moist on the moor, melts on the mountains;
    every hill has a hat, a mist-mantle huge.
    Brooks break and boil on braes all about,
    bright bubbling on their banks where they bustle downwards.
    Very wild through the wood is the way they must take,
    until soon comes the season when the sun rises
      that day.
    On a high hill they abode,
    white snow beside them lay;
    the man that by him rode
    there bade his master stay.

84 'For so far I have taken you, sir, at this time,
   and now you are near to that noted place
   that you have enquired and questioned so curiously after.
   But I will announce now the truth, since you are known
           to me,
   and you are a lord in this life that I love greatly,
   if you would follow my advice you would fare better.
   The place that you pass to, men perilous hold it,
   the worst wight in the world in that waste dwelleth;
   for he is stout and stern, and to strike he delights,
   and he mightier than any man upon middle-earth is,
   and his body is bigger than the four best men
   that are in Arthur's house, either Hestor or others.
   All goes as he chooses at the Green Chapel;
   no one passes by that place so proud in his arms
   that he hews not to death by dint of his hand.
   For he is a man monstrous, and mercy he knows not;
   for be it a churl or a chaplain that by the Chapel rideth,
   a monk or a mass-priest or any man besides,
   he would as soon have him slain as himself go alive.
   And so I say to you, as sure as you sit in your saddle,
   if you come there, you'll be killed, if the carl has his way.
   Trust me, that is true, though you had twenty lives
           to yield.
       He here has dwelt now long
       and stirred much strife on field;
       against his strokes so strong
       yourself you cannot shield.

85 And so, good Sir Gawain, now go another way,
   and let the man alone, for the love of God, sir!
   Come to some other country, and there may Christ keep you!
   And I shall haste me home again, and on my honour I promise
   that I swear will by God and all His gracious saints,
   so help me God and the Halidom, and other oaths a plenty,
   that I will safe keep your secret, and say not a word
   that ever you fain were to flee for any foe that I knew of.'
   'Gramercy!' quoth Gawain; and regretfully answered:

'Well, man, I wish thee, who wishest my good,
and keep safe my secret, I am certain thou wouldst.
But however heedfully thou hid it, if I here departed
fain in fear now to flee, in the fashion thou speakest,
I should a knight coward be, I could not be excused.
Nay, I'll fare to the Chapel, whatever chance may befall,
and have such words with that wild man as my wish is
to say, come fair or come foul, as fate will allot
    me there.
    He may be a fearsome knave
    to tame, and club may bear;
    but His servants true to save
    the Lord can well prepare.'

86 'Marry!' quoth the other man, 'now thou makest it so clear
that thou wishest thine own bane to bring on thyself,
and to lose thy life hast a liking, to delay thee I care not!
Have here thy helm on thy head, thy spear in thy hand,
and ride down by yon rock-side where runs this same track,
till thou art brought to the bottom of the baleful valley.
A little to thy left hand then look o'er the green,
and thou wilt see on the slope the selfsame chapel,
and the great man and grim on ground that it keeps.
Now farewell in God's name, Gawain the noble!
For all the gold in the world I would not go with thee,
nor bear thee fellowship through this forest one foot further!'
With that his bridle towards the wood back the man turneth,
hits his horse with his heels as hard as he can,
gallops on the greenway, and the good knight there leaves
    alone,
    Quoth Gawain: 'By God on high
    I will neither grieve nor groan.
    With God's will I comply,
    Whose protection I do own.'

87 Then he put spurs to Gringolet, and espying the track,
thrust in along a bank by a thicket's border,
rode down the rough brae right to the valley;

and then he gazed all about: a grim place he thought it,
and saw no sign of shelter on any side at all,
only high hillsides sheer upon either hand,
and notched knuckled crags with gnarled boulders;
the very skies by the peaks were scraped, it appeared.
Then he halted and held in his horse for the time,
and changed oft his front the Chapel to find.
Such on no side he saw, as seemed to him strange,
save a mound as it might be near the marge of a green,
a worn barrow on a brae by the brink of a water,
beside falls in a flood that was flowing down;
the burn bubbled therein, as if boiling it were.
He urged on his horse then, and came up to the mound,
there lightly alit, and lashed to a tree
his reins, with a rough branch rightly secured them.
Then he went to the barrow and about it he walked,
debating in his mind what might the thing be.
It had a hole at the end and at either side,
and with grass in green patches was grown all over,
and was all hollow within: nought but an old cavern,
or a cleft in an old crag; he could not it name
        aright.
    'Can this be the Chapel Green,
    O Lord?' said the gentle knight.
    'Here the Devil might say, I ween,
    his matins about midnight!

88 On my word,' quoth Wawain, ''tis a wilderness here!
This oratory looks evil. With herbs overgrown
it fits well that fellow transformed into green
to follow here his devotions in the Devil's fashion.
Now I feel in my five wits the Fiend 'tis himself
that has trapped me with this tryst to destroy me here.
This is a chapel of mischance, the church most accursed
that ever I entered. Evil betide it!'
With high helm on his head, his lance in his hand,
he roams up to the roof of that rough dwelling.
Then he heard from the high hill, in a hard rock-wall

beyond the stream on a steep, a sudden startling noise.
How it clattered in the cliff, as if to cleave it asunder,
as if one upon a grindstone were grinding a scythe!
How it whirred and it rasped as water in a mill-race!
How it rushed, and it rang, rueful to harken!
Then 'By God,' quoth Gawain, 'I guess this ado
is meant for my honour, meetly to hail me
  as knight!
 As God wills! Waylaway!
 That helps me not a mite.
 My life though down I lay,
 no noise can me affright.'

89 Then clearly the knight there called out aloud:
'Who is master in this place to meet me at tryst?
For now 'tis good Gawain on ground that here walks.
If any aught hath to ask, let him hasten to me,
either now or else never, his needs to further!'
'Stay!' said one standing above on the steep o'er his head,
'and thou shalt get in good time what to give thee I vowed.'
Still with that rasping and racket he rushed on a while,
and went back to his whetting, till he wished to descend.
And then he climbed past a crag, and came from a hole,
hurtling out of a hid nook with a horrible weapon:
a Danish axe newly dressed the dint to return,
with cruel cutting-edge curved along the handle –
filed on a whetstone, and four feet in width,
'twas no less – along its lace of luminous hue;
and the great man in green still guised as before,
his locks and long beard, his legs and his face,
save that firm on his feet he fared on the ground,
steadied the haft on the stones and stalked beside it.
When he walked to the water, where he wade would not,
he hopped over on his axe and haughtily strode,
fierce and fell on a field where far all about
  lay snow.
 Sir Gawain the man met there,
 neither bent nor bowed he low.

The other said: 'Now, sirrah fair,
I true at tryst thee know!'

90 'Gawain,' said that green man, 'may God keep thee!
On my word, sir, I welcome thee with a will to my place,
and thou hast timed thy travels as trusty man should,
and thou hast forgot not the engagement agreed on
           between us:
at this time gone a twelvemonth thou took'st thy
           allowance,
and I should now this New Year nimbly repay thee.
And we are in this valley now verily on our own,
there are no people to part us – we can play as we like.
Have thy helm off thy head, and have here thy pay!
Bandy me no more debate than I brought before thee
when thou didst sweep off my head with one swipe only!'
'Nay,' quoth Gawain, 'by God that gave me my soul,
I shall grudge thee not a grain any grief that follows.
Only restrain thee to one stroke, and still shall I stand
and offer thee no hindrance to act as thou likest
     right here.'
  With a nod of his neck he bowed,
  let bare the flesh appear;
  he would not by dread be cowed,
  no sign he gave of fear.

91 Then the great man in green gladly prepared him,
gathered up his grim tool there Gawain to smite;
with all the lust in his limbs aloft he heaved it,
shaped as mighty a stroke as if he meant to destroy him.
Had it driving come down as dour as he aimed it,
under his dint would have died the most doughty man ever.
But Gawain on that guisarm then glanced to one side,
as down it came gliding on the green there to end him,
and he shrank a little with his shoulders at the sharp iron.
With a jolt the other man jerked back the blade,
and reproved then the prince, proudly him taunting.

'Thou'rt not Gawain,' said the green man, 'who is so
      good reported,
who never flinched from any foes on fell or in dale;
and now thou fleest in fear, ere thou feelest a hurt!
Of such cowardice that knight I ne'er heard accused.
Neither blenched I nor backed, when thy blow, sir,
      thou aimedst,
nor uttered any cavil in the court of King Arthur.
My head flew to my feet, and yet fled I never;
but thou, ere thou hast any hurt, in thy heart quailest,
and so the nobler knight to be named I deserve
     therefore.'
    'I blenched once,' Gawain said,
    'and I will do so no more.
    But if on floor now falls my head,
    I cannot it restore.

92 But get busy, I beg, sir, and bring me to the point.
Deal me my destiny, and do it out of hand!
For I shall stand from thee a stroke and stir not again
till thine axe hath hit me, have here my word on't!'
'Have at thee then!' said the other, and heaved it aloft,
and watched him as wrathfully as if he were wild with rage.
He made at him a mighty aim, but the man he touched not,
holding back hastily his hand, ere hurt it might do.
Gawain warily awaited it, and winced with no limb,
but stood as still as a stone or the stump of a tree
that with a hundred ravelled roots in rocks is embedded.
This time merrily remarked then the man in the green:
'So, now thou hast thy heart whole, a hit I must make.
May the high order now keep thee that Arthur gave thee,
and guard thy gullet at this go, if it can gain thee that.'
Angrily with ire then answered Sir Gawain:
'Why! lash away, thou lusty man! Too long dost thou threaten.
'Tis thy heart methinks in thee that now quaileth!'
'In faith,' said the fellow, 'so fiercely thou speakest,
I no longer will linger delaying thy errand
    right now.'

Then to strike he took his stance
and grimaced with lip and brow.
He that of rescue saw no chance
was little pleased, I trow.

93 Lightly his weapon he lifted, and let it down neatly
with the bent horn of the blade towards the neck that was bare;
though he hewed with a hammer-swing, he hurt him no more
than to snick him on one side and sever the skin.
Through the fair fat sank the edge, and the flesh entered,
so that the shining blood o'er his shoulders was shed on
      the earth;
and when the good knight saw the gore that gleamed on
      the snow,
he sprang out with spurning feet a spear's length and more,
in haste caught his helm and on his head cast it,
under his fair shield he shot with a shake of his shoulders,
brandished his bright sword, and boldly he spake –
never since he as manchild of his mother was born
was he ever on this earth half so happy a man:
'Have done, sir, with thy dints! Now deal me no more!
I have stood from thee a stroke without strife on this spot,
and if thou offerest me others, I shall answer thee promptly,
and give as good again, and as grim, be assured,
      shall pay.
But one stroke here's my due,
as the covenant clear did say
that in Arthur's halls we drew.
And so, good sir, now stay!'

94 From him the other stood off, and on his axe rested,
held the haft to the ground, and on the head leaning,
gazed at the good knight as on the green he there strode.
To see him standing so stout, so stern there and fearless,
armed and unafraid, his heart it well pleased.
Then merrily he spoke with a mighty voice,
and loudly it rang, as to that lord he said:
'Fearless knight on this field, so fierce do not be!

No man here unmannerly hath thee maltreated,
nor aught given thee not granted by agreement at court.
A hack I thee vowed, and thou'st had it, so hold thee content;
I remit thee the remnant of all rights I might claim.
If I brisker had been, a buffet, it may be,
I could have handed thee more harshly, and harm could have
      done thee.
First I menaced thee in play with no more than a trial,
and clove thee with no cleft: I had a claim to the feint,
for the fast pact we affirmed on the first evening,
and thou fairly and unfailing didst faith with me keep,
all thy gains thou me gavest, as good man ought.
The other trial for the morning, man, I thee tendered
when thou kissedst my comely wife, and the kisses
      didst render.
For the two here I offered only two harmless feints
    to make.
   The true shall truly repay,
   for no peril then need he quake.
   Thou didst fail on the third day,
   and so that tap now take!

95 For it is my weed that thou wearest, that very woven girdle:
my own wife it awarded thee, I wot well indeed.
Now I am aware of thy kisses, and thy courteous ways,
and of thy wooing by my wife: I worked that myself!
I sent her to test thee, and thou seem'st to me truly
the fair knight most faultless that e'er foot set on earth!
As a pearl than white pease is prized more highly,
so is Gawain, in good faith, than other gallant knights.
But in this you lacked, sir, a little, and of loyalty came short.
But that was for no artful wickedness, nor for wooing either,
but because you loved your own life: the less do I blame you.'
The other stern knight in a study then stood a long while,
in such grief and disgust he had a grue in his heart;
all the blood from his breast in his blush mingled,
and he shrank into himself with shame at that speech.
The first words on that field that he found then to say

were: 'Cursed be ye, Coveting, and Cowardice also!
In you is vileness, and vice that virtue destroyeth.'
He took then the treacherous thing, and untying the knot
fiercely flung he the belt at the feet of the knight:
'See there the falsifier, and foul be its fate!
Through care for thy blow Cowardice brought me
to consent to Coveting, my true kind to forsake,
which is free-hand and faithful word that are fitting to knights.
Now I am faulty and false, who afraid have been ever
of treachery and troth-breach: the two now my curse
    may bear!
  I confess, sir, here to you
  all faulty has been my fare.
  Let me gain your grace anew,
  and after I will beware.'

96 Then the other man laughed and lightly answered:
'I hold it healed beyond doubt, the harm that I had.
Thou hast confessed thee so clean and acknowledged
    thine errors,
and hast the penance plain to see from the point of my blade,
that I hold thee purged of that debt, made as pure and as clean
as hadst thou done no ill deed since the day thou wert born.
And I give thee, sir, the girdle with gold at its hems,
for it is green like my gown. So, Sir Gawain, you may
think of this our contest when in the throng thou walkest
among princes of high praise; 'twill be a plain reminder
of the chance of the Green Chapel between chivalrous knights.
And now you shall in this New Year come anon to my house,
and in our revels the rest of this rich season
    shall go.'
  The lord pressed him hard to wend,
  and said, 'My wife, I know,
  we soon shall make your friend,
  who was your bitter foe.'

97 'Nay forsooth!' the knight said, and seized then his helm,
and duly it doffed, and the doughty man thanked:

'I have lingered too long! May your life now be blest,
and He promptly repay you Who apportions all honours!
And give my regards to her grace, your goodly consort,
both to her and to the other, to mine honoured ladies,
who thus their servant with their designs have subtly beguiled.
But no marvel it is if mad be a fool,
and by the wiles of woman to woe be brought.
For even so Adam by one on earth was beguiled,
and Solomon by several, and to Samson moreover
his doom by Delilah was dealt; and David was after
blinded by Bathsheba, and he bitterly suffered.
Now if these came to grief through their guile, a gain 'twould
      be vast
to love them well and believe them not, if it lay in man's
      power!
Since these were aforetime the fairest, by fortune most blest,
eminent among all the others who under heaven bemused
    were too,
  and all of them were betrayed
  by women that they knew,
  though a fool I now am made,
  some excuse I think my due.

98 But for your girdle,' quoth Gawain, 'may God you repay!
That I will gain with good will, not for the gold so joyous
of the cincture, nor the silk, nor the swinging pendants,
nor for wealth, nor for worth, nor for workmanship fine;
but as a token of my trespass I shall turn to it often
when I ride in renown, ruefully recalling
the failure and the frailty of the flesh so perverse,
so tender, so ready to take taints of defilement.
And thus, when pride my heart pricks for prowess in arms,
one look at this love-lace shall lowlier make it.
But one thing I would pray you, if it displeaseth you not,
since you are the lord of yonder land, where I lodged
      for a while
in your house and in honour – may He you reward
Who upholdeth the heavens and on high sitteth! –

how do you announce your true name? And then nothing
      further.'
'That I will tell thee truly,' then returned the other.
'Bertilak de Hautdesert hereabouts I am called,
[who thus have been enchanted and changed in my hue]
by the might of Morgan le Fay that in my mansion dwelleth,
and by cunning of lore and crafts well learned.
The magic arts of Merlin she many hath mastered;
for deeply in dear love she dealt on a time
with that accomplished clerk, as at Camelot runs
      the fame;
   and Morgan the Goddess
   is therefore now her name.
   None power and pride possess
   too high for her to tame.

99 She made me go in this guise to your goodly court
    to put its pride to the proof, if the report were true
    that runs of the great renown of the Round Table.
    She put this magic upon me to deprive you of your wits,
    in hope Guinevere to hurt, that she in horror might die
    aghast at that glamoury that gruesomely spake
    with its head in its hand before the high table.
    She it is that is at home, that ancient lady;
    she is indeed thine own aunt, Arthur's half-sister,
    daughter of the Duchess of Tintagel on whom doughty
        Sir Uther
    after begat Arthur, who in honour is now.
    Therefore I urge thee in earnest, sir, to thine aunt return!
    In my hall make merry! My household thee loveth,
    and I wish thee as well, upon my word, sir knight,
    as any that go under God, for thy great loyalty.'
    But he denied him with a 'Nay! by no means I will!'
    They clasp then and kiss and to the care give each other
    of the Prince of Paradise; and they part on that field
       so cold,
     To the king's court on courser keen
     then hastened Gawain the bold,

and the knight in the glittering green
to ways of his own did hold.

100 Wild ways in the world Wawain now rideth
on Gringolet: by the grace of God he still lived.
Oft in house he was harboured and lay oft in the open,
oft vanquished his foe in adventures as he fared
which I intend not this time in my tale to recount.
The hurt was healed that he had in his neck,
and the bright-hued belt he bore now about it
obliquely like a baldric bound at his side,
under his left arm with a knot that lace was fastened
to betoken he had been detected in the taint of a fault;
and so at last he came to the Court again safely.
Delight there was awakened, when the lords were aware
that good Gawain had returned: glad news they thought it.
The king kissed the knight, and the queen also,
and then in turn many a true knight that attended to
        greet him.
About his quest they enquire, and he recounts all the marvels,
declares all the hardships and care that he had,
what chanced at the Chapel, what cheer made the knight,
the love of the lady, and the lace at the last.
The notch in his neck naked he showed them
that he had for his dishonesty from the hands of the
        knight in blame.
    It was torment to tell the truth:
    in his face the blood did flame;
    he groaned for grief and ruth
    when he showed it, to his shame.

101 'Lo! Lord,' he said at last, and the lace handled,
'This is the band! For this a rebuke I bear in my neck!
This is the grief and disgrace I have got for myself
from the covetousness and cowardice that o'ercame me there!
This is the token of the troth-breach that I am detected in,
and needs must I wear it while in the world I remain;
for a man may cover his blemish, but unbind it he cannot,

for where once 'tis applied, thence part will it never.'
The king comforted the knight, and all the Court also
laughed loudly thereat, and this law made in mirth
the lords and the ladies that whoso belonged to the Table,
every knight of the Brotherhood, a baldric should have,
a band of bright green obliquely about him,
and this for love of that knight as a livery should wear.
For that was reckoned the distinction of the Round Table,
and honour was his that had it evermore after,
as it is written in the best of the books of romance.
Thus in Arthur his days happened this marvel,
as the Book of the Brut beareth us witness;
since Brutus the bold knight to Britain came first,
after the siege and the assault had ceased at Troy,
　　　I trow,
　　many a marvel such before,
　　has happened here ere now.
　　To His bliss us bring Who bore
　　the Crown of Thorns on brow!　　　　　　　AMEN

HONY SOYT QUI MAL PENCE

PEARL

Pearl of delight that a prince doth please
    To grace in gold enclosed so clear,
I vow that from over orient seas
Never proved I any in price her peer.
So round, so radiant ranged by these,
So fine, so smooth did her sides appear
That ever in judging gems that please
Her only alone I deemed as dear.
Alas! I lost her in garden near:
Through grass to the ground from me it shot;
I pine now oppressed by love-wound drear
For that pearl, mine own, without a spot.

2 Since in that spot it sped from me,
   I have looked and longed for that precious thing
   That me once was wont from woe to free,
   to uplift my lot and healing bring,
   But my heart doth hurt now cruelly,
   My breast with burning torment sting.
   Yet in secret hour came soft to me
   The sweetest song I e'er heard sing;
   Yea, many a thought in mind did spring
   To think that her radiance in clay should rot.
   O mould! Thou marrest a lovely thing,
   My pearl, mine own, without a spot.

3 In that spot must needs be spices spread
   Where away such wealth to waste hath run;
   Blossoms pale and blue and red
   There shimmer shining in the sun;
   No flower nor fruit their hue may shed
   Where it down into darkling earth was done,
   For all grass must grow from grains that are dead,
   No wheat would else to barn be won.

From good all good is ever begun,
And fail so fair a seed could not,
So that sprang and sprouted spices none
From that precious pearl without a spot.

4 That spot whereof I speak I found
When I entered in that garden green,
As August's season high came round
When corn is cut with sickles keen.
There, where that pearl rolled down, a mound
With herbs was shadowed fair and sheen,
With gillyflower, ginger, and gromwell crowned,
And peonies powdered all between.
If sweet was all that there was seen,
Fair, too, a fragrance flowed I wot,
Where dwells that dearest, as I ween,
My precious pearl without a spot.

5 By that spot my hands I wrung dismayed;
For care full cold that had me caught
A hopeless grief on my heart was laid.
Though reason to reconcile me sought,
For my pearl there prisoned a plaint I made,
In fierce debate unmoved I fought;
Be comforted Christ Himself me bade,
But in woe my will ever strove distraught.
On the flowery plot I fell, methought;
Such odour through my senses shot,
I slipped and to sudden sleep was brought,
O'er that precious pearl without a spot.

6 From that spot my spirit sprang apace,
On the turf my body abode in trance;
My soul was gone by God's own grace
Adventuring where marvels chance.
I knew not where in the world was that place
Save by cloven cliffs was set my stance;
And towards a forest I turned my face,

Where rocks in splendour met my glance;
From them did a glittering glory lance,
None could believe the light they lent;
Never webs were woven in mortal haunts
Of half such wealth and wonderment.

7 Wondrous was made each mountain-side
With crystal cliffs so clear of hue;
About them woodlands bright lay wide,
As Indian dye their boles were blue;
The leaves did as burnished silver slide
That thick upon twigs there trembling grew.
When glades let light upon them glide
They shone with a shimmer of dazzling hue.
The gravel on ground that I trod with shoe
Was of precious pearls of the Orient:
Sunbeams are blear and dark to view
Compared with that fair wonderment.

8 In wonder at those fells so fair
My soul all grief forgot let fall;
Odours so fresh of fruits there were,
I was fed as by food celestial.
In the woods the birds did wing and pair,
Of flaming hues, both great and small;
But cithern-string and gittern-player
Their merry mirth could ne'er recall,
For when they beat their pinions all
In harmony their voices blent:
No delight more lovely could men enthrall
Than behold and hear that wonderment.

9 Thus arrayed was all in wonderment
That forest where forth my fortune led;
No man its splendour to present
With tongue could worthy words have said.
I walked ever onward well-content;
No hill was so tall that it stayed my tread;

More fair the further afield I went
Were plants, and fruits, and spices spread;
Through hedge and mead lush waters led
As in strands of gold there steeply pent.
A river I reached in cloven bed:
O Lord! the wealth of its wonderment!

10 The adornments of that wondrous deep
Were beauteous banks of beryl bright:
Swirling sweetly its waters sweep,
Ever rippling on in murmurous flight.
In the depths stood dazzling stones aheap
As a glitter through glass that glowed with light,
As streaming stars when on earth men sleep
Stare in the welkin in winter night;
For emerald, sapphire, or lewel bright
Was every pebble in pool there pent,
And the water was lit with rays of light,
Such wealth was in its wonderment.

11 The wondrous wealth of down and dales,
Of wood and water and lordly plain,
My mirth makes mount: my mourning fails,
My care is quelled and cured my pain.
Then down a stream that strongly sails
I blissful turn with teeming brain;
The further I follow those flowing vales
The more strength of joy my heart doth strain.
As fortune fares where she doth deign,
Whether gladness she gives or grieving sore,
So he who may her graces gain,
His hap is to have ever more and more.

12 There more was of such marvels thrice
Than I could tell, though I long delayed;
For earthly heart could not suffice
For a tithe of the joyful joys displayed.
Therefore I thought that Paradise

Across those banks was yonder laid;
I weened that the water by device
As bounds between pleasances was made;
Beyond that stream by steep or slade
That city's walls I weened must soar;
But the water was deep, I dared not wade,
And ever I longed to, more and more.

13 More and more, and yet still more,
I fain beyond the stream had scanned,
For fair as was this hither shore,
Far lovelier was the further land.
To find a ford I did then explore,
And round about did stare and stand;
But perils pressed in sooth more sore
The further I strode along the strand.
I should not, I thought, by fear be banned
From delights so lovely that lay in store;
But a happening new then came to hand
That moved my mind ever more and more.

14 A marvel more did my mind amaze:
I saw beyond that border bright
From a crystal cliff the lucent rays
And beams in splendour lift their light.
A child abode there at its base:
She wore a gown of glistening white,
A gentle maid of courtly grace;
Erewhile I had known her well by sight.
As shredded gold that glistered bright
She shone in beauty upon the shore;
Long did my glance on her alight,
And the longer I looked I knew her more.

15 The more I that face so fair surveyed,
When upon her gracious form I gazed,
Such gladdening glory upon me played
As my wont was seldom to see upraised.

Desire to call her then me swayed,
But dumb surprise my mind amazed;
In place so strange I saw that maid,
The blow might well my wits have crazed.
Her forehead fair then up she raised
That hue of polished ivory wore.
It smote my heart distraught and dazed,
And ever the longer, the more and more.

16   More than I would my dread did rise.
I stood there still and dared not call
With closed mouth and open eyes,
I stood as tame as hawk in hall.
A ghost was present, I did surmise,
And feared for what might then befall,
Lest she should flee before mine eyes
Ere I to tryst could her recall.
So smooth, so seemly, slight and small,
That flawless fair and mirthful maid
Arose in robes majestical,
A precious gem in pearls arrayed.

17   There pearls arrayed and royally dight
Might one have seen by fortune graced
When fresh as flower-de-luces bright
She down to the water swiftly paced
In linen robe of glistening white,
With open sides that seams enlaced
With the merriest margery-pearls my sight
Ever before, I vow, had traced.
Her sleeves hung long below her waist
Adorned with pearls in double braid;
Her kirtle matched her mantle chaste
All about with precious pearls arrayed.

18   A crown arrayed too wore that girl
Of margery-stones and others none,

With pinnacles of pure white pearl
That perfect flowers were figured on.
On head nought else her hair did furl,
And it framed, as it did round her run,
Her countenance grave for duke or earl,
And her hue as rewel ivory wan.
As shredded sheen of gold then shone
Her locks on shoulder loosely laid.
Her colour pure was surpassed by none
Of the pearls in purfling rare arrayed.

19 Arrayed was wristlet, and the hems were dight
At hands, at sides, at throat so fair
With no gem but the pearl all white
And burnished white her garments were;
But a wondrous pearl unstained and bright
She amidst her breast secure did bear;
Ere mind could fathom its worth and might
Man's reason thwarted would despair.
No tongue could in worthy words declare
The beauty that was there displayed,
It was so polished, pure, and fair,
That precious pearl on her arrayed.

20 In pearls arrayed that maiden free
Beyond the stream came down the strand.
From here to Greece none as glad could be
As I on shore to see her stand,
Than aunt or niece more near to me:
The more did joy my heart expand.
She deigned to speak, so sweet was she,
Bowed low as ladies' ways demand.
With her crown of countless worth in hand
A gracious welcome she me bade.
My birth I blessed, who on the strand
To my love replied in pearls arrayed.

21 'O Pearl!' said I, 'in pearls arrayed,
   Are you my pearl whose loss I mourn?
Lament alone by night I made,
Much longing I have hid for thee forlorn,
Since to the grass you from me strayed.
While I pensive waste by weeping worn,
Your life of joy in the land is laid
Of Paradise by strife untorn.
What fate hath hither my jewel borne
And made me mourning's prisoner?
Since asunder we in twain were torn,
I have been a joyless jeweller.'

22 That jewel in gems so excellent
Lifted her glance with eyes of grey,
Put on her crown of pearl-orient,
And gravely then began to say:
'Good sir, you have your speech mis-spent
To say your pearl is all away
That is in chest so choicely pent,
Even in this gracious garden gay,
Here always to linger and to play
Where regret nor grief e'er trouble her.
"Here is a casket safe" you would say,
If you were a gentle jeweller.

23 But, jeweller gentle, if from you goes
Your joy through a gem that you held lief,
Methinks your mind toward madness flows
And frets for a fleeting cause of grief.
For what you lost was but a rose
That by nature failed after flowering brief;
Now the casket's virtues that it enclose
Prove it a pearl of price in chief;
And yet you have called your fate a thief
That of naught to aught hath fashioned her,
You grudge the healing of your grief,
You are no grateful jeweller.'

24 Then a jewel methought had now come near,
    And jewels the courteous speech she made.
    'My blissful one,' quoth I, 'most dear,
    My sorrows deep you have all allayed.
    To pardon me I pray you here!
    In the darkness I deemed my pearl was laid;
    I have found it now, and shall make good cheer,
    With it dwell in shining grove and glade,
    And praise all the laws that my Lord hath made,
    Who hath brought me near such bliss with her.
    Now could I to reach you these waters wade,
    I should be a joyful jeweller.'

25 'Jeweller,' rejoined that jewel clean,
    'Why jest ye men? How mad ye be!
    Three things at once you have said, I ween:
    Thoughtless, forsooth, were all the three.
    You know not on earth what one doth mean;
    Your words from your wits escaping flee:
    You believe I live here on this green,
    Because you can with eyes me see;
    Again, you will in this land with me
    Here dwell yourself, you now aver;
    And thirdly, pass this water free:
    That may no joyful jeweller.

26 I hold that jeweller worth little praise
    Who well esteems what he sees with eye,
    And much to blame his graceless ways
    Who believes our Lord would speak a lie.
    He promised faithfully your lives to raise
    Though fate decreed your flesh should die;
    His words as nonsense ye appraise
    Who approve of naught not seen with eye;
    And that presumption doth imply,
    Which all good men doth ill beseem,
    On tale as true ne'er to rely
    Save private reason right it deem.

27 Do you deem that you yourself maintain
   Such words as man to God should dare?
   You will dwell, you say, in this domain:
   'Twere best for leave first offer prayer,
   And yet that grace you might not gain.
   Now over this water you wish to fare:
   By another course you must that attain;
   Your flesh shall in clay find colder lair,
   For our heedless father did of old prepare
   Its doom by Eden's grove and stream;
   Through dismal death must each man fare,
   Ere o'er this deep him God redeem.'

28 'If my doom you deem it, maiden sweet,
   To mourn once more, then I must pine.
   Now my lost one found again I greet,
   Must bereavement new till death be mine?
   Why must I at once both part and meet?
   My precious pearl doth my pain design!
   What use hath treasure but tears to repeat,
   When one at its loss must again repine?
   Now I care not though my days decline
   Outlawed afar o'er land and stream;
   When in my pearl no part is mine,
   Only endless dolour one that may deem.'

29 'But of woe, I deem, and deep distress
   You speak,' she said. 'Why do you so?
   Through loud lament when they lose the less
   Oft many men the more forgo.
   'Twere better with cross yourself to bless,
   Ever praising God in weal and woe;
   For resentment gains you not a cress:
   Who must needs endure, he may not say no!
   For though you dance as any doe,
   Rampant bray or raging scream,
   When escape you cannot, to nor fro,
   His doom you must abide, I deem.

30 Deem God unjust, the Lord indict,
    From his way a foot He will not wend;
    The relief amounts not to a mite,
    Though gladness your grief may never end.
    Cease then to wrangle, to speak in spite,
    And swiftly seek Him as your friend.
    Your prayer His pity may excite,
    So that Mercy shall her powers expend.
    To your languor He may comfort lend,
    And swiftly your griefs removed may seem;
    For lament or rave, to submit pretend,
    'Tis His to ordain what He right may deem.'

31 Then I said, I deem, to that damosel:
      'May I give no grievance to my Lord,
    Rash fool, though blundering tale I tell.
    My heart the pain of loss outpoured,
    Gushing as water springs from well.
    I commit me ever to His mercy's ward.
    Rebuke me not with words so fell,
    Though I erring stray, my dear adored!
    But your comfort kindly to me accord,
    In pity bethinking you of this:
    For partner you did me pain award
    On whom was founded all my bliss.

32 Both bliss and grief you have been to me,
    But of woe far greater hath been my share.
    You were caught away from all perils free,
    But my pearl was gone, I knew not where;
    My sorrow is softened now I it see.
    When we parted, too, at one we were;
    Now God forbid that we angry be!
    We meet on our roads by chance so rare.
    Though your converse courtly is and fair,
    I am but mould and good manners miss.
    Christ's mercy, Mary and John: I dare
    Only on these to found my bliss.

33 In bliss you abide and happiness,
   And I with woe am worn and grey;
   Oft searing sorrows I possess,
   Yet little heed to that you pay.
   But now I here yourself address,
   Without reproach I would you pray
   To deign in sober words express
   What life you lead the livelong day.
   For delighted I am that your lot, you say,
   So glorious and so glad now is;
   There finds my joy its foremost way,
   On that is founded all my bliss.'

34 'Now bliss you ever bless!' she cried,
   Lovely in limb, in hue so clear,
   'And welcome here to walk and bide;
   For now your words are to me dear.
   Masterful mood and haughty pride,
   I warn you, are bitterly hated here.
   It doth not delight my Lord to chide,
   For meek are all that dwell Him near.
   So, when in His place you must appear,
   Be devout in humble lowliness:
   To my Lord, the Lamb, such a mien is dear,
   On whom is founded all my bliss.

35 A blissful life you say is mine;
   You wish to know in what degree.
   Your pearl you know you did resign
   When in young and tender years was she;
   Yet my Lord, the Lamb, through power divine
   Myself He chose His bride to be,
   And crowned me queen in bliss to shine,
   While days shall endure eternally.
   Dowered with His heritage all is she
   That is His love. I am wholly His:
   On His glory, honour, and high degree
   Are built and founded all my bliss.'

36 'O Blissful!' said I, 'can this be true?
        Be not displeased if in speech I err!
Are you the queen of heavens blue,
    Whom all must honour on earth that fare?
We believe that our Grace of Mary grew,
    Who in virgin-bloom a babe did bear;
And claim her crown: who could this do
    But one that surpassed her in favour fair?
And yet for unrivalled sweetness rare
    We call her the Phoenix of Araby,
That her Maker let faultless wing the air,
    Like to the Queen of Courtesy.'

37 'O courteous Queen,' that damsel said,
    Kneeling on earth with uplifted face,
'Mother immaculate, and fairest maid,
    Blessed beginner of every grace!'
Uprising then her prayer she stayed,
    And there she spoke to me a space:
'Here many the prize they have gained are paid,
    But usurpers, sir, here have no place.
That empress' realm doth heaven embrace,
    And earth and hell she holds in fee,
From their heritage yet will none displace,
    For she is the Queen of Courtesy.

38 The court where the living God doth reign
    Hath a virtue of its own being,
That each who may thereto attain
    Of all the realm is queen or king,
Yet never shall other's right obtain,
    But in other's good each glorying
And wishing each crown worth five again,
    If amended might be so fair a thing.
But my Lady of whom did Jesu spring,
    O'er us high she holds her empery,
And none that grieves of our following,
    For she is the Queen of Courtesy.

39 In courtesy we are members all
Of Jesus Christ, Saint Paul doth write:
As head, arm, leg, and navel small
To their body doth loyalty true unite,
So as limbs to their Master mystical
All Christian souls belong by right.
Now among your limbs can you find at all
Any tie or bond of hate or spite?
Your head doth not feel affront or slight
On your arm or finger though ring it see;
So we all proceed in love's delight
To king and queen by courtesy.'

40 'Courtesy,' I said, 'I do believe
And charity great dwells you among,
But may my words no wise you grieve,
. . . .
You in heaven too high yourself conceive
To make you a queen who were so young.
What honour more might he achieve
Who in strife on earth was ever strong,
And lived his life in penance long
With his body's pain to get bliss for fee?
What greater glory could to him belong
Than king to be crowned by courtesy?

41 That courtesy gives its gifts too free,
If it be sooth that you now say.
Two years you lived not on earth with me,
And God you could not please, nor pray
With Pater and Creed upon your knee –
And made a queen that very day!
I cannot believe, God helping me,
That God so far from right would stray.
Of a countess, damsel, I must say,
'Twere fair in heaven to find the grace,
Or of lady even of less array,
But a queen! It is too high a place.'

42 'Neither time nor place His grace confine,'
Then said to me that maiden bright,
'For just is all that He doth assign,
And nothing can He work but right.
In God's true gospel, in words divine
That Matthew in your mass doth cite,
A tale he aptly doth design,
In parable saith of heaven's light:
"My realm on high I liken might
To a vineyard owner in this case.
The year had run to season right;
To dress the vines 'twas time and place.

43 All labourers know when that time is due.
The master up full early rose
To hire him vineyard workers new;
And some to suit his needs he chose.
Together they pledge agreement true
For a penny a day, and forth each goes,
Travails and toils to tie and hew,
Binds and prunes and in order stows.
In forenoon the master to market goes,
And there finds men that idle laze.
'Why stand ye idle?' he said to those.
'Do ye know not time of day nor place?'

44 'This place we reached betimes ere day,'
This answer from all alike he drew,
'Since sunrise standing here we stay,
And no man offers us work to do.'
'Go to my vineyard! Do what ye may!'
Said the lord, and made a bargain true:
'In deed and intent I to you will pay
What hire may justly by night accrue.'
They went to his vines and laboured too,
But the lord all day that way did pace,
And brought to his vineyard workers new,
Till daytime almost passed that place.

45 In that place at time of evensong,
   One hour before the set of sun,
   He saw there idle labourers strong
   And thus his earnest words did run:
   'Why stand ye idle all day long?'
   They said they chance of hire had none.
   'Go to my vineyard, yeomen young,
   And work and do what may be done!'
   The hour grew late and sank the sun,
   Dusk came o'er the world apace;
   He called them to claim the wage they had won,
   For time of day had passed that place.

46 The time in that place he well did know;
   He called: 'Sir steward, the people pay!
   Give them the hire that I them owe.
   Moreover, that none reproach me may,
   Set them all in a single row,
   And to each alike give a penny a day;
   Begin at the last that stands below,
   Till to the first you make your way.'
   Then the first began to complain and say
   That they had laboured long and sore:
   'These but one hour in stress did stay;
   It seems to us we should get more.

47 More have we earned, we think it true,
   Who have borne the daylong heat indeed,
   Than these who hours have worked not two,
   And yet you our equals have decreed.'
   One such the lord then turned him to:
   'My friend, I will not curtail your meed.
   Go now and take what is your due!
   For a penny I hired you as agreed,
   Why now to wrangle do you proceed?
   Was it not a penny you bargained for?
   To surpass his bargain may no man plead.
   Why then will you ask for more?

48 Nay, more – am I not allowed in gift
    To dispose of mine as I please to do?
    Or your eye to evil, maybe, you lift,
    For I none betray and I am true?'
    "Thus I," said Christ, "shall the order shift:
    The last shall come first to take his due,
    And the first come last, be he never so swift;
    For many are called, but the favourites few."
    Thus the poor get ever their portion too,
    Though late they came and little bore;
    And though to their labour little accrue,
    The mercy of God is much the more.

49 More is my joy and bliss herein,
    The flower of my life, my lady's height,
    Than all the folk in the world might win,
    Did they seek award on ground of right.
    Though 'twas but now that I entered in,
    And came to the vineyard by evening's light,
    First with my hire did my Lord begin;
    I was paid at once to the furthest mite.
    Yet others in toil without respite
    That had laboured and sweated long of yore,
    He did not yet with hire requite,
    Nor will, perchance, for years yet more.'

50 Then more I said and spoke out plain:
    'Unreasonable is what you say.
    Ever ready God's justice on high doth reign,
    Or a fable doth Holy Writ purvey.
    The Psalms a cogent verse contain,
    Which puts a point that one must weigh:
    "High King, who all dost foreordain,
    His deserts Thou dost to each repay."
    Now if daylong one did steadfast stay,
    And you to payment came him before,
    Then lesser work can earn more pay;
    And the longer you reckon, the less hath more.'

51 'Of more and less in God's domains
No question arises,' said that maid,
'For equal hire there each one gains,
Be guerdon great or small him paid.
No churl is our Chieftain that in bounty reigns,
Be soft or hard by Him purveyed;
As water of dike His gifts He drains,
Or streams from a deep by drought unstayed.
Free is the pardon to him conveyed
Who in fear to the Saviour in sin did bow;
No bars from bliss will for such be made,
For the grace of God is great enow.

52 But now to defeat me you debate
That wrongly my penny I have taken here;
You say that I who came too late
Deserve not hire at price so dear.
Where heard you ever of man relate
Who, pious in prayer from year to year,
Did not somehow forfeit the guerdon great
Sometime of Heaven's glory clear?
Nay, wrong men work, from right they veer,
And ever the ofter the older, I trow.
Mercy and grace must then them steer,
For the grace of God is great enow.

53 But enow have the innocent of grace.
As soon as born, in lawful line
Baptismal waters them embrace;
Then they are brought unto the vine.
Anon the day with darkened face
Doth toward the night of death decline.
They wrought no wrong while in that place,
And his workmen then pays the Lord divine.
They were there; they worked at his design;
Why should He not their toil allow,
Yea, first to them their hire assign?
For the grace of God is great enow.

54 Enow 'tis known that Man's high kind
    At first for perfect bliss was bred.
    Our eldest father that grace resigned
    Through an apple upon which he fed.
    We were all damned, for that food assigned
    To die in grief, all joy to shed,
    And after in flames of hell confined
    To dwell for ever unréspited.
    But soon a healing hither sped:
    Rich blood ran on rough rood-bough,
    And water fair. In that hour of dread
    The grace of God grew great enow.

55 Enow there went forth from that well
    Water and blood from wounds so wide:
    The blood redeemed us from pains of hell,
    Of the second death the bond untied;
    The water is baptism, truth to tell,
    That the spear so grimly ground let glide.
    It washes away the trespass fell
    By which Adam drowned us in deathly tide.
    No bars in the world us from Bliss divide
    In blessed hour restored, I trow,
    Save those that He hath drawn aside;
    And the grace of God is great enow.

56 Grace enow may the man receive
    Who sins anew, if he repent;
    But craving it he must sigh and grieve
    And abide what pains are consequent.
    But reason that right can never leave
    Evermore preserves the innocent;
    'Tis a judgement God did never give
    That the guiltless should ever have punishment.
    The guilty, contrite and penitent,
    Through mercy may to grace take flight;
    But he that to treachery never bent
    In innocence is saved by right.

57 It is right thus by reason, as in this case
   I learn, to save these two from ill;
   The righteous man shall see His face,
   Come unto him the harmless will.
   This point the Psalms in a passage raise:
   "Who, Lord, shall climb Thy lofty hill,
   Or rest within Thy holy place?"
   He doth the answer swift fulfil:
   "Who wrought with hands no harm nor ill,
   Who is of heart both clean and bright,
   His steps shall there be steadfast still":
   The innocent ever is saved by right.

58 The righteous too, one may maintain,
   He shall to that noble tower repair,
   Who leads not his life in folly vain,
   Nor guilefully doth to neighbour swear.
   That Wisdom did honour once obtain
   For such doth Solomon declare:
   She pressed him on by ways made plain
   And showed him afar God's kingdom fair,
   As if saying: "That lovely island there
   That mayst thou win, be thou brave in fight."
   But to say this doubtless one may dare:
   The innocent ever is saved by right.

59 To righteous men – have you seen it there? –
   In the Psalter David a verse applied:
   "Do not, Lord, Thy servant to judgement bear;
   For to Thee none living is justified."
   So when to that Court you must repair
   Where all our cases shall be tried,
   If on right you stand, lest you trip beware,
   Warned by these words that I espied.
   But He on rood that bleeding died,
   Whose hands the nails did harshly smite,
   Grant you may pass, when you are tried,
   By innocence and not by right.

60 Let him that can rightly read in lore,
Look in the Book and learn thereby
How Jesus walked the world of yore,
And people pressed their babes Him nigh,
For joy and health from Him did pour.
"Our children touch!" they humbly cry,
"Let be!" his disciples rebuked them sore,
And to many would approach deny.
Then Jesus sweetly did reply:
"Nay! let children by me alight;
For such is heaven prepared on high!"
The innocent ever is saved by right.

61 Then Jesus summoned his servants mild,
And said His realm no man might win,
Unless he came there as a child;
Else never should he come therein.
Harmless, true, and undefiled,
Without mark or mar of soiling sin,
When such knock at those portals piled,
Quick for them men will the gate unpin.
That bliss unending dwells therein
That the jeweller sought, above gems did rate,
And sold all he had to clothe him in,
To purchase a pearl immaculate.

62 This pearl immaculate purchased dear
The jeweller gave all his goods to gain
Is like the realm of heaven's sphere:
So said the Lord of land and main;
For it is flawless, clean and clear,
Endlessly round, doth joy contain,
And is shared by all the righteous here.
Lo! amid my breast it doth remain;
There my Lord, the Lamb that was bleeding slain,
In token of peace it placed in state.
I bid you the wayward world disdain
And procure your pearl immaculate!'

63 'Immaculate Pearl in pearls unstained,
　　Who bear of precious pearls the prize,
　　Your figure fair for you who feigned?
　　Who wrought your robe, he was full wise!
　　Your beauty was never from nature gained;
　　Pygmalion did ne'er your face devise;
　　In Aristotle's learning is contained
　　Of these properties' nature no surmise;
　　Your hue the flower-de-luce defies,
　　Your angel-bearing is of grace so great.
　　What office, purest, me apprise
　　Doth bear this pearl immaculate?'

64 'My immaculate Lamb, my final end,
　　Beloved, Who all can heal,' said she,
　　'Chose me as spouse, did to bridal bend
　　That once would have seemed unmeet to be.
　　From your weeping world when I did wend
　　He called me to his felicity:
　　"Come hither to me, sweetest friend,
　　For no blot nor spot is found in thee!"
　　Power and beauty he gave to me;
　　In his blood he washed my weeds in state,
　　Crowned me clean in virginity,
　　And arrayed me in pearls immaculate.'

65 'Why, immaculate bride of brightest flame,
　　Who royalty have so rich and rare,
　　Of what kind can He be, the Lamb you name,
　　Who would you His wedded wife declare?
　　Over others all hath climbed your fame,
　　In lady's life with Him to fare.
　　For Christ have lived in care and blame
　　Many comely maids with comb in hair;
　　Yet the prize from all those brave you bear,
　　And all debar from bridal state,
　　All save yourself so proud and fair,
　　A matchless maid immaculate.'

66 'Immaculate, without a stain,
   Flawless I am,' said that fair queen;
   'And that I may with grace maintain,
   But "matchless" I said not nor do mean.
   As brides of the Lamb in bliss we reign,
   Twelve times twelve thousand strong, I ween,
   As Apocalypse reveals it plain:
   In a throng they there by John were seen;
   On Zion's hill, that mount serene,
   The apostle had dream divine of them
   On that summit for marriage robed all clean
   In the city of New Jerusalem.

67 Of Jerusalem my tale doth tell,
   If you will know what His nature be,
   My Lamb, my Lord, my dear Jewel,
   My Joy, my Bliss, my Truelove free.
   Isaiah the prophet once said well
   In pity for His humility:
   "That glorious Guiltless they did fell
   Without cause or charge of felony,
   As sheep to the slaughter led was He,
   And as lamb the shearer in hand doth hem
   His mouth he closed without plaint or plea,
   When the Jews Him judged in Jerusalem."

68 In Jerusalem was my Truelove slain,
   On the rood by ruffians fierce was rent;
   Willing to suffer all our pain
   To Himself our sorrows sad He lent.
   With cruel blows His face was flain
   That was to behold so excellent:
   He for sin to be set at naught did deign,
   Who of sin Himself was innocent.
   Beneath the scourge and thorns He bent,
   And stretched on a cross's brutal stem
   As meek as lamb made no lament,
   And died for us in Jerusalem.

69 In Jerusalem, Jordan, and Galilee,
As there baptized the good Saint John,
With Isaiah well did his words agree.
When to meet him once had Jesus gone
He spake of Him this prophecy:
"Lo, the Lamb of God whom our trust is on!
From the grievous sins He sets us free
That all this world hath daily done."
He wrought himself yet never one,
Though He smirched himself with all of them.
Who can tell the Fathering of that Son
That died for us in Jerusalem?

70 In Jerusalem as lamb they knew
And twice thus took my Truelove dear,
As in prophets both is record true,
For His meekness and His gentle cheer.
The third time well is matched thereto,
In Apocalypse 'tis written clear:
Where sat the saints, Him clear to view
Amidst the throne the Apostle dear
Saw loose the leaves of the book and shear
The seven signets sewn on them.
At that sight all folk there bowed in fear
In hell, in earth, and Jerusalem.

71 Jerusalem's Lamb had never stain
Of other hue than whiteness fair;
There blot nor blemish could remain,
So white the wool, so rich and rare.
Thus every soul that no soil did gain
His comely wife doth the Lamb declare;
Though each day He a host obtain,
No grudge nor grievance do we bear,
But for each one five we wish there were.
The more the merrier, so God me bless!
Our love doth thrive where many fare
In honour more and never less.

72 To less of bliss may none us bring
   Who bear this pearl upon each breast,
   For ne'er could they think of quarrelling
   Of spotless pearls who bear the crest.
   Though the clods may to our corses cling,
   And for woe ye wail bereaved of rest,
   From one death all our trust doth spring
   In knowledge complete by us possessed.
   The Lamb us gladdens, and, our grief redressed,
   Doth at every Mass with joy us bless.
   Here each hath bliss supreme and best,
   Yet no one's honour is ever the less.

73 Lest less to trust my tale you hold,
   In Apocalypse 'tis writ somewhere:
   "The Lamb," saith John, "I could behold
   On Zion standing proud and fair;
   With him maidens a hundred-thousand fold,
   And four and forty thousand were,
   Who all upon their brows inscrolled
   The Lamb's name and His Father's bare.
   A shout then I heard from heaven there,
   Like many floods met in pouring press;
   And as thunder in darkling tors doth blare,
   That noise, I believe, was nowise less.

74 But nonetheless, though it harshly roared,
   And echo loud though it was to hear,
   I heard them note then new record,
   A delight as lovely to listening ear
   As harpers harping on harps afford.
   This new song now they sang full clear,
   With resounding notes in noble accord
   Making in choir their musics dear.
   Before God's very throne drawn near
   And the Beasts to Him bowed in lowliness
   And the ancient Elders grave of cheer
   They sang their song there, nonetheless.

75 Yet nonetheless were none so wise
    For all the arts that they ever knew
    Of that song who could a phrase devise,
    Save those of the Lamb's fair retinue;
    For redeemed and removed from earthly eyes,
    As firstling fruits that to God are due,
    To the noble Lamb they are allies,
    Being like to Him in mien and hue;
    For no lying word nor tale untrue
    Ever touched their tongues despite duress.
    Ever close that company pure shall sue
    That Master immaculate, and never less." '

76 'My thanks may none the less you find,
    My Pearl,' quoth I, 'though I question pose.
    I should not try your lofty mind,
    Whom Christ to bridal chamber chose.
    I am but dirt and dust in kind,
    And you a rich and radiant rose
    Here by this blissful bank reclined
    Where life's delight unfading grows.
    Now, Lady, your heart sincere enclose,
    And I would ask one thing express,
    And though it clown uncouth me shows,
    My prayer disdain not, nevertheless.

77 I nonetheless my appeal declare,
    If you to do this may well deign,
    Deny you not my piteous prayer,
    As you are glorious without a stain.
    No home in castle-wall do ye share,
    No mansion to meet in, no domain?
    Of Jerusalem you speak the royal and fair,
    Where David on regal throne did reign;
    It abides not here on hill nor plain,
    But in Judah is that noble plot.
    As under moon ye have no stain
    Your home should be without a spot.

78 This spotless troop of which you tell,
   This thronging press many-thousandfold,
   Ye doubtless a mighty citadel
   Must have your number great to hold:
   For jewels so lovely 'twould not be well
   That flock so fair should have no fold!
   Yet by these banks where a while I dwell
   I nowhere about any house behold.
   To gaze on this glorious stream you strolled
   And linger alone now, do you not?
   If elsewhere you have stout stronghold,
   Now guide me to that goodly spot!'

79 'That spot,' that peerless maid replied,
   'In Judah's land of which you spake,
   Is the city to which the Lamb did ride,
   To suffer sore there for Man's sake.
   The Old Jerusalem is implied,
   For old sin's bond He there let break.
   But the New, that God sent down to glide,
   The Apocalypse in account doth take.
   The Lamb that no blot ever black shall make
   Doth there His lovely throng allot,
   And as His flock all stains forsake
   So His mansion is unmarred by spot.

80 There are two spots. To speak of these:
   They both the name "Jerusalem" share;
   "The City of God" or "Sight of Peace",
   These meanings only doth that bear.
   In the first it once the Lamb did please
   Our peace by His suffering to repair;
   In the other naught is found but peace
   That shall last for ever without impair.
   To that high city we swiftly fare
   As soon as our flesh is laid to rot;
   Ever grow shall the bliss and glory there
   For the host within that hath no spot.'

81 'O spotless maiden kind!' I cried
To that lovely flower, 'O lead me there,
To see where blissful you abide,
To that goodly place let me repair!'
'God will forbid that,' she replied,
'His tower to enter you may not dare.
But the Lamb hath leave to me supplied
For a sight thereof by favour rare:
From without on that precinct pure to stare,
But foot within to venture not;
In the street you have no strength to fare,
Unless clean you be without a spot.

82 If I this spot shall to you unhide,
Turn up towards this water's head,
While I escort you on this side,
Until your ways to a hill have led.'
No longer would I then abide,
But shrouded by leafy boughs did tread,
Until from a hill I there espied
A glimpse of that city, as forth I sped.
Beyond the river below me spread
Brighter than sun with beams it shone;
In the Apocalypse may its form be read,
As it describes the apostle John.

83 As John the apostle it did view,
I saw that city of great renown,
Jerusalem royally arrayed and new,
As it was drawn from heaven down.
Of gold refined in fire to hue
Of glittering glass was that shining town;
Fair gems beneath were joined as due
In courses twelve, on the base laid down
That with tenoned tables twelve they crown:
A single stone was each tier thereon,
As well describes this wondrous town
In Apocalypse the apostle John.

84 These stones doth John in Writ disclose;
    I knew their names as he doth tell:
    As jewel first the jasper rose,
    And first at the base I saw it well,
    On the lowest course it greenly glows;
    On the second stage doth sapphire dwell;
    Chalcedony on the third tier shows,
    A flawless, pure, and pale jewel;
    The emerald fourth so green of shell;
    The sardonyx, the fifth it shone,
    The ruby sixth: he saw it well
    In the Apocalypse, the apostle John.

85 To them John then joined the chrysolite,
    The seventh gem in the ascent;
    The eighth the beryl clear and white;
    The twin-hued topaz as ninth was pent;
    Tenth the chrysoprase formed the flight;
    Eleventh was jacinth excellent;
    The twelfth, most trusty in every plight,
    The amethyst blue with purple blent.
    Sheer from those tiers the wall then went
    Of jasper like glass that glistening shone;
    I knew it, for thus did it present
    In the Apocalypse the apostle John.

86 As John described, I broad and sheer
    These twelve degrees saw rising there;
    Above the city square did rear
    (Its length with breadth and height compare);
    The streets of gold as glass all clear,
    The wall of jasper that gleamed like glair;
    With all precious stones that might there appear
    Adorned within the dwellings were.
    Of that domain each side all square
    Twelve thousand furlongs held then on,
    As in height and breadth, in length did fare,
    For it measured saw the apostle John.

87   As John hath writ, I saw yet more:
      Each quadrate wall there had three gates,
So in compass there were three times four,
The portals o'erlaid with richest plates;
A single pearl was every door,
A pearl whose perfection ne'er abates;
And each inscribed a name there bore
Of Israel's children by their dates:
Their times of birth each allocates,
Ever first the eldest thereon is hewn.
Such light every street illuminates
They have need of neither sun nor moon.

88   Of sun nor moon they had no need,
For God Himself was their sunlight;
The Lamb their lantern was indeed
And through Him blazed that city bright
That unearthly clear did no light impede;
Through wall and hall thus passed my sight.
The Throne on high there might one heed,
With all its rich adornment dight,
As John in chosen words did write.
High God Himself sat on that throne,
Whence forth a river ran with light
Outshining both the sun and moon.

89   Neither sun nor moon ever shone so sweet
As the pouring flood from that court that flowed;
Swiftly it swept through every street,
And no filth nor soil nor slime it showed.
No church was there the sight to greet,
Nor chapel nor temple there ever abode:
The Almighty was their minster meet;
Refreshment the Victim Lamb bestowed.
The gates ever open to every road
Were never yet shut from noon to noon;
There enters none to find abode
Who bears any spot beneath the moon.

90 The moon therefrom may gain no might,
   Too spotty is she, of form too hoar;
   Moreover there comes never night:
   Why should the moon in circle soar
   And compare her with that peerless light
   That shines upon that water's shore?
   The planets are in too poor a plight,
   Yea, the sun himself too pale and frore.
   On shining trees where those waters pour
   Twelve fruits of life there ripen soon;
   Twelve times a year they bear a store,
   And renew them anew in every moon.

91 Such marvels as neath the moon upraised
   A fleshly heart could not endure
   I saw, who on that castle gazed;
   Such wonders did its frame immure,
   I stood there still as quail all dazed;
   Its wondrous form did me allure,
   That rest nor toil I felt, amazed,
   And ravished by that radiance pure.
   For with conscience clear I you assure,
   If man embodied had gained that boon,
   Though sages all assayed his cure,
   His life had been lost beneath the moon.

92 As doth the moon in might arise,
   Ere down must daylight leave the air,
   So, suddenly, in a wondrous wise,
   Of procession long I was aware.
   Unheralded to my surprise
   That city of royal renown so fair
   Was with virgins filled in the very guise
   Of my blissful one with crown on hair.
   All crowned in manner like they were,
   In pearls appointed, and weeds of white,
   And bound on breast did each one bear
   The blissful pearl with great delight.

93 With great delight in line they strolled
   On golden ways that gleamed like glass;
   A hundred thousands were there, I hold,
   And all to match their livery was;
   The gladdest face could none have told.
   The Lamb before did proudly pass
   With seven horns of clear red gold;
   As pearls of price His raiment was.
   To the Throne now drawn they pacing pass:
   No crowding, though great their host in white,
   But gentle as modest maids at Mass,
   So lead they on with great delight.

94 The delight too great were to recall
   That at His coming forth did swell.
   When He approached those elders all
   On their faces at His feet they fell;
   There summoned hosts angelical
   An incense cast of sweetest smell:
   New glory and joy then forth did fall,
   All sang to praise that fair Jewel.
   The strain could strike through earth to hell
   That the Virtues of heaven in joy endite.
   With His host to laud the Lamb as well
   Indeed I found a great delight.

95 Delight the Lamb to behold with eyes
   Then moved my mind with wonder more:
   The best was He, blithest, most dear to prize
   Of whom I e'er heard tales of yore;
   So wondrous white was all His guise,
   So noble Himself He so meekly bore.
   But by His heart a wound my eyes
   Saw wide and wet; the fleece it tore,
   From His white side His blood did pour.
   Alas! thought I, who did that spite?
   His breast should have burned with anguish sore,
   Ere in that deed one took delight.

96 The Lamb's delight to doubt, I ween,
    None wished; though wound He sore displayed,
    In His face no sign thereof was seen,
    In His glance such glorious gladness played.
    I marked among His host serene,
    How life in full on each was laid –
    Then saw I there my little queen
    That I thought stood by me in the glade!
    Lord! great was the merriment she made,
    Among her peers who was so white.
    That vision made me think to wade
    For love-longing in great delight.

97 Delight there pierced my eye and ear,
    In my mortal mind a madness reigned;
    When I saw her beauty I would be near,
    Though beyond the stream she was retained.
    I thought that naught could interfere,
    Could strike me back to halt constrained,
    From plunge in stream would none me steer,
    Though I died ere I swam o'er what remained.
    But as wild in the water to start I strained,
    On my intent did quaking seize;
    From that aim recalled I was detained:
    It was not as my Prince did please.

98 It pleased Him not that I leapt o'er
    Those marvellous bounds by madness swayed.
    Though headlong haste me heedless bore,
    Yet swift arrest was on me made,
    For right as I rushed then to the shore
    That fury made my dream to fade.
    I woke in that garden as before,
    My head upon that mound was laid
    Where once to earth my pearl had strayed.
    I stretched, and fell in great unease,
    And sighing to myself I prayed:
    'Now all be as that Prince may please.'

99 It pleased me ill outcast to be
So suddenly from that region fair
Where living beauty I could see.
A swoon of longing smote me there,
And I cried aloud then piteously:
'O Pearl, renowned beyond compare!
How dear was all that you said to me,
That vision true while I did share.
If it be true and sooth to swear
That in garland gay you are set at ease,
Then happy I, though chained in care,
That you that Prince indeed do please.'

100 To please that Prince had I always bent,
Desired no more than was my share,
And loyally been obedient,
As the Pearl me prayed so debonair,
I before God's face might have been sent,
In his mysteries further maybe to fare.
But with fortune no man is content
That rightly he may claim and bear;
So robbed of realms immortally fair
Too soon my joy did sorrow seize.
Lord! mad are they who against Thee dare
Or purpose what Thee may displease!

101 To please that Prince, or be pardon shown,
May Christian good with ease design;
For day and night I have him known
A God, a Lord, a Friend divine.
This chance I met on mound where prone
In grief for my pearl I would repine;
With Christ's sweet blessing and mine own
I then to God it did resign.
May He that in form of bread and wine
By priest upheld each day one sees,
Us inmates of His house divine
Make precious pearls Himself to please.   *Amen Amen*

SIR ORFEO

We often read and written find,
as learned men do us remind,
that lays that now the harpers sing
are wrought of many a marvellous thing.
Some are of weal, and some of woe,
and some do joy and gladness know;
in some are guile and treachery told,
in some the deeds that chanced of old;
some are of jests and ribaldry,
10 and some are tales of Faërie.
Of all the things that men may heed
'tis most of love they sing indeed.
    In Britain all these lays are writ,
there issued first in rhyming fit,
concerning adventures in those days
whereof the Britons made their lays;
for when they heard men anywhere
tell of adventures that there were,
they took their harps in their delight
20 and made a lay and named it right.
    Of adventures that did once befall
some can I tell you, but not all.
Listen now, lordings good and true,
and 'Orfeo' I will sing to you.

    Sir Orfeo was a king of old,
in England lordship high did hold;
valour he had and hardihood,
a courteous king whose gifts were good.
His father from King Pluto came,
30 his mother from Juno, king of fame,
who once of old as gods were named
for mighty deeds they did and claimed.
Sir Orfeo, too, all things beyond

of harping's sweet delight was fond,
and sure were all good harpers there
of him to earn them honour fair;
himself he loved to touch the harp
and pluck the strings with fingers sharp.
He played so well, beneath the sun
40 a better harper was there none;
no man hath in this world been born
who would not, hearing him, have sworn
that as before him Orfeo played
to joy of Paradise he had strayed
and sound of harpers heavenly,
such joy was there and melody.
This king abode in Tracience,
a city proud of stout defence;
for Winchester, 'tis certain, then
50 as Tracience was known to men.
There dwelt his queen in fairest bliss,
whom men called Lady Heurodis,
of ladies then the one most fair
who ever flesh and blood did wear;
in her did grace and goodness dwell,
but none her loveliness can tell.

It so did chance in early May,
when glad and warm doth shine the day,
and gone are bitter winter showers,
60 and every field is filled with flowers,
on every branch the blossom blows,
in glory and in gladness grows,
the lady Heurodis, the queen,
two maidens fair to garden green
with her she took at drowsy tide
of noon to stroll by orchard-side,
to see the flowers there spread and spring
and hear the birds on branches sing.
There down in shade they sat all three
70 beneath a fair young grafted tree;

and soon it chanced the gentle queen
fell there asleep upon the green.
Her maidens durst her not awake,
but let her lie, her rest to take;
and so she slept, till midday soon
was passed, and come was afternoon.
Then suddenly they heard her wake,
and cry, and grievous clamour make;
she writhed with limb, her hands she wrung,
80 she tore her face till blood there sprung,
her raiment rich in pieces rent;
thus sudden out of mind she went.

    Her maidens two then by her side
no longer durst with her abide,
but to the palace swiftly ran
and told there knight and squire and man
their queen, it seemed, was sudden mad;
'Go and restrain her,' they them bade.
Both knights and ladies thither sped,
90 and more than sixty damsels fled;
to the orchard to the queen they went,
with arms to lift her down they bent,
and brought her to her bed at last,
and raving there they held her fast;
but ceaselessly she still would cry,
and ever strove to rise and fly.

    When Orfeo heard these tidings sad,
more grief than ever in life he had;
and swiftly with ten knights he sped
100 to bower, and stood before her bed,
and looking on her ruefully,
'Dear life,' he said, 'what troubles thee,
who ever quiet hast been and sweet,
why dost thou now so shrilly greet?
Thy body that peerless white was born
is now by cruel nails all torn.
Alas! thy cheeks that were so red
are now as wan as thou wert dead;

thy fingers too, so small and slim,
110 are stained with blood, their hue is dim.
Alas! thy lovely eyes in woe
now stare on me as on a foe.
A! lady, mercy I implore.
These piteous cries, come, cry no more,
but tell me what thee grieves, and how,
and say what may thee comfort now.'
   Then, lo! at last she lay there still,
and many bitter tears did spill,
and thus unto the king she spake:
120 'Alas! my lord, my heart will break.
Since first together came our life,
between us ne'er was wrath nor strife,
but I have ever so loved thee
as very life, and so thou me.
Yet now we must be torn in twain,
and go I must, for all thy pain.'
   'Alas!' said he, 'then dark my doom.
Where wilt thou go, and go to whom?
But where thou goest, I come with thee,
130 and where I go, thou shalt with me.'
   'Nay, nay, sir, words avail thee naught.
I will tell thee how this woe was wrought:
as I lay in the quiet noontide
and slept beneath our orchard-side,
there came two noble knights to me
arrayed in armour gallantly.
"We come," they said, "thee swift to bring
to meeting with our lord and king."
Then answered I both bold and true
140 that dared I not, and would not do.
They spurred then back on swiftest steed;
then came their king himself with speed;
a hundred knights with him and more,
and damsels, too, were many a score,
all riding there on snow-white steeds,
and white as milk were all their weeds;

I saw not ever anywhere
a folk so peerless and so fair.
The king was crowned with crown of light,
150 not of red gold nor silver white,
but of one single gem 'twas hewn
that shone as bright as sun at noon.
And coming, straightway he me sought,
and would I or no, he up me caught,
and made me by him swiftly ride
upon a palfrey at his side;
and to his palace thus me brought,
a dwelling fair and wondrous wrought.
He castles showed me there and towers,
160 Water and wild, and woods, and flowers,
and pastures rich upon the plain;
and then he brought me home again,
and to our orchard he me led,
and then at parting this he said:
"See, lady, tomorrow thou must be
right here beneath this grafted tree,
and then beside us thou shalt ride,
and with us evermore abide.
If let or hindrance thou dost make,
170 where'er thou be, we shall thee take,
and all thy limbs shall rend and tear –
no aid of man shall help thee there;
and even so, all rent and torn,
thou shalt away with us be borne."'

When all those tidings Orfeo heard,
then spake he many a bitter word:
'Alas! I had liever lose my life
than lose thee thus, my queen and wife!'
He counsel sought of every man,
180 but none could find him help or plan.
On the morrow, when the noon drew near,
in arms did Orfeo appear,
and full ten hundred knights with him,

all stoutly armed, all stern and grim;
and with their queen now went that band
beneath the grafted tree to stand.
A serried rank on every side
they made, and vowed there to abide,
and die there sooner for her sake
190　than let men thence their lady take.
And yet from midst of that array
the queen was sudden snatched away;
by magic was she from them caught,
and none knew whither she was brought.

　　Then was there wailing, tears, and woe;
the king did to his chamber go,
and oft he swooned on floor of stone,
and such lament he made and moan
that nigh his life then came to end;
200　and nothing could his grief amend.
His barons he summoned to his board,
each mighty earl and famous lord,
and when they all together came,
'My lords,' he said, 'I here do name
my steward high before you all
to keep my realm, whate'er befall,
to hold my place instead of me
and keep my lands where'er they be.
For now that I have lost my queen,
210　the fairest lady men have seen,
I wish not woman more to see.
Into the wilderness I will flee,
and there will live for evermore
with the wild beasts in forests hoar.
But when ye learn my days are spent,
then summon ye a parliament,
and choose ye there a king anew.
With all I have now deal ye true.'

　　Then weeping was there in the hall,
220　and great lament there made they all,
and hardly there might old or young

for weeping utter word with tongue.
They knelt them down in company,
and prayed, if so his will might be,
that never should he from them go.
'Have done!' said he. 'It must be so.'

    Now all his kingdom he forsook.
Only a beggar's cloak he took;
he had no kirtle and no hood,
230 no shirt, nor other raiment good.
His harp yet bore he even so,
and barefoot from the gate did go;
no man might keep him on the way.
    A me! the weeping woe that day,
when he that had been king with crown
went thus beggarly out of town!
Through wood and over moorland bleak
he now the wilderness doth seek,
and nothing finds to make him glad,
240 but ever liveth lone and sad.
He once had ermine worn and vair,
on bed had purple linen fair,
now on the heather hard doth lie,
in leaves is wrapped and grasses dry.
He once had castles owned and towers,
water and wild, and woods, and flowers,
now though it turn to frost or snow,
this king with moss his bed must strow.
He once had many a noble knight
250 before him kneeling, ladies bright,
now nought to please him doth he keep;
only wild serpents by him creep.
He that once had in plenty sweet
all dainties for his drink and meat,
now he must grub and dig all day,
with roots his hunger to allay.
In summer on wildwood fruit he feeds,
or berries poor to serve his needs;

in winter nothing can he find
260 save roots and herbs and bitter rind.
All his body was wasted thin
by hardship, and all cracked his skin.
A Lord! who can recount the woe
for ten long years that king did know?
His hair and beard all black and rank
down to his waist hung long and lank.
His harp wherein was his delight
in hollow tree he hid from sight;
when weather clear was in the land
270 his harp he took then in his hand
and harped thereon at his sweet will.
Through all the wood the sound did thrill,
and all the wild beasts that there are
in joy approached him from afar;
and all the birds that might be found
there perched on bough and bramble round
to hear his harping to the end,
such melodies he there did blend;
and when he laid his harp aside,
280 no bird or beast would near him bide.

There often by him would he see,
when noon was hot on leaf and tree,
the king of Faërie with his rout
came hunting in the woods about
with blowing far and crying dim,
and barking hounds that were with him;
yet never a beast they took nor slew,
and where they went he never knew.
At other times he would descry
290 a mighty host, it seemed, go by,
ten hundred knights all fair arrayed
with many a banner proud displayed.
Each face and mien was fierce and bold,
each knight a drawn sword there did hold,
and all were armed in harness fair

and marching on he knew not where.
Or a sight more strange would meet his eye:
knights and ladies came dancing by
in rich array and raiment meet,
300 softly stepping with skilful feet;
tabour and trumpet went along,
and marvellous minstrelsy and song.

And one fair day he at his side
saw sixty ladies on horses ride,
each fair and free as bird on spray,
and never a man with them that day.
There each on hand a falcon bore,
riding a-hawking by river-shore.
Those haunts with game in plenty teem,
310 cormorant, heron, and duck in stream;
there off the water fowl arise,
and every falcon them descries;
each falcon stooping slew his prey,
and Orfeo laughing loud did say:
'Behold, in faith, this sport is fair!
Fore Heaven, I will betake me there!
I once was wont to see such play.'
He rose and thither made his way,
and to a lady came with speed,
320 and looked at her, and took good heed,
and saw as sure as once in life
'twas Heurodis, his queen and wife.
Intent he gazed, and so did she,
but no word spake; no word said he.
For hardship that she saw him bear,
who had been royal, and high, and fair,
then from her eyes the tears there fell.
The other ladies marked it well,
and away they made her swiftly ride;
330 no longer might she near him bide.
'Alas!' said he, 'unhappy day!
Why will not now my death me slay?

Alas! unhappy man, ah why
may I not, seeing her, now die?
Alas! too long hath lasted life,
when I dare not with mine own wife
to speak a word, nor she with me.
Alas! my heart should break,' said he.
'And yet, fore Heaven, tide what betide,
340   and whithersoever these ladies ride,
that road I will follow they now fare;
for life or death no more I care.'
     His beggar's cloak he on him flung,
his harp upon his back he hung;
with right good will his feet he sped,
for stock nor stone he stayed his tread.
Right into a rock the ladies rode,
and in behind he fearless strode.
He went into that rocky hill
350   a good three miles or more, until
he came into a country fair
as bright as sun in summer air.
Level and smooth it was and green,
and hill nor valley there was seen.
A castle he saw amid the land
princely and proud and lofty stand;
the outer wall around it laid
of shining crystal clear was made.
A hundred towers were raised about
360   with cunning wrought, embattled stout;
and from the moat each buttress bold
in arches sprang of rich red gold.
The vault was carven and adorned
with beasts and birds and figures horned;
within were halls and chambers wide
all made of jewels and gems of pride;
the poorest pillar to behold
was builded all of burnished gold.
And all that land was ever light,
370   for when it came to dusk of night

from precious stones there issued soon
a light as bright as sun at noon.
No man may tell nor think in thought
how rich the works that there were wrought;
indeed it seemed he gazed with eyes
on the proud court of Paradise.

    The ladies to that castle passed.
Behind them Orfeo followed fast.
There knocked he loud upon the gate;
380 the porter came, and did not wait,
but asked him what might be his will.
'In faith, I have a minstrel's skill
with mirth and music, if he please,
thy lord to cheer, and him to ease.'
The porter swift did then unpin
the castle gates, and let him in.

    Then he began to gaze about,
and saw within the walls a rout
of folk that were thither drawn below,
390 and mourned as dead, but were not so.
For some there stood who had no head,
and some no arms, nor feet; some bled
and through their bodies wounds were set,
and some were strangled as they ate,
and some lay raving, chained and bound,
and some in water had been drowned;
and some were withered in the fire,
and some on horse, in war's attire,
and wives there lay in their childbed,
400 and mad were some, and some were dead;
and passing many there lay beside
as though they slept at quiet noon-tide.
Thus in the world was each one caught
and thither by fairy magic brought.
There too he saw his own sweet wife,
Queen Heurodis, his joy and life,
asleep beneath a grafted tree:
by her attire he knew 'twas she.

When he had marked these marvels all,
410 he went before the king in hall,
and there a joyous sight did see,
a shining throne and canopy.
Their king and lord there held his seat
beside their lady fair and sweet.
Their crowns and clothes so brightly shone
that scarce his eyes might look thereon.
When he had marked this wondrous thing,
he knelt him down before the king:
'O lord,' said he, 'if it be thy will,
420 now shalt thou hear my minstrel's skill.'
The king replied: 'What man art thou
that hither darest venture now?
Not I nor any here with me
have ever sent to summon thee,
and since here first my reign began
I have never found so rash a man
that he to us would dare to wend,
unless I first for him should send.'
'My lord,' said he, 'I thee assure,
430 I am but a wandering minstrel poor;
and, sir, this custom use we all
at the house of many a lord to call,
and little though our welcome be,
to offer there our minstrelsy.'
Before the king upon the ground
he sat, and touched his harp to sound;
his harp he tuned as well he could,
glad notes began and music good,
and all who were in palace found
440 came unto him to hear the sound,
and lay before his very feet,
they thought his melody so sweet.
He played, and silent sat the king
for great delight in listening;
great joy this minstrelsy he deemed,
and joy to his noble queen it seemed.

At last when he his harping stayed,
this speech the king to him then made:
'Minstrel, thy music pleaseth me.
450 Come, ask of me whate'er it be,
and rich reward I will thee pay.
Come, speak, and prove now what I say!'
'Good sir,' he said, 'I beg of thee
that this thing thou wouldst give to me,
that very lady fair to see
who sleeps beneath the grafted tree.'
'Nay,' said the king, 'that would not do!
A sorry pair ye'd make, ye two;
for thou art black, and rough, and lean,
460 and she is faultless, fair and clean.
A monstrous thing then would it be
to see her in thy company.'
     'O sir,' he said, 'O gracious king,
but it would be a fouler thing
from mouth of thine to hear a lie.
Thy vow, sir, thou canst not deny,
Whate'er I asked, that should I gain,
and thou must needs thy word maintain.'
The king then said: 'Since that is so,
470 now take her hand in thine, and go;
I wish thee joy of her, my friend!'
     He thanked him well, on knees did bend;
his wife he took then by the hand,
and departed swiftly from that land,
and from that country went in haste;
the way he came he now retraced.
     Long was the road. The journey passed;
to Winchester he came at last,
his own beloved city free;
480 but no man knew that it was he.
Beyond the town's end yet to fare,
lest men them knew, he did not dare;
but in a beggar's narrow cot
a lowly lodging there he got

both for himself and for his wife,
as a minstrel poor of wandering life.
He asked for tidings in the land,
and who that kingdom held in hand;
the beggar poor him answered well
490 and told all things that there befell:
how fairies stole their queen away
ten years before, in time of May;
and how in exile went their king
in unknown countries wandering,
while still the steward rule did hold;
and many things beside he told.
　　Next day, when hour of noon was near,
he bade his wife await him here;
the beggar's rags he on him flung,
500 his harp upon his back he hung,
and went into the city's ways
for men to look and on him gaze.
Him earl and lord and baron bold,
lady and burgess, did behold.
'O look! O what a man!' they said,
'How long the hair hangs from his head!
His beard is dangling to his knee!
He is gnarled and knotted like a tree!'
　　Then as he walked along the street
510 He chanced his steward there to meet,
and after him aloud cried he:
'Mercy, sir steward, have on me!
A harper I am from Heathenesse;
to thee I turn in my distress.'
The steward said: 'Come with me, come!
Of what I have thou shalt have some.
All harpers good I welcome make
For my dear lord Sir Orfeo's sake.'
　　The steward in castle sat at meat,
520 and many a lord there had his seat;
trumpeters, tabourers there played
harpers and fiddlers music made.

Many a melody made they all,
but Orfeo silent sat in hall
and listened. And when they all were still
he took his harp and tuned it shrill.
Then notes he harped more glad and clear
than ever a man hath heard with ear;
his music delighted all those men.

530   The steward looked and looked again;
the harp in hand at once he knew.
'Minstrel,' he said, 'come, tell me true,
whence came this harp to thee, and how?
I pray thee, tell me plainly now.'
'My lord,' said he, 'in lands unknown
I walked a wilderness alone,
and there I found in dale forlorn
a man by lions to pieces torn,
by wolves devoured with teeth so sharp;

540   by him I found this very harp,
and that is full ten years ago.'
'Ah!' said the steward, 'news of woe!
'Twas Orfeo, my master true.
Alas! poor wretch, what shall I do,
who must so dear a master mourn?
A! woe is me that I was born,
for him so hard a fate designed,
a death so vile that he should find!'
Then on the ground he fell in swoon;

550   his barons stooping raised him soon
and bade him think how all must end –
for death of man no man can mend.

King Orfeo now had proved and knew
his steward was both loyal and true,
and loved him as he duly should.
'Lo!' then he cried, and up he stood,
'Steward, now to my words give ear!
If thy king, Orfeo, were here,
and had in wilderness full long

560   suffered great hardship sore and strong,

had won his queen by his own hand
out of the deeps of fairy land,
and led at last his lady dear
right hither to the town's end near,
and lodged her in a beggar's cot;
if I were he, whom ye knew not,
thus come among you, poor and ill,
in secret to prove thy faith and will,
if then I thee had found so true,
570 thy loyalty never shouldst thou rue:
nay, certainly, tide what betide,
thou shouldst be king when Orfeo died.
Hadst thou rejoiced to hear my fate,
I would have thrust thee from the gate.'

    Then clearly knew they in the hall
that Orfeo stood before them all.
The steward understood at last;
in his haste the table down he cast
and flung himself before his feet,
580 and each lord likewise left his seat,
and this one cry they all let ring:
'Ye are our lord, sir, and our king!'
To know he lived so glad they were.
To his chamber soon they brought him there;
they bathed him and they shaved his beard,
and robed him, till royal he appeared;
and brought them in procession long
the queen to town with merry song,
with many a sound of minstrelsy.
590 A Lord! how great the melody!
For joy the tears were falling fast
of those who saw them safe at last.

    Now was King Orfeo crowned anew,
and Heurodis his lady too;
and long they lived, till they were dead,
and king was the steward in their stead.
    Harpers in Britain in aftertime
these marvels heard, and in their rhyme

a lay they made of fair delight,
600 and after the king it named aright,
'Orfeo' called it, as was meet:
good is the lay, the music sweet.
   Thus came Sir Orfeo out of care.
God grant that well we all may fare!

GLOSSARY

For *Sir Gawain and the Green Knight*, *Pearl* and *Sir Orfeo*

This glossary provides no more than the meanings of some archaic and technical words used in the translations, and only the meanings that the translator intended in those contexts (which in a very few cases may be doubtful). In the stanzas describing the breaking-up of the deer he employed some of the technical terms of the original which are debatable in meaning, and in such cases (e.g. *Arber*, *Knot*, *Numbles*) I have given what I believe was his final interpretation. References to *Sir Gawain* (G) and *Pearl* (P) are by stanza, and to *Sir Orfeo* (O) by line.

Arber Paunch, first stomach of ruminants, G 53.

Assay The testing of the fat of a deer, and the proper point at which to make the test, G 53.

Assoiled Absolved, G 75.

Baldric A belt passing over one shoulder and under the other, supporting a sword or a horn, G 100, 101; a strap to suspend the shield, G 27.

Barbican A strong outer defence of a castle, over a bridge or gate, connected with the main work, G 34.

Barrow Mound, G 87.

Beaver Moveable front part of a helmet, protecting the face, G 26.

Blazon Shield, G 27, 35.

Blear Dim, P 7.

Brawn Flesh, G 64, 65.

Buffet Blow, G 94.

Caitiff Boor, one of base mind and conduct, G 71.

Capadoce This word is taken from the original; it apparently meant a short cape, that could be buttoned or clasped round the throat, G 9, 25.

Caparison Ornamented cloth covering of a horse, G 26.

Carl Man, G 84.

Carols	Dances accompanied by song, G 3; cf. *carol-dances*, G 66, 75, and *they carolled*, G 42.
Childermas	The feast of the Holy Innocents, on the 28th of December, G 42.
Chine	Backbone, G 54.
Churl	Common man, G 84.
Cincture	Girdle, G 98.
Cithern	Stringed instrument, P 8.
Coat-armour	Surcoat worn over the armour, embroidered with distinctive heraldic devices, G 25, 81.
Cognisance	literally 'recognition', i.e. a personal badge by which the wearer could be known (referring to the Pentangle), G 81.
Coif	Head-dress, G 69.
Corses	Bodies, P 72.
Crenelles	Battlements, G 34 (strictly, the indentations in the battlements, alternating with the raised parts, the 'merlons').
Crupper	Leather strap passing round a horse's hind-quarters and fastened to the saddle to prevent it from slipping forward, G 8, 26.
Cuisses	Armour for the thighs, G 25.
Demeaned her	Behaved, G 51.
Dolour	Sorrow, P 28.
Doted	Gone out of their wits, G 78.
Ellwand	Measuring-rod an ell (45 inches) long, G 10.
Empery	Absolute dominion, P 38.
Eslot	Hollow above the breastbone at the base of the throat, G 53; = *neck-slot*, G 63.
Fain	Glad, G 35.
Featly	Neatly, G 34; deftly, skilfully, G 51.
Feigned	Formed, fashioned, P 63.
Fells	Skins, G 37, 69; *fox-fell*, G 77.
Finials	Ornamental pinnacles on roofs or towers, G 34.
Flower-de-luce	iris (in the translation specifically a white iris), P 17, 63.
Fore-numbles	The original has '*avanters*', part of the numbles of a deer, see *Numbles*; G 53.

Frore Very cold, frosty, P 90.

Gittern Stringed instrument, P 8.

Glair White of egg, P 86.

Glamoury Enchantment (enchanted being), G 99.

Gledes Live coals, G 64.

Gramercy Thank you, G 35, 42, 85.

Greaves Armour for the legs, G 25.

Greet Weep, O 104.

Grue Shuddering horror, G 95.

Guerdon Reward, recompense, G 72, 82; P 51, 52.

Guisarm Battle-axe, G 13, 15, 17, 91.

Gules Heraldic name for red, G 27, 28.

Halidom In the oath '*So help me God and the Halidom*', '*the Halidom*' referred to something of reverence or sanctity on which the oath was taken; G 85.

Handsels Gifts at New Year, G 4.

Hap Fortune, P 11.

Hastlets Edible entrails of a pig, G 64.

Heathenesse The heathen lands, O 513.

Hie Hasten, G 53.

Holt Wood, G 68.

Ingle Fire burning on the hearth, G 66.

Keep (*probably*) guard, protect, O 233.

Kerchiefs Head-coverings, G 39.

Kirtle A short coat or tunic reaching to the knees, G 73, P 17.

Knot Technical term applied to two pieces of fat in the neck and two in the flanks, G 53.

Latchet Loop, lace, fastening, G 26.

Lemman Lover, mistress, G 71.

Liever Rather, G 50, O 177.

Link-men Torch-carriers, G 79.

List Wished, G 61.

Loopholes Narrow slits in a castle-wall, G 34.

Ma fay! By my faith! G 59.

Marge Edge, G 87.

Margery-pearls Pearls, P 17.

Margery-stones Pearls, P 18.

Maugre   In spite of; *maugre his teeth*, in spite of all he could do to resist, G 62.

Meed   Reward, P 47.

Mellay   Close hand-to-hand combat, G 63.

Molains   Ornamented bosses on a horse's bit, G 8.

Numbles   Pieces of loin-meat, probably the tenderloin or fillet, G 53.

Oratory   Chapel, G 88.

Palfrey   Small saddle-horse (especially for the use of women), O 156.

Pauncer   Armour protecting the abdomen, G 80.

Pease   Pea, G 95.

Pisane   Armour for upper breast and neck, G 10.

Pleasances   Pleasure gardens, P 12.

Point-device   To perfection, G 26.

Poitrel   Breast-armour of a horse, G 8, 26.

Polains   Pieces of armour for the knees, G 25.

Popinjays   Parrots, G 26.

Port   Bearing, G 39.

Prise   literally capture, taking, G 64; notes blown on the horn at the taking or felling of the hunted beast, G 54.

Purfling   Embroidered border, P 18.

Quadrate   Square, P 87.

Quarry   Heap of slain animals, G 53.

Quest   Searching of hounds after game; *cried for a quest*, called for a search (by baying), G 57.

Rewel   Some kind of ivory, P 18.

Rood   Cross, P 54, 59, 68.

Ruth   Remorse, G 100.

Sabatons   Steel shoes, G 25.

Sendal   A fine silken material, G 4.

Sheen   Bright, P 4.

Slade   Valley, P 12.

Surnape   Napkin, *or* overcloth to protect tablecloth, G 37.

Tables   Horizontal courses, the stepped tiers of the foundation, P 83.

Tabour   Small drum, O 301.

Tabourers Players on the tabour, O 521.

Tenoned Closely joined, P 83.

Tines Pointed branches of a deer's horn, G 34.

Tors High hills, P 73.

Tressure Jewelled net confining the hair, G 69.

Vair Variegated (grey and white) squirrel's fur, O 241.

Weasand Oesophagus, gullet, G 53.

Weed Garment, G 95; *weeds*, P 64, O 146.

Welkin Heavens, sky, G 23, P 10.

Wight Being, G 84.

Wist Knew, G 61.

Worms Dragons, serpents, G 31.

Wrack Drifting cloud, G 68.

This glossary was compiled by Christopher Tolkien.

APPENDIX

The Verse-forms of *Sir Gawain and the Green Knight* and *Pearl*

The word 'alliterative', as applied to the ancestral measure of England, is misleading; for it was not concerned with *letters*, with *spelling*, but with *sounds*, judged by the ear. The sounds that are important are those that *begin* words – more precisely, those that begin the stressed syllables of words. Alliteration, or 'head-rhyme', is the agreement of stressed syllables within the line in beginning with the same consonantal sound (sound, not letter), or in beginning not with a consonant but with a vowel. Any vowel alliterates with any other vowel: the alliterative pattern is satisfied if the words in question do *not* begin with a consonant.

'Apt alliteration's artful aid,' said an eighteenth-century writer. But to a fourteenth-century poet in this mode three only of those four words alliterated. Not *alliteration* itself; for its first strong syllable is *lit*, and so it alliterates on the consonant *l*. *Apt*, *artful*, and *aid* alliterate; not because they begin with the same *letter*, *a*, but because they agree in beginning with no consonant; and that was alliteration enough. 'Old English art', where the words begin with three different letters, would be just as good.

But a line of this verse was not verse simply because it contained such alliterations; *rum ram ruf*, as Chaucer's parson mocked it, is not a line. It also had some structure.

The poet begins his poem with a very regular line, of one of his favourite varieties:

> Siþen þe sege and þe assaut watz sesed at Troye
>
> When the siege and the assault had ceased at Troy

This kind of line falls into two parts: 'When the siege and the assault' and 'had ceased at Troy'. There is nearly always a breath-pause between them, corresponding to some degree of pause in the sense. But the line was welded into a metrical unit by alliteration; one or more (usually two) of the chief words in the first part were linked by alliteration with the *first* important word in the second part. Thus, in the line above, *siege, assault*; *ceased*. (As it is the stressed syllable that counts, *assault* runs on *s*, not on a vowel).

Each of these parts had to contain two syllables (often whole words, like *siege*) that were in their place sufficiently stressed to bear a 'beat'. The other syllables should be lighter and quieter. But their number was not counted, nor in this medieval form was their placing strictly ordered. This freedom has one marked effect on rhythm: there might be no intervening light syllable between the stresses. It is of course an effect far easier to produce in English than to avoid, being normal in natural speech. Verse that uses it can accommodate easily many natural phrasings. The medieval poets used it especially in the second part of their lines; examples from the translation are

Tirius went to Tuscany   and tówns fóunded   (stanza 1)

Indeed of the Table Round   all those tríed bréthren   (stanza 3)

The alliteration may be at a minimum, affecting only one word in each part of the line. This is not frequent in the original (and in some places of its occurrence mistakes in the manuscript may be suspected); it is somewhat more so in the translation. Far more often, the alliteration is increased. Mere excess, when both of the stresses in the second part alliterate, is seldom found; two examples occur in consecutive lines in stanza 83:

þay *b*oȝen bi *b*onkkez   þer *b*oȝes are *b*are,

þay *c*lomben bi *c*lyffez   þer *c*lengez þe *c*olde

and are preserved in the translation. This is an excess, a rum-ram-ruf-*ram*, that soon cloys the ear.

Increased alliteration is usually connected with increase in weight and content of the line. In very many verses the first part of the line has thee heavy syllables or beats (not necessarily, nor indeed usually, of equal force). It is convenient to look at this sort of rhythm in this way. Natural language does not always arrange itself into the simple patterns:

> the siege and the assault   had ceased at Troy
>
> Tirius to Tuscany   and towns founded

There might be more 'full words' in a phrase. 'The king and his kinsman/and courtly men served them.' (see stanza 21, line 16) is well enough and is a sufficient line. But you might wish to say: 'The king and his good kinsman/and quickly courtly men served them.' As far as the second half of the line went, you restrained your wish and did not allow the language to have its head; you kept the ends of lines simple and clear. At most you would venture on 'and courtiers at once served them' avoiding double alliteration and putting the adverb where in natural narration it could be subordinated in force and tone to *court-* and *served*, leaving them plainly as the beats. But in the first part of the line 'packing' was much practised.

In 'The king and his good kinsman' *good* is not of much importance, and can be reduced in tone so as hardly to rise up and challenge the main beats, *king* and *kin*. But if this element joins in the alliteration, it is brought into notice, and then one has a triple type: 'The king and his kind kinsman'. This variety, in which there is a third beat inserted before the second main beat, to which it is subordinated in tone and import, but with which it nonetheless alliterates, is very common indeed. Thus the second line of the poem:

> And the *f*ortress *f*ell in *f*lame   to *f*irebrands and ashes

But the added material may come at the beginning of the line. Instead of 'In pomp and pride/he peopled it first' (see the ninth line of the poem) you may say: 'In great pomp and pride'. This will lead easily to another variety in which there is a third beat before the first main stress, to which it is subordinate, but with which it alliterates; so in the eighth line of the poem:

> Fro *r*iche *R*omulus to *R*ome   *r*icchis hym swyþe
>
> When *r*oyal *R*omulus to *R*ome his   *r*oad had taken

Less commonly a full but subordinate word may be put instead of a weak syllable at the end of the first part of the line; thus in stanza 81:

> þe gordel of þe grene silke,   þat gay wel bisemed
> That girdle of green silk,   and gallant it looked

If this is given an alliteration, one gets the type:

> And *f*ar over the *F*rench *f*lood   *F*elix Brutus   (stanza 1)

Further varieties will then develop; for example, those in which the third beat is not really subordinate, but either phonetically, or in sense and vividness, or in both, a rival to the others:

> But *w*ild *w*eathers of the *w*orld, a*w*ake in the land

> The *r*ings *r*id of the *r*ust   on his *r*ich byrnie   (both from stanza 80)

It may sometimes occur that the added beat bears the alliteration and the phonetically or logically more important word does not. In the translation, this type is used in order to provide an alliteration when a main word that cannot be changed refuses to alliterate. Thus in the first line of stanza 2 the translation has:

> And when *ʃ*air Britain was *ʃ*ounded   by this *ʃ*amous lord

for the original

> Ande quen þis *B*retayn watz *b*igged   bi þis *b*urn rych(e) –

since 'Britain' was inescapable, but neither *bigged* (founded) nor *burn* (knight, man) have any modern counterparts to alliterate with it.

As was said earlier, alliteration was by ear, and not by letter; the spelling is not concerned.

> *J*usted ful *j*olilé   þise *g*entyle kniȝtes   (stanza 3, line 6)

alliterated, despite the spelling with *g* and *j*. Quite another matter is 'licence'. The poet allowed himself certain of these: where neither the spelling nor the sound were the same, but the sounds were at least *similar*. He could occasionally disregard the distinction between voiced and voiceless consonants, and thus equate *s* with *z*, or *f* with *v*, and (often) words beginning with *h* with words beginning with a vowel. In the translation the same licences are allowed when necessary – a translator needs even more help than one composing on his own.

Thus:

> Quen Zeferus syflez hymself   on sedez and erbez

When Zephyr goes sighing   through seeds and herbs   (stanza 23)

and:

Though you yourself be desirous   to accept it in person   (stanza 16)

where the second stress is the 'zire' of *desirous*, and the third is the 'sept' of *accept*.

The cases where the alliteration is borne not by the first but by the second element in a compound word (such as *eyelid* or *daylight* in lines alliterating on *l*) are really not different metrically from those in which a separate but subordinate word usurps the alliteration. For example:

> And unlouked his yȝe-lyddez,   and let as him wondered

He lifted his eyelids   with a look as of wonder   (stanza 48)

One variety is frequently used in the translation which is not often found in clear cases in the original; that is 'crossed alliteration'. In this, a line contains two alliterative sounds, in either the arrangement *abab* or *abba*. These patterns are used in the translation because they satisfy the requirements of simple alliteration and yet add more metrical colour to make up for the cases where triple or quadruple alliteration in the original cannot be rivalled in modern English. Thus:

All of *g*reen were they *m*ade,   both *g*arments and *m*an   (stanza 8)

Towards the *f*airest at the *t*able   he *t*wisted the *f*ace   (stanza 20)

In the following line the pattern is *f/s/s/f*:

And since *f*olly thou hast *s*ought,   thou de*s*ervest to *f*ind it
   (stanza 15)

The frequent occurrence in the translation of 'Wawain' for 'Gawain' follows the practice of the original. Both forms of the name were current; and of course the existence of an alternative form of the name of a principal character, beginning with another consonant, was a great help to an alliterative poet.

But in *Sir Gawain* there is end-rhyme as well, in the last lines of each stanza. The author had the notion (so it may probably be said, for nothing quite like it is found elsewhere) to lighten the monotony and weight of some 2,000 long alliterating lines on end. He broke them up into groups (hardly really 'stanzas', as they are very variable in length), and at the end of each he put a patch of rhyme. This consists of four three-beat lines rhyming alternately (now known as the 'wheel') and a one-beat tag (known as the 'bob') to link the 'wheel' with the preceding stanza. The bob rhymes with the second and fourth lines of the wheel. There is no doubt of the metrical success of this device; but since the rhymed lines had also to alliterate, and there is not much room to move in the short lines of the wheel, the author set himself a severe technical test, and the translator a worse one. In the translation, the attempt to alliterate as well as rhyme has had to be abandoned a little more often than in the original. As an example of the bob and wheel both in the original and in the translation, this is the end of stanza 2:

> If ӡe wyl lysten þis laye bot on littel quile
> I schal telle hit astit, as I in toun herde,
> > with tonge,
> > As hit is stad and stoken
> > In stori stif and stronge,
> > With lel letteres loken,
> > In londe so hatz ben longe.

> If you will listen to this lay but a little while now,
> I will tell it at once as in town I have heard
> > it told,
> > as it is fixed and fettered
> > in story brave and bold,
> > thus linked and truly lettered
> > as was loved in this land of old.

II PEARL

In *Pearl* the author adopted a twelve-line rhyming stanza in which alliteration is used as well. The line in *Pearl* is a French line, modified primarily (a) by the difference of English from French generally, and (b) by the influence of inherited metrical practices and taste, especially in the areas where the alliterative tradition was still strong. The essential features of the ancient English alliterative practice are wholly unlike, in effect and aim, what is found in *Pearl*. In the old alliterative verse the 'line' had no repeated or constant accentual rhythm which gave it its metrical character; its units were the half-lines, each of which was independently constructed. The line was internally linked by alliteration; but this linking was deliberately used *counter* to the rhetorical and syntactic structure. The chief rhetorical or logical pauses were normally placed (except at the end of a verse period of several lines) in the middle of the line, between the alliterations; and the second half-line was most frequently more closely connected in sense and syntax to the following line.

In complete contrast to all this, there is in *Pearl* a basic and model accentual rhythm of alternating strong/loud – weak/soft syllables; the poem being written to a scheme:

$$x \, / \, x \, / \, x \, / \, x \, / \, (x)$$

Þay songen wyth a swete asent   (line 94 of the original).

'Model' lines of this kind make up about a quarter of the lines in the poem; but if those lines are included in which there occurs the simple variation of allowing one of the 'falls' to contain *two* weak syllables, the proportion rises to about three-fifths, and higher still if two such two-syllable falls are allowed. In all these cases (since only those in which the metrically unstressed elements are genuinely 'weak' are counted) the metrical pattern of alternating strong-loud and weak-soft syllables is clearly maintained. And in spite of the 'variations' that are used, and of the doubt concerning the presence or absence of final -*e*, this pattern remains indeed so frequent and insistent as to impart to the metrical effect of the whole a certain monotony, which combined with the emphasis of alliteration can (at any rate to a modern listener) become almost soporific. This is increased by the poet's preference for making the last beat, which is a rhyming syllable, share in the alliteration.

In *Pearl* the *total line* is the unit, and is usually 'locked up in itself'; in the vast majority of cases, the major marks of punctuation must be placed at the line-ends. Even 'commas', when phonetically used (that is, when not used simply by custom, to mark off phrases which are not naturally marked off even by light pauses in speech) are infrequent within the line; while 'run-ons' from one line to the next are extremely rare.

And finally, alliteration in the verse-form of *Pearl* plays *no* structural part in the line at all. It may be divided among the four stresses in any order or amount from two to four, and where there is only one pair these may be placed together as *ab* or as *cd*, leaving the other half alliteratively blank. And it may be absent altogether; in the 1,212 lines of the poem, over 300 are quite blank. Moreover, unless the number of blank lines is to be made even larger, syllables may assist in alliteration that do not bear the main metrical stresses, or are in the structure of the line relatively weak. In other words, alliteration is in *Pearl* a mere 'grace' or decoration of the line, which is sufficiently defined as such, and as being 'verse', without it. And this decoration is provided according to the skill of the poet, or linguistic opportunity, without guiding rule or other function.

Each stanza of *Pearl* has twelve lines, containing only three rhymes, always arranged *ab* in the first eight and then *bcbc* in the last four. The whole poem would contain 100 stanzas in twenty groups of five, if the fifteenth group (which begins with stanza 71) did not contain six. It has been argued that a stanza has been included in the manuscript which the author meant to strike out; but against this is the fact that the extra stanza in *Pearl* gives the poem a total of 101, and there are 101 stanzas in *Sir Gawain*.

The groups of five stanzas (which are indicated in the manuscript by an ornamental coloured initial at the beginning of each group) are constituted in this way. The last word in each stanza reappears in the first line of the following one (so stanza 1 ends in the original 'Of þat pryuy perle wythouten *spot*', and stanza 2 begins 'Syþen in þat *spote* hit fro me sprange'). This link-word reappears in the first line of the first stanza of the following group (so stanza 6 begins 'Fro *spot* my spyryt þer sprang in space'), and the new link-word appears at the end of that stanza (so stanza 6 ends 'Of half so dere adubbemente', and stanza 7 begins 'Dubbed wern alle þo downez sydez'). As this last instance shows, the link need not be precisely the same, but may be constituted from different parts of the same verb, from noun and adjective with the same stem, and so on. The linkage fails in the original at the beginning of stanza 61, as it does in the translation.

Thus not only are the stanzas linked together internally as groups, but the groups are linked to each other; and the last line of the poem, 'And precious perlez vnto his pay' (where *pay* means 'pleasure') echoes the first, 'Perle, plesaunte to prynces paye.' This echoing of the beginning of the poem in its end is found also in *Sir Gawain*, and in *Patience*.

This form was not easy to compose in, but very much more difficult to translate in; since the rhyme-words used by the poet rarely still fit in modern English, and the alliterating words fit as seldom. In the translation, satisfaction of the rhyme-scheme is of course given the primacy, and the alliteration is less rich than in the original. But the effect of the translation on the modern ear is probably that of its original on a contemporary ear in this respect, since we no longer habitually expect alliteration as an essential ingredient in verse, as the people of the North and West of England once did.

GAWAIN'S LEAVE-TAKING

Now Lords and Ladies blithe and bold,
    To bless you here now am I bound:
I thank you all a thousand-fold,
    And pray God save you whole and sound;
    Wherever you go on grass or ground,
        May he you guide that nought you grieve,
    For friendship that I here have found
        Against my will I take my leave.

For friendship and for favours good,
    For meat and drink you heaped on me,
The Lord that raised was on the Rood
    Now keep you comely company.
    On sea or land where'er you be,
        May he you guide that nought you grieve.
    Such fair delight you laid on me
        Against my will I take my leave.

Against my will although I wend,
    I may not always tarry here;
For everything must have an end,
    And even friends must part, I fear;
    Be we beloved however dear
        Out of this world death will us reave,
    And when we brought are to our bier
        Against our will we take our leave.

Now good day to you, goodmen all,
    And good day to you, young and old,
And good day to you, great and small,
    And gramercy a thousand-fold!
    If ought there were that dear ye hold,
        Full fain I would the deed achieve –
    Now Christ you keep from sorrows cold
        For now at last I take my leave.

This book is set in CASLON, designed and engraved by William Caslon of WILLIAM CASLON & SON, Letter-Founders in London, around 1740. In England at the beginning of the eighteenth century, Dutch type was probably more widely used than English. The rise of William Caslon put a stop to the importation of Dutch types and so changed the history of English typecutting.